Books by Andrew Billingsley

Black Families in White America
(with Amy Tate Billingsley)

Children of the Storm
(with Jeanne Giovannoni)

Black Families and the Struggle for Survival

The Evolution of Black Families

The Role of the Social Worker
in a Child Protective Agency

Climbing Jacob's Ladder

THE ENDURING LEGACY
OF AFRICAN-AMERICAN
FAMILIES

by

Andrew Billingsley, Ph.D.

Foreword by Paula Giddings

SIMON & SCHUSTER

New York   London   Toronto   Sydney   Tokyo   Singapore

Simon & Schuster
Simon & Schuster Building
Rockefeller Center
1230 Avenue of the Americas
New York, New York 10020

Designed by Irving Perkins Associates
Manufactured in the United States of America

1   3   5   7   9   10   8   6   4   2

Library of Congress Cataloging-in-Publication Data

Billingsley, Andrew.
Climbing Jacob's ladder : the enduring legacy of African-American families
/ by Andrew Billingsley; foreword by Paula Giddings.
p.   cm.
Includes bibliographical references and index.
1. Afro-American families.   I. Title.
E185.86.B522   1993
306.85′0896073—dc20   92-27967
CIP
ISBN 0-671-67708-X

Grateful Acknowledgment is given to the following for permission to quote from previously published material:
"Blacks as a Percentage of All Officers and Enlisted Personnel in the U.S. Military, 1971–1981" (Table 1) and "Blacks as a Percentage of the U.S. Armed Forces, by Service 1981" (Table 2). Joint Center for Political and Economic Studies Conference Report, "Blacks and the Military." No. 1 (August 1982): 2–3.
Bennett Harrison and Barry Bluestone. *The Deindustrialization of America.* (New York: Basic Books, a Division of HarperCollins Publishers).
Allen W. Jones. "The Black Press in the 'New South': Jesse C. Duke's struggle for Justice and Equality." *Journal of Negro History.* LXIV (Summer 1969): 215–228.
Asa G. Hilliard III, Larry Williams, and Nia Damali, eds. *The Teachings of Ptahhotep: The Oldest Book in the World.* (Atlanta: Blackwood Press, 1987) 17–35.
Bart Landry. *New Black Middle Class.* Copyright © 1987, The Regents of the University of California, 228.   *(continued at back of book)*

with the assistance of

Amy Tate Billingsley
Executive Assistant
Poverty and Race Research Action Council

and

Robert B. Hill
Director
Institute for Urban Research
Morgan State University

Contents

Part IV
FAMILY STRUCTURE IS ADAPTIVE

Part V
THE AFRICAN-AMERICAN COMMUNITY IS GENERATIVE

Part VI
THE FUTURE IS ALREADY HERE

STILL I RISE

You may write me down in history
With your bitter, twisted lies,
you may trod me in the dirt
But still, like dust, I'll rise . . .

—Maya Angelou

WE ARE CLIMBING JACOB'S LADDER

We are climbing Jacob's ladder
We *are* climbing Jacob's ladder
We are *climbing* Jacob's ladder
Soldiers of the cross.

Every round goes higher, higher
Every round goes higher, higher
Every round goes higher, higher
Soldiers of the cross.

Do you think I'll make a soldier?
Do you think I'll make a soldier?
Do you think I'll make a soldier?
Soldier of the cross?

—Traditional Spiritual

Foreword

by Paula Giddings

I remember feeling my mind expand in the late 1960s and 1970s when I read what the new generation of black sociologists—Andrew Billingsley among them—had to say about the black family. Where a previous generation of scholars saw deviation and weakness, the new scholars saw resourcefulness and resilience. It was the latter who refuted past notions of the black family being hopelessly trapped, like Tar Baby, in the quagmire of a slave past. It was still a racist present, they assured us, which accounted for most of the extant problems. If black families were in difficulty, it was not some inherent, cultural condition which was at the "heart of its deterioration" but socioeconomic factors pressing in from the outside. And where the older generation of scholars saw the strength of women as dysfunctional, the newer scholars saw their strength as indispensable to their families' health and survival.

This new perspective was not meant to mask the very real problems of black families, but to offer more effective solutions to remedy them. For those of us interested in history, the perspective was also a powerful tool in rendering a usable past. For looking at the African-American family through the lens of what it has done, against all odds, to sustain its coherence brings one to a very different conclusion than looking at it as merely a deficit model. And in reading Andrew Billingsley's *Climbing Jacob's Ladder*, one is

11

reminded of how much of our history has been shaped by the determination of black families to live their lives together.

The African-American family stayed surprisingly intact even through slavery, historians such as Herbert Gutman have found. Despite involuntary separations, large numbers of slave couples lived in long marriages, and the majority lived in double-headed households. After Emancipation, Union soldiers testified to how blacks, whose "wives and husbands the rebels had driven off, firmly refused to form new connections and declared their purpose to keep faith to absent ones." Those who had married as slaves exercised their first social act as freed men and women to marry again under the auspices of the Freedmen's Bureau. Knowledge of this phenomenon prompted a judge, Albion Tourgee, to speculate in 1890 that if the marriage bonds were dissolved throughout the state of New York in his time, "It may be doubted if as large a proportion of her intelligent white citizens would choose again their old partners."

Children, too, had to be recovered. Apprenticeship laws in many Southern states allowed former slave masters to expropriate children of their former slaves if the courts determined that they would be "better off" being apprenticed to whites than remaining in their own families. Freedmen's Bureau records contain petitions from fathers requesting the bureau to get their children back. And a Maryland administrator noted that "Not a day passes without some unfortunate mother walking sometimes ten or twenty miles to the Bureau offices to try to get her children's release."

In the early days of Reconstruction, women—with the cooperation of their husbands—refused to work Southern cotton fields so that they might spend more time with their families. Boston cotton brokers, inquiring into the disastrous cotton crop of 1867–68, concluded that the greatest loss resulted from the decision of "growing numbers of Negro women to devote their time to their homes and children." When it became impossible to sustain their position as non-wage-earners, their undiminished determination was probably the reason sharecropping took precedence over other kinds of collective labor, concluded historian Jacqueline Jones, because it allowed the whole family to work together.

Before the end of Reconstruction, it seemed that black families would outdistance the legacy of slavery. As the former abolitionist Frances Ellen Harper wrote after her tour of the South in 1870, blacks were "getting homes for themselves, and putting money in the bank."

Throughout the first half of the twentieth century, heroic efforts to keep kith and kin together were also required when, driven by disenfranchisement, lynching, depression, and sexual exploitation in the South and economic opportunity in the North, hundreds and thousands of black families trekked there to urban cities. There, too, when possible, the labor force was bent to family needs. Domestic workers, for example, asserted their determination to work day jobs instead of live-in work, so that a more coherent family life could be maintained. Welfare, initiated during Franklin D. Roosevelt's administration, was welcomed by African-American women for the same reason, as Jones observed. With it, domestic workers—the majority of black women workers—could stay home with children instead of leaving to work, and having the hours that they could spend there being subjected to the whims of white employers.

The North, with its fickle and discriminatory employment practices, housing convenants, and violent response to economic competition from blacks, was not the mecca prophesied in earlier years. Nonetheless, studies of black migrants in the North revealed that families managed to ride out the vagaries that disorganized family life. In the 1920s, for example, black infant mortality went down, as did out-of-wedlock births. A 1930 study by sociologist Irene Graham showed that a smaller percentage of black children in Chicago lived in broken homes than their white peers. Ninety percent of black children lived with their own parents; and a portion of the remaining tenth lived with relatives.

The integrity of black families would be challenged again during the Depression, when, based on the principle that black families needed less to live on than whites, they received less in relief payments. Nevertheless, such leaders as Walter White of the NAACP, Mary McLeod Bethune of the National Council of Negro Women, and A. Philip Randolph of the Brotherhood of Sleeping Car Porters and Maids helped break down barriers to the economic opportunities, and there would be ushered in the first appearance of the black middle class. However, unlike its white counterpart, it was a middle class whose status primarily depended not only on earnings from employment in the professions (as compared to business ownership), but on a dual income. This extraordinary achievement precipitated the rising expectations that would launch the contemporary civil rights movement in the

1950s. That black women so depended on city buses to take them to work across town to white neighborhoods, and bring them back again to families, made public transportation a particularly potent symbol of resistance for the Montgomery Boycott.

Indeed, much of African-American history has been shaped by the determination of black families to live their lives together. Of course, such a perspective is rare in the annals of social science, which tends to focus on the unique tragedy of slavery and racism and thus on the unique quality of various "aberrations" in black family life. What makes Dr. Billingsley's work so refreshing—and so much more accurate, in my opinion—is an alternative conceptual framework, a framework informed by not just sociology but history. A framework that does not see the black family in aberrant isolation to be measured by an imagined white middle-class norm, but rather as a product of society that both shapes and is shaped by it. Thus today, as in the past, the behavior and various configurations of the black family are a direct response, adaptation, and reflection of the society around it.

This point of view makes for a clearer and more comprehensive vision of the African-American family. Seeing non-nuclear families in terms of their own integrity also allows a more comprehensive look at the tremendous variety of black families in composition, health, and even categories of class that extend beyond the standard designations. Billingsley shows us that even poor, inner-city black families are far from the monolith that Moynihanian-influenced studies and television documentaries reduce them to.

This perspective also allows us to focus on the working-class family which is virtually invisible in most studies. While the deficit models concentrate on upper and lower economic classes, it is the working class, Billingsley makes clear, that is the key to whether the status of African-American families as a whole will improve or decline. They have always been the backbone of the black community, he says, and the group which will either move up to increase the numbers of the middle class or down and become a part of the poorer economic classes. And it is they, of course, who have been the most devastated by the public policies and restructuring of the economy in the last decade.

Finally, this framework helps us look at "problems" of the African-American family differently. For example, the growing number of female single heads of households should not be seen only as evidence of some kind of intrafamily breakdown, but also as a means to adapt to and cope with the buffeting forces of contemporary life. History implies that where black women, of any class, have faith in the prospect of upward mobility, they have fewer out-of-wedlock births.

These realizations and others in *Climbing Jacob's Ladder* have profound implications for public policy as well as personal perception. More aid that specifically targets the working class and working poor would seem to have far-reaching implications. And for single-headed households, less attention should be paid to the configuration of the family and more to empowering the mother with adequate child care so that she might remain in school and adequate health care for her and her children. This would seem to be more effective than making welfare conditional on some meaningless labor force participation. And it certainly would be more effective than only focusing on the marital disincentives of unemployed males; or encouraging women to shift their dependence from the welfare rolls to that of a male breadwinner—as if the real problem is the lack of patriarchal dominance. And in the long run, of course, a meaningful future is the only truly effective public policy.

Climbing Jacob's Ladder provides us with important data, information, and analysis; it corrects misconceptions and stereotypes about black family life; and it provides a framework which helps us to squarely and constructively confront the problems and challenges of the family at the cusp of the twenty-first century. As such the book is not only illuminating, but enabling for all who read it.

Introduction

The African-American family is neither dead nor dying, nor vanishing. Instead, the family remains a resilient and adaptive institution reflecting the most basic values, hopes, and aspirations of the descendants of African people in America. But to say that black families are alive is not to say that they are all faring well.

It would be naive in the extreme to ignore the many pressures bearing down and compromising the ability of many to meet the basic needs of their members. But there is another side to the story. And we argue in this book that this other side—enduring, positive, and powerful—is more important because it is more generative. It can continually renew and sustain this vital sector of American society in the years ahead.

Many scholars have argued that African-American family structure is weak. We have argued that African-American family structure is strong. In this regard, *Climbing Jacob's Ladder* is both a sequel and a companion to *Black Families in White America,* first published in 1968 and reissued in a twentieth-anniversary edition in 1988 by Simon & Schuster. In this new work, we argue that African-American families are both weak and strong but their strengths are by far more powerful and contain the seeds of their survival and rejuvenation.

From time to time, people inside as well as outside the black community depict it as a small, insignificant minority, "only" 12

17

percent of the nation's population, characterized by poverty, dysfunctional families, and general powerlessness. In the early 1990s, for instance, we heard that black voters, constituting "only" 28 percent of the electorate in Louisiana, could not prevent the election of David Duke, who was running on a racist platform for United States Senator and, later, for governor. Most commentators did not anticipate that a unified, inspired black minority would lead a coalition that defeated Duke both times.

How could a presumably insignificant minority prevail? In part, because they did not define themselves as such. They chose instead to identify with their strengths, which were myriad. The lesson that emerges from this experience applies equally well outside the political arena. Its relevance to family policy and family development is striking, particularly in light of the dramatic changes we have witnessed in black families during the past twenty-five years.

We believe that black families have arrived at a point of maximum danger, which is also a point of maximum opportunity. A proper understanding of this watershed era is absolutely essential, not only for sustaining African-American families, but other family groups as well.

Our approach is wholistic in the sense that it takes into account the totality of African-American family life. Our analysis includes two-parent families, single-parent families, and no-parent families. It includes upper-income as well as middle- and low-income families. It embraces highly achieving families as well as marginal and troubled families. It recognizes the changing family dynamics throughout the life cycle. For scholars and others who argue whether it was slavery or contemporary racism that cripples African-American families, we argue that it is both and more. We search for the impact of both historical and contemporary social forces on patterns of family life. And to the argument whether it is poverty or racial discrimination (both of which are on the rise) that threaten black families more, we urge that economic deprivation is as invidious as racial discrimination and just as powerful. Yet other factors are at work too. Forged by the heritage and contemporary status of the African-American people themselves, these factors include their values, survival techniques, records of achievement, and capacity to work with others, as well as their often underestimated levels of economic, political, and social power. How to capture this generative power and how to use it in helping families realize their inherent potential: these are our deepest concerns.

The book is organized into six parts, each exploring a theoretical proposition. Part I explores the proposition that the whole of African-American family life is greater than its parts. Any particular aspect of family structure cannot be meaningfully interpreted in isolation. Here we set forth the wholistic perspective which guides the rest of the book.

Part II is titled "History Is Prologue." Students of the African-American family who give any attention at all to history generally begin and end with slavery, and focus on what the European people did to the African people. While that is an important aspect of African-American history, we hold that it is not the whole of that history and heritage which has affected the development of African-American families. We explore selected aspects of the evolution of African-American families from their origins in Africa, through the slave trade, and the period immediately following slavery. Each of these epochs reveals particular sources of strength which have helped to insure the African people's ability to survive and contribute to family life and to the larger society.

In Part III we explore the proposition that "Society Has the Upper Hand." It reflects our view that in relations between families and their society, though the influence is mutual, society has greater power to shape the outcome. The question here is how do the forces, institutions, and systems of the larger society impact both positively and negatively on family viability? The health care, education, and military systems offer a variety of insights.

In Part IV we examine the proposition that African-American families are adaptive. They adapt their structures and their patterns of operation according to the pressures and opportunities of the larger society in their constant effort to meet the needs of their members. One chapter examines the persistence of married-couple families, the functions of marriage, the place of other types of family structure, and the patterns of interaction among family members. Another chapter explores the manner in which African-Americans adapt to the changing racial climate by embracing interracial marriages in increasing numbers. A third chapter explores the relative adaptability of native-born African-American families and those of Caribbean descent in adjusting to the conditions of life imposed on both groups by discrimination.

Part V addresses the proposition that the African-American community is generative. Its internal spiritual, intellectual, cultural, social, physical, economic, and political resources constitute the building blocks for upward mobility and for strong families. We show that in coalescing around a set of values and aspirations, working-class, middle-class, and upper-class families intersect in striking ways.

Part VI explores the proposition that the future of African-American families is already here emerging from their present situation. While some scholars hold that blacks need to abandon their traditional values, institutions, organizations, and leaders, and seek greater assimilation into white institutions, organizations, and ways of life (culture), we hold quite to the contrary. It is by building strong institutions, organizations, and alliances based on traditional values and their history and heritage that blacks have already entered the mainstream of national and world society as equals. The question is, therefore, not whether to build black institutions or to integrate into white institutions. The object is to see the value of both strategies and to seek a newer world that moves beyond race, race prejudice, and racial discrimination to greater levels of equality and equalitarianism.

The chapters in Part VI explore the manner in which black churches, business enterprise, economic and political development, cultural expression, and a broad array of black leadership and organizations already operative hold the key to black family viability. It is from this base that the ideas, commitment, energy, and know-how will come that can bring social reform that will enable more African-American families to rise above the odds arrayed against them.

We take sharp issue with those who hold that the underclass is permanent or self-perpetuating; or that nothing can be done to rescue families caught in its web; or that racism only affects poor people; or that only the government can make a difference. We do not accept the conventional view that the spectacular rise of the black middle class, accompanied by the even more spectacular rise in the underclass, is a puzzling paradox. As we reflect on history and contemplate the future, nothing could be further from the truth.

It will be apparent throughout that we do not invariably use white families as a comparison or normative group, despite the widely held view among social scientists that the only way to describe black families is to show their similarities to or differences from white families. We sometimes use the black-white comparison when it helps to clarify a point, but we do not feel bound to do so on every characteristic.

What white families believe, how they act, and how they are structured do not constitute controlling norms for African-American people. All people participate in fashioning the norms of contemporary society. If we are interested in social change, the black-white comparison not only distorts the reality, complexity, and diversity among black families but often serves as a disincentive to reform. If comparisons are warranted, then comparisons of black families in different situations are much more helpful.

True reform must come from within people themselves. And no true reform can be based on a people's weakness; it must be based on their strengths. Thus it is much more important to compare poor black families who are dysfunctional with poor black families who are functional. And it is much more helpful if we compare poor black families with black families in the working class, the middle class, and upper class than to compare them with middle-class whites. The reason is that with effort and the right set of policies and opportunities, poor black families have a chance of becoming nonpoor black families as many have done before them.

There are more than three times as many nonpoor blacks as there are poor blacks. Every black community is peopled with them. The underclass is only half of that poor third. A majority of black working-class and middle-class individuals live in the inner cities of the nation and not in the white suburbs. There are more black adults who have graduated from high school and who know how to read and write than there are black high school dropouts. There are three times as many black youths who have managed to stay out of the criminal justice system than the celebrated 25 percent who have become engulfed in it. There are far more black persons who grew up in viable, stable, upward-striving black families than otherwise. And as we see in several chapters in this book, they have millions of achieving, successful role models.

The black community is not only rich in talent, but rich in numbers as well. The population, which stood at 400,000 at the end of slavery and at just 1 million at the time of the first census in 1790 and only 10 million at the turn of this century, had reached more than 30 million by 1990 and is expanding at a much more rapid rate than the nation as a whole. The future viability of

African-American families requires greater recognition and utilization of the strengths of that community, among which is the strength in numbers.

Our wholistic perspective helps us to see that major societal transitions affect all institutions, including families. We will argue throughout this book that many contemporary black family patterns can be viewed as adaptations to those conditions. In this context, we will give particular attention to changing technology and the rise and decline of the black working class.

We conclude that while all African-American families are not in a state of crisis, the many who do suffer inordinately are not so much in crisis as they are engulfed by a set of crisis conditions, most of which emanate from society itself.

This book reflects our belief that one cannot understand contemporary patterns of African-American family life without placing them in their broad historical, societal, and cultural context. We seek, therefore, to expand on our 1968 social systems approach to the study of African-American family life and make some additional contribution toward a general theory of African-American family development.

Some readers may consider our views overly optimistic, or even naive. They will take issue with our insistence on looking at the positive as well as the negative. And they may reject out of hand our assertion that the African-American community and its families are strong entities—weak, too, but more strong than weak, containing within their heritage, their history of achievement against the odds, their values, their humanitarianism, their resilience, and adaptability, those forces which can insure a viable future. Some readers may tend toward the view that American society is too rigid, too decadent, too racist, too self-centered, and as James Baldwin might say, too scared to change and make an equitable place for its African-American citizens.

Readers who approach this book with such skeptical views may be pardoned. For much of what they have read about the African-American people suggests that they are too weak, poor, problem-ridden, dependent, and other-worldly to exercise the force necessary to overturn the status quo. After all, it can be argued, if Frederick Douglass, Marcus Garvey, Martin Luther King, Jr., and Fannie Lou Hamer could not rouse the black race to its full potential, how can lesser leaders expect to succeed? And as for changing the American society, if Abraham Lincoln couldn't do it by freeing the slaves, and if Lyndon Johnson and Earl Warren with the Great Society and the proactive Supreme Court could not implement Daniel Patrick Moynihan's dream of stable black families, what can be expected in the era of Reagan-Bush conservatism and the more reactionary Supreme Court? All legitimate doubts. But the strength of the black experience is underestimated in part by underestimating the length and depth of it, the variety and complexity of it, but especially, the regenerative power of it.

Our view, however, is that a sufficiently broad and deep understanding of the black experience in the world and in the nation will reveal that there are values and adaptive capacities as well as social, economic, and political structures, movements, and personages already in place attesting to the possibility of harnessing the enormous resources of this people, connecting them with the forces of the larger society in ways to make family life more viable. The resourceful black grandmother, the vital black church, the effective black school, the successful black business enterprise, the authentic black scholar, the hardworking, long-suffering black masses, the upwardly mobile sectors: all hold important keys to the regeneration of our families, our communities, and our society—not only for our own benefit, but for the enhancement of that larger sense of community that Martin Luther King, Jr., dreamed about.

We urge the reader to consider this larger view. And we bring to the task a certain amount of faith. We find support for this view in the writings of the founding elders of our discipline: W.E.B. Du Bois, Charles S. Johnson, and E. Franklin Frazier. And we share the view recently expressed by John Hope Franklin, who wrote in *Race and History: Selected Essays,* "If one believes in the power of his own words and in the words of others, one must also hope and believe that the world will be a better place for our having spoken or written those words."

The poet Maya Angelou understands the regenerative quality in African-American culture much better than many social scientists. This is why she can sing so eloquently, "And still I rise." Large numbers of ordinary black people understand it too, which is why they can sing, "We are climbing Jacob's ladder."

PART I

The Whole
Is Greater
Than Its Parts

Chapter 1

In Intimate Association:
Tradition and Transitions in
African-American Family Structure

For years the technological revolution has been driving American families to adopt new patterns for survival. As industrial society gives way to the new information society and the blue-collar manufacturing economy gives way to the white-collar service economy, nontraditional lifestyles have become commonplace. Nearly everyone knows that divorce, adult singlehood, cohabitation, childless couples, and single parenthood have surged. The greatest manifestations of these structural changes are no respecters of race, color, or social class.

Many of the profound recent changes in African-American family life that spring from this transformation in society are likely to persist into the new century. Any serious effort to judge what they mean, however, requires a considerably broader perspective than most observers bring to bear.

Too many discussions of African-American families focus exclusively on single-parent families or on the underclass or on children in trouble as if these phenomena were characteristic of African-American families. Inadvertently, they contribute to stereotypical thinking that sets these families apart from other American families. The result is an absurd and counterproductive tendency to see African-American families in isolation, out of the context of their communities and the larger society.

We take a different view. It begins with a concise but rather complex definition.

What do we mean by "African-American family"? Essentially, it is an *intimate association* of persons of African descent who are *related to one another* by a variety of means, including blood, marriage, formal adoption, informal adoption, or by appropriation; sustained by a history of common residence in America; and deeply embedded in a network of social structures both internal to and external to itself. Numerous interlocking elements come together, forming an extraordinarily resilient institution.

Blood ties or lineage constitute the strongest element in the African-American kinship system. (At the beginning of the slave trade, families were defined more by blood ties [sanguinity] than by marital ties [conjugality], while in seventeenth-century European culture it was just the opposite.) Among women, who are the primary culture bearers for the group, it often happens that if a choice must be made between allegiance to blood relatives, including siblings, parents, or children, or to marital partners, the latter allegiance must give way. Wise and mature black men understand this and strive mightily to avoid such confrontations.

The primacy of blood ties, however, does not mean that marriage ties are unimportant. Both relationships are highly valued and highly honored. Indeed, at every time period since the end of slavery until about 1980, a majority of African-American families have been married-couple families.

The value placed on marriage is still so strong that a majority of African-American youths and adults want to be married. Even when one marriage is dissolved, a majority seek still another. Many persons who are separated and divorced continue to believe that marriage is preferable.

This has led sociologist Hylan Lewis to conclude that there is no need to focus on teaching values of marriage and stability to African-American youths. They already exist. The need instead is to create the conditions which make it possible to consummate and sustain the marital bond which they value.[1]

Marriage in the African tradition is not simply a union between two people but between groups of people. The kinship unit expands to embrace another whole set of kinfolk. Much of that tradition is still alive among contemporary African-American families. While marriage no longer requires the permission of parents, it is common to treat marriage as an event involving the sanction and support of the two families. When that does not occur an element of instability is introduced. Moreover, the relationship between members of the two families is often so close that even after divorce of a couple, one member will continue close relations with the family of the former spouse.

Another element in the formation and perpetuation of African-American families is formal adoption. This is the procedure by which black adults, married or single, go through legal procedures sanctioned by the courts to claim responsibility for a child not necessarily related to them by blood or marital ties. Formal adoption is highly valued and frequently practiced among the African-American people. This is not always understood by the wider society or by social agencies. When in the 1960s and 1970s some social agencies began recruiting white couples to adopt black children, some social scientists assured them that African-American people had a cultural aversion to adopting these children, many of whom were born out of wedlock. It is perhaps the height of irony that while social scientists were describing black families as being characterized by a tendency toward female-headed families with children born out of wedlock, they were also assuring the public that blacks rejected these children. At the very same time the transracial adoption movement was being championed as a solution to the problem, blood relatives accepted a majority of these children into their families. This is still the case today.

While it is not generally reported, middle-income African-American families adopt children at a higher rate than their white counterparts. This fact is often obscured by the practice of comparing black and white families from samples composed primarily of low-income black families and middle-income white families. Indeed, if black married-couple families are compared with similar white families, the formal adoption rate is higher among the black couples.[2] And since the evolution of black adoption agencies and programs beginning with Sydney Duncan's Homes for Black Children in Detroit in the 1960s, the formal adoption rates for black married and single persons have increased. Formal adoption has a long and honorable tradition among African-American families. This is part of the reason Father George H. Clements, a black Catholic priest, has been so successful in getting black churches to encourage black families to adopt black children. Within a decade after he adopted two boys and launched his one-church, one-child movement, more than 10,000 children have been adopted through this program alone.

It is in the realm of informal adoptions, however, where the

TABLE 1.1
**Children Living in Households of Grandparents
1970–1989**

	1970	1979	1989
Number of informally adopted children	1,302,000	1,363,000	1,232,000
Percentage of all children	13.3	14.9	16.5
Total percentage	100	100	100
Both parents present	11	4	4
Mother only	21	18	56
Father only	2	1	2
Neither parent present	66	77	38

SOURCE: U.S. Bureau of the Census, *Current Population Reports, Household and Family Characteristics 1970, 1979, and 1989.*

black extended family has excelled. Most black children born out of wedlock are cared for by extended families, generally their grandmothers, without the benefit of legal adoption. Robert Hill found that 90 percent of black babies born out of wedlock are reared in three-generational families headed by their grandparents. Moreover, the number of informally adopted children living with extended kin increased from 1.3 million in 1970 to 1.4 million in 1979. Nearly 15 percent of all black children are informally adopted. Reynolds Farley and Walter Allen found in an analysis of 1980 census data that a third of all African-American families were extended in the sense that at least one other relative lived with a nuclear family core. Robert Hill has estimated that by 1990 some 40 percent of African-American families were extended. According to Hill the U.S. Census shows that the number of children living in households of extended kin (informal adoption) rose from 13.3 percent of all black children in 1970 to 14.9 percent in 1979 and to 16.5 percent in 1989. Thus at a time when there was a prevailing view that extended families were on the decline, they were in fact increasing as a proportion of all black families.[3]

This is due to the persistence of informal adoption. Hill has shown the extent of this phenomenon. The number of informally adopted children by extended kin stood at 1.4 million in 1979, accounting for some 15 percent of all black children, and at 1.2 million in 1989, constituting 16.5 percent of all black children (Table 1.1).

Grandparents continue to be the primary agents of informal

adoption. The U.S. Census for 1989 reports that some 1.2 million black children lived with their grandparents. In 38 percent of the families where grandparents presided neither of the children's parents lived in the home. In some 56 percent of these families the children's mother was also present, while in another 2 percent their fathers only were present and in 4 percent both parents were present.

Our definition of the African-American family includes the relationship of appropriation. These are unions without blood ties or marital ties. People can become part of a family unit or, indeed, form a family unit simply by deciding to live and act toward each other as family.

Reverend Otis Moss of Cleveland, Ohio, remembers that his mother died when he and the other children were young. His father worked hard to sustain the family unit. Then a few short years later his father was killed in an auto accident. While young Otis was standing viewing the wreckage, a woman completely unrelated to him took him by the arm and said, "Come home with me." He grew up as a member of her family. He graduated from high school, was inducted into the army, and went off to college, experiencing a very important and not uncommon form of African-American family life, even though there were neither blood ties, marriage ties, nor formal adoption.

The propensity to care for other people's children has led naturally into involvement in the foster care system where black families have distinguished themselves. Though the payments from the governmental authorities for caring for these children are generally inadequate, many black families have raised these children for long periods of time. Often they become the only families the children recognize. At any one time, nearly a third of black children are being reared in foster families.[4]

There is an element in African-American family life which Carol Stack calls "fictive kin" and others call "play mother, brother or sister, aunt, uncle, or cousin." This can still be a strong basis for family unity in the African-American community. Indeed, our own children have so many "aunts," "uncles," and "cousins" unrelated to them by blood that they can hardly keep track of them. Whenever they are in need, however, or reach a particular transition in their lives, they can count on assistance from these "appropriated" family members.

Finally, in our definition of African-American family organiza-

TABLE 1.2
African-American Family Structures

| | MAJOR STRUCTURES | | |
| | | | |
Primary Members	*Nuclear Families (Primary Members)*	*Extended Families (Primary members Plus Other Relatives)*	*Augmented Families (Primary Members Plus Nonrelatives)*
Married couple with no children	Incipient Nuclear	Incipient Extended	Incipient Augmented
Married couple with children	Simple Nuclear	Simple Extended	Simple Augmented
Unmarried mother with children	Segmented Nuclear I	Segmented Extended I	Segmented Augmented I
Unmarried father with children	Segmented Nuclear II	Segmented Extended II	Segmented Augmented II

SOURCE: Andrew Billingsley

tion, people do not have to live in the same household in order to function as a family unit. They only need share some history of common residence with some part of the family at some time in the past. Persons living in different households often function as members of the same intergenerational kinship unit.

African-American families tend to be caught between conflicting demands—the economic, physical, social, psychological, and spiritual demands of their members on the one hand, and the demands of society on the other. In an effort to resolve this conflict, they have adopted a wide variety of family structures. The three major structures that have emerged—nuclear families, extended families, and augmented families—have given rise to twelve different subtypes, depending on gender and marital status of family heads, and the presence or absence of children, other relatives, or nonrelatives (Table 1.2).[5] This twelve-part typology was developed in our earlier work and has been widely replicated and modified by other scholars.[6]

Among these studies, the work of Isabel Payton is most extensive. Utilizing a national sample taken from the U.S. Department of Agriculture's Consumer Expenditure Survey, she was able to replicate parts of our original typology. Her analysis of the various types of female-headed households found more than a half dozen subtypes (Table 1.3). Moreover, in such an extensive and sophis-

TABLE 1.3
Typology of Single-Parent-Headed Households

Type	Example
MODIFIED NUCLEAR (only head and children in the home)[1]	
1. Natural parent[2] Own children—all related to the head by blood, marriage, or adoption	Divorced, separated, widowed, or never-married parent raising his/her own children.
2. Surrogate parent Other children—all children other than the head's own	Lone adult raising his/her grandchildren, younger siblings, nieces, nephews, cousins, or foster children.
3. Natural surrogate parent Own *and* other children	Divorced, separated, widowed, or never-married parent raising his/her own children *and* grandchildren, younger siblings, nieces, nephews, cousins, or foster children.
MODIFIED EXTENDED (head, children, and additional adults in the home)	
Natural parent—own children	
4. Own adult children—all adults related to the head by blood, marriage, or adoption	Divorced, separated, widowed, or never-married parent sharing his/her home with only own children *and* adult children.
5. Other adults—all adults other than the head's own adult children	Divorced, separated, widowed, or never-married parent sharing his/her home with own children, *and* other adults, such as siblings, parents, nieces, nephews, cousins, and/or friends of either sex.
6. Multi-adults—own adult children *and* other adults	Divorced, separated, widowed, or never-married parent sharing his/her home with own children *and* adult children *and* other adults, such as siblings, parents, nieces, nephews, cousins, and/or friends of either sex; spouses of adult children and/or other relatives.
Surrogate parent—other children	
7. Own adult children—all adults related to the head by blood, marriage, or adoption	Adult head sharing his/her home with grandchildren, younger siblings, nieces, nephews, cousins, or foster children *and* adult children.

TABLE 1.3 (*continued*)

Type	Example
8. Other adults—all adults other than the head's own adult children	Adult head sharing his/her home with grandchildren, younger siblings, nieces, nephews, cousins, or foster children *and* other adults, such as siblings, parents, nieces, nephews, cousins, and/or friends of either sex.
9. Multi-adults—own adult children *and* other adults	Adult head sharing his/her home with grandchildren, younger siblings, nieces, nephews, cousins, or foster children *and* adult children *and* other adults, such as siblings, parents, nieces, nephews, cousins, and/or friends of either sex; spouses of adult children and/or other relatives.
Natural-surrogate parent—own *and* other children	
10. Own adult children—all adults related to the head by blood, marriage, or adoption	Divorced, separated, widowed, or never-married parent sharing his/her home with own children *and* grandchildren, siblings, nieces, cousins, or foster children *and* adult children.
11. Other adults—all adults other than the head's own adult children	Divorced, separated, widowed, or never-married parent sharing his/her home with own children *and* grandchildren, siblings, nieces, nephews, cousins, or foster children *and* other adults, such as siblings, parents, nieces, nephews, cousins, and/or friends of either sex.
12. Multi-adults—own adult children and other adults	Divorced, separated, widowed, or never-married parent sharing his/her home with own children *and* grandchildren, siblings, nieces, nephews, cousins, or foster children *and* other adults, such as siblings, parents, nieces, nephews, cousins, and/or friends of either sex; spouses of adult children and/or other relatives.

[1] Children are all persons less than 18 years of age regardless of their relationship to the head. Adults are all persons 18 or more years of age.

[2] All of the children are the head's own children; this is considered as the traditional nuclear single-parent household.

SOURCE: Isabel Payton, 1982, p. 12.

ticated analysis much of the racial differences disappeared. Specifically Payton found that some two-thirds of single-parent families were modified nuclear and one-third were modified extended. Both these types involved several subtypes, with natural parents playing a role in the majority of instances. In another replication, William Dressler, Susan Haworth-Hoeppner, and Barbara Pitts developed a four-way typology with twelve subtypes.[7]

Dressler and his associates point out that the most commonly studied female-headed household consisting of a mother and her children or grandchildren accounted for only 22.2 percent of the families in the community they studied. Other types of female-headed households consisted of women living alone (12 percent); women living with other relatives or nonrelatives (3.8 percent, but not their children); and women living with their own parents or grandparents (2.4 percent). And while this essentially adds up to the 41 percent female-headed households commonly reported in the literature, Dressler reminds us that different types of female-headed families have different meanings. And perhaps different causes and different consequences as well.

On the basis of these and other recent findings, William Cross concluded:

> Thus, the evolution of the urban, poor black single-parent household is more a function of the unique stresses and supports these families face in urban areas, than an outgrowth of a historically matrilocal culture, the problems of transition to life in cities, or the development of a culture of poverty. In short, the nemesis of black life is not the black family, it is the black struggle with unemployment, racism, and a containment-oriented welfare system.[8]

What these scholars find is that the single-parent family is not generated from within African-American culture or values but from forces in the wider society, largely beyond their immediate control.

This research enables us to see that the structure of African-American family life is purposive, that is, it is not accidental, haphazard, or mysterious. It is an adaptive strategy for meeting the basic needs of its members given the situation they face in contemporary society.

In short, the common misconception that African-American families are characterized by single-parent, female-headed structures is as misleading as is the widespread assumption that they got that way because of factors internal to their culture.

FAMILY STRUCTURE DIVERSITY

For the hundred-year period between the end of slavery and the aftermath of World War II the structure of African-American family life was characterized by a remarkable degree of stability. Specifically, the core of the traditional African-American family system has been the nuclear family composed of husband and wife and their own children. Divorce was rare and couples stayed together till the death of a spouse. Children lived with their parents until maturity, then started their own families. As late as 1960 when uneducated black men could still hold good-paying blue-collar jobs in the industrial sector, 78 percent of all black families with children were headed by married couples (Figure 1.1). By 1970 only 64 percent of African-American families with children were headed by married couples. This declined steadily to a minority of 48 percent by 1980; and to 39 percent by 1990. This trend is likely to continue into the future.

Meanwhile, the incidence of one of the alternatives to the traditional family, the female-headed single-parent family, has escalated enormously over the past generation. Consisting of a minority of 20 percent of families with children in 1960, this

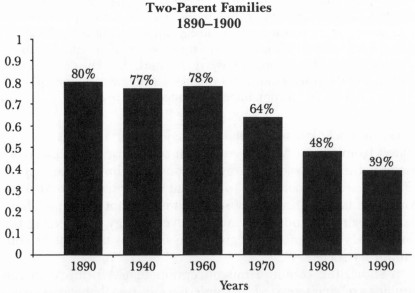

FIGURE 1-1
Two-Parent Families
1890–1900

SOURCE: U.S. Bureau of the Census, *Current Population Studies, The Black Population in the U.S. 1790–1978, January 1980* and U.S. Bureau of the Census, *Current Population Reports Household and Family Characteristics, 1980 and 1990.*

family form had increased to 33 percent by 1970, to 49 percent by 1980, and to a whopping 57 percent by 1990. Over the same period single fathers bringing up their own children increased from 2 percent to 4 percent.[9]

Beginning in 1980 for the first time in history, female-headed families with children outnumbered married-couple families with children. For the first time since slavery, a majority of black children lived in single-parent families. Thus the nuclear, extended, and augmented family forms which were adopted after slavery and which were to serve the African-American people well for 125 years are all in a rapid state of decline. The major observation here is that both black men and women have been avoiding or abandoning marriage in record numbers during recent years. But this is more a shift in the marriage relation than in the family.

Marriage, as has been pointed out above, is only one of several bases for family formation and endurance. The allegiance to family is still so strong that on any given day the overwhelming majority of African-American people will be found living in families of one type or another. In 1990, for example, 70 percent of the 10.5 million African-American households were family households with persons related by blood, marriage, or adoption. Contrary to popular belief, this is about the same as the proportion of whites who live in families. (Though among Hispanics a high 84 percent still lived in family households.)

What has taken the place of the traditional family system? A number of alternative family structures have arisen in postindustrial America to characterize the contemporary pattern of African-American family diversity.[10]

Single-Person Households

Increasing numbers of African-American adults are living in single-person households. They are single either because they have never been married or have been married and separated, widowed, or divorced. Young persons are delaying marriage longer than in former years. Many are deciding to forgo marriage altogether. The norms of society no longer require that persons be married in order to live respectable, healthy, and happy lives.

The world of black adult singles has expanded enormously in recent years. As late as 1975, only 11 percent of black men ages thirty-five to forty-four were still single. These figures had not changed appreciably since 1890. The proportion of black adult single women was slightly lower and also steady at about 8 percent over this period.

After 1980, however, the population of adult black singles would rise dramatically. Not only were large numbers remaining unmarried but a substantial proportion of those were choosing to live apart from their families in single-person households.

In 1983, of the 8.9 million black households in the nation, a total of 2,054,000 were single-person households with adults living alone. This represented 23 percent of all black households. Women outnumbered men slightly at 1,120,000 to 934,000.

By 1986, these numbers had increased to 2,500,000, constituting 21 percent of the 9.8 million black households in that year. Single females living alone continued to outnumber men. By 1990 some 25 percent of the 10.5 million black households were occupied by single adults.

This does not mean, of course, that these singles are without family relationships; they may have strong family ties, relationships, and responsibilities without living in the same household. Still, it is a growing phenomenon which helps to accentuate the relative decline in married-couple families. It is important to note that this is a relative decline and not an absolute decline in black married-couple families. The actual numbers of married-couple families continue to increase, rising from 3.3 million in 1970 to 3.4 million in 1980 and to over 3.8 million by 1990. At the same time, however, other types of family structures and other living arrangements have expanded much more rapidly.

Cohabitation

Small but expanding numbers of adults are choosing to live with another person of the opposite sex and sometimes of the same sex in a marriage-like relationship without benefit of legal marriage. While less than 5 percent of black adults live in cohabitation relationships, the numbers are expanding rapidly. Some do so as a prelude to marriage. Others do so in the aftermath of marriage. Still others pursue cohabitation as an alternative to marriage. Social norms have changed so drastically in recent years that even in the black community cohabitation, which has a long history, referred to as "shacking up," has come to be acceptable and almost respectable. These arrangements tend, however, to be short-lived and less stable than conventional marriages.

The number of cohabitating couples is difficult to know. In

TABLE 1.4
Cohabitation Experience of Women Aged 15–44
1988

Age	Cohabitated Before First Marriage (%)	Ever Cohabitated (%)	Ever Married (%)
All Ages	29.3	35.0	47.1
15–19	3.7	3.7	1.5
20–24	28.6	29.0	23.6
25–29	44.3	47.8	47.7
30–34	42.0	52.1	69.0
35–39	34.3	45.0	75.1
40–44	19.4	32.8	83.5

SOURCE: Division of Vital Statistics, National Center for Health Statistics, Public Health Service, U.S. Department of Health and Human Services, 1988.

addition to the unmarried persons living in the single-person households described above, large numbers live in two-person households with persons to whom they are not married and not related. In 1983, there were 266,000 such couples, representing 3 percent of all black households.

By 1986, these numbers had increased to 297,000, accounting for 3.2 percent of all living arrangements. By 1990 these numbers had risen to 315,000, still about 3 percent of the 10.5 million black households at that time. This is the most likely pool where cohabitating couples may be found.

While the practice of cohabitation, defined as "not married but living with a partner or boyfriend," may involve less than 5 percent of black households at any one time, a study conducted by the National Center for Health Statistics in 1988 shows that cohabitation is a phase through which increasing numbers of black women pass at some time in their lives.[11]

A number of findings with respect to black women illustrate some important changes in this practice. One finding relates to the ages of the women (Table 1.4). Data show that the most extensive cohabitation is among women aged twenty-five to thirty-nine. Nearly half of these women indicate that they have engaged in sexually based cohabitation with a man at some time in their lives. Better than a third indicate that they cohabitated with their first husband prior to marriage. Among younger women and older women the practice is less common. Even so, nearly a third of women aged twenty to twenty-four and aged forty to forty-four indicate a cohabitation experience.

TABLE 1.5
Status of Women Who Have Ever Cohabitated
1988

Status	(%)
All women cohabitants	100
Still intact cohabitation	9.2
Intact marriage	26.5
Dissolved marriage	15.6
Dissolved cohabitation	48.7

SOURCE: Division of Vital Statistics, National Center for Health Statistics, Public Health Service, U.S. Department of Health and Human Services, 1988.

Another observation is that cohabitation often leads to marriage. Among ever-married black women, some 29 percent report that they cohabitated with their first husband prior to marriage. This was less likely for married women forty and over, but it was especially pronounced for those between twenty-five and thirty-four.

Cohabitation does not always lead to marriage, however, and when it does not it is considerably less stable than marriage (Table 1.5). Among black women who ever cohabitated only 9.2 percent were still in those cohabitation relationships in 1988. Some 26.5 percent were in an intact marriage. Another 15.6 percent were married and divorced, while a significant 48.7 percent of cohabitational relationships had not led to marriage nor were the participants intact as cohabitating couples.

Children, No Marriage

Among the most rapidly expanding family structures are those where there are children without marriage. In 1983, there were 3,043,000 black single-parent households (as compared with 3,486,000 married-couple households and 2,386,000 nonfamily households). These constituted some 33 percent of the 8.9 million black households. Of these, 1,989,000 were single parents with children under eighteen. In these households, 127,000 were male-headed families and 1,862,000 were female headed. The 872,000 female-headed families whose children are eighteen and over must surely be distinguished from the 1.8 million who have children under eighteen. They do not share the same responsibilities and resources.

What is the source of their single-parent status? Among both men and women, the major source is primarily never-married parenthood, and also divorce, separation, and widowhood. Among men, 98,000 were never married, 79,000 were divorced, 68,000 were widowed, and 64,000 were married with absent spouse due to incarceration, long-term illness, or desertion.

Among women a similar pattern is obtained. The number never married comprised 655,000. Divorced mothers were also 655,000, followed by those married with absent spouses at 646,000, and 534,000 widows with children.

By 1986, single-parent families from all sources had expanded. Overall, the numbers had increased to 3,242,000, representing 33 percent of the 9.8 million black households. By 1990 these had increased to 3.7 million, accounting for 35 percent of the 10.5 million total black households.

Marriage, No Children

A further deviation from traditional families is married couples without children. In 1983, there were 1,585,000 black married couples without children. This represented 18 percent of all 8.9 million black households. By 1986, this had increased to 1,683,000, representing 17 percent of 9.8 million households. By 1990, of the 3.8 million total black married couples some 1.8 million had no children of their own under 18. This represented 17 percent of the 10.5 million black households.

Who are these couples without children? They are generally the more highly educated, higher-income, two-earner families. Not only is this a sizable family form but it is a highly satisfactory one. Our studies show that married partners without children have higher levels of personal satisfaction, family satisfaction, satisfaction with life in general, and self-esteem than any other type of family structure.

Marriage and Children

Finally, we come to a family pattern that approaches the traditional. These are married couples with children. And despite the relative decline of this form in relation to other forms it is still quite prevalent. In 1983, there were 1,901,000 such families, exceeding slightly the number of couples without children. Altogether, they accounted for 21 percent of the 8.9 million black households that year.

By 1986, despite population growth, there were still only 1,997,000 married-couple families with children. This amounted to a relatively stable 20 percent of the 9.8 million black households. By 1990, the nearly 2 million black married couples with children under eighteen still represented only 19 percent of the 10.5 million black households. While this 3 percent decline since 1983 is not as dramatic as popular discussion would suggest, when considered in the context of the rapid expansion of other living arrangements it is clear that this simple nuclear family form has not been holding its formerly preeminent place among African-American family structures.

Children and Grandparents

Parents are not the only persons to head families. Grandparents still play an important role in extended families. There were some 1.2 million children living with grandparents in 1989 (Table 1.6). Altogether some 465,000, or 38 percent, of these children were being reared by their grandparents with neither of their parents present. For some 56 percent of them only 691,000 or the mother was present, in 2 percent only fathers were present, for 4 percent both parents were present, though grandparents were the householders.

Blended Families

Even among married-couple families new patterns have emerged in the years since 1970. Among these are blended families, dual-earner families, commuter-couple families, and aug-

TABLE 1.6
Children Living in Households of Grandparents
1989

	INFORMALLY ADOPTED CHILDREN	
	Number	(%)
Total children	1,232,000	100
Both parents present	44,000	4
Mother only	691,000	56
Father only	31,000	2
Neither parent present	465,000	38

SOURCE: U.S. Bureau of the Census, *Current Population Reports, Household and Family Characteristics, 1989.*

mented families with nonrelatives sharing the family household. A married couple, one or both of whom have been married previously and often with children of a prior relationship—sometimes referred to as a blended family, or reconstituted family— forms a part of the whole picture. The escalating divorce rate and the increasing remarriage rate are the sources of this family form. In addition, unmarried mothers with children often get married later to men who are not the children's father. Sometimes these men are divorced with their own children. Thus it is not uncommon for children to have two sets of grandparents and one or more sets of step-grandparents. Sometimes the step-grandparents take a greater interest in the children than the natural grandparents.

Dual-Earner Families

Married-couple families increasingly depart from the traditional relationship of husband working in the labor force and the wife a full-time homemaker. Among African-American families, dual-earner families have a long history but the numbers have accelerated in recent years. Since dual-earner families have such higher earnings than single-earner ones, it is understandable why the latter, more traditional pattern is vanishing. Indeed, black dual-earner families under thirty-five who live outside the South constitute the only category of black family whose earnings have reached parity with their white counterparts. Even this is due, in part, to the fact that black wives have a longer and more consistent history of full-time work than white wives. Often, however, this arrangement places extra strains on the wife, who must work both in the labor force and at home. Husbands do not share equitably the responsibility of child care and housework, even when wives work outside the home. This, in turn, puts additional stress on the marriage.

Commuter-Couple Families

Another alternative to tradition is the commuter-couple family. Under this structural arrangement, the husband works and lives for the work week in one city while the wife and the children live in a different city, usually where the wife has a career.

Augmented Families

Augmented families, those family units where nonrelatives live with the nuclear or extended family core, continue to play an important role in African-American family life.

By 1990 there were some 756,000 augmented families with nonrelatives sharing the living quarters with family members. This constituted nearly 8 percent of the 10.5 million black households. This represented an expansion over 1986, when there were 607,000 augmented families, accounting for some 6 percent of total black households.

All this makes clear that African-American family life is not characterized by any single type of family structure. It is instead characterized by a wide variety. Nuclear families of primary relatives exist along with extended families with secondary relatives and augmented families containing nonrelatives. They break down into a dozen different types of family structure. Some of the major ones as well as the changing nature of their relative proportions have been discussed above.

The traditional two-parent, or simple, nuclear family which arose at the height of the industrial era has given way dramatically in relative terms to various alternative family structures. Among the most prominent alternative living arrangements which have arisen are single-person households, cohabiting couples, married couples without children, unmarried persons with children, and grandparents rearing grandchildren without the children's parents.

Does this mean, as some suggest, that the African-American family is vanishing? Not at all. It means instead that families are doing what they always do. They are adapting as best they can to the pressures exerted upon them from their society in their gallant struggle to meet the physical, emotional, moral, and intellectual needs of their members. It is a struggle for existence, viability, and a sense of worth. Families that are less able to avoid or resist these societal pressures must adapt their structures in order to survive. That the overwhelming majority of African-American people continue to live in families, and to form new ones as the old ones lose their vitality, must be counted among the strengths of African-American families. It is a testament to their adaptive capacity. Such adaptation is not, of course, without tremendous costs. Without such adaptation, however, the costs would be much greater for the families and their members as well as for their community and their society. All these diverse family structures, now common and growing, constitute the essence of contemporary African-American family life. Some are involuntary, some temporary and transitional. Some are filled with pain and suffering. All, however, have arisen to fill some need and function.

Moreover, none of the types of structures that have evolved are exclusive to the African-American people. Because these structures are driven by larger forces which affect the entire population, they appear in other groups as well. For example, in absolute numbers a majority of female-headed families are whites. If the patterning is different among African-American than other American families, it is not because blacks are peculiar or deviant, as many people still believe, but because of the reality of the American experience. In short, single-parent families do not arise from the history or culture or genes of the African-American people but from their adaptation to the pressures of their contemporary economic, political, and social circumstances. Both the structure of families and their functioning are determined significantly by large-scale societal forces. It is important to note that whites are not immune from these forces. If they are more resistant to the destructive forces of society it is because they are more privileged and protected.

The key to understanding African-American family structure is to see the whole picture with its many variations and to note its flexibility. Almost no one remains throughout life in any one of these structures. The public policy implications of viewing family structure in this manner are enormous. Daniel Patrick Moynihan understands this much better now than he did in 1965 and much better than many other social scientists; and of course, scholar-activists such as Marian Wright Edelman understand it even better.[12]

The diverse and evolving African-American families represent, in part, the fallout from the decimation of the traditional family forms. They also represent, however, the capacity to hold on to the spirit and the experience of family even in the face of vanishing tradition.

SOCIAL-CLASS DIVERSITY

If the African-American people are characterized by diverse and rapidly changing patterns of family structure—rather than any one family structure—this diversity is equally true with respect to social class.

TABLE 1.7
Social-Class Structure of Families
1969–1986

Class Strata	1969		1983		1986	
	N	(%)	N	(%)	N	(%)
Total families	4,823,000	100	6,681,000	100	7,096,000	100
Upper class ($50,000 and over)	239,000	5	401,000	6	639,000	9
Middle class ($25,000–$49,999)	1,289,000	27	1,670,000	25	1,916,000	27
Working-class nonpoor ($10,000–$24,999)	2,053,000	42	2,338,000	35	2,413,000	34
Working-class poor (under $10,000)	621,000	13	869,000	13	852,000	12
Nonworking poor (under $10,000)	621,000	13	1,403,000	21	1,277,000	18

SOURCE: U.S. Bureau of the Census, *Current Population Reports, Income and Poverty Status of Individuals and Families, 1969–1986.* Median Income in 1986 dollars.

In our own work, we have identified distinct social-class strata in the African-American community. Based primarily on level of family income complemented by education, occupation, and style of life these strata include: (1) The nonworking poor, consisting of poor families where no member has a permanent attachment to the work force; (2) the working poor, who despite working for low wages are not able to earn above the poverty line; (3) the nonpoor working class composed of unskilled and semiskilled workers with earnings above the poverty line; (4) the middle class, comprised primarily of skilled and professional workers with family income above the median for all families; and (5) a small black upper class of families with high incomes and substantial wealth as well as social and economic influence. Relying primarily on median combined family incomes converted into 1986 dollars, we have identified these five social-class strata at three points in time, 1969, 1983, and 1986, revealing a dynamic social-class structure in the African-American community (Table 1.7). It has changed over recent decades. At the very bottom of the structure, the nonworking poor, often described as the "underclass," expanded substantially from 13 percent of all black families in 1969 to a high of 21 percent in 1983 and to 18 percent in 1986. These figures refer to the nation as a whole. Some studies, notably those by

William Julius Wilson and his associates, have found that in selected Northern and Midwestern cities this group has expanded
even more extensively.[13]

Over the same period, working-poor families remained at between 12 and 13 percent of all black families, as families move into
and out of this stratum.

The most dramatic change occurred over this period in the
ranks of working-class nonpoor families. They fell from a high of
42 percent of all black families in 1969 to 35 percent in 1983 and
to 34 percent in 1986. Since 1986 the ranks of the black working-
class nonpoor families have continued to erode. By 1990, for
example, while the working poor had continued to expand, the
nonpoor working class had declined farther to a twenty-year low
of 31 percent of all black families. Some families move up into the
middle and even upper classes, while others plunge downward
into the ranks of the working poor and even the nonworking
poor. The erosion of the nonpoor working class will be discussed
extensively in two of the chapters which follow.

The black middle class, composed largely of families of white-
collar workers with incomes distinctly above the poverty level,
maintained its size throughout this period at between 25 and 27
percent of all black families. And by 1990 it was 29 percent.

Concomitant with the expansion of the nonworking poor at the
bottom of the socioeconomic scale over this period was an expansion of the small upper class at the top of the scale. Families with
median incomes of $50,000 and above expanded from 5 percent
of all black families in 1969 to 6 percent in 1983 and to an impressive 9 percent by 1986. By 1990 they had reached 14 percent
of all black families.

Nonworking Poor

Poor families where no member has a secure and productive niche
in the work force are at the bottom of the social structure. This
group has expanded substantially over the past two decades. They
were overwhelmingly single-parent families, with 75 percent single parents and only 25 percent husband-wife families. Where did
they come from? Some families moved into this stratum by persons leaving one family and creating another family without bet-
tering their conditions. The birth of children to persons who
moved out of their parents' home forming new families is an-

other. But just as surely large numbers of these families were downwardly mobile from the working poor and the nonpoor working class as the rapid march of technological change has thrown millions of unskilled, uneducated, and inexperienced workers out of work.

A profile of these families also reveals that they are more likely than any other stratum to have children under eighteen. Eighty percent have dependent children. They are also concentrated in the younger age range. An overwhelming 80 percent of the heads of these families are under sixty-five, and they are largely uneducated with a majority having not completed high school. A fifth of these family heads cannot find work and have given up looking for it. Public assistance is the major means of support for 70 percent of these families. A quarter of them receive Social Security and about 12 percent receive Supplemental Security income.

While this group of families is described as occupying the bottom rung of the social structure, it is not a static or uniform entity. These families encompass a substantial degree of variety both as to characteristics and conditions, both of which are undoubtedly reflected in different patterns of behavior as well.

Working Poor

Moving up the socioeconomic ladder, just above the nonworking poor, are the working poor. These are families headed by men and women who work regularly but for such low wages that they cannot escape poverty. It is important to note that these are almost as numerous as the nonworking poor families. Moreover, if we combine the nonworking poor with the working poor, we note that African-American families in poverty, after declining dramatically from 46 percent of all families in 1959 to 26 percent by 1969, expanded again to 34 percent by 1983 before declining slightly to 30 percent in 1986. Consequently, poor black families nearly doubled, increasing from 1.2 million families in 1969 to more than 2.2 million by 1983, with a slight decline to 2.1 million by 1986. These absolute numbers help to show the magnitude of the poverty phenomenon and the human suffering it causes. Such numbers also show the enormous cost of eradicating poverty. The up-and-down trends reveal that poverty is not permanent and intractable, however. It responds to changes of technology and policy changes in the larger society. But by 1990, the situation had not improved. Instead, poverty was on the rise again.

Who are these working poor? They are those families where at least one member is employed. They have median incomes below the poverty line due to low wages, including a minimum wage which has not kept pace with inflation. Even the rise in the minimum wage passed by the Congress in 1988 is so far below inflation that it will lift few families out of poverty.

Only one-third of these working-poor families are husband-wife families and as many have working husbands and wives.

Working-poor families are even more likely to have children than their nonworking-poor counterparts. Ninety percent of working-poor families have children under eighteen. They are also clustered in the younger age range. Fully 95 percent of these families are headed by persons under sixty-five. Because they are working class all have at least one member in the work force, and a third of them have two or more earners. Even with multiple earners, they are not able to move out of poverty. They typically work in low-paying jobs, in industries with high turnover, and few job benefits. As a consequence, some 25 percent of working-poor families have their incomes supplemented by welfare, while 15 percent draw Social Security and another 10 percent receive Supplemental Security income.

They are not well educated as a rule. Only 40 percent are high school graduates and 60 percent are dropouts.

Again, the majority are working single mothers under sixty-five. They account for 57 percent of the total. A second group is composed of single fathers under sixty-five. They make up 28 percent of the total. Single-parent families, therefore, account for 85 percent of working-poor families. A third group of 10 percent is composed of family heads under sixty-five without children. Only 5 percent are elderly with or without children.

If the working nonpoor and the working poor are combined, it can be seen that the working class continues to comprise the largest sector of the African-American community but is in decline. It ranged downward from 54 percent of all African-American families in 1970 to 48 percent by 1983 and declined further to 46 percent by 1986. Where did they go? Some moved up to the expanding middle and upper classes. More, however, moved down to the expanding nonworking poor. The rise and decline of the black working class is discussed later.

Nonpoor Working Class

Above the working poor in the socioeconomic structure is the nonpoor working class. The nonpoor (or near poor) working class is composed of families with combined family incomes ranging from just above the poverty line of $10,000 in 1986 dollars to just under $25,000. Composed largely of blue-collar skilled and unskilled workers, these families are less dependent on dual earners than the middle and upper classes. Only 45 percent have working wives and husbands. Most have a high school education.

This largely working class group of nonpoor has declined dramatically since 1970. That year some 40 percent of African-American families were in this class, comprising some 2.1 million families. This was and still is the largest single stratum, and is the economic, social, and political backbone of the black community. By 1983, this stratum had declined to 35 percent of all African-American families and to 34 percent by 1986. The strength of this social class is reflected in the fact that 60 percent were husband-wife families as late as 1986. This is at once the most important and vulnerable of all sectors of the class structure. A fortification and growth of this stratum would have two effects simultaneously. It would help to stem the downward flow into the underclass and resume the upward flow into the middle and upper classes.

Who are these nonpoor working-class families? They are largely headed by persons in their middle adult years. Ninety percent are under sixty-five. A majority have children. Sixty percent are husband-wife families with some 40 percent headed by single parents. And while all have some working member, one-half of them have two or more earners.

They are predominantly high school graduates; 60 percent have finished high school and 30 percent have received some college education. They work mostly in blue-collar jobs in the primary industrial sector in crafts and protective services. They are over represented, however, in those industries vulnerable to job loss due to imports, automation, and plant relocation to the Sunbelt and low-wage countries.[14]

Middle Class

Middle-class families are those with family incomes between $25,000 and $50,000 in 1986 dollars. They tend to be dual-earner families. Indeed, as Harriette McAdoo has pointed out, black middle-class husbands often maintain their level not only by having a second working person in the family but a second job as well, generally on a part-time basis.

While the proportion of middle-class families doubled during the decade of the 1960s from 12 percent to 25 percent, reaching an all-time high of 29 percent in 1978, there has been a decline in recent years. By 1986 there were 1.9 million black families in this sector, constituting 27 percent of all African-American families.

The black middle class also tends to have high proportions of husband-wife family structures. An overwhelming majority of 83 percent of families in this sector were husband-wife families. Working wives and mothers are the keys to the viability of the black middle class, as 78 percent of these families have working wives, more than any of the other five socioeconomic sectors. The financial contribution the wives make to the family income is increasing and is substantially higher than in white families.

Who are these middle-class families? They are largely younger parents with children; 90 percent are under sixty-five and most have children under eighteen. Most are husband-wife families, with 17 percent headed by single parents.

The black middle class tends to be highly educated. At a time when 10 percent of blacks and 25 percent of white adults are college graduates, 40 percent of these black middle-class families are headed by persons with some college and 25 percent are college graduates.

They tend to work in the upper tier of the primary economic sector in professional, managerial, and technical positions. Women are more numerous than men in professional positions but tend to cluster in the lower-level professions, such as elementary school teachers and nurses. The black middle class is heavily dependent on government employment, as 66 percent of women and one-half of male professionals work for government agencies.

Upper Class

Finally, at the peak of the African-American social-class structure is a small and growing upper class. This sector has expanded dramatically over the past two decades.

Upper-class families are those with median family incomes ranging upward from $50,000 to above $200,000 and who possess substantial wealth and economic power. We define economic power as the capacity to create jobs and wealth. It is not the income alone, however, but the accumulated wealth which distinguishes the black upper class from the middle class. Wealth or net worth is measured as total assets owned minus total debts owed. Overall, the average black-family wealth is less than 10 percent of average white-family wealth, nearly $4,000 for black families and $40,000 for whites. Even among middle-class black families, it is $18,000 constituting only a third of similar white families. However, a few black families, those with earnings above $50,000, have amassed accumulated wealth allowing them to rise distinctly above the white median. Thus some 12 percent of black families have accumulated wealth above $50,000. Four percent of all black families have accumulated family wealth above $100,000, a position they share with 24 percent of white American families. These families tend to be headed by highly educated parents in middle- and high-status occupations and to involve a high proportion of two working partners in the labor force. A relatively high proportion own their own business or professional practice.

Wealth Accumulation

It has been widely reported in the press and elsewhere that according to a study by the U.S. Census the median net worth of black families in 1984 and 1988 was less than 10 percent of the median net worth of white families.[15] The other part of the picture is that there is enormous variation in net worth among black families. It is this diversity of both levels and sources of wealth accumulation, perhaps more than the diversity of income, education, and occupation, that truly distinguishes the diversity of economic well-being among African-American families.

Levels of Wealth

With respect to levels of wealth, while median net worth for African-American families was $3,800 in 1984 and $4,200 in 1988 there were altogether five levels of wealth that may be identified (Tables 1.8 and 1.9). First, at the very bottom of the economic scale are some 30 percent of all African-American families in both 1984 and 1988 with zero or negative net worth. That means that when these families compare what they own with what they owe they end up dead even, or still in debt.

A second group consisting of another 30 percent of all black families had somewhat higher levels of wealth ranging upward from $1 to just under $10,000. A third group, consisting of a

TABLE 1.8
Net Worth of Families
1984–1988

Distribution	% of Families 1984	% of Families 1988
Zero or Negative	30.5	29.1
$1–$9,999	30.7	30.9
$10,000–$49,999	25.7	24.5
$50,000–$99,999	9.3	10.3
$100,000–$250,000 +	3.9	5.2

SOURCE: U.S. Bureau of the Census, *Current Population Reports, Household Economic Studies, 1984 and 1988.*

quarter of all black families, had net worth ranging upward from $10,000 to just under $50,000. A fourth group, consisting of 10 percent of the total, had net worth in the middle range from $50,000 to just under $100,000. Finally, at the very top of the wealth pyramid is a small group of families, rising from 4 percent of the total in 1984 to 5 percent in 1988. These families had net worth ranging from $100,000 to over $250,000. In 1984 there were some 380,000 African-American families in this top group and by 1988 the number had expanded to some 515,000 families.

Wealth varies according to level of income, occupation, and education of family members. It also varies according to age and marital status and from year to year. Wealth, however, is a much

TABLE 1.9
Median Net Worth by Family Structure
1984–1988

Family Structure	NUMBER OF HOUSEHOLDS (MILLIONS)		MEDIAN NET WORTH*	
	1984	1988	1984	1988
Total households	9.5	10.3	$3,800	$4,200
Married-couple households	3.5	3.6	14,900	15,700
Female-headed households	4.4	4.8	729	757
Male-headed households	1.6	1.9	3,400	1,500

* Median net worth in 1988 dollars.
SOURCE: U.S. Bureau of the Census, *Current Population Reports, Household Economic Status, 1984 and 1988.*

more stable and powerful index of economic well-being than annual or monthly income alone, much of which goes right out
again to pay for expenses.

One basis of net worth variation among African-American families is age of the family head, or householder. Families with youthful heads (those under thirty-five years of age) have the lowest net
worth, which rose slightly from $600 in 1984 to $800 in 1988.
Families with heads aged thirty-five to forty-four saw their median net worth rise slightly from $3,881 to $4,487. In the middle
of the age distribution, those families with heads in the age range
forty-five to fifty-four years had substantially higher net worth of
$15,000 in 1984, which declined dramatically to $10,100 in 1988.
Finally, in the age range fifty-five to sixty-four, families had the
highest net worth. This, too, declined, however, from $25,700 in
1984 to $20,500 in 1988.

The declines in average net worth of these experienced workers
reflect the softness in the economy. In both established blue-collar
and white-collar occupations, black workers lost ground during
the latter part of the 1980s. Layoffs, stagnation of benefits, combined with the rising costs of their goods and services caused these
well-established families to lose ground. They are still much better
off, however, than younger families and persons over sixty-five.
Another drain on their relative net worth has been the necessity
of helping out their own (often grown) children, and helping out
their elderly relatives. Refinancing a home to meet some of these
responsibilities represents a sharp decline in net worth even
though the monthly income may remain the same or rise slightly.

Another important basis of the variations in levels of family net
worth is family structure. In general, married-couple families
have higher net worth than either female-headed families or
single-male-headed families. This is partly because they generally
have multiple earners, in part because of the economy of pooling
resources, and in part because on average black men have higher
earnings than black women.

Sources of Wealth Accumulation

What are the financial instruments that African-American families have found useful in the accumulation of the varying levels of
wealth described above? There are principally ten instruments
used to accumulate wealth (Table 1.10).

Numerically of the types of assets owned by African-American
families, motor vehicles rank at the top. Some 65 percent of all

TABLE 1.10
Assets of Households
1984–1988

	PERCENTAGE HOUSEHOLDS OWNING	
Asset	1984	1988
Motor vehicles	65	65
Interest-earning assets	46	46
Own home	44	43
Regular checking accounts	32	30
U.S. Savings Bonds	7	5
Rental property	7	7
Stocks and mutual funds	5	7
IRA or KEOGH	5	7
Other rental estate	3	4
Own business or profession	4	4
Other assets	2	1
Total households	9.5 million	10.3 million

SOURCE: U.S. Bureau of the Census, *Current Population Reports, Household Economic Studies, 1984 and 1988.*

African-American families owned motor vehicles in both 1984 and 1988 (this does not mean that they are fully paid for, as we shall see below). Second to motor vehicles comes interest-earning assets, primarily in financial institutions. The third most frequently held asset is home ownership. In 1988, 43 percent of families owned equity in their own homes. Fourth is regular checking accounts, which are held by 30 percent of these families. These four constitute the major financial investments of African-American families. Other investments, each of which is utilized by less than 10 percent of African-American families, include U.S. Savings Bonds, stocks, mutual funds, IRA and KEOGH retirement accounts, ownership of own business and professional firms, and other real estate.

There is, however, a substantial difference between the number or percent of families owning a given asset and the value of that asset (Table 1.11). When value of assets is considered, a different ordering of these ten assets results. By far, the most valuable asset held by African-American families is rental property, which had a mean (average) value of $38,100 in 1984 that rose to $40,800 in 1988.

In second place comes ownership of a business or professional practice. Only about 4 percent of African-American families own their own business or professional practice, but for the roughly 400,000 families that do, this is quite a valuable asset, ranking

TABLE 1.11
Mean Value of Assets
1984–1988

	MEAN VALUE*	
Type of Asset	*1984*	*1988*
Rental property	$38,100	$40,800
Equity in business/profession	34,000	25,200
Equity in own home	30,000	36,800
Other real estate property	14,400	16,400
Equity in motor vehicles	3,400	4,000
IRA/KEOGH	3,400	5,600
Interest-earning deposits	3,100	4,400
Stock/mutual funds	2,800	3,700
Regular checking accounts	600	700
U.S. Savings Bonds	550	1,000

* Mean Value in 1988 dollars.
SOURCE: U.S. Bureau of the Census, *Current Population Reports, Household Economic Studies, 1984 and 1988.*

second only to rental property. In 1984, the mean value of business ownership was $34,000. By 1988, however, the value of this holding among African-American families had declined to $25,200. This is another reflection of the precarious economic climate during the latter part of the 1980s.

The third most valuable asset is home ownership. The 44 percent of those families who owned their own homes amounted to some 4 million families. The average value of the equity they held in their homes was $30,000 in 1984, which appreciated to some $36,800 in 1988. Closely tied in the economy to home ownership is ownership of rental property. While owned by less than 10 percent of African-American families, rental property ranks fourth in value as an asset. The mean value of equity in real estate held by these families was $14,400 in 1984, increasing slightly to $16,400 in 1988.

After these four major sources of wealth, other instruments have values all ranging under $6,000. These include motor vehicles, IRA and KEOGH retirement accounts, interest-earning deposits, stocks and mutual funds, regular checking accounts, and U.S. Savings Bonds.

These findings present a rather conservative investment posture on the part of African-American families, focused as it is so closely on property ownership of home and business. But it also shows a tested and successful investment strategy, one which has enabled an appreciable number of African-American families to

TABLE 1.12
Social-Class and Family Structure
1986

	FAMILY STRUCTURE		
Class	Married-Couple Families (%)	Single-Parent Families (%)	Working Wife (%)
Upper class	96	4	50
Middle class	83	17	78
Working class (nonpoor)	60	40	45
Working class (poor)	33	67	33
Nonworking poor	25	75	25

SOURCE: U.S. Bureau of the Census, *Current Population Reports, Income and Poverty Status of Individuals and Families 1969–1986.*

accumulate wealth over and above their indebtedness and daily needs. The other instruments show some increase in value between 1984 and 1988. Taken together they are all important in the search of African-American families for economic viability, family stability, and upward mobility.

Why Social-Class Stratification Matters

The higher up the social-class structure families are, the more likely they are to be husband-wife families. They are also more likely to have working wives helping to sustain this status. Social class and family status are directly related (Table 1.12).

At the lowest level among the nonworking poor, only 25 percent are husband and wife families. This rises to 33 percent among the working poor and to a majority of 60 percent of the working nonpoor. Among the black middle and upper classes husband and wife families rise to 83 percent and 96 percent respectively.

In sum, socioeconomic class stratification is an important, if often overlooked, dimension of African-American family life. A wholistic approach which understands the full range of socioeconomic statuses in the black community can teach the following lessons crucial to the well-being of black families.

First there is, indeed, room at the top and all along the socioeconomic ladder in legitimate enterprises for black Americans to channel their talents, interests, and skills. They can achieve their aspirations in a wide variety of fields and be rewarded if they also get the help they need.

Another view of the entire socioeconomic structure reveals that individual achievement is not incompatible with stable family development, but, instead, they often go hand-in-hand.

Moreover, these findings call attention to the fact that a remarkable concomitant to financial, occupational, and educational success is the ability to make a contribution to others. Bill Cosby, Oprah Winfrey, Reginald Lewis, and George Russell are outstanding examples of wealthy blacks who continue to contribute to a variety of community uplift projects and institutions.

There is still some dispute among scholars as to whether there is a distinct black upper class. Some hold that in terms of socioeconomic resources, particularly wealth and economic power, it may be more appropriate to consider the highest-ranked black families as upper-middle class rather than upper class. In any event, for black parents, teachers, family professionals, and others in a position to help socialize black children, both the rise of this top stratum and the barriers they still face can provide meaningful insights that will be explored in subsequent chapters.

AGE STRUCTURE DIVERSITY

After noting the diversity of family forms and social classes in the African-American community, it is important to recognize the diverse and changing age structure and its impact on both the needs and the resources of these families.

While the elderly population will continue to expand through the year 2000, the declining birth rate will produce a steady decline in persons at the younger end of the life cycle.

Infants and Toddlers

In the totality of the life span, each age range presents its own special challenges to African-American families (Table 1.13). There were some 3.1 million black infants and toddlers in the nation in 1985, evenly divided between males and females. These numbers expanded to 3.2 million in 1990 and are projected to decline to 3.1 million again in the year 2000. A major challenge for their families at this stage is infant mortality, where despite the substantial changes over the last half century the rate is still twice as high for black children as for children in the nation as a whole. A second challenge is to avoid the preventable illnesses that inflict children not regularly exposed to high-quality prenatal and post-

TABLE 1.13
Age Structure Through the Life Span
1985–2000
(in millions)

Age Range	1985 N	1985 (%)	1990 N	1990 (%)	2000 N	2000 (%)
All ages	29.1	100	31.4	100	35.8	100
Male	13.8		14.9		17.0	
Female	15.3		16.5		18.7	
Infants/toddlers, under 5	*3.1*	*11*	*3.2*	*10*	*3.1*	*9*
Male	1.5		1.6		1.6	
Female	1.5		1.6		1.5	
Childhood, 5–9	*2.5*	*8*	*3.1*	*10*	*3.2*	*9*
Male	1.3		1.6		1.6	
Female	1.2		1.5		1.6	
Early adolescence, 10–14	*2.5*	*8*	*2.5*	*8*	*3.2*	*9*
Male	1.3		1.3		1.6	
Female	1.2		1.2		1.6	
Late adolescence, 15–19	*2.7*	*9*	*2.5*	*8*	*3.1*	*9*
Male	1.4		1.3		1.6	
Female	1.3		1.3		1.5	
Young adulthood, 20–24	*3.0*	*10*	2.7	*9*	2.6	*7*
Male	1.5		1.4		1.3	
Female	1.5		1.4		1.3	
Adulthood 25–39	*7.1*	*24*	8.2	*26*	*8.3*	*23*
Male	3.4		3.9		4.1	
Female	3.8		4.3		4.2	
Middle years, 40–64	*5.8*	*20*	*6.5*	*21*	*9.2*	*26*
Male	2.7		2.8		4.2	
Female	3.1		3.7		5.0	
Seniors, 65–84	*2.2*	*8*	*2.2*	*7*	*2.6*	*7*
Male	1.0		.8		.9	
Female	1.3		1.4		1.7	
Elders, 85 and over	*189**	*1*	*257**	*1*	*412**	*1*
Male	60*		77*		110*	
Female	129*		180*		302*	
Median	*26.2*		*27.7*		*30.2*	

*thousands
SOURCE: U.S. Bureau of the Census, *Current Population Reports, Projections of Population of the U.S. by Sex, 1983–2080.*

natal care. The third major challenge is to provide the type of socialization experiences, protection, and guidance that will enable the children to develop strong self-esteem as well as positive individual and group identity. Finally, parents need to prepare infants and toddlers for the progessive learning and mastery experiences required for successful integration into the world of childhood.

Childhood

When children reach the age range five to nine, they become schoolchildren and have new needs. In the nation as a whole, there were some 2.5 million black children in this age range in 1985, again one-half male and one-half female. By 1990, these numbers had increased to 3.1 million and are projected to increase to 3.2 million by the year 2000. Most of these children have working mothers. This means extraordinary efforts to provide adult supervision after school, a problem black working parents have long faced. In years past, they could count on a great deal of support from the extended families. Now these, mostly grandmothers, are themselves in the work force. Latchkey children—those who come home after school with no adults present—who have recently drawn special attention in the white community, have a long history among African-American parents. Recent studies suggest a great need for high-quality and affordable after-school programs.

Early Adolescence

The next age group in the life cycle is grossly neglected in social policy and programs. These are the 2.5 million black early adolescents between the ages of ten and fourteen. This group, too, is expected to expand to 3.2 million by the year 2000. A recent comprehensive study by the Carnegie Corporation shows that parents, schools, and other community institutions are failing these children severely in almost every one of their developmental needs. The report focused on the need to restructure the junior high schools to make them more compatible to the developmental and learning needs and styles of this age group. At the same time, it called on parents and other community agencies for more cooperation in focusing on the needs of this age, which has often been neglected in our concern over teen pregnancy, juvenile delinquency, and other behaviors associated with the older adolescents.[16]

Late Adolescence

The late adolescent years between fifteen and nineteen are the most challenging. Like most parents, African-American parents face keeping their teens in clothes, food, and school. The challenge is most severe for the low-income families. If parents have been successful in instilling a set of personal values about bodily care and correct conduct, adolescents will have a stronger set of armor with which to fight the efforts of the peer groups, the streets, and the mass media to reduce their appetites and conduct to the lowest common denominator. If families have nurtured a set of skills and high aspirations, they will have even more protection. If the family and the youths are tied into social, economic, and political institutions in the community, additional protection will provide for their growth and development. The key for adolescents, however, is whether they have developed by then a love for learning and whether they are placed in a supportive and demanding learning environment.

It is at this stage that young people desert their family traditions with seeming reckless abandon. Religion, personal conduct codes, sexual codes, dress codes, language codes, all become brittle and are often toppled by the influence of the mainstream culture, popular media, and commercial exploitation. Youths will spend as much for the right type of jeans or sweater as their fathers paid for an entire suit of clothes.

It is also at the impressionable teenage years that the drug culture can be attractive and gang life stands poised to replace home life and church life.

In the years ahead after at first a slight decline there will then be a sharp growth in the number of late adolescents, from 2.7 million in 1985 to 2.5 million in 1990 and then up to 3.1 million by the year 2000.

Young Adulthood

If young people can pass successfully through the challenges of adolescence, with a high school education, positive skills, and positive attitudes; and if they can face an opportunity structure which beckons and welcomes them; they can then move into the years of young adulthood, aged twenty to twenty-four, full of promise. The numbers in this age group will decline steadily from 3 million in 1985 and 2.7 million in 1990 to 2.6 million by 2000.

If they can look forward confidently to college, trade school, the military, or a meaningful entry-level job, they can become the best and most productive of citizens. Postponing marriage, living the life of adult singles, often in cohabitation relations with other youths, they can prepare for the transition into adulthood with all flags flying. Unfortunately, all too many of these young adults face the consequences of failure to make the transition from adolescence. Many will be convicted of crimes and serve long jail sentences. By 1990 some 25 percent of black males aged twenty to twenty-five were in the custody of the criminal justice system. A three-fourths majority of African-American families, however, kept their young men out of the criminal justice system. Some will spend years of their lives in unemployment or drifting from one unfulfilling situation to another. Often they will find that they cannot be self-supporting and will return to live with their parents. Young, unmarried mothers will inevitably seek the protection of their mothers' and grandmothers' homes. The extended family will be taxed often beyond its limits.

The upside and the downside of young adulthood cause many parents to extend their parental role and concern well beyond the age of majority of their offspring. We have come to witness a type of reverse empty-nest phenomenon as many young adults find it more comfortable to return to their parents' home.

The Middle Years

Those who survive with their persons, values, and their opportunity structure intact move into middle adulthood, ages twenty-five to thirty-nine, ready to tackle higher education, to achieve occupational stability, and to enter the realm of marriage and childrearing. This group will expand from 7.1 million in 1985 and 8.2 million in 1990 to 8.3 million by 2000. If their first priority is establishing their occupational and economic stability, their second priority is socializing their children along the lines indicated above and protecting them from the hazards of life, including racism. Whatever their social class, they face enormous challenges in the areas of housing, health care, and education for their children.

They share these concerns with the mature group aged forty to sixty-four, which will expand from 5.8 million in 1985 and 6.5 million in 1990 to 9.2 million by the year 2000, where they will constitute the largest and most stable segment of the black community. They will comprise the classic sandwich generation with concern for both their children and their parents.

Seniors

Family members are living longer and creating a larger older group of dependents. The number of African-American persons over sixty-five years is projected to expand from 2.4 million in 1985 to over 3 million by the year 2000. The numbers over eighty-five will expand even more rapidly, from 189,000 to more than 412,000. Finally, though not singled out in the table, there were 6,000 blacks aged one hundred and over in 1985. This number will expand to over 10,000 by the year 2000.

At the same time, many of the elderly are less dependent economically because of improved Social Security and pension benefits. And because of improved health care, many of the elderly are not physically dependent until they reach advanced years. The black elderly, as a number of scholars have pointed out, are not only a source of dependency to their families but also a source of assistance to them. Grandmothers are the most characteristic family support in that they provide a great deal of the child care, particularly for the increasing numbers of working mothers.

One of the most striking changes in the African-American population during this century has been in the age structure, represented especially by the aging of the black population. In 1900, the average life expectancy of black males was thirty-two and a half years, and for females it was thirty-five. In 1985, this had expanded to over sixty-five years for black men and over seventy years for black women. By 1990, however, this expansion in the life span had been arrested particularly among black males due in part to premature fatalities among youth.

THE WHOLISTIC PERSPECTIVE

Our definition of family in the African-American tradition is somewhat broader, more inclusive, and more flexible than the usual definition of family.

We have described a pattern of family structures that moves considerably beyond the usual focus on single-parent families.

The wide variety of family types which exist among African-Americans has changed over time in response to society's conditions and demands. African-American family diversity extends also to social-class diversity. Beyond the families at the bottom of the socioeconomic scale exists a more elaborate social-class structure in five levels, from the nonworking poor to the black upper class. We have shown that black families at successively higher social-class levels are more stable and more functional. Finally, we have described a more elaborate age structure than is generally found in studies of African-American families.

Candor about their problems is vital. But the whole of African-American family life is greater and more generative than any of its parts. The practice of focusing on any one aspect must give way to a perspective that embraces the whole. If we isolate the problems of children, we are less likely to notice that they are connected to the problems of the elderly. If we look only at low-income, single-parent, female-headed families in poverty, we may be led to assume that their single-parent status is the major cause of their predicament or to overlook the expanding black male population. If we concentrate on the similarities and differences black families have in comparison with white families, we risk missing the more important distinctions among black families themselves.

By insisting on a wholistic perspective we are reasserting a line of analysis established by the earliest and best of African-American scholarship on the family. W.E.B. Du Bois, the pioneering African-American scholar, eloquently insisted on taking a broad and inclusive approach to analyzing African-American families. In a paper before the American Academy of Political and Social Science in 1898, he argued that it is not possible to understand black life in America without systematically assessing the influence of broad historical, cultural, social, economic, and political forces:

> We should seek to know and measure carefully all the forces and conditions that go to make up these different problems, to trace the historical development of these conditions and discover as far as possible the probable trend of further development.[17]

Chapter 2

Family, Community, and Society

The supreme test of how well families function is how well they care for their members, particularly their dependent members, and most especially their children. The same test may be applied to the community and the larger society that surrounds them.

Children are the centerpiece of African-American family life. As we will see, they depend on adult family members in various and changing family structures. The ability of their families to care for them depends in turn on the resources of their surrounding community and social policies emanating from the larger society. But by the early 1990s not only African-American families but significant sectors of their communities and the larger society had become acutely concerned.

THE AFRICAN-AMERICAN FAMILY CRISIS

"Today, compared to 1980," declared Marian Wright Edelman of the Children's Defense Fund in 1990, "black children are *more* likely to be born into poverty, lack early prenatal care, have a single mother, have an unemployed parent, be unemployed themselves as teenagers, and not go to college after high school graduation."[1] Moreover, the following national trends affect black children in startling proportions:

· Today, the United States ranks eighteenth in the world behind Spain and Singapore in overall infant mortality. Amer-

ican black infant mortality rates place the United States
twenty-eighth in the world, behind the overall rates of Cuba
and Bulgaria.

- A black baby born in Indianapolis, Detroit, or in the shadow
  of the White House and Capitol was more likely to die in the
  first year of life in 1986 than a baby born in Jamaica, Trinidad
  and Tobago, Chile, Panama, Romania, or the Soviet Union.
  Black infant mortality rates in 1986 were equivalent to white
  infant mortality rates in 1970.
- If recent trends continue, in the year 2000 more than a third
  of all black births will be to a mother who did not receive early
  prenatal care.
- One in five of all American children has a single parent and
  one child in five is poor. By the year 2000, one in four will
  have a single parent and one in four will be poor.[2]

What is happening to black children? One of the best barometers is suggested by changes in their living arrangements over
the past few decades. As late as 1960 some 67 percent of black
children under eighteen lived with both parents (Table 2.1). By
1988 this proportion had declined to 38.6 percent. Meanwhile
the proportion living with their mothers only rose from nearly
20 percent in 1960 to over 51 percent by 1988. Over the same
period the proportion of black children living with their fathers
only rose from 2 percent to 3 percent. Meanwhile those living
with other relatives declined from nearly 10 percent to just over
6 percent, while those living with nonrelatives declined slightly
from 1.5 percent to 1 percent. With all these changes, however,
it is notable that as late as 1988 some 99 percent of all black
children lived with adults who were related to them. Such is the
elasticity of the black family. Yet when other barometers are
checked, one fact stands out: children are not the only ones in
jeopardy.

Internal strife has made homicide the leading cause of death
for young black men, just ahead of preventable accidents and just
behind suicide. Domestic strife causes unprecedented numbers of
African-American mothers and fathers to war against their own
children, against each other, and against their parents. Child
abuse, sibling abuse, spouse abuse, elder abuse, and fratricide—
while by no means unique to black people—are relatively new in
such numbers.

TABLE 2.1
Living Arrangements of Children
1960–1988

	DISTRIBUTION	
Living Arrangement	*Number*	*%*
Total children under 18		
1960	8,650,000	100.0
1970	9,422,000	100.0
1980	9,375,000	100.0
1988	9,699,000	100.0
Living with 2 parents		
1960	5,795,000	67.0
1970	5,508,000	58.5
1980	3,956,000	42.2
1988	3,739,000	38.6
Living with mother only		
1960	1,723,000	19.9
1970	2,783,000	29.5
1980	4,117,000	43.9
1988	4,959,000	51.1
Living with father only		
1960	173,000	2.0
1970	213,000	2.3
1980	180,000	1.9
1988	288,000	3.0
Living with other relatives		
1960	827,000	9.6
1970	820,000	8.7
1980	999,000	10.7
1988	620,000	6.4
Living with nonrelatives only		
1960	132,000	1.5
1970	97,000	1.0
1980	123,000	1.3
1988	94,000	1.0

SOURCE: U.S. Bureau of the Census, *Current Population Reports, Population Characteristics, Marital Status and Living Arrangements,* March 1988.

More young black males go to jail than to college, and it costs five times as much per year to keep them there. By the end of the 1980s a definitive report from Jewelle Taylor Gibbs of the University of California at Berkeley on the status of young black males concluded that they are "an endangered species." A brilliant series of analyses led her to conclude, "In American society today, no single group is more vulnerable, more victimized, and more violated than young black males in the age range 15 to 24."[3] In a scholarly essay on the plight of black men, the poet Haki Madhubuti remarked with unmistakable feeling, "The major piece of education I absorbed after twelve years of public education was that I was a problem, inferior, ineducable, and a victim. And as a victim I began to see the world through the eyes of a victim."[4]

By the end of the 1980s, stimulated in part by the findings of the 1980 census, many family specialists, black leaders, professionals, public officials, and people in the media began to discuss the African-American family crisis. The idea of such a "crisis" was buttressed by research findings. Essentially it consisted of a cluster of conditions with devastating consequences reflected in Figure 2.1. They include family problems such as divorce, stress, marital conflict, domestic violence, and teen pregnancy; and dependent children behavioral problems such as school failure. Other conditions include substance abuse, sexually transmitted diseases and

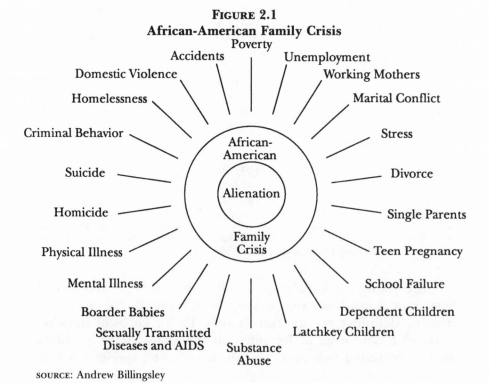

FIGURE 2.1
African-American Family Crisis

SOURCE: Andrew Billingsley

AIDS, physical and mental illness, criminal behavior, homicide, suicide, homelessness, and accidents.

Several characteristics stand out. First, almost all the conditions are more common and crippling among African-American families than among families in the nation as a whole.

Second, none of these conditions is exclusive or indigenous to African-American families. All of them afflict other American families as well. Numerically, most of the victims of these conditions are white. The proportion of sufferers, however, is higher among the black population.

Third, all of these conditions seem to have become more widespread, and more severe, in the decades since the 1960s. To some extent, this is because of greater social awareness of them. But mostly, the conditions themselves have worsened.

Fourth, each is either caused directly or aggravated substantially by social conditions. The United States leads many of the other industrial societies in the incidence of the problems, but trails many other industrialized nations in institutionalizing prevention and treatment. These conditions do not arise, exist, or operate in isolation. They often work together. Poverty, unemployment, and stress are highly interrelated. Reinforcing each other, they impact on divorce, single parenthood, teen pregnancy, and school failure. Substance abuse, illness, and domestic violence interact to produce dependent children, boarder babies, and marital conflict. Antisocial behavior such as crime in general and homicide in particular, as well as suicide and accidents, intertwine with other problems. Homelessness is the evidence of a whole cluster of problems. With so many elements overlapping, the crisis can seem overwhelming. A growing sense of alienation or estrangement leads to a hopelessness which often borders on despair.

One final point comes through nonetheless. Not one of these problems affects all or even a majority of African-American families. For example, the most widespread problem, unemployment, affects about a third.

As Patricia Raybon observed succinctly in a letter published in *Newsweek* in 1989:

Day after day, week after week, this message—that black America is dysfunctional and unwhole—gets transmitted across the American landscape. Sadly, as a result, America never learns the truth about what is actually a wonderful, vibrant, creative community of people.

Most black Americans are not poor. Most black teenagers are not crack addicts. Most black mothers are not on welfare. Indeed, in sheer numbers, more white Americans are poor and on welfare than are blacks. Yet one never would deduce that by watching television or reading American newspapers and magazines.

Why does the American media insist on playing this myopic, inaccurate picture game?

. . . I want America to know us—all of us—for who we really are. To see us in all of our complexity, our subtleness, our artfulness, our enterprise, our specialness, our liveliness, our American-ness. That is the real portrait of black Americans—that we are strong people, surviving people, capable people. That may be the best kept secret in America. If so, it's time to let the truth be known.[5]

THE AFRICAN-AMERICAN COMMUNITY

One of the most powerful truths about families is that they cannot be strong unless they are surrounded by a strong community. Can black families look to their communities for assistance in meeting their responsibilities, particularly to their children? What is the capability and the responsibility of the black community? These are questions on which knowledgeable analysts differ markedly. The African-American community, as a context for helping families protect their children and youth, has itself undergone enormous changes during recent decades. Some analysts hold that as an organized entity, with guiding norms, values, and institutions, this community has virtually ceased to exist. Others point to the many dysfunctional aspects of community life. And while all these characterizations are based on fact, they in no sense constitute the whole truth.

The fact is that the African-American community exists, and is both weak and strong. Even as it is undergoing constant change, major generative elements endure. The community is capable of providing resources and assistance. Any community composed of 30 million people, most of whom live in families, most of whom are no longer poor, with combined annual income exceeding $300 billion, more than 400,000 black-owned business firms, some 75,000 black-owned churches, a hundred black colleges, and numerous other organizations, with a common history, common identity, and successful struggles against the adversities of life, cannot reasonably be defined as impotent.

A community cannot be accurately defined by its limitations alone. A wholistic definition includes its strengths as well. Nor are these the worst of times for African-American families. Slavery, Jim Crow, and abject poverty were all much worse. Neither is it necessary to wait for another Harriet Tubman, Frederick Douglass, Marcus Garvey, Ida B. Wells, Earl Warren, Rosa Parks, Martin Luther King, Jr., Malcolm X, Lyndon B. Johnson, or Thurgood Marshall to usher in reforms. Scholars, leaders, organizations, and citizens generally—both black and white—who grasp the generative features of the African-American experience can harness this resource. With it, they can build communities that can sustain families that will be better able to protect, guide, and care for their children and youth.

What specifically do we mean by "African-American community"? According to James Blackwell:

> The black community can be perceived as a social system. Within the community value consensus and congruence exists; a significant segment of its constituents share norms, sentiments, and expectations. . . . Even though diversity exists within the community, its members are held together by adherence to commonly shared values and goals.[6]

Thus, the black community is not just isolated individuals and families as presented by most sociological studies.

We take issue, however, with another of Blackwell's views, that the African-American community is held together by "white oppression and racism." There is strong evidence to support our view that the African-American people have reasons of their own to cling together, quite apart from external oppression. For example, the black church does not exist simply because the white church is oppressive. Black religion is a qualitatively different experience altogether and exists parallel with but not subservient to white religion. The black fraternal organizations might have been necessary because of exclusion from white organizations, but their persistence and growth are driven by forces internal to the black experience as much as by external hostility.

People of African descent in America constitute a community in four respects. First, geographically, most black families live in neighborhoods where most of their neighbors are also black. In conducting a national survey of black Americans in 1989, we found that 80 percent of a national sample of black adults live in neighborhoods that are predominantly black. This occurs sometimes out of economic necessity, and sometimes because of racist

exclusionary practices which prevent people from exercising freedom of choice. Whatever the reasons, there are African-American
communities in every part of the nation which exist as enclaves.

A second sense of community among African-Americans that is
less widely known or accepted in the larger society is a shared set
of values, which helps to define them.

The traditional values of the community, many of them intact
today, have been articulated by a number of scholars. One group
of black scholars headed by John Hope Franklin, Eleanor Holmes
Norton, and twenty-eight others summarized these values in a
statement published by the Joint Center for Political and Economic Studies in 1987. In an era when many public officials and
even scholars were asserting an absence of values among the
African-American people, these scholars wrote:

> Blacks have always embraced the central values of the society, aug-
> mented those values in response to the unique experiences of slav-
> ery and subordination, incorporated them into a strong religious
> tradition, and espoused them fervently and persistently. These val-
> ues—among them, the primacy of family, the importance of edu-
> cation, and the necessity for individual enterprise and hard work—
> have been fundamental to black survival. These community values
> have been matched by a strong set of civic values, ironic in the face
> of racial discrimination—espousal of the rights and responsibilities
> of freedom, commitment to country, and adherence to the demo-
> cratic creed.[7]

Thirdly, most black people, wherever they live, continue to identify with their heritage to some considerable degree. Many persons who move out of black neighborhoods or who never lived in
one have relatives and friends who have stayed; others return to
go to churches, barber shops, and beauty parlors. Even individuals who seldom visit these neighborhoods have a potentially powerful connection with black causes and issues.

For example, witness their response on Sunday, February 18,
1990, as Nelson Mandela was released from twenty-seven years of
imprisonment for fighting against the apartheid system in South
Africa. Roger Wilkins captured the spirit of the occasion in an
op-ed article in *The New York Times* a few days later:

> When the son of an African noble house goes defiantly to prison to
> continue his struggle for freedom, part of us goes with him. And
> when we get reports of his growth, stubborn dignity, calm, com-

manding presence and wisdom, we swell again and think of our
ancient heritage and bonds of blood.

There was a surge of pride when the world for the first time gave
a black man his regal due during his lifetime. So when the day
finally came, we clapped, cheered and cried at the sight of a king—
our cousin, the king—walking in the sunshine.[8]

Finally, it is appropriate to speak of an African-American community in terms of a set of institutions and organizations which
grow out of the African-American heritage, identify with it, and
serve primarily African-American people and families. The repeated assertion that the black community is not organized misses
the mark. Organization is widespread. There is an organization,
agency, or institution for every conceivable function in the black
community today. They are, however, sometimes small and un-
coordinated, and uncooperative with others. And they sometimes
spring up and dissolve too soon to complete their missions. But
they anchor the community and can be galvanized into collective
action when circumstances or leadership commands.

Four sets of organizations have been preeminent throughout
the history of the community. These are the church, the school,
the business enterprise, and the voluntary organization. All these
have undergone enormous change since the end of World War II.
Even so, a majority of African-American adults belong.

Fully 70 percent of black adults belong to just one, namely the
black church, which is easily the strongest and most representative. The black church embodies all the four senses of community.
Ordinarily located in neighborhoods where a majority of the families are of African-American descent, it embraces traditional
African-American values. It identifies with both the struggles and
achievements of African-American people, and it is institutionalized with an enduring organizational structure and mission.

It is appropriate, then, to speak of the African-American community in either, all, or any combination of the above respects.
The African-American community, at bottom, is the organized or
collective expression of the African-American people in the
United States.

Robert Bellah, in *Habits of the Heart*, has given voice to the concept that a real community is "one that does not forget its past. In
order not to forget that past, a community is involved in retelling
its story, its constitutive narrative, and in so doing, it offers examples of the men and women who have embodied and exem-

plified the meaning of the community. These stories of collective history and exemplary individuals are an important part of the tradition that is so central to a community of memory."[9] He could be speaking directly of the African-American community as he observes: "At times, neighborhoods, localities, and regions have been communities in America, but that has been hard to sustain in our restless and mobile society. Families can be communities, remembering their past, telling the children the stories of parents' and grandparents' lives, and sustaining hope for the future—though without the context of a larger community that sense of family is hard to maintain."[10]

This definition raises several questions. For instance, does the African-American community include persons of West Indian ancestry? In our conception it does as long as they live in the United States, since they are obviously of African descent. And while there are individuals from time to time of West Indian or Caribbean ancestry living in the United States who do not wish to identify with the African-American community, that is an individual matter and we are speaking of collectivities.

What about individual African-American natives of the United States who choose not to identify with the African-American community? Certain blacks wish to distance themselves from their heritage. More than one such individual has been heard to say that he or she is an American who just happens to be black. We have found that this is an acute minority view. In a national study of black households, adults were asked how they prefer to be identified. A small minority of 8 percent want to be called just "American." Nearly three times as many, or some 20 percent, prefer just "black." In keeping with the double consciousness Du Bois wrote about, an overwhelming 70 percent preferred the identity of black *and* American.[11]

Nothing in this definition has referred to skin color, texture of hair, or rhythm in the stride. While these may indicate African heritage, they are not the same thing. The real thing is the sense of peoplehood with a common anchor in African history and the American experience.

THE LARGER SOCIETY

Every American family insures the well-being of its children with the help of policies, programs, and resources generated within the larger society. Full employment, certain Constitutional guarantees, education, and health care, for example, require resources far beyond the ones that can be generated within any limited community. Therefore, the African-American community has a major responsibility to use its resources to focus the attention of the wider society on the needs of its families and children. Through organized, persistent efforts, the community has to enlighten, persuade, cooperate, pressure, and lead in order to make sure that the appropriate national resources flow its way and are channeled effectively.

Any minority community which allows the larger society's majority community to define its character, determine its needs, and design policies and programs to meet those needs is likely to suffer perpetual disadvantage. At the same time, any community which proposes to ignore the collaboration of forces in that larger society and go it alone is likely to suffer the same fate. Joint action is complex, taxing, and difficult, but clearly indispensable to progress.

The public sector, the private for-profit sector, the voluntary nonsectarian sector, and the religious sector all control resources to which African-American people continue to make enormous contributions. It is not a question of blacks being supplicants, or begging alms of others. Blacks do more than their fair share of the hard work, pay more than their fair share of taxes, contribute more than their fair share of personnel to the military, spend most of their income to keep the consumer economy going, contribute great amounts to charity and to voluntary service, to culture and leisure activities, and provide many of the customers and clients for private and nonprivate enterprises. They are entitled to the resources they need to maintain their independence, stability, and their viability. Blacks, in other words, are an intricate and contributing part of this amorphous national society. But what is the nature of this society? How does it go about influencing African-American families for good and for ill?

We have identified twelve key systems through which society influences African-American families. These are the economic system, the political system, the health system, the housing system, the educational system, the welfare system, the criminal justice system, and the military system, as well as the transportation, recreation, communications, and religious systems. They may be conveniently considered in four major sectors: government, private business, voluntary nonsectarian, and religious. They often collaborate and interact.

The government sector includes politics and government at all levels. The private business sector includes the profit-making enterprises. Many of the twelve societal systems are subsystems of these two sectors, sometimes independently and sometimes jointly. For example, the military system is part of the government sector, as is the criminal justice system. Other systems such as health, welfare and education, and transportation are derivatives of both the government and private business sectors. The government sector plays a preeminent role because it, more than any other sector, has historically stood as an obstacle to the freedom, independence, and opportunity available to African-American families. And conversely, government leadership has enabled the greatest measure of progress over the past century.

The private business sector consists of ideas, practices, and institutions, which control the production and distribution of goods and services. When it works optimally it provides jobs, income, and wealth, distributed on an equitable basis. Profits earned are used to perpetuate the business and to distribute rewards to those eligible. The private business sector provides most of the jobs for African-American people that make it possible for families to meet their basic obligations. It is dependent on vigorous family functioning in both its instrumental domain, providing food, clothing, shelter, and other basic necessities; and in its more expressive domain, providing love and care for all its members.

The voluntary sector is the largest sector of all. As President George Bush's theme of "the thousand points of light" suggests, it has enormous power, status, and place in American society. It consists of those ideas, practices, and institutions which operate for the general welfare of the people without pursuing a profit and without pursuing a sectarian purpose. This is the fastest growing sector of American society, and it virtually exploded with the onset of the postindustrial era. The United Way, the American Red Cross, family agencies, foundations, and a plethora of professional associations are typical of the voluntary sector.

Finally, there is the religious sector. This is composed of a wide range of ideas, values, institutions, and practices oriented to particular religious and spiritual traditions. Most have at bottom a set of moral values, which are humanitarian and family oriented. They have been, are, and can be even more helpful in the struggle of African-American families for viability.

Systems of Contemporary Society

Figure 2.2 sketches out the broad implications of this analysis. It suggests that knowing the truth about black families today requires a profound appreciation of certain large-scale influences. First, a careful observer recognizes that the family which surrounds and sustains the child is in turn surrounded and sustained by the black community and by the wider American society. Whatever considerable influence history has had, it is moderated through these forces of contemporary society. A dozen segments of the wider society are identified. Each has an impact. In addi-

FIGURE 2.2
A Wholistic Perspective

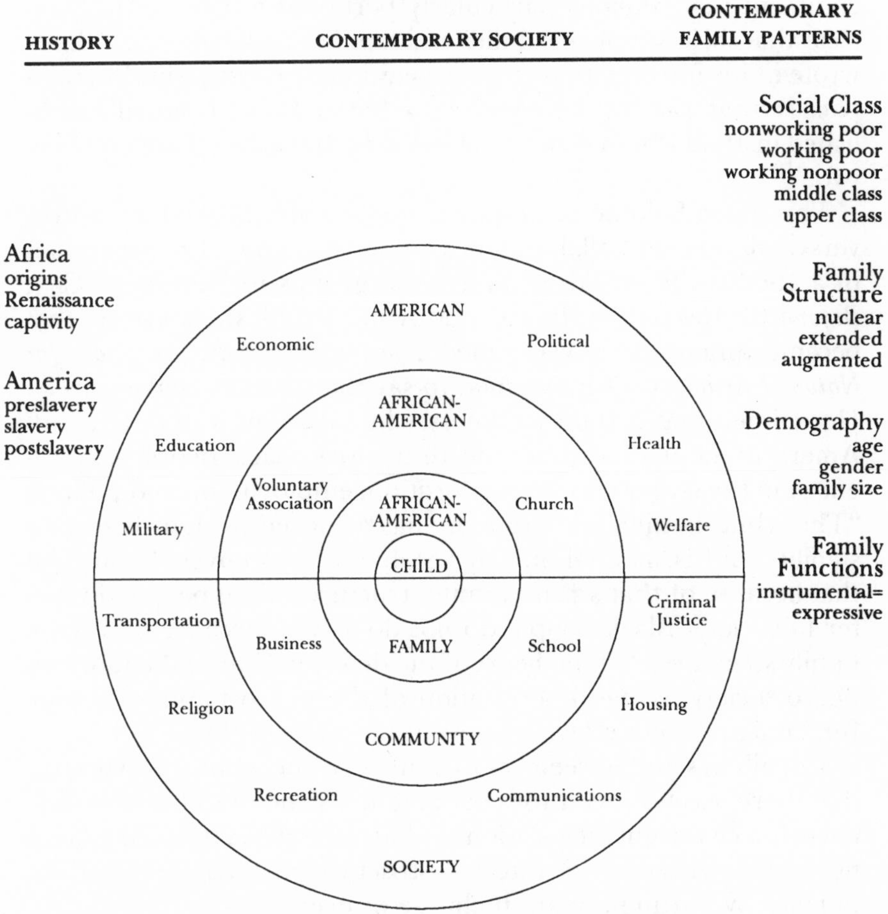

HISTORY	CONTEMPORARY SOCIETY	CONTEMPORARY FAMILY PATTERNS

Social Class
nonworking poor
working poor
working nonpoor
middle class
upper class

Africa
origins
Renaissance
captivity

Family
Structure
nuclear
extended
augmented

America
preslavery
slavery
postslavery

Demography
age
gender
family size

Family
Functions
instrumental=
expressive

AMERICAN
Economic   Political
AFRICAN-
AMERICAN
Education   Health
Voluntary
Association   AFRICAN-   Church
Military   AMERICAN
CHILD   Welfare
Transportation   Criminal
Justice
Business   FAMILY   School
Religion   Housing
COMMUNITY
Recreation   Communications
SOCIETY

SOURCE: Andrew Billingsley

tion, there are certain segments or institutions within the African-American community which are particularly powerful in their effects on family life. Finally, as a consequence of how society and the community operate, certain distinct patterns of family life emerge. These are reflected in social class, family structure, age structure, and gender distinctions.

SOCIETY'S ADVANTAGE

Working through its various sectors, society both assists and blocks families in their efforts to meet their basic responsibilities even though families are not passive entities and also influence society. In the late 1960s, prominent sociologist Nathan Glazer made a comment that remains particularly pertinent to this point. "It is clear that society makes families and families make society," Glazer wrote in his introduction to a new edition of E. Franklin Frazier's pace-setting *The Negro Family in the United States,* originally published in 1939, "but what is not clear is the relative influence of the two."[12]

This was a Solomonic response to a raging theoretical controversy. Glazer had collaborated with Senator Daniel P. Moynihan in a 1963 study on ethnic and racial groups in New York City, *Beyond the Melting Pot.* In 1965, Moynihan published a study that became infamous. It was called *The Negro Family: The Case for National Action.* In it he seemed to say that families make society. He claimed that certain weaknesses he identified within African-American families caused the difficulties black people experienced in the larger society in education, employment, and politics. "The white family," he argued, "has achieved a high degree of stability and is maintaining that stability." Moreover, he argued that because of that strong family structure, white people do better in society. Black people do not do as well because of a weak family structure. "At the heart of the deterioration of the fabric of negro society, is the deterioration of the negro family. It is the fundamental source of weakness at the present time."[13]

Moynihan's thesis seemed to reinforce the policy perspective that there was less need for changing the structure of society, less need for civil rights legislation and affirmative action, and more need for changing the internal structure of African-American families by putting a man in charge of every house.

We argued, along with others, that Moynihan had it all backward. We argued that society makes families and that it was the difficulties experienced by African-Americans in the wider society (their economic, political, and educational deprivation) which caused the patterns of instability within families that Moynihan identified. Consequently, we argued that by changing the structure of social institutions so that they would function as well for blacks as they do for whites, and as well for female-headed families as they do for male-headed families, and as well for poor families as they do for more privileged families, both family stability and more effective family functioning would follow.

After reflecting on two decades of research in the social sciences since then, we would now state our position somewhat differently. Recent studies of African-American families seem to bear out Nathan Glazer.[14] However, to avoid the either-or mode of thought, we propose that families make society and society makes families. We add to that observation, however, the view that while the influence between families and society flows in both directions, society has the advantage. This is, in part, because society is older, larger, stronger, more continuous and, thus, more powerful and has more resources at its command. Though contemporary analysts of African-American families still have some difficulty with the idea of the supremacy of society over families, this proposition is really not new. Aristotle expressed it this way: "The state is by nature clearly prior to the family and to the individual, since the whole is of necessity prior to the part."[15] It is an idea which can help us all understand better both the structure and the functioning of contemporary African-American families as these intimate associations struggle to help their members adapt to the pressures and opportunities inherent in their communities and their larger society. The so-called black family crisis is not of their own making; nor is it the worst crisis they ever faced and survived.

We will show that within the range of family structures, within the range of community institutions and initiatives, and within the larger society, there are enormous pressures making it difficult for families to be strong. Just as important, however, we will identify a set of strengths and resources in family, community, and society, with the potential for generating policies, programs, and practices which can help families meet their responsibilities.

In the next section we ask what we can learn from the history of the African-American people that will help us understand better the value they place on family life. What struggles have they faced in trying to protect and enhance their families? What successful efforts can they look back to for guidance and inspiration? Reflecting on their past, we uncover ideas that could help more families meet the future effectively. We also gain more insight into the way that society's influence works.

PART II

History Is Prologue

Chapter 3

The African Heritage of African-American Families

Questions about the meaning of their African heritage have long circulated among the African-American people. The sociologist E. Franklin Frazier argued that Africa had no meaning for this people, all traces of African heritage having been blotted out by the experience of American slavery.[1] The anthropologist Melville Herskovitz argued just as forcefully that important traces of African culture did indeed survive the holocaust of slavery.[2]

Alex Haley, in his book and television series *Roots*, has traced his ancestral lineage from seventeenth-century Gambia in West Africa to the present time. Our 1968 book *Black Families in White America* described the impact of the seventeenth-century West African culture on contemporary African-American family patterns.

Until recently, however, the prevailing scholarship has been on the side of Frazier and not Herskovitz. As late as 1963 two leading social scientists would go unchallenged in their assertion that, while other ethnic groups had historical and cultural backgrounds to help define them, African-Americans were without such historical and cultural context. "The Negro is only an American and nothing else," they concluded. "He has no history and culture to guard and protect."[3] Contemporary scholars, however, have demonstrated that the history and the heritage of the African-

83

American people does not begin or end with slavery. It goes far back into ancient Africa, back to the origins of all humankind and the rise of civilization.

In this chapter, three eras of that early heritage are described: the African Genesis of human civilization at least four million years ago; the African Renaissance, in the Nile Valley civilizations some three-and-a-half centuries before the flowering of Greek and Roman civilizations; and the African Captivity, showing how slavery disrupted West African societies between the fifteenth and eighteenth centuries A.D. at the time of the slave trade.

AFRICAN GENESIS

In 1974 archaeologists, working in Ethiopia in a place called Hadsar, found sufficient fossil remains to piece together the most complete skeleton of a two-legged upright walking human ancestor ever unearthed. A female, they named her Lucy. She was about three feet tall, weighed about sixty pounds as an adult, and was approximately 3.5 million years old. It was the oldest complete skeleton of a human ancestor ever found.[4] It was also the latest in a long line of discoveries pioneered by Louis and Mary Leaky, who first discovered East African man in 1959.

The next year in the same location they found enough fossils to represent thirteen individuals: men, women, and at least four children. They named this "The First Family." In 1981, about forty-five miles away from Hadsar in another region in Ethiopia, other archaeologists found other fossils which showed life that reached back to 4 million years, a half-million years older than Lucy and her kin. Still, they belonged to the same species.

Less spectacular, perhaps, but no less meaningful was the discovery in 1984 of the skeletal remains of a twelve-year-old boy in the Lake Turkana region of Kenya in East Africa. Judged to be a member of the *Homo erectus* species, the boy was found to have lived 1.6 million years ago.[5]

A remarkable feature of Turkana Boy is that he looked very much like contemporary African and African-American people. The scientists found that if Turkana Boy had been clothed in modern dress, with a cap over his forehead to obscure the low forehead and beetle brow, he could walk the streets today without being particularly noticed in a crowd containing African and African-American people.

Eve and Her Children

Until recently, the support for the theory of the African genesis of modern humanity came exclusively from archaeological excavations and the examination of fossil remains. A few years ago, major breakthroughs in laboratory research by molecular biologists, chemists, and geneticists revolutionized the study of human evolution.[6] Operating independently in three different universities in different parts of the country, laboratory scientists have verified the findings of paleontologists with respect to the African genesis. Examining cell structures over time through the process of DNA research, these laboratory scientists have been able to trace the evolution of modern human beings from the present generation back in time to more than 200,000 years ago to a common female ancestor in black Africa, whom some scientists are calling "Eve."

Berkeley scientists, analyzing samples from the placentas donated by 147 women who had new babies and who represent all the races of humankind, were able to trace their common ancestry back through time and establish that all the people alive on earth today are direct descendants of one African woman who lived 200,000 years ago.

> Mitochondrial DNA from 147 people, drawn from five geographic populations, has been analyzed by restriction mapping. All these mitochondrial DNAs stem from one woman, who is postulated to have lived about 200,000 years ago. Probably in Africa. All the populations examined except the African population have multiple origins, implying that each area was colonized repeatedly.[7]

Working independently, another group of scientists at Emory University, by studying DNA through blood samples from 700 women of all races and regions of the world, came to essentially the same conclusion—a single female ancestor who lived about 200,000 years ago. Another group at Yale University confirmed this finding.[8]

What was Eve like? She was a dark-haired, dark-skinned, dark-eyed woman of about twenty-five years when she died. Scientists say that she was as muscular as contemporary tennis star Martina Navratilova but probably stronger. She lived in a family group of about twenty-five people. They roamed the hot savannah region of Africa in search of food. They were able to use stone tools, which had been invented by their ancestors. She was sturdy and fruitful. Her descendants fanned out all over the world and survived. Her genes are now in all of the 5 billion living people in the world, without regard to race, creed, color, or national origin. She has been said to be our ten-thousandth great-grandmother.[9]

The Races of Humankind

These findings not only verify the African genesis and the common human heritage, they also sharply contradict the earlier theory about the different races originating and evolving in various regions of the world and of one race as superior or more advanced than the others.

Additionally, these findings support the origin and evolution of humanity as having occurred in Africa and the migration of people from Africa to other parts of the world and over time taking on the characteristics which enabled them to survive and prosper in those climates and regions. Scientists know, for example, that it takes only about a thousand years for color and other physical features to change completely. We now know that somewhere between 90,000 and 180,000 years ago, African people, the descendants of Eve, migrated from the African homeland and settled in other parts of the world. As they moved out to Europe, for example, they lost their pigmentation and skin color, their curly hair, and other features which protected them from the hot sun. In short, they took on characteristics which enabled them to adapt to their new climates. But the basic cell structure, the center of their humanity, did not change. Thus they might look different, act differently, and speak different languages, but the essence of their humanity, gained in ancient Africa, did not change over hundreds of thousands of years.

Dr. Stephen Jay Gould, the Harvard University paleontologist and essayist, put the matter even more cogently: "It makes us realize that all human beings, despite differences in external appearance, are really members of a single entity that's had a very recent origin in one place. There is a kind of biological brotherhood that's much more profound than we ever realized."[10]

AFRICAN RENAISSANCE: THE NILE VALLEY CIVILIZATION

When Herodotus, the father of history, visited Egypt in the fifth century B.C. he wrote that "nowhere are there so many marvellous things, nor in the whole world beside are there to be seen so many things of unspeakable greatness."[11]

It has often been said by Western scholars that the origin, the color, and other important features of the ancient Egyptians are unknown. John Anthony West put it this way: "No one is sure who the ancient Egyptians were, where they came from or how they got there. All that is known is that in the not so very distant past, Egypt was not the desert it is today. The vast, trackless, lifeless expanse of the Sahara Desert was green savannah as recently as 15,000 B.C."[12]

Although still a controversial aspect of African history, this African civilization is rapidly gaining authoritative chroniclers. Among the leading students of this era have been the late Professor Cheikh Anta Diop, Director of the Radiocarbon Laboratory and the Fundamental Institute of Black Africa at the University of Dakar in West Africa; Martin Bernal, Professor of Government Studies at Cornell University; Dr. Yosef ben-Jochannan, formerly Adjunct Professor of History and Egyptology at Cornell University; Ivan Van Sertima, Professor of African Studies at Rutgers University; Dr. Asa Hilliard, Calloway Professor of Education and Psychology at Georgia State University; and Charles S. Finch, M.D., Professor of Community Medicine at the Morehouse School of Medicine in Atlanta.

These scholars have identified several means of verifying Egyptians' African identity. Primary among these are the portraits of themselves which they left showing African features. Moreover, in their own writings they identified their origin as black Africa. Indeed, until about 200 years ago, the Greeks, Romans, Hebrews, and others who studied in ancient Egypt had no difficulty attributing this advanced civilization to native Africans. Martin Bernal's two-volume study is perhaps the most definitive in establishing the link between the ancient Egyptian civilization and the later Greek and Roman civilizations.[13]

These black Egyptians were remarkably gifted original and creative scientists, engineers, astronomers, mathematicians, artists, philosophers, teachers. This African renaissance was so well accepted by early Western scholars that the very science of chemistry takes its name from Kemet, the name the ancient Egyptians gave their homeland.

They were deeply religious or spiritual and saw no distinction between the spiritual, the intellectual, and the physical elements of the universe and of man.

They were strongly devoted to the family as a pattern of organization. Statues, carvings, drawings, and paintings of almost all the gods, kings, noblemen, and priests show them with wives, children, sisters, brothers, or extended kin.

They were extraordinary farmers, horticulturists, orchardists, and arborists. Because the annual flooding of the Nile made the richest soil of the region, ancient Egypt became the breadbasket for the whole area and much of Europe and the Middle East.

They were master builders. The pyramids and temples they built have not been equaled since. The great Karnak Temple, near Luxor on the west bank of the Nile, built some thirty-three centuries ago, was a vast complex of structures that extended more than a mile into the desert. It was here that the Temple of Ipet Isut served as a center of learning where early European scholars came to study with the priests and learned men of Egypt. It was built by King Akhenaten, who is known primarily because of his espousal of one supreme God. One expert has called him "the world's first idealist . . . the earliest monotheist, and the first prophet of internationalism—the most remarkable figure of the Ancient World before the Hebrews."[14]

NILE VALLEY CIVILIZATION

Figure 3.1 shows Professor Asa Hilliard's 1983 outline of the history of ancient Egypt, which was called Kemet by the founding natives, and later named Egypt by the Greeks who had a profound appreciation for this civilization. They learned a great deal from it and communicated what they learned to the rest of the world. Indeed, much of what is known about ancient Egypt is due to the scholarship of the early Greeks, following the conquest of Alexander the Great. Hilliard shows the four golden ages of this ancient civilization from about 2600 B.C. to about 650 B.C. It was during these four golden ages that much of the birth of learning, art, mathematics, architecture, philosophy, and science took place. The first of these periods is called the Pyramid Age and lasted from roughly 2665 to 2160 B.C. It was during this period that the major pyramids and other important monuments were built. The

FIGURE 3.1
Nile Valley Civilization
Related to Other Important African Events
Dynasty 1 (3100)

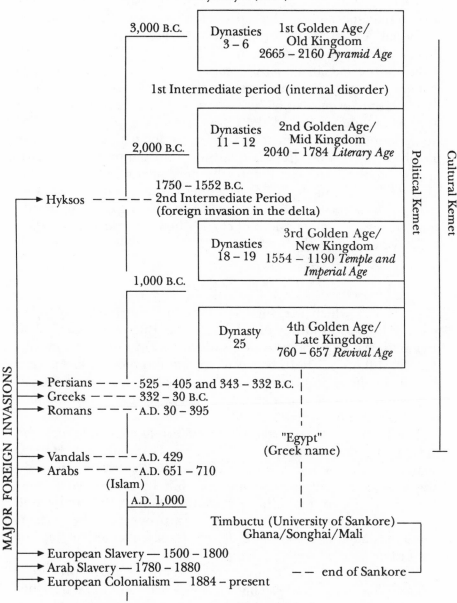

SOURCE: Asa G. Hilliard, 1983.

second is the Literary Age, which commenced about 2040 B.C. and lasted to 1784 B.C. During this period much of the ancient Egyptian contribution to literature and philosophy flowered, to be discovered later recorded on huge scrolls of papyrus, a plant native to the Nile Valley. The third golden age was the Temple and Imperial Age, and it lasted from 1554 B.C. to 1190 B.C. when many of the temples and other religious cities were built and which witnessed an expansionist period when Egypt sought to conquer neighboring peoples. Finally, the Revival Age, which lasted from 760 B.C. to 657 B.C., witnessed a recapitulation of all the major innovations of the three previous ages. During these four periods when ancient Egypt was under native African rule much of Egypt's progress and lasting contribution to world civilization took place, well before the permanent conquest of this civilization by outsiders. Between these four golden ages, however, history records that outsiders did rule Egypt temporarily and there were some periods of chaos when there seemed to be no effective central authority.

Family Code

One area in which the ancient Egyptians contributed to world civilization was in family life. E. A. Wallis Budge has said, "The Egyptian was in all periods of his history a lover of his home and family, and the relations between parents and their children were usually of the most affectionate character. His world was the village where his home was and his kinsfolk were the only inhabitants that counted in his sight."[15]

The family code consisted of the following elements: first, the role of the man, husband, and father was paramount. He was master of the house, breadwinner. Second, however, the wife was in some respects more important. She bore the children and brought them up, providing for continuation of the family. She preserved his name, safeguarded his property. The ancient tombs usually bear the name of the deceased's mother but not his father.

Third, marriage was highly sanctioned and regularly practiced. To found a family and establish a house was held to be the duty of every right-minded man. The first step was marriage. Most of the fine stone statues of African kings showed them with their wives. The great statue of Ramses II and his southern-born wife is an outstanding example. Fourth, children were highly valued.

As among all African peoples, it was generally held that every man who could afford to keep a wife should marry, and that every woman should give her husband offspring.

Fifth, despite or alongside polygamy, strong emphasis was placed on love and honor between husband and wife. Ptah Hotep, one of the most venerable Egyptian priests, who lived about 2500 years before Christ, laid down certain guidelines for the family:

> If thou wouldst be wise [or prosperous] establish a house for thyself [get married]. Love thou thy wife in the house wholly and rightly. Fill her belly and clothe her back; oil for anointing is the medicine for her limbs. Make her heart to rejoice as long as thou livest; she is a field profitable to her lord. Enter not into disputes with her. She will withdraw herself before violence. Make her to prosper permanently in thy house.[16]

Sixth, men were advised by the ancient Egyptian wise men to avoid relationships with strange women. Ptah Hotep says:

> If thou wishest to maintain a permanent friendship in the house to which thou art in the habit of going, whether as master, or whether as brother, or whether as friend, or in fact any place to which thou hast the entry, strive against associating with the women there. The place which they frequent is not good [for thee]; but the imprudent man follows them in their quest of what is beautiful. A man is made a fool of by their dazzling limbs, which turn into things that are harder than quartzite sandstone. The pleasure lasts only for a brief moment, and it is even as a dream, and when it is ended a man finds death through having experienced it.[17]

A seventh principle governs parent-child relations. A father claimed implicit obedience from his son, but Egyptians thought a boy owed more to his mother than to his father. It was, therefore, his duty not only to obey her but to love her and to give her constant proof of his devotion to her.

Eighth, boys were preferred to girls. Boys were sent to school at age four, for a period of ten to twelve years. There were other schools for girls. Boys prepared for professions chosen by their fathers. A schoolmaster often taught children in his own house.

Moreover, this greatest scribe of all, Ptah Hotep, includes in his original instructions found in a cave some 2500 years before the Christian era the ten-point code in figure 3.2 pertaining to family life:[18]

Figure 3.2

Ancient African Family Code According to Ptah Hotep

- If God gives you children, don't impose on one who has no children. Neither should you decry or brag about having your own children, for there is many a father who has grief, and many a mother with children who is less content than another. . . .

- If you are a wise man train up a son who will be pleasing to God. If he is straight and takes after you, take good care of him. Do everything that is good for him. . . . Don't withdraw your heart from him. But an offspring can make trouble.

- If your son strays and neglects your counsel and disobeys all that is said, with his mouth spouting evil speech, then punish him for all his talk. God will hate him who crosses you. His guilt was determined in the womb. He who God makes boastless cannot cross the water.

- If you want friendship to endure in the house that you enter, the house of a master, of a brother or a friend, then, in whatever place you enter beware of approaching the women there. Unhappy is the place where this is done.

- If you want to have perfect conduct, to be free from every evil, then above all guard against the vice of greed. Greed is a grievous sickness that has no cure. There is no treatment for it. It embroils fathers, mothers, and the brothers of the mother. It parts the wife from the husband. Greed is a compound of all the evils.

- Do not be greedy in the division of things. Do not covet more than your share. Don't be greedy toward your relatives. . . . Poor is the person who forgets his relatives. He is deprived of their company. Even a little bit of what is wanted will turn quarreler into a friendly person.

- Be circumspect in matters of sexual relations.

- If you take for a wife a good-time woman who is joyous and who is well known in the town, if she is fickle and seems to live for the moment, do not reject her. Let her eat. The joyful person brings happiness.

- Useful is hearing to a son who hears. . . . How good it is for a son to understand his father's words. The son will reach old age through those words.

- Every man teaches as he acts. He will speak to his children so that they will speak to their children. He will set an example and not give offense. So if justice stands firm, your children will live. As to the first child who gets into trouble, when people see it, they will say about the child "that is just like him" and they will also say when they even hear a rumor about the child "that is just like him too."

AFRICAN DIASPORA

As the African people spread out from the Nile Valley, they settled in other regions of Africa, the Middle East, and Europe. Much of this settlement took place in West Africa. Chief among the West African kingdoms which arose after this migration were ancient Ghana, Mali, Songhay, and the Mossi States, which came to be known as Upper Volta, and now Burkina-Faso.

Ghana's known history extends back as far as the 25th dynasty or the seventh century B.C. Known as the "Land of Gold" because of the abundance of this precious metal, it also boasted sufficient resources in agricultural products such as cotton, wheat, millet, corn, yams, and cattle. In addition, there was mining, and a thriving iron industry, and many craftsmen, among them blacksmiths, goldsmiths, coppersmiths, stone masons, brick masons, water diviners, carpenters, weavers, sandalmakers, dyers, cabinet-makers, and potters.

The family was central to this flourishing commerce, both as a producer and beneficiary. Often entire families, extended families, lineages, and even whole villages would be involved with a particular trade. Each family member had a role to play. Trades helped bind families together.

This empire fell from the same forces of external invasions, climatic changes, and internal strife that destroyed other great African kingdoms.

Around A.D. 1050, after the decline of Ghana, Mali, whose history dates to paleolithic times, rose to preeminence. Its black king embraced Islam and the nation prospered, especially during the thirteenth century A.D. With strong leadership, unity, and favorable foreign trade, Mali continued to prosper until 1550 when foreign Muslim influence gained ascendancy.

The Songhay empire became the greatest empire in all of Africa during the fifteenth and sixteenth centuries. Its history went back to at least the seventh century A.D. Two of Africa's world-famous centers of learning, at Timbuktu and Jenne, were located in the northern and western sectors of Songhay. Trade was the primary basis of its wealth and power. By 1591, however, Muslim armies had virtually destroyed this once great kingdom. It lasted another seventy years or so in splinter groups struggling against the superior firepower of the invaders.

By A.D. 1500, the Mossi had succeeded Songhay and had become the most powerful and most industrial state in the region.

Basically a farming society, it survived as a native African state for over 500 years until overrun by France in the twentieth century. By July 1896, as France captured the Mossi nation, the Europeans were firmly in control of all West Africa. Mossi was the last of the great black West African states to surrender. Even though conquered by Europeans, the culture was not obliterated but mingled with European culture and persisted among the African captives transported to the New World.

As John Hope Franklin has written, "When the Arabs swept into North and West Africa in the seventh century, they found a civilization that was already thousands of years old."[19] The Arabs would fasten their hold on the Egyptian people for centuries until the advent of the European exploitations in the fifteenth century, which led to the Atlantic slave trade and brought more than 15 million Africans to the New World.

A number of African family patterns survived the American experience, diluted and transformed by it, but not destroyed. Primary among these African family features is the primacy given to blood ties over all types of relationship, including marriage. The anthropologist Niara Sudarkasa has found that "the most far-reaching difference between African and European families stems from their differential emphasis on consanguinity and conjugality. . . . In Africa, unlike in Europe, in many critical areas of family life the concrete core group rather than the conjugal pair was paramount."[20]

A second distinctive feature of African family patterns which survived in America was the primacy given to extended families versus nuclear families. The primacy was given to the extended family, including relatives beyond the nuclear core, to include grandparents, aunts, uncles, cousins, nieces, nephews, siblings, and the like.

A third feature of African family patterns was the strong value placed on children. A child-centered society meant that the children were not only the responsibility of the biological parents but the entire extended family. A fourth distinctive feature of African family patterns was the reverence and respect held for the elderly and other members. A fifth feature was role reciprocity among family members. While there was women's work, men's work, and children's work, there was a great deal of flexibility and interchange and no stigma attached to men doing women's work and vice versa, depending on the situation and circumstances.

A sixth distinctive feature of African family life was restraint.

Restraint means that the rights of any person must always be balanced against the requirements of the family or the larger group and the rights of others. In the family this holds in patterns of consumption, verbal communication, the management of connubial relations, and the needs of the children. Responsibility, a seventh feature of African family relations, refers to the assumption of obligations for the well-being of others beyond one's own selfish needs and desires.

Finally, a distinctive and often misunderstood feature of African family patterns was the acceptance of polygynous marriages. Supported by long-standing and highly honored traditions, rules, and regulations, a husband took plural wives. This often occurred when there was a shortage of men. In African societies where there was a shortage of women, the practice of plural husbands, called polyandry, was also sanctioned. In either situation, the rights, responsibilities, and duties of each member of the family were understood and protected. From all indications, polygynous marriages were as functional as monogamous ones.

The two types of families often existed side by side in the same community. Sudarkasa has found that they functioned well: "The cohesion of the polygynous Yoruba family derived in large measure from the existence of explicit rules or codes defining appropriate behavior for all persons in the group."[21] She also observed: "Even though there was some rivalry and competition among wives of the same husband, the relationships among wives of the entire compound were characterized by considerable camaraderie and cooperation."[22]

Overall, reflection on the African heritage suggests strong support for the views of Herskovitz over those of Frazier. As Du Bois put it: "There is a distinct nexus between Africa and America which, though broken and perverted, is nevertheless not to be neglected by the careful student."

Serious analysis of the relevance of the ancient African world to contemporary African-American families would prove exceedingly fruitful. It might help to allay some of the despair which often accompanies analysis of the major disruption in traditional family patterns in recent years. The long view of history might well suggest that the very idea of family is so deeply ingrained that black families sustain themselves in part during periods of transition by clinging tenaciously to certain basic values.

Chapter 4

The Way of the New World: The Triumph Over Slavery

There is abundant evidence that the slave trade destroyed all semblance of family ties among the Africans captured and sold into slavery. Yet a revisionist approach to history reveals that families, though broken by the slave trade and degraded by the slave experience, were revived and sustained by large numbers of the Africans in America. This can be seen particularly among those who were free during the slave era.

FAMILY PATTERNS AMONG FREE BLACKS DURING SLAVERY

A major pattern is that nearly half, or some 45 percent of free blacks lived in families (Table 4.1). In eight of the twelve states for which we have complete figures, a majority lived in families. Only in Virginia, Pennsylvania, Maine, and Vermont did less than half of free blacks live in families.

Although not shown in the table, in each of the twelve states for which we have complete figures, the overwhelming majority of these families had both husbands and wives as family heads. Altogether 85 percent had male-female heads and approximately 15 percent had female heads only. In the New England region the incidence of male and female–headed families was extremely common, ranging from a high of 97.2 percent in Maine to 89.6 percent in Connecticut, with the other states somewhere between

TABLE 4.1
**Enslaved and Free Black Population
and Free Blacks in Families by States, 1798**

States and Territories	Enslaved N	Free N	Free Blacks in Families N	Percentage of Free Blacks in Families
Connecticut	2,759	2,801	2,069	74
Delaware	8,887	3,899	NA	—
Georgia	29,264	398	NA	—
Kentucky	11,830	114	NA	—
Maine	—	538	167	31
Maryland	103,036	8,043	5,423	67
Massachusetts	—	5,463	3,251	60
New Hampshire	158	630	393	62
New Jersey	11,423	2,762	NA	—
New York	21,324	4,654	3,201	69
North Carolina	100,572	4,975	3,623	73
Pennsylvania	3,737	6,537	2,119	32
Rhode Island	952	3,469	2,179	63
South Carolina	107,094	1,801	1,431	79
Tennessee	3,417	361	NA	—
Vermont	17	255	119	47
Virginia	293,427	12,766	2,758	22
Total	697,897	59,466	26,733	45

NA = Not available.

SOURCE: J.D.B. DeBow, *Statistical View of the United States,* Compendium of the Seventh Census, Washington, 1854; Records of the United States Census, Record Group 29, National Archives, Washington, D.C.

these proportions. In the states of Pennsylvania and New York the presence of two-parent families stood at 91.8 percent and 83.5 percent respectively. In the Southern states with the largest free black populations and also the strongest and most oppressive economic, political, and social conditions, the prevalence of male-female families was somewhat less than in the other regions. Even so, however, they were the overwhelming majority, ranging from a high of 87 percent in Virginia to a relative low of 73 percent in South Carolina.

The specter of black people owning slaves, and particularly the idea of buying and selling slaves, while always a tiny aspect of the slave system, has always fascinated, angered, and embarrassed most African-American people. A striking example of this was the campaign for governor of Louisiana in 1873. While black delegates were in the majority, mostly former slaves, the black candidate for governor, Francis F. Dumas, lost to the white candidate by a narrow vote of forty-five to forty-three. A major factor against him was that he had been a slaveholder. And though he had valiantly taken his slaves into battle on the side of the victorious forces which resulted in freedom for all, he was nevertheless resented.[1]

There is still another aspect, however, to black persons owning one or two slaves in the United States at that time. Free blacks often were permitted to purchase relatives, offspring, wives or husbands, and they were not always in a position to set them free at will. They could only provide better care and protection for them than would the ordinary slaveholders. Men often purchased the freedom of their wives even while they were themselves still enslaved, in part so that they could be protected from further abuse and, in part, in order that their children could have the legal status of the mother and be free.[2]

Marriage Patterns Among Free Blacks

When we search for factors which contributed to such an overwhelming existence of stable patterns of family life among these early Africans in America two stand out. First is the strong commitment and attachment to family among African peoples. This commitment is so pervasive that whenever opportunities exist and barriers are relaxed, they establish and maintain these close family ties. Great and unusual sacrifices will be endured for the sake of establishing, maintaining, and reestablishing family relationships. A second factor is that the social, economic, and political environment encouraged the development of families among free black populations. Religious values, economic opportunities, and patterns of settlement all tended to encourage family organization and to discourage the more individualistic patterns of life and social relationships.

Free blacks followed several patterns of marriage and family life, all heavily influenced by the prevailing conditions and opportunities in the area where they lived.[3] They sometimes married other free blacks; sometimes they married enslaved blacks. At other times they married white partners or Native Americans.

Free Black Partners

In New England, two of the leading black women of the literary world, Phillis Wheatley and Lucy Terry, married free black husbands, as did Elizabeth Freeman, who challenged successfully the legal foundations of slavery in Massachusetts.

Phillis Wheatley, who was already a world-famous poet by the time she was freed in 1773, was not married until 1778 when she married John Peters, a free black man. His difficulties in providing for her and her three children were characteristic of the experience of many black families then and today.

Lucy Terry, a somewhat lesser known poet than Phillis Wheatley, is best remembered by historians and literary scholars as the author of "Bar's Fight," a poem about an Indian Massacre of whites in her little Deerfield, Massachusetts, community. On May 17, 1756, she married a free black man named Abijah Prince. She was twenty-six; he was fifty-two. They moved from Deerfield to Guilford, Vermont, where he was owner of a hundred-acre farm. They were more than once threatened with violence by their white neighbors. They had six children, who were rejected by New England colleges because of their race. Two of their sons fought in the War of Independence. In 1794, Abijah died at the age of ninety-four. Lucy died eighteen years later, at the age of ninety-one. In order to protect the family land, she once appeared personally and argued her case successfully before the United States Supreme Court.

Elizabeth Freeman is best known because of her abolitionist activities before the movement gained fame nationally. She was born a slave in Massachusetts about 1742. Both her parents had been born in Africa. She was married sometime before the Revolutionary War to a free black man who was killed in that war. In about 1781, as a forty-year-old widow with a young daughter, she sued for her own freedom and won. She died in 1829 when she was about eighty-five years old. It is said that she lived "to a ripe old age ... surrounded by her grandchildren and great-grandchildren." In her will, she left to her daughter "a black silk gown, a gift of her African father, and a short gown that her African mother had worn."[4]

Nonblack Partners

A number of prominent black men during this period married nonblack women. Paul Cuffee, an eighteenth-century New England merchant, shipbuilder, seaman, and early Pan-Africanist, married a Native American woman in 1784, as his own father had done forty years before. He died in 1817 after a distinguished career, including being a pioneer in the black American resettlement in Sierra Leone. Jean-Baptiste Pointe Du Sable, the founder of Chicago, also married a Native American woman named Catherine in 1788, after they had lived together for a number of years and she had borne him two children. Catherine died shortly after the turn of the century and he died sometime after 1814, while living in the home of his granddaughter. He died a pauper.

Prominent among the free blacks who married whites was Lemuel Hays, a free black man who was a longtime minister of white congregations in New England. Born in 1753 in Hartford, he was placed as an infant with a white family as an indentured servant until he was twenty-one. In 1783, he married a white schoolteacher, Elizabeth Babbit, whom he had helped to convert to Christianity. They had ten children and she stood by him through hardships and racial discrimination and triumphed over it until his death in 1833.

Slave Partners

Among the free blacks who married slaves were Venture Smith and Amos Fortune. Venture Smith, born in Africa, was captured and brought to this country and sold into slavery. In 1765, he was able to purchase his freedom at the age of thirty-six, but his wife and children were still slaves. He worked hard as a woodsman, saved his money, and purchased his pregnant wife, his daughter, two sons, and three friends. He died in 1805 at the age of seventy-seven.

One of the most colorful examples of family life among the free black population of the eighteenth century is the family of Amos Fortune. He was born in Africa, and as a slave in Massachusetts, he was taught the trades of bookbinding and tannery. In 1770, after serving one master for forty years, he was permitted to purchase his freedom when he was sixty years old. When he was sixty-eight, he purchased a slave woman named Lydia Somerset and married her. She died a few months later in the midst of the Revolutionary War. He then purchased another slave, Violate Baldwin, and married her. They were to have a long and fruitful life together. He died in 1801 at the age of ninety-one. She died a year later at the age of seventy-three. They were buried side by side in a cemetery in Jaffrey, New Hampshire, with handsome gravestones on which the following epitaphs, composed by him, are inscribed: For his headstone: "SACRED, to the memory of Amos Fortune, who was born free in Africa, a slave in America; he purchased liberty, professed Christianity, lived reputably, and died hopefully, November 17, 1801." And on her headstone: "SACRED, to the memory of Violate, by sale the slave of Amos Fortune, by marriage his wife, by her fidelity his friend and solace, she died his widow, September 13, 1802."

These are only a few of the free blacks of the eighteenth century who carved out a family life for themselves and their people, and who laid the groundwork for the institutional forms the black family followed for centuries to come.

FAMILY LIFE AMONG THE ENSLAVED POPULATION

What about the enslaved population? What evidence do we have about the existence of family patterns among them?

Contemporary scholarly assertions about the absence of family life among black people during slavery often refer to the works of Frazier, principally his *The Negro Family in the United States*, published originally in 1939 by the University of Chicago Press.[5] Such references to Frazier's work reflect a superficial reading of it and an almost total ignorance of his earlier, more definitive studies as reflected in his three slender works, "The Negro Slave Family," *The Free Negro Family*, and *The Negro Family in Chicago*.[6] For in each of these works the existence of family among the enslaved population is generally recognized.

In concluding one study, Frazier observed: "Where the plantation system was breaking down and Negro artisans achieved a semi-free status and acquired property the slave family tended to become stabilized."[7] This was a remarkable sociological insight which holds true to this very day. Economic viability and social status lead in turn to stable patterns of family life. The manner in which they came forward to register their marriages with the authorities after the Civil War attests to the long-standing practice of slave families.[8]

In November of 1866 Charles West and Henrietta Chase, both ex-slaves, had their marriage registered by the Reverend R.H. Robinson in the District of Columbia. They had been married since 1836, when they were given permission to do so by their owner, but without benefit of ceremony. At the time they registered, they had nine children and had lived together for nearly thirty years.

During the same month in 1866, Isaac Diggs and Letty Smith, both ex-slaves, had their marriage registered by the Reverend J.A. Jones in the District of Columbia. They had been married for thirty years, since they were first joined together by the Reverend Mr. Breckinbridge in Prince George's County, Maryland, in 1826 with the permission of their owner. At the time they registered they also had nine children.

In May of 1867, George Washington and Mary Shanklin had their marriage registered by M.V. Wright in the District of Columbia. They had been married in 1847 in King George County, Virginia, in a ceremony conducted by Moses Myers. They were the parents of nine children.

Between November 1866 and July 1867, 843 couples who had been married and lived together during slavery came to have their marriages legalized and registered in the District of Columbia (Table 4.2). Ten of these couples had been married for over fifty years, two since 1813, and eight since 1815.

In Vicksburg, Mississippi, between 1864 and 1866, another 4,638 couples who had been married during slavery had their marriages registered. The Vicksburg data show that a relatively large number of both the men and women in these couples had been married at least one time previous to their present marriage (Tables 4.3 and 4.4).

Moreover, large numbers of these couples had been married for long periods of time. Nearly 50 percent of the men and 45 percent of the women had been married for more than five years to their previous spouse.

Most couples had children by their previous spouses. Fifty-seven percent of the men and 56 percent of the women reported one or more children. In addition, the dissolution of the previous marriage was due to the death of the spouse or to forced separation because of the sale of one partner (Table 4.5). Among the women, death of their previous husbands accounted for the dissolution in 60 percent of the instances. Among the men, forced sales accounted for the larger share of family breakups; others

TABLE 4.2
Number of Marriages Registered in the District of Columbia
November 1866 Through July 1867 and Year of Original Marriage

Year of Marriage	Number of Families	Year of Marriage	Number of Families
1813	2	1844	7
1815	8	1845	19
1818	1	1846	14
1820	11	1847	54
1821	1	1848	12
1823	1	1849	8
1825	1	1850	29
1826	2	1851	21
1827	12	1852	36
1828	1	1853	21
1830	4	1854	36
1831	4	1855	65
1832	4	1856	26
1834	2	1857	54
1835	3	1858	28
1836	10	1859	42
1837	29	1860	80
1838	3	1861	63
1839	1	1862	55
1840	27	1863	18
1841	12	1864	1
1842	7	1865	4
1843	3	1867	1
Total	149		694

SOURCE: Old Military Branch, Bureau of Refugees, Freedmen and Abandoned Lands, District of Columbia Marriage Record, Asst. Com'r. of D.C., 1866 and 1867, Record Group 105, The National Archives, Washington, D.C.

were caused by desertion, common consent, and other reasons.

What the data in tables 4.3, 4.4, and 4.5 show from both the Washington, D.C., and the Vicksburg, Mississippi, registries is that the existence of family life among black people during slavery was not confined to free black families or any one section of the country.

Finally, George Rawick provides strong support for our proposition about the mutually enhancing role of the family and achievement among the African captives. After examining thousands of slave narratives, Rawick concluded: "Indeed, the activity of the slaves in creating patterns of family life that were functionally integrative did more than merely prevent the destruction of

Table 4.3
Men with Previous Spouses
Vicksburg, 1864–1866

	N	(%)
No previous spouse	2,586	55.8
Yes previous spouse	1,893	40.8
Indicated having children previously, but gave no information on previous spouse	159	3.4
Total	4,638	100
Number of Years with Previous Spouse		
1 or less	272	13.3
2–4	599	29.2
5–10	635	31.0
11 or more	387	18.8
Did not state	159	7.7
Total	2,052	100
Number of Children by Previous Marriage		
None	879	42.8
One	371	18.1
2–4	552	26.9
5–10	215	10.5
11 or more	35	1.7
Total	2,053	100

SOURCE: Marriage Records, Asst. Com'r., Vicksburg, Mississippi, 1863–1866, RG 105, NA.

personality. . . . It was part and parcel . . . of the social process out of which came black pride, black identity, black culture, the black community, and black rebellion in America."[9]

In Their Own Words

The re-creation of a new form of family in the minds and experiences of the African captives during slavery is graphically depicted in the interviews conducted with these survivors in the 1930s. They were interviewed as part of the government-sponsored Federal Writers Project designed to provide work for unemployed writers.[10]

Table 4.6 shows a sample of these interviews in four different regions of the South. In the South Carolina region, for example,

TABLE 4.4
Women with Previous Spouses
Vicksburg, 1864–1866

	N	(%)
No previous spouse	2,409	51.9
Yes previous spouse	2,038	43.9
Indicated having children, previously, but gave no information on previous spouse	191	4.2
Total	4,638	100
Number of Years with Previous Spouse		
1 or less	333	14.9
2–4	709	31.8
5–10	703	31.6
11 or more	293	13.1
Did not state	191	8.6
Total	2,234	100
Number of Children by Previous Marriage		
None	968	44.0
One	434	19.7
2–4	607	27.6
5–10	192	8.7
11 or more	28	—
Total	2,201	100

SOURCE: Marriage Records, Asst. Com'r., Vicksburg, Mississippi, 1863–1866, RG 105, NA.

153 ex-slaves were interviewed in 1937. Some 130 of them representing 85 percent of the total had vivid recollections of their mother. In like manner 116, or 76 percent, had recollections of their father. Altogether seventy, or 46 percent, spoke of their own children, while fifty-nine, or 39 percent, spoke of their brothers and sisters. Thus each of the three generations—parents, siblings, and children—were firmly fixed in the experiences and recollections of these ex-slaves. There were other ways too that they revealed the meaning of family life for them during slavery. A total of sixty-one, or 40 percent, referred to their own husband or wife during slavery while ninety-eight, or 64 percent, referred to marriage in general among the captives. Finally it will be noted that twenty-one, or 14 percent, referred to families in general while seventy-five, or 49 percent, referred to other relatives. Even eight

TABLE 4.5
Reason for Separation
Vicksburg, 1864–1866

	Male N	(%)	Female N	(%)
Death	775	41.6	1,103	55.8
Forced separation by owner	872	46.9	688	34.8
Desertion	95	5.1	90	4.5
Mutual consent	97	5.2	81	4.1
Other	24	1.2	14	.8
Total	1,863	100	1,976	100

SOURCE: Marriage Records, Asst. Com'r., Vicksburg, Mississippi, 1863–1866, RG 105, NA.

persons, or 5 percent, referred to their relationships with fictive kin, that is people treated like family even though not related by blood or marriage.

A similar pattern was revealed by ex-slaves in each of the other regions, Georgia, Kentucky, and Texas.

What this demonstrates is that neither the idea nor the experience of family was obliterated by slavery. Instead the family was re-created and reconstructed based on the family ideals, values, and yearnings the Africans brought with them in their memories and sustained through the harsh realities of slave life in European-oriented North America.

The centrality of the mother as a basis for the often noted and often misunderstood matricentrism in African-American families is also revealed. In the experience and recollection of these former slaves, their own mothers had a central place. More people know and remember their mother than any other relationship. For example, in South Carolina 85 percent mentioned their mothers as compared with 76 percent who mentioned their fathers and 64 percent marriage in general. A total of 46 percent mentioned their own children. Moreover, mothers were mentioned on average 3.0 times as compared with 2.4 times for fathers. It must also be noted, however, that matricentrism does not obliterate the father from the experiences and memories of the people. In all regions the father was the next most frequent reference after the mother.

Finally the importance of the extended family concept will be noted in these narratives. In the South Carolina narratives, for example, seventy-five, or nearly 50 percent, of the ex-slaves mentioned other relatives outside the nuclear core. Moreover the rudiments of the augmented family structure that would emerge after the war can be seen. Even in slavery it was present. In the South Carolina narratives, some 5 percent of the ex-slaves spoke of family-like relationships with nonkin.

While the African-American family evolved during slavery in all regions of the South, there were some regional differences. The Texas narratives, for example, show substantially more family recollections than the regions along the Atlantic coast. In Texas fully 98 percent of ex-slaves had recollections of their mother and 85 percent had recollections of their father. While in Georgia the proportions were 68 and 62 percent. This may well reflect regional differences in their impact on black family formation. Texas was not admitted to the Union until 1845, after the slave trade had been officially abolished. As John Hope Franklin has pointed out, however, the 1808 law abolishing the external slave trade (but not trading within the country) was so weak and so weakly enforced that during the great westward expansion after 1812 slavery flourished.[11]

Prior to its admission to the Union, Texas had been an independent territory, and before that a province of Mexico. The slave tradition may not have been as firmly established and thus not as effective in stifling family formation as in the East. Moreover, Franklin has pointed out that most of the slave plantations in the West, after cotton became king, were huge plantations with hundreds of slaves as contrasted with most of the plantations in the East which were small with fewer than twenty slaves and where nearly two-thirds of the plantations had fewer than five slaves. The opportunity for cultural continuity, social intercourse, and family formation were obviously greater on the larger plantations.

In general, the analysis of these slave narratives, from the words, ideas, and direct expression of the African captives themselves, reveals strong support for the proposition that the African-American family was re-created and reconstructed during slavery. It was not the African family, nor the European family, nor the American family. It was and is a more distinctive aggregation, the African-American family. It is characterized now as then by its matricentrism, its extended families, and its remarkable flexibility, adaptability, and resilience.

TABLE 4.6
Recollections of Family Relations During Slavery by Ex-Slaves Interviewed in the 1930s

	Number of People Interviewed	NUMBER AND PERCENTAGE WITH STRONG MEMORIES OF:								
		Mother	Father	Sibling	Spouse	Children	Other Relatives	Fictive Kin	Marriage in General	Family in General
Region 1—South Carolina										
Number of persons	153	130	116	59	61	70	75	8	98	21
Percentage of persons	100%	85%	76%	39%	40%	46%	49%	5%	64%	14%
Number of references	1,503	388	275	116	113	143	208	10	213	37
Average number of references	10.1	3.0	2.4	2.0	1.9	2.0	2.8	1.3	2.2	1.8
Region 2—Georgia										
Number of persons	50	34	31	22	17	22	23	7	20	8
Percentage of persons	100%	68%	62%	44%	34%	44%	46%	14%	40%	16%
Number of references	337	74	57	40	29	37	47	8	30	12
Average number of references	6.7	2.2	1.8	1.8	1.7	1.7	2.0	1.1	1.5	1.5
Region 3—Kentucky										
Number of persons	34	28	17	17	11	12	19	1	21	12
Percentage of persons	100%	82%	50%	50%	32%	35%	56%	3%	62%	35%
Number of references	333	102	43	36	16	29	49	1	42	15
Average number of references	9.8	3.6	2.5	2.1	1.5	2.4	2.6	1.0	2.0	1.3

TABLE 4.6 (continued)

	Number of People Interviewed	NUMBER AND PERCENTAGE WITH STRONG MEMORIES OF:							Marriage in General	Family in General
		Mother	Father	Sibling	Spouse	Children	Other Relatives	Fictive Kin		
Region 4—Texas										
Number of persons	122	120	104	85	90	82	65	2	101	37
Percentage of persons	100%	98%	85%	70%	74%	67%	53%	2%	83%	30%
Number of references	1,684	381	308	186	201	163	179	2	211	53
Average number of references	13.8	3.2	3.0	2.2	2.2	2.0	2.8	1.0	2.1	1.4
Total References for All Regions	3,854	945	683	378	359	372	483	21	496	117
Total Interviewees for All Regions	359	312	268	183	179	186	182	18	240	78
Total Percentage of Persons for All Regions	87%	87%	75%	51%	50%	52%	51%	5%	67%	22%

SOURCE: George Rawick, *The American Slave* (Westport, Conn.: Greenwood Publishing, 1970).

Beyond Patriarchy: The Role of Women in Slave Families

There is still another issue about slave families which the historians have barely begun to consider. Did the existence of husband-wife families during slavery indicate male dominance? Or were slave families egalitarian, with men and women fairly equal in their power, status, role, and function in the family? Or were slave families dominated by women? Earlier scholars had ignored or overlooked the role of men in slave families. More recent scholars have documented the presence of men. Unfortunately, most scholars, who are males, have tended to assume that if a man was in the family the man was dominant, and tended to conclude that it is a good and proper thing when men are dominant in the family. What they have ignored in these assumptions is the systemic nature of the slave regime. For to say that the slave family survived, was allowed to survive, or insisted on surviving and to say that captive men played a role is not to say that the family fared well. Moreover, this is certainly not to say that the slave family was the same as or similar to white families. For as strong as the family is in influencing the development of a people, it is not strong enough to overcome the social system, especially one based on force and violence and almost absolute power.

In support of this view, Dr. Deborah Gray White has found that black families, despite the presence of males, females, and marriage, did not follow the same power relationships as did the white families.[12] They were not essentially male-dominated nor were they essentially egalitarian. They were essentially and primarily female centered.

This is not to say that slave families were "matriarchal" in the sense that women exercised inordinate and dominant power over their husbands. What is clear, on reflection, is that the power in the slave family resided in neither the slave husband nor the slave wife but with the white owner, often delegated to the white overseer and supported by the force and violence of the slave system. Thus, while the head of the white family was the white man, the head of the black slave family was also the white man.

Indeed the slave system required that the mother rather than the father serve as the central focus of the family, again contrary to the pattern in white families. For however strong were the bonds and relationships between husband and wife, it was the bonds between mother and child which were paramount.

And although only a minority of women bore children without

an identifiable father, the acceptance of these children by the slave community was markedly different from the concept of "illegitimacy" which inflicted these children in the white community.[13]

Deborah Gray White found strong cultural continuity in the role of the African-American mother even during slavery:

> What black women did was very much in the pattern of their female African ancestors who had for generations stood at the center of the African family. Slave women did not dominate slave marriage and family relationships; they did what women all over the world have done and been taught to do from time immemorial. Acting out a very traditional role, they made themselves a real bulwark against the destruction of the slave family's integrity.[14]

WHO FREED THE CAPTIVES?

"Studies of slavery," Herbert Gutman once told me, "are primarily about what whites have done *to* blacks. Some attention is paid to what whites did *for* blacks. But very little attention is given to what blacks did for *themselves*."[15] Still another dimension of slavery is what black people did *for others*, including what they did for the nation which misused them so egregiously.

Harriet Jacobs

A classic example of what whites did to blacks comes down to us from Harriet Jacobs, in one of the few slave narratives written by a woman.[16] She provides an excruciating account of her predicament as a house slave. The relentless sexual harassment by her owner, a physician, and the persecution of his jealous wife drove her to extreme measures. Falling in love with another slave offered her no way out. In desperation, she took a white man as a lover because "it seemed less degrading to give one's self than to submit to compulsion." And though she deliberately bore two children by this man, she found no peace from her owner-suitor. Only by running away and hiding for seven years in her grandmother's attic was she able to break the bonds of exploitation and eventually escape to freedom.

To be sure, there were numerous examples of slaveholders who were kind to their slaves even within the inherently exploitative slave system. There were exceptional white persons in the United

States who violated the slave codes because of self-interest, paternalism, humanitarianism, or a combination of all three.

James Rapier

A conspicuous example is the case of the slave James Rapier, who was later to serve as a U.S. Congressman from Alabama.[17] Rapier's white owner was also his father. Born in Florence, Alabama, in 1839, a full generation before the end of slavery, Rapier benefited from his parentage. His black mother gave him loving care and upbringing, while his white father, contrary to the pattern among most men who fathered children by their slaves, acknowledged Rapier as his son, gave protection and support for him until he was of age, and provided private instruction for him. Then when he was of age, his father sent him to Canada to attend Montreal College and to Scotland to attend the University of Glasgow.

Rapier would return to Alabama after the end of the Civil War and become active in the civic, educational, and political affairs of the state and nation. He served as a labor union organizer, was elected to the Alabama Constitutional Convention, edited a newspaper in Montgomery, the capital city, and became Secretary of the Alabama Equal Rights League, which celebrated the ratification of the Fifteenth Amendment to the United States Constitution granting the right to vote to male ex-slaves. He served one term in the United States House of Representatives as a Republican in 1872–74 and for a long time thereafter as Collector of Internal Revenue, beginning in 1878 until he was removed from office by President Chester A. Arthur during the resurgence of white supremacy. Soon thereafter he left the state and moved to St. Louis, Missouri, where he died on May 31, 1883, a fighter for human rights until the end.

But other slaveholders were not as kind to their black offspring as Rapier's father. Conspicuous among them was Thomas Jefferson.[18] The leading thinker and statesman of his era, he failed to treat his slave mistress Sally Hemmings and their five children as persons "whom God had given life and liberty at the same time."

Ellen and William Craft

What the slaves did for themselves and others is dramatically illustrated by Ellen and William Craft, two slaves from a Georgia plantation. They escaped to Philadelphia by public transportation, riding in the white sections of the train.[19] Their ingenious disguise and daring escape as a family endeared them to the abolitionist movement. Because Ellen was sufficiently light-skinned to pass for white, they arranged it so that she would pass for a white man in ill health supposedly going north for medical treatment accompanied at every turn on "his" trip north by a faithful slave servant who was, in fact, William Craft, her husband.

They tied a bandage around her head and face so that she could not speak. More than once they were nearly detected. With the help of the Quakers and other members of the Underground Railroad, they were able to establish their family in Philadelphia. Later they moved to England, raised a family, and helped to establish schools for Africans in London and on the African Continent. After the war, they would return to their native Georgia and establish a school, which would prosper for many years, for the newly freed Africans.

Robert Smalls and His Family

Another outstanding example of self-help to combat the slave system was the life and work of Robert Smalls and his family.[20]

Smalls was born into slavery, but because his mother was a favorite house slave, she was allowed to keep him around the house as a baby and young boy. The strong family bonds between mother and son became legendary. She taught him the evils of the slave system, even though he and she were allowed to escape its worst features. She had him watch other slaves being flogged. She had him spend time on a slave plantation as a guest to observe the people and the conditions. She succeeded in instilling in him a revulsion to slavery.

His mother's teachings bore fruit years later in Charleston, South Carolina, where his new owner had moved to participate in the commercial renaissance of the early 1880s. Following a common practice he allowed Robert to hire himself out and work for others around the harbor. With an unusual degree of generosity, the slave owner allowed Smalls to keep a portion of his earnings. When Smalls earned $15 a month, the owner allowed him to keep one dollar. Robert saved his money, bought goods and sold them to men working on the docks and bided his time. When he fell in love with a slave woman, he persuaded both his owner and hers to permit them to get married, but not before he had persuaded his wife's owner to agree to another unusual commercial transaction. Smalls, who by then had demonstrated his commercial acumen around the town, proposed to his wife's master that he purchase his wife on the installment plan. The matter was agreed to. So Smalls, himself a slave, became the owner of his wife. Their first daughter came and then a second.

What is not generally known or appreciated is that Smalls stole a Confederate warship, *Planter,* and delivered it into the hands of the Union, with his family in tow. (One of the benefits of his stealing the Rebel ship and helping the North win the war is that he never had to finish making his last installments on his wife's freedom.)

Just before daybreak on Tuesday, May 13, 1862, Smalls, his family, and five other slaves and their families made their daring move. A number of accounts of this feat have been recorded, beginning with Smalls's own accounts in oral and written form. One early morning while the crew was on shore leave:

> Smalls quietly secreted his family and a few chosen associates [and their families] aboard his master's vessel and in the faint dawn of Tuesday morning, the thirteenth of May [1862] stole out of Charleston harbor, bound for Port Royal. Carefully giving the appropriate signal at Fort Sumter, two long whistles and a short, Smalls cut through the inland waterway until he encountered a [Northern navy] blockade ship off Otter Island. The crew ran up a bedsheet and the Federal Flag and gave three cheers for the Union. He was thus allowed to pass through. In the evening of the same day Smalls reached Hilton Head, delivering his vessel and its expensive cargo of Confederate artillery to the [Union] authorities. He found himself a hero within the hour, and his story circulated widely through newspapers.[21]

For the rest of the war Smalls served as captain of this ship. At the war's end he was permitted to sail into Charleston Harbor and to Fort Sumter where the war had begun. On board were Smalls and all his family, plus a delegation of the leading abolitionists of the day.

The Underground Railroad and Harriet Tubman

An estimated 100,000 African captives braved the elements, the slaveholders, the government, and often their own people to quit the slave system during the first half of the nineteenth century.[22] It has been estimated that nearly half that number passed through Ohio alone. In defying the slave system and the nation and risking their very lives for the cause of freedom, they were doing for themselves and their people a hundred thousand daring deeds which helped to undermine and overthrow the slave system. They did not accomplish this feat alone but with help of their families, friends, and strangers. While the work of the Quakers and other religious people as accomplices in the Underground Railroad has become well known, the important work by younger persons is not as well known. In Ohio, for example, students at Lane Theological Seminary in Cincinnati, Oberlin College in Ohio, and Western Reserve University in Cleveland participated actively in this movement. Franklin has observed that "At no other time in American history had the colleges played such an important part in a program of social reform."[23] It was an action that would not be equaled for more than a hundred years until the civil rights and antiwar movements of the 1960s.

The Underground Railroad got its name because one hapless slaveholder pursuing an escapee lost track of his property after he crossed the Ohio River and concluded in public that the successful fugitive "must have gone off on an underground railroad." Actually, the "railroad" consisted of individuals and groups of African captives who against the law and the contracts on their lives escaped slavery and made their way over land, through backwoods, and under the cover of night to places along the way from the slave South to the free North and to Canada. How they knew where they would find help and sympathy along the way is still not totally clear.

Among the estimated 30,000 blacks and whites in the North and South who helped the slaves to escape, none was more effective or colorful than Harriet Tubman, whose name is virtually synonymous with the Underground Railroad.

The impact of the Underground Railroad in helping to topple the slave system has been chronicled by Franklin: "Perhaps nothing did more to intensify the strife between North and South and to emphasize in a most dramatic way the determination of the abolitionists to destroy slavery than the Underground Railroad."[24]

Harriet Tubman was born about 1829. So large was her impact on the economy of slavery that at one time as much as $40,000 was offered as reward for her capture. She was widely known for carrying a pistol and for her willingness to use it on enemy or on fainthearted followers who might want to turn back. The reward money was never paid, she was never captured, she never killed an enemy, and she never lost a passenger.

During her early years, she saw two of her older sisters sold to a chain gang and taken away, never to be seen again. Then one day, sick in bed, she learned that as soon as she was well, she and two of her brothers would be sold to the chain gang going South. This was the signal to Harriet that the time had come for a dash to freedom.[25] She and her two brothers started off together, but the men got scared and turned back. For Harriet there was no turning back. As firm in her resolve as Patrick Henry, she was determined to gain liberty or to die trying. On arriving safely in the free territory of the North, she worked and saved her money and bided her time. Then nineteen times she returned to the South to rescue a total of between 300 and 400 others—including more members of her family.

This much is clear. While in bondage the African captives made families. They also made revolution. The two strivings, the yearning for a sense of belonging and the yearning for freedom, went hand in hand and fortified each other. While the African captives had a great deal of assistance both in making families and in making revolution, it is inconceivable that either would have been successful without their own desire, initiative, sacrifice, and leadership. The families they made were different from the African families of their ancestors and different from free white families. These families were, however, just as functional for them as the conditions of life permitted. They were just as moral and honorable. And their central feature, beyond patriarchy, beyond matriarchy, beyond egalitarianism, was their matrifocality. African-American families were focused around women. Women, mothers, and grandmothers were the glue that held these families together, though neither they (nor their men) had the power, authority, or resources commensurate with this responsibility. Surely this was the most intelligent response possible to the deep yearnings within the Africans for a sense of belonging and kinship.

Chapter 5

After Appomattox: The Struggle for Stability

The victory over slavery was sweet, but the forces of oppression rose swiftly. The former captives were willing to accept forty acres of land and a mule in exchange for 250 years of free labor so that they could become self-supporting. They believed that they were entitled to safety and protection from abuse and molestation. They believed that this was their chance to enter the mainstream of American society. But such was not to be. Despite the heroic efforts of the freedmen and their friends in the North and the passage of the Thirteenth, Fourteenth, and Fifteenth amendments to the Constitution, they would have only six brief years of Reconstruction before the struggle for political and economic power would be lost for a century.

It would be difficult to overestimate the national crisis in which 4 million new African-Americans were required to find their way. John Hope Franklin has said, "In few periods of our history has the whole fabric of American life been altered so drastically as during the Civil War and the period immediately following it."[1] Some of the economic, political, social, and ideological changes had exceedingly mixed consequences, some of which were only dimly seen at the time. For example, the economy of the South was in total collapse. At the same time the Civil War had brought the industrial revolution to the North in a manner to pit North against South for another hundred years. And most of the Africans were Southerners. After the military war between the states was settled, the political war between the President and the Congress would take center stage.

President Lincoln had expressed the hope that large numbers of the Africans would leave the country after Emancipation. But they and their allies had other ideas. A convention of the colored people of North Carolina in 1865 expressed their determination to remain in the country and in the South:

> Though associated with many memories of suffering as well as enjoyment, we have always loved our homes, and dreaded as the worst of evils, a forcible separation from them. Now that freedom and a new career are before us, we love this land and people more than ever before. Here we have toiled and suffered; our parents, wives, and children are buried here, and in this land we will remain, unless forcibly driven away.[2]

Arnold Taylor has found that "the role and status of former slaves in the social order of the South was the central issue of the Reconstruction era."[3] After 1877, however, a short decade after the war, this era of reform would be over. The forces of repression won out and the Africans would be subjected to economic, political, and social oppression similar to slavery for the next century.

Black leaders were aware of this danger. Shortly before Lee surrendered to Grant at Appomattox, the *New Orleans Tribune,* a black newspaper, expressed the warning that black freedom might be almost meaningless without complete economic, political, and social equality.[4]

How, then, did the new African-Americans respond to their situation?

All over the South the ex-slaves had the same common aspirations. First, they sought to solidify their families. They searched far and wide for relatives from whom they had been separated by slavery or by the war. They legalized their marriages and adopted surnames different from their former owners'. In large numbers women withdrew from working under the white overseers. In order to sustain their families, they sought to own a piece of land on which they could farm, build a house, and grow their own cotton, other crops, and gardens.

The ex-slaves sought to further the formal education of their children. All over the South, the initiatives of the Africans and the support of sympathetic and largely Northern and religious whites established schools. In the state of Georgia alone, less than two years after the end of the Civil War, more than 236 schools had been established for black children.[5] The majority of these were supported entirely or partly by the African-Americans, who also owned many of the buildings. And while there was no compulsory school attendance law in Georgia until 1916, black parents insisted on sending their children to school. In Dougherty County, Georgia, some 20 percent of black children aged ten to twelve were in schools in 1870. By 1900 the proportion in school had risen to 61 percent and substantially exceeded the proportion of white children of a similar age who were in school.[6]

THE EXODUS

The first major as well as first truly voluntary migration of the African-American people commenced in 1880. Labeled "the Great Exodus" this was migration westward to Kansas, Missouri, and Ohio, during which they took their families with them.[7]

Later they would spread to all parts of the nation. At the end of the Civil War, eleven of every twelve blacks lived in the South.

In the decade 1870–80 net migration of blacks out of the South was 60,000 persons, meaning 60,000 more blacks moved out of the South than moved into the region. This net out migration rose to 454,000 in the decade of the 1920s and to a peak of 1,599,000 in the 1940s. Most of these settled in the northeast and north central regions of the country. The northward movement declined gradually after 1950 until during the 1980s more blacks moved into the South than out.[8]

FAMILY LIFE IN THE SOUTH AND NORTH

While there were some differences in the conditions of life for African-American families in the rural South, the urban South, and the urban North, there were some distinct similarities as well. Vivid portraits of the regional forces affecting African-American family life, the family patterns which developed in response to these forces, and their effects on the lives of the people have emerged in three locations. One is rural Dougherty County, Georgia. Another is a Southern city, Hampton, Virginia, and a third is a Northern city, Cleveland, Ohio.

Rural South

Dougherty County is in the heart of the old slave plantation country.[9] It was dominated by 150 large plantations which held more than 6,000 slaves who produced some 20,000 bales of cotton annually prior to the war. Despite an oppressive postwar economic system of tenant farming, blacks worked hard, built churches, schools, and other institutions. In the areas of education and family formation they achieved remarkable successes with no public support. The phenomenal success the ex-slaves achieved in establishing institutional forms of family life was such that, despite adverse conditions, by 1880 the structure of black families closely resembled the structure of white families. Thus in 1880 51.6 percent of black families were husband-wife families as compared to 42 percent of white families. A decade later the proportions were 42.8 percent for black families and 44.4 percent for white families. Other family forms were also comparable between the two groups. Herbert Gutman found even stronger family structures among blacks in three counties of Virginia in 1865–66. The proportion of husband-wife families was 72 percent in Montgomery, 79 percent in York, and 79 percent in Princess Ann counties.[10]

Urban South

In the up south city of Hampton, Virginia, Robert Francis Engs found that during the twenty years between 1870 and 1890 blacks made tremendous strides in achieving their goals after emancipation:

> During this progressive decade, nearly a fifth of black families owned property. They owned half of the businesses on Main Street. In the political process they elected a majority of the city council but deliberately supported a white for mayor. Their majority electorate sent blacks to all other local offices and the state legislature. In the occupational sphere, blacks held jobs across the entire spectrum from laborer to skilled craftsman to professional. In education they built, supported and controlled the local elementary school and secondary schools for their children which were open to others as well. Many sent their children to college including Hampton Institute and to graduate schools in the North. Some of these returned to become involved in local and state politics. Moreover, Hampton blacks established a wide range of community institutions which they controlled. Among these were five churches, several fraternal

organizations, women's associations, young people's groups, and temperance societies.[11]

By 1890, however, the pendulum began to swing against the African-American people in Hampton:

In that year, blacks began to suffer major setbacks after more than twenty years of progress. Native whites, in alliance with northern white immigrants, launched an onslaught against black office-holding which removed blacks from local office and marked the beginning of black Hampton's decline as a unique and successful entity. The end of this remarkable experiment in black equality was ignored by most Americans.[12]

Engs reports:

Even in political and economic defeat, black Hampton's first free generation could look with pride at its major achievement: its children. They were well-educated, ambitious, sophisticated in business, in education, and in the ways of the world, white as well as black, northern as well as southern. They and their descendants would continue to play a major role in American black life long after accommodation had been repudiated.[13]

What does the Hampton experience tell us about the evolution of African-American family life? First, the experience shows that the political system, the economic system, the educational system—all emanating from the larger society—have an interactive and decisive influence on the well-being of the African-American community. When blacks gained political power, they shared it with the whites and all benefited. Even though blacks had a majority of the voters, they held only five of the nine top political offices, not including mayor. When the whites regained political power, on the other hand, they removed all the black elected officials and eventually completely disenfranchised the blacks.

Blacks have a deep humanitarian streak which encourages co-operation and sharing of resources. It paid off in the good will and mutual progress of the races for a period of twenty years, or as long as the blacks held political power. Some blacks also have short memories. At the height of black political power and inter-racial cooperation, the black revenue commissioner, R.M. Smith, was quoted as saying, "I do not believe our white brethren would do this [persecute] to us again, had they the power."[14] Engs writes that "Smith was wrong; two years later, whites once again had the power, and Smith was driven from his position along with most black office holders."[15]

A second lesson taught by the Hampton experience is the value of economic power—not just full employment, which is important, but jobs throughout the spectrum of the economy. In 1880, 40 percent of black workers were in the skilled crafts, 5 percent held professional and business positions, 10 percent were farmers, and 45 percent unskilled laborers. By 1896, the occupational distribution was still impressive, though slightly less so. Even then, 36 percent of black workers were in the skilled crafts, including oystermen, teamsters, waiters, carpenters, cooks, shoemakers, firemen, seamstresses, plasterers, painters, butchers, blacksmiths, brick masons, and related skills. Another 12 percent were in professional and business careers, mainly barbers, teachers, restaurant owners, grocery owners, schoolteachers, ministers, saloon keepers, insurance agents, lawyers, and doctors. By this time, however, farmers had declined to about 1 percent and unskilled laborers had increased to 50 percent of the black work force. Still, the occupational distribution in Hampton at this time was much greater than was to be found in large numbers of other cities, even to the present time.[16]

But as important as having a job—and having a good job—is to the economic well-being of a community, the accumulation of wealth is a more important indicator of well-being. In this regard, too, the African-American families of Hampton, in the golden years after the Civil War, were much better off than those in many other communities and far better off than they would be later on.

The ownership of half the businesses in town plus their fair share of political power provided African-American families the basis for both stability and viability with important lessons for today. Finally, education was understood by the African-American families in Hampton to be absolutely critical for the advancement of their children, themselves, and the race, as well as the general community. From elementary schools through high schools, both public and private, and on to Hampton Institute, these newly freed citizens took to education with a vengeance.

Moreover, the ultimate lesson learned from the Hampton experience is that with the support, protection, and resources provided by the federal government, the Northern missionaries, and their own political, economical, and educational power, they could extract a measure of cooperation and support—not to speak of harmonious relationships—with the local white population that was the envy of other localities and other generations. Behind this massive phalanx of external support, they were then free to develop their own strong African-American institutions, including churches, clubs, lodges, businesses, and strong, stable African-American families. For generations, the sons and daughters of postbellum Hampton have been leaders in every walk of life in the nation. They have produced strong middle-class, highly achieving black families.

The meaning of the Hampton experience is that the stability, viability, and productivity of African-American family life depends heavily on the functioning of the systems of the larger society, to the extent that they are sensitive to and supportive of the aspirations—to include providing empowerment—to the black community generally. Primary among these are the political system, the economic system, and the educational system.

Urban North

The transition of African-American families from the South to the West and North provided many opportunities denied them in the deep South. The growing black population was accompanied by a gradual closing of many of these opportunities. The situation in Cleveland, Ohio, provides insight into this phenomenon and its impact on African-American families.[17]

Before the Civil War and in the early years of Emancipation, prior to 1870, blacks were "almost equal" to whites in Cleveland. They exercised and experienced an enormous degree of freedom and economic and social opportunity and acceptance. It was in Cleveland where John Brown was openly embraced as a hero after his raid on Harper's Ferry in 1859 and was sheltered by the local population, even after the President of the United States had declared him a fugitive. This was just one indication of the positive state of race relations and opposition to slavery.

There was no racial discrimination in public facilities. In the economic sphere, blacks enjoyed substantial dispersion in occupations. In 1870, 32 percent of black workers in Cleveland were in skilled occupations. Another 5 percent were in professional or business enterprises. Fifteen percent were in semiskilled occupations. Another 30 percent were in unskilled occupations and 15 percent in domestic service. This occupational profile was comparable to that of both foreign-born and native-born whites. It was somewhat higher than the profile for Irish immigrants. As late as 1870, blacks, though living mainly in three areas of the city, were not rigidly segregated and lived scattered throughout those areas.

Between 1870 and 1915, however, with the enormous local expansion of the African-American population as a result of migration from the South, the black ghetto began to take hold. The ghetto grew because of a combination of factors. One was the growth of the black population and a tendency to live with and near other relatives. A second was the accompanying growth in racial hostility on the part of white settlers. These were years of enormous expansion in urban America. By 1900, the bulk of the African-American population of Cleveland had recently migrated from the South. And by 1910 blacks were rigidly segregated in separate neighborhoods.

Along with the rise of the ghetto in Cleveland and elsewhere came more rigid patterns of segregation and discrimination in all aspects of life. This process was aided by the actions of the federal government. A series of Republican administrations in Washington seemed to abandon the newly emancipated blacks. The Supreme Court in 1883 declared the Civil Rights Act of 1875 unconstitutional and by 1896 had established the *Plessy* v. *Ferguson* doctrine of separate but equal, which was to hold for half a century until unanimously outlawed by the Supreme Court in 1954, under the leadership of Republican Earl Warren. In Cleveland, conditions for African-Americans began to worsen substantially in response to this national climate. Integrated facilities and economic opportunities began a precipitous decline.

Whereas in 1870, 26 percent of the African-American workers were in skilled occupations and 22 percent in domestic service, by 1890 this had changed to 12 percent in skilled occupations and 40 percent in domestic service. Moreover, home ownership among blacks in Cleveland took a nosedive between 1870 and 1910.[18]

As blacks poured into Cleveland toward the end of the nineteenth century, a social-class structure began to develop much like the social-class structure Du Bois had found in Philadelphia in the 1890s in his classic study *The Philadelphia Negro*.[19] So, too, the rise of black institutions, organizations, and associations.

The great exodus came to Cleveland as to other Northern cities around the time of World War I.[20] Three factors were paramount in this migration. First, the war in Europe cut off the supply of

European immigrants. Second, the industrial might of the North needed workers, particularly for its war-related undertakings, and unskilled blacks were recruited from the South to meet this need. Third, dissatisfaction with race relations in the South, particularly the violence perpetrated against blacks, also played an important role. In addition, the spread of the boll weevil slowed cotton production and caused widespread unemployment. Again during the 1920s after the war, with the return of economic prosperity, the migration from the South resumed. Between 1920 and 1930, Cleveland's black population doubled again. It was during this period that, according to Kenneth Kusmer, "racism in Cleveland rose to high tide."[21]

The Cleveland experience casts considerable doubt on the Frazier thesis that the movement from the rural South to the urban North resulted in greater family instability. Indeed, Kusmer holds that the sharp rise in proportion of female-headed families among urban blacks "is more a product of the post–World War II era than of the Great Migration period."[22]

In keeping with this challenge to the Frazier thesis, Kusmer found that in 1930 the percentage of African-American families headed by women in the Northern urban areas of Ohio, Illinois, New York, and in the urban and rural areas of the Southern states of Alabama and Georgia were so similar as to refute the thesis that the move to Northern urban areas is what brought on the deterioration of African-American family structure.

A similar and even more comprehensive picture of the evolution of African-American structure in the Ohio Valley after emancipation has been drawn by Paul J. Lammermeier.[23] Adapting some concepts of diverse family structure that we developed in *Black Families in White America,* Lammermeier showed the changes in black family structure on both sides of the Ohio River. These changes were pronounced in both Cincinnati, Ohio, and Louisville, Kentucky, over a twenty-year period spanning the Civil War (Table 5.1). The simple nuclear family form consisting of a married couple and their children was the most prevalent form as early as 1850 in both cities. The extended and augmented family forms, with relatives and nonrelatives, were also well developed. Change over time is reflected in the finding that the simple nuclear family form expanded in Cincinnati from nearly 27 percent of all families in 1850 to an impressive 34.2 percent by 1880. In the Southern city the simple nuclear family was similar, rising from 26.2 percent in 1850 to nearly 37 percent by 1870.

TABLE 5.1
Changing Family Structure in the Urban Ohio Valley
Percentage of All Families, 1850–1870

	CINCINNATI			LOUISVILLE		
	1850 (%)	1860 (%)	1870 (%)	1850 (%)	1860 (%)	1870 (%)
NUCLEAR FAMILIES						
Incipient nuclear	11.8	12.9	16.7	13.0	10.8	12.6
Simple nuclear	26.7	28.8	34.2	26.2	27.0	36.8
Attenuated nuclear (father)	0.5	1.0	1.9	1.8	2.2	1.3
Attenuated nuclear (mother)	14.0	15.5	13.7	20.3	19.5	11.4
TOTAL NUCLEAR FAMILIES	53.0	58.2	66.5	61.3	59.5	62.1
EXTENDED-AUGMENTED FAMILIES						
Incipient extended-augmented	14.5	13.3	9.4	8.7	5.8	8.4
Simple extended-augmented	22.2	17.0	15.7	16.6	19.7	19.3
Attenuated extended-augmented	1.7	0.7	0.6	—	1.7	1.4
Attenuated extended-augmented	8.6	10.8	7.8	13.4	13.3	8.8
TOTAL EXTENDED-AUGMENTED	47.0	41.8	33.5	38.7	40.5	37.9

SOURCE: Paul Lammermeier, "The Urban Black Family of the Nineteenth Century," 1973.

The problem of freedom for African-Americans was four-fold: how to stabilize their families and provide for their integrity, how to establish an independent economic existence on the land, then how to establish permanent institutions to carry on their social development, and finally how to secure their political liberty through active participation in the political process. In the rural South, the urban South, and the urban North, the struggle for viability was filled with ups and downs, hope and disappointment. After a brief decade or so of reform, after the passage of the Fifteenth Amendment to the Constitution, after the Republican Congress asserted its leadership over the reluctant President, a new reign of terror descended over the South which toppled its newly interracial governments, ended Reconstruction, and fastened a system of servitude and subservience on the Africans that would last for nearly a century.

In subtle, blatant, or benignly neglectful ways, the society in which African-Americans found themselves failed to live up to the promises of the Thirteenth, Fourteenth, and Fifteenth amendments to the Constitution or to the Civil Rights Act of 1875. Yet throughout this period the ex-slaves held on to their families and their religion. It was in reflecting on this period that the poet James Weldon Johnson and his brother J. Rosamond would write:

> God of our weary years
> God of our silent tears
> Thou who has led us thus far on the way
> Thou who has by thy might
> Led us into the light
> Keep us forever in thy path, we pray.[24]

Chapter 6

The Impact of Technology: The Rise and Decline of the Black Working Class

The massive migration of blacks from the rural South to the urban North has been the subject of much scholarly interpretation. Nicholas Lehman is among those who have emphasized the negative and destructive impact of this migration on African-American families. Indeed, Lehman holds that this migration was a proximate cause of the rise of the pockets of poverty and disenfranchisement that have come to be called the black urban underclass.[1] Our own view is that this migration had both positive and negative effects for African-American families and the balance lies on the side of the positive. More important still is the need to appreciate the impact of technology in the generation of this migration and its attendant impact on the rise and decline of the black working class and on the structure of African-American families.

During the ninety years between 1890 and 1980, a far-reaching set of changes in society required families to make serious adjustments. In 1890, for example, better than 90 percent of all African-American families lived in the rural South; most of the workers were farmers. Their family life was consistent with the demands of this period. Large extended families were dominant, anchored by married couples at the center, other relatives in close proximity, with augmented family members (those not related by blood or marriage) playing important roles in the family system.

128

Husband-wife families were at the core of 80 percent of all African-American households within the first generation after slavery.

Less than a hundred years later, the situation had changed markedly. A majority of African-American families no longer lived in the rural South. They were scattered to all parts of the nation. Nearly 90 percent now lived in urban areas in the South, the North, and the West. Society had made the transition from the agricultural era to the industrial era and into the postindustrial era.

We believe with Alvin Toffler that the small nuclear family is a creature of industrial society and was most suited to that society, just as the large extended family was a creature of agricultural society. Prior to that the wandering nomadic bands were suited to the hunting and gathering era before the agricultural revolution. Now that industrial society is being superseded by a new postindustrial society based on modern technological changes, social institutions, including families, are being reshaped to conform to the demands of the new society.[2]

The traditional nuclear family form of husband and wife and their children, with the husband in the work force and the wife-mother as full-time homemaker may not have been made in heaven after all. It may be more accurately perceived as a transitory human response to changing technology.

One of the earliest sociologists to herald the coming of the postindustrial era was Daniel Bell in a pathbreaking book, *The Coming of Post Industrial Society,* first published in 1973. In later editions he has continued to elaborate on the characteristics of these changing technologically driven eras.

> A pre-industrial sector is primarily *extractive,* its economy based on agriculture, mining, fishing, timber, and other resources such as natural gas or oil. An industrial sector is primarily fabricating, using energy and machine technology, for the manufacture of goods. A postindustrial sector is one of processing in which telecommunications and computers are strategic for the exchange of information and knowledge.[3]

This definition helps us to appreciate the dominance of machine technology in the industrial era and the rise to prominence of intellectual and communications technology in the postindustrial era. Another sociologist who has helped to show the relevance of these eras for the structure and functioning of families is

Amitai Etzioni. He believes that technological change often disrupts social institutions including families, and their ability to perform their essential functions. He observes, "The family is widely considered the 'first' institution, the elementary call of social life."[4]

As one of the most basic social institutions, the family is affected by technological and economic changes in its environment. For African-American families, these changes are complicated by racial and ethnic discrimination and economic marginality. In their recent and comprehensive analysis of the quality of life for African-American people, the sociologists Reynolds Farley and Walter Allen remind us that "racial and ethnic competition has been a hallmark of American society from the moment the first European settlers arrived to discover an established native American presence."[5] Moreover, they observe that "economic status is critical in the lives of Americans generally and the lives of black Americans in particular."[6] As a result, African-American families are altered by technological changes earlier, more extensively, and in a more negative way than families of other groups.

There are two major reasons for this. On the one hand, they are more vulnerable, less powerful, and less protected; and on the other, out of historical necessity they are more flexible and adaptive. An understanding of the experience of African-American families will to a large extent reveal much about other families as well. As these large-scale technological and social forces increasingly impact on even more powerful and favored people, they too are beginning to show the same deviations from traditional forms of family life as African-American families are. Some conspicuous examples of the changes are mothers in the work force, single-parent families, high divorce rates, teen pregnancy, and substance abuse. While all these conditions are more prevalent among black families, they may no longer be considered uniquely black or as emanating from within African-American culture. This is why in 1985, just twenty short years after his initial report, Daniel Moynihan said that what he thought was a peculiarly black family problem in 1965 "has now become the general condition."[7] He explains:

> In 1965 . . . non-white families with a female head had reached 21 percent. By 1984 for white families with children this proportion had reached nearly 20 percent. . . . What was a crisis condition for one group in 1965 is now the general condition.[8]

All of which led Moynihan to conclude in a burst of optimism that such changes "would free the subject of family from the issue of race—or ought to."[9]

What Moynihan saw more clearly in 1985 than he had in 1965 was that the source of this changing family structure was not inside black families. And since white families had not endured 200 years of slavery and could not reasonably be labeled matriarchal there must be something else—something in the larger society that was driving these structural changes in the family. Much of that something else has to do with the technological changes in society which escalated in the mid-1950s.

There can be little doubt about the benefits technological development has brought to society or to the African-American people. It has removed much of the drudgery of hard physical labor. New advances in nutrition, public health, environmental control, education, and medical science have increased the average life span of blacks from about thirty-five years at the turn of the century to over sixty-five today. Indeed, black women have now surpassed white men and are second only to white women in average longevity. Moreover, advances in technology have brought down the black infant mortality rate from 73 deaths per 1,000 live births in 1940 to 20 by 1981, where it remains today. Only persons who grew up in pre–World War II America can fully appreciate the revolution technology has brought to the modern kitchen or the modern bathroom, the two areas of the home most enhanced by technology.

Even in the face of such progress, however, the racial factor persists. Blacks benefit less from the positive consequences of technological change than whites and suffer more from the negative consequences of such change. For example, during the same period white infant mortality was reduced from 43 per 1,000 live births to ten. Infant mortality among blacks today is at the same level it was among whites two decades ago.

At the same time that it brings such enormous benefits, technological change also brings problems. The negative consequences of technology are not as well known, and their impact on African-American families is known hardly at all. The technological revolution has encouraged the view that efficiency is everything and faster is better. Such an attitude can lead to persons and relationships being treated as means to selfish ends rather than enhancing the quality of life.[10]

The Deindustrialization of America

In the mid-1950s, for the first time in American history, more people were employed in white-collar jobs than in blue-collar jobs, driven by the relative decline of the manufacturing sector and the explosion of the service sector. That was the turning point when America became a middle-class society for the first time. Until the decade after World War II, the manufacturing sector was the dominant sector of the economy, having largely supplanted the agricultural economy. Beginning in the 1950s, however, at first gradually, then markedly, the manufacturing sector was replaced by the service sector just as it had replaced the agricultural sector (Table 6.1). In the nation at large, in 1940 blue-collar workers outnumbered white-collar workers by 36 percent to 32 percent.

Table 6.1
Occupations of Employed Persons of All Races, Aged 14 and Over 1940–1970

	1940 (%)	1960 (%)	1970 %
BOTH SEXES			
All races	100	100	100
White-collar	32	41	46
Blue-collar	36	37	33
Farm	18	6	3
Service	13	12	12
Not reported	1	4	6
MEN			
All races	100	100	100
White-collar	28	35	38
Blue-collar	41	46	44
Farm	23	8	4
Service	7	7	8
Not reported	1	4	6
WOMEN			
All races	100	100	100
White-collar	45	54	58
Blue-collar	20	17	16
Farm	4	2	1
Service	29	22	19
Not reported	2	5	6

SOURCE: U.S. Bureau of the Census, *Current Population Studies, The Black Population in the U.S. 1790–1978, January 1980.*

TABLE 6.2
Occupations of Employed African-Americans
Aged 14 and Over
1940–1970

	1940 (%)	1960 (%)	1970 (%)
BOTH SEXES	100	100	100
White-collar	6	13	24
Blue-collar	27	38	37
Farm	32	8	3
Service	34	32	25
Not reported	1	9	11
MEN	100	100	100
White-collar	5	11	17
Blue-collar	38	54	53
Farm	41	11	4
Service	15	15	14
Not reported	1	9	12
WOMEN	100	100	100
White-collar	6	17	32
Blue-collar	7	14	17
Farm	16	3	1
Service	70	57	38
Not reported	1	9	12

SOURCE: U.S. Bureau of the Census, *Current Population Studies, The Black Population in the U.S. 1790–1978, January 1980.*

By 1960, however, white-collar workers outnumbered blue-collar workers by 41 percent to 37 percent. For the first time in history, the U.S. became an essentially white-collar society. Women workers made the major contribution to this transition.

For black workers, however, there was a time lag in this transition (Table 6.2). In the black community as late as 1960, blue-collar workers still outnumbered white-collar workers by 38 percent to 13 percent, and in 1970 by 37 percent to 24 percent. The enormous increase in the black middle class, which would double from 13 percent in 1960 to 24 percent by 1980, represented a delayed development. Moreover, black women made the transition before black men. Already by 1960 white-collar workers among black women outnumbered blue-collar workers by 17 percent to 14 percent. This trend continued to 1970 at 32 percent versus 17 percent. In 1960, among black men white-collar workers were only 11 percent as compared with 54 percent who were blue-collar workers. By

1970 the trend had accelerated to 17 percent versus 53 percent.

The next major consequence of technological change was driven by the first. It was in the mid-1950s that for the first time in history unemployment among African-Americans became twice as high as among white Americans (Table 6.3).

Before 1954, unemployment rates for black persons aged sixteen and over had never been as high as twice the rate for whites. Since 1954, until the present time, the rates have seldom been as low as twice the white rates.

This technology-driven economic transition, more than any other factor or cluster of factors, drove millions of black men from the stable blue-collar work force and simultaneously drove millions of wives and mothers out of the home and into the expanding service sector and white-collar labor force. The impact of this transition on African-American families has been devastating, beginning in the decade after the end of World War II. This has been the

TABLE 6.3
Unemployment Rates for Persons 16 Years and Over
Blacks and Whites, 1948–1985

	Blacks (%)	Whites (%)	Black/White Ratio
1948	5.9	3.5	1.7
1950	9.0	4.9	1.8
1952	5.4	2.8	1.9
1954	9.9	5.0	2.0
1956	8.3	3.6	2.3
1958	12.6	6.1	2.1
1960	10.2	4.9	2.1
1962	10.9	4.9	2.2
1964	9.6	4.6	2.1
1966	7.3	3.3	2.2
1968	6.7	3.2	2.1
1970	8.2	4.5	1.8
1972	10.0	5.0	2.1
1974	9.9	5.0	2.0
1979	12.3	5.1	2.4
1981	15.6	6.7	2.3
1983	19.5	8.4	2.3
1985	15.1	6.2	2.3

SOURCE: U.S. Bureau of the Census, *The Social and Economic Status of the Black Population in the United States: An Historical View, 1790–1978* (Current Population Reports, Special Studies Series P–23, No. 80), and U.S. Bureau of Labor Statistics, June 1985, pp. 71–72; and Employment and Earnings, November 1986, p. 38.

major cause of expanding black joblessness, expanding black single-parent families, and an expanding sense of hopelessness.

The greatest impact of this transition is that it has produced a sharp decline in the stable black working class, which had evolved slowly since World War I in the basic industries of coal, iron, steel, rubber, and auto making. At the same time it has produced an expansion in the somewhat more precarious black middle class. Black men suffer most in this transition, which has been called the deindustrialization of America.

The impact has been devastating for black youth. In 1955 the employment rates for black and white youth aged sixteen to nineteen were similar at about 52 percent. Since then, employment rose rapidly for white youth to about 56 percent by 1980 while declining even more rapidly for black youth to about 28 percent. Over the same period employment declined from 78 percent to 55 percent for black males twenty to twenty-four.[11] This is why there are massive numbers of black men aged twenty-five to thirty who have never had a good, steady job. It is a major reason for the downturn in their marriage rates and the upturn in unmarried parenthood.

It is perhaps ironic that the traditional family system that slavery could not destroy during 200 years may be dismantled in a few short years by the modern industrial transition.

Change is sweeping Western society. The General Electric Company, which during the 1970s expanded its payroll by 5,000 workers, did so, however, by expanding their overseas work force by 30,000 and abolishing 25,000 jobs in the United States. In a similar manner, the RCA Corporation increased its overseas work force by 19,000 and cut United States jobs by 14,000. The Ford Motor Company spent 40 percent of its capital budget outside the United States during that period. General Motors expanded substantially in Spain while contracting in the United States.[12]

While many families feel the impact, black families often suffer disproportionately. In St. Louis, Missouri, a laundry chain had a work force in 1964 that was 75 percent black. It began to decentralize during the 1970s and opened thirteen new branches in suburban areas and reduced its operations in downtown St. Louis. As a consequence, its work force went from 75 percent black to only 5 percent black by 1975. Another example comes from Detroit. One manufacturing company moved its plants just over the line into rural Ohio. The salaried employees, most of whom were white, were offered assistance in relocating to different jobs. The hourly wage employees, most of whom were black, were offered no such assistance. Thus the work force of this one company went from 40 percent black to 2 percent black.[13] Such layoffs and the sustained idleness it generates have been devastating to African-American families.

The negative consequences of layoffs for the workers and their families in the society at large are demonstrated in a study conducted by Dr. Harvey Brenner of Johns Hopkins University. He found on examining the history of layoffs over the period 1940 through 1973 that a 1 percent increase in unemployment, extended over a six-year period, results in the following casualties:

- 500 deaths from cirrhosis of the liver
- 650 deaths by homicide
- 920 deaths by suicide
- 37,000 deaths by a variety of other means
- 4,000 admissions to mental hospitals
- 3,300 admissions to state prisons[14]

This particular study does not cite the substantial increase in family tension, domestic violence, and divorce which are also heightened by unemployment and economic dislocation.

Unless wise and brave leadership arises to enable the nation to manage it, this technologically driven, economic transition will continue to take its natural course of feeding the individualistic aspirations of the privileged, the wealthy, and the powerful to the detriment of the common good.

As a consequence of racial discrimination black families suffer disproportionately from all the above effects of sustained unemployment. A study by the United States Department of Health and Human Services for the period 1979 to 1981 found that during this two-year period, if blacks had died of all causes at the same rates as whites there would have been 58,942 more black men and women still alive today.[15]

As more and more black men are thrown out of work and find it hard to make the transition to new jobs, ever larger numbers are likely to turn to drugs and alcohol, to family violence, and to experience automobile accidents, all causing untold misery and unnecessary loss of life. While some analysts look to the victims themselves for the sources of this fatalistic behavior, a more potent source may be the negative and destructive consequences of technological change combined with the racial preference enjoyed by white men.

Rise and Decline of the Black Working Class

The black unskilled industrial working class had its origin in slavery. It expanded appreciably at the end of the Civil War. It was not, however, until the great exodus out of the South around the time of World War I that the black industrial working class really took hold. Both World War I and the postwar restrictive immigration legislation of 1924 caused a dramatic rise in the number of black workers and their families in the North, Midwest, and West. Until then the rapidly expanding industrial revolution and its resultant jobs in steel foundries, textile plants, slaughterhouses, automobile plants, rubber plants, and coal mines were not available to blacks in any appreciable numbers. Industrial leaders preferred Europeans and imported them in large numbers from the end of the Civil War to the onset of World War I. Blacks would only make the transition from the agricultural South to the industrial North after 1915. Thereafter, the black working class expanded rapidly.

There are indications that the decline in the manufacturing sector which set in after World War II, the decline in the black working class, and the decline in the black nuclear families all go hand in hand. Moreover, these longterm trends seem destined to continue into the future unless there are dramatic changes in public policies to cope more effectively with changing technology and racial exclusion.

The rise of the black working class is supported by U.S. Census data (Table 6.4). In 1910, for example, the bulk of black workers

TABLE 6.4
Changes in the Black Working Class
1910–2000

	1910 (%)	1960 (%)	1976 (%)	1981 (%)	1990 (%)	2000 (%)
Unskilled working class	39	45	46	31	25	20
Skilled working class	8	26	26	30	26	23
Combined working class	47	71	72	61	51	43

SOURCE: U.S. Census: *The Social and Economic Status of the Black Population in the United States: An Historical View 1790–1978*; also *The Black Population in the U.S. March 1990 and 1989*.

were still farmworkers, the unskilled working class consisting of 39 percent, and the skilled working class only 8 percent of all workers. In his pioneering study, *The New Black Middle Class,* Bart Landry estimates that middle-class workers constituted 3 percent. By 1960, however, the unskilled working class had risen to 45 percent and the skilled working class to 26 percent. Thus while the combined skilled and unskilled black working class was 47 percent of all black workers in 1910, it increased to 71 percent of all workers over the next half century.

In recent years the working class has been in steady decline. The combined working class had been reduced from 71 percent of all workers in 1960 to 61 percent by 1981 and to 51 percent by 1990. It is projected to decline further to 43 percent by the year 2000. Thus in the span of less than a century, the black working class has expanded from 47 percent of the black labor force in 1910 to 71 percent in 1960 and will decline dramatically to a new low of 43 percent by the year 2000. The decline in the black working class since 1960 has been the single most important force responsible for the decline in the nuclear-family structure over this period, from a high of 78 percent in 1960 to 44 percent by 1990.

The source of this destabilizing influence on African-American families is to be found deep in the larger society and not within the black community. A study published by the Joint Center for Political Studies in 1989 shows the impending trends in the continued shift from a manufacturing economy to a service economy, which will adversely affect the black working-class families.[16]

The study observed that despite the expected slowdown in the growth of the labor force because of the leveling off of white women's participation, and despite the fact that the labor force will increasingly consist of black and other minorities, the situation for working-class blacks will not necessarily improve. These new jobs will go largely to middle-class workers and white workers and increasingly to workers imported from abroad. The reason is partly that blacks are not well represented in the occupations that are expected to grow the fastest between 1986 and 2000, such as medical assistants and computer programmers. On the other hand, blacks are overrepresented in the slow-growing or declining occupations, such as machine operators and assemblers. Moreover, as new immigrants come into the country from Latin America and Asia, and perhaps from Eastern Europe as well, there will be even keener competition for low-skilled jobs. "Immigrants," the study observed, "are expected to account for about 23 percent of the increase in the labor force during the next 15 years."[17]

Another finding was that black working-class workers have been the backbone of the stable black community with earnings substantially above the poverty level for a number of years. "Between 1940 and 1975," for example, "the job opportunities within manufacturing were a major means for black families to move up into the middle-income bracket."[18] However, there has been a major decline in manufacturing jobs in the postwar years. While in 1947 one-third of all U.S. workers were in manufacturing, this declined by 40 percent by 1985. According to the Bureau of Labor Statistics, the manufacturing jobs will decline by another 40 percent between 1986 and 2000. By then, manufacturing will account for only 14 percent of all jobs, as compared with 33 percent in 1947.

Black employment fell much faster than overall employment in the manufacturing sector in five of the seven declining manufacturing industries.[19]

While there has been an expansion of upper-level administrative, skilled clerical, technical, and other such jobs, the black men displaced in the goods-producing sector do not generally have the skills, work experience, and education to qualify for these jobs in the fast-growing technological and service-producing sectors. Indeed, there is a pending shortage of workers in these sectors while there is a surplus of unskilled workers.

Civil Rights and Affirmative Action

A number of analysts, including most notably Bart Landry, have observed that the small black middle class, which comprised some 13 percent of all black workers as late as 1960, expanded rapidly to 25 percent during the single decade.[20] The reasons for this were, in part, the expanding economy of the 1960s and the expanding middle-class occupations. It had also to do, however, with affirmative action policies spawned by the civil rights movement. Landry shows, for example, that during the 1950s there was an expanding economy but no affirmative action. The black middle class did not expand appreciably during that time. During the 1960s, there was both an expanding economy and affirmative action policies. As a consequence, the black middle class expanded enormously, nearly doubling during that period. In the decade of the 1970s, when there was still affirmative action, but no longer an expanding economy, there was stagnation in the black middle class.

In the 1980s, the economy turned up again after the worst recession since the 1930s. But affirmative action policies were thwarted by public and political pressures. As a consequence, while the underclass continued to spread, the expanded black middle class lost ground. The consequence of all this for African-American family structure is that the erosion in traditional patterns continued to be driven by the demise of the working class and the expansion of the nonworking poor.

Black Women and Work

Technological change has also factored in large numbers of women leaving the home to join the work force. While African-American women have traditionally worked in the labor force and in the home simultaneously, the expansion of black women in the labor force during the last two decades has outstripped that of black men. According to economist Bernard Anderson, "Black women will make up the largest share of the increase in the non-white work force during the next decade and will outnumber black men in the work force—a contrast to the pattern among white workers, where men outnumber women almost three to two."[21]

Even among husband-wife families, the expansion of working wives and mothers has been both functional and dysfunctional. The partnership of working together for the economic viability of the family has had the effect of strengthening the stability in some families. We know, for example, that economic viability bears the strongest relationship to family stability. Working-class families are stronger than underclass families. The decline of the stable, nonpoor working class has led to the decline in traditional family structures. For the women themselves, opportunities for work outside the home have provided meaningful options for the use of talents and energies long denied by the structure of society. Most important of all, the expanding opportunities for paid work for black women have enabled their families to be self-supporting and to avoid much of the consequences of dire poverty.

Despite the full and active participation of black women in the labor force, they are a long way from receiving equality of treatment. They earn less than other workers, are most likely to be unemployed, and are still confined to more traditional and dead-end jobs without adequate career advancement. This is not something these working women have brought on themselves. They are not powerful enough to create such a system of exploitation. Moreover, while they tend to be of relatively low formal education, it is the educational system that has failed them and not they themselves.

TECHNOLOGY IN THE HOME

The mixed impact of all technology on African-American families has no more dramatic symbol than television. On the upside, television brings great joy into the homes of millions of families. In addition to its entertainment value and its function as baby-sitter, it has brought positive role models to the African-American people as they watch with pride the ascendancy of Bill Cosby, Oprah Winfrey, Bryant Gumbel, Carl Rowan, Arsenio Hall, and dozens of local news, weather, and sports personalities. Moreover, television was of enormous assistance to the civil rights movement. And for the past generation, television has documented the rise of African-American athletes to dominant positions on the playing field if not yet in the front office.

There is, though, a downside to television as well. Television is like a thief in the night. It sneaks into family life and robs parents of their capacity to teach their children to think critically. Numerous studies have shown that black children watch television many more hours of the day than other children. While the positive aspect of this is that busy, overworked, and harassed parents are able to provide television entertainment and a certain instruction for their children, the negative effect is that most of what they see is destructive of their healthy growth and development. Primarily, TV excludes black people, and were it not for the Bill Cosby show and "Roc" starring the incomparable Charles Dutton and company there would be no continuous positive image of black families. Worse still, the constant dose of violence, irresponsible sex, and mainstream opulence virtually drown out the few positive programs.

Popular culture, an area which has provided enormous opportunities for black talent, provides relatively few positive role models that black parents can use with their children via television. It has been estimated that by age twelve the average child has witnessed 10,000 acts of violence on television. Moreover, research has shown that the more people watch certain types of shows the more they adopt the attitudes and values portrayed by those shows.[22]

James Comer has explained that existing images of blacks on television often convey the impression that "Blacks are unworthy, are not able and do not desire to share in the mainstream activities of the society."[23] This creates ambivalence among blacks about their identity. Gordon Berry notes that television images often have an adverse impact on children's conceptions of themselves, their families, and the people of other races and nations. They see themselves on television as inferior to other people. Such television programming he argues can have unintended consequences which must be recognized and understood.[24] Television's tremendous potential as a positive force for the rearing of African-American children has only begun to be appreciated by parents, scholars, and policymakers.[25]

CONSTRUCTION TECHNOLOGY

Another important area of technological change affecting African-American families operates at the community level. Technological advances in the automobile, the superhighway, and construction technology all combined to produce the suburb, which in post–World War II America affected American family life profoundly. Driven by the baby boom, a surge in the economy, and the transition from manufacturing to service occupations, these spatial developments gave new meaning to the rapidly expanding American middle-class family life. As a consequence, most white families now live in the suburbs while a majority of black families live in the inner cities.

At first, designed to provide an escape from city life for residential purposes while enabling families to commute to the city for work and leisure, the suburbs became synonymous with middle-class white flight. Later, they would become home to the flight of industry from the cities as well. Finally, they would begin to serve grudgingly and gradually a trickle of the black middle-class families.

With enormous subsidies from the government, the suburban expansion provided a haven for the upwardly mobile, simple, nuclear families. Better schools, playgrounds, and fresh air added to the positive impact of suburbia on American family life. Soon, however, there emerged a downside to suburbia. The isolation and loneliness and longing for the amenities of urban life caused much family and marital unhappiness. Eventually, family conflict, violence, divorce, youth alienation, school dropouts, and youth unemployment became facts of life in suburbs as well as the cities. Still, single-family homes on a small plot of land with grass and trees, better schools, and no black neighbors, all continue to hold a central place in middle-class white America.

The few African-American families in suburbia often found themselves rejected and isolated by their new neighbors. Often they also felt estranged from the friends, relatives, and associates they left behind. As with other technological advances, suburbanization is capable of bringing both pleasure and pain.

The priority the nation placed on suburban development for middle-class families has drained resources from the cities. The reallocation of massive amounts of government and private investment, the movement of substantial numbers of middle-class white families, followed by the flight of industry, then the trickle of black middle-class and working-class families, have all left the inner cities of the nation impoverished. This combination of societal forces has been directly responsible in large measure for the expansion of black underclass neighborhoods in the central cities which sooner or later will impact on the suburbs in a variety of ways.

In this manner, the suburban rings around American cities become symbols of the results of technological innovation. They also become symbols of America's tendency toward racial and class exclusiveness. Yet their gradual opening to black families after civil rights legislation, which aided the expansion of the black middle class, must be considered as positive.

Throughout history, forces of change have created conditions that simultaneously hold both danger and promise for black families. In the next section we will take a closer look at the implications. As the larger society, through its various systems, maintains its dominant position, it becomes increasingly urgent to reassess how it makes progress possible. Clearly, it can ill afford to obstruct the development of strong black families.

—

PART III

Society Has the Upper Hand

Chapter 7

The Struggle for Life

Helping one another run the gauntlet from birth to old age has brought out the best in African-American families throughout history. Turning to their relatives, neighbors, friends, institutions in their community, and systems of the larger society when necessary, they have readily accepted their responsibility to generate, protect, and sustain life and health. In recent years, however, the struggle has intensified. Whose fault is it that so many black families face critical health problems and inadequate health care? Whose responsibility is it to correct the situation? The answer is the same to both questions. And as we will see, it is multiple.

At the beginning of the life cycle, black families contribute vigorously to the future work force, and to future taxpayers, consumers, and defenders of the nation. Births in the black community, though declining somewhat, are ahead of the national average.

In 1960, 602,000 black babies were born (Table 7.1). The numbers declined each year to 1975 when it reached a low of 512,000. Thereafter, however, the numbers increased steadily to 642,000 by 1987. The birth rates (the number of births per 1,000 black women) also declined from a high of 31.9 in 1960 to 21.6 by 1987.

By 1988 the proportion of black married women who were childless reached a low of 13.6 percent rising to an appropriate high of 48 percent for married women under twenty and 29.7

Table 7.1
Births and Birth Rates
1960–1987

	N	Rate (per 1,000 Population)
1960	602,000	31.9
1965	581,000	27.7
1970	572,000	25.3
1975	512,000	20.7
1980	590,000	22.1
1985	608,000	21.1
1987	642,000	21.6

source: U.S. Bureau of the Census, *Statistical Abstract of the U.S., 1990.*

percent for those twenty to twenty-four. But for those twenty-five and over childlessness increased dramatically (Table 7.2).

Meanwhile, children ever born to married women stood at the rate of 2,099 for every 1,000 married women. The rate was a proper low of 613 per thousand for black married women under twenty and rose to 2,527 for every 1,000 black married women aged thirty-five to thirty-nine. Overall, very few married women were childless except the very young, and the usual number of children per married woman was two, again except for the very young.

We know, of course, that the number of children born is not the same as the number of children conceived (Table 7.3).

Abortion has long been viewed with disapproval in the black

Table 7.2
Childlessness and Children Ever Born Among Married Women
1988

	Percentage Childless Among Women Ever-Married	Children Ever Born (per 1,000 Ever-Married Women)
Age:		
Total	13.6	2,099
18–19	48.2	613
20–24	29.7	1,342
25–29	17.5	1,748
30–34	11.2	1,980
35–39	7.6	2,527
40–44	12.5	2,436

source: U.S. Bureau of the Census, *Statistical Abstract of the U.S., 1990.*

community. Better to let the child arrive and have relatives help rear it or place it for adoption, so the attitude goes. Still, beginning in the 1970s the number of legal abortions would rise dramatically from a little over 6,000 a year in 1972 to over 9,000 by 1985. The rate of abortions per 1,000 live births would show a similar rise from 223 in 1972 to 659 in 1985. This phenomenon caused great consternation among African-American families. It often separated the older generation from the younger and the working class from the middle; Southerners from Northerners, and those in the city from their country cousins. Also, however, when it could be done legally and safely abortion eased the problem of unwanted pregnancy and premature childbearing.

The black community and the nation had reasons to be pleased with the steady decline in the black infant mortality rates over the past century (Table 7.4). As late as 1940, on the eve of World War II, of every 1,000 black live births an astounding 73 died before the second birth date. By 1970 the infant death rate had been cut in half. During the next seventeen years it was cut in half again, falling from the 73 per 1,000 in 1940 to 18 per 1,000 by 1987. Why did these rates decline so dramatically? Improved public health and sanitation conditions in the larger society as well as in African-American communities helped. So did advances in immunization and nutritional standards. Education and health awareness among the families themselves increased. Moreover, these families have given high priority to the well-being of their

TABLE 7.3
Legal Abortions Among Women, Aged 15–44
1972–1985

	N	*Rate per 1,000 Live Births*
1972	6,056	223
1975	6,749	565
1976	7,000	638
1977	7,247	679
1978	7,493	665
1979	7,750	625
1980	8,106	642
1981	8,407	645
1982	8,630	646
1983	8,834	670
1984	9,038	646
1985	9,242	659

SOURCE: U.S. Bureau of the Census, *Statistical Abstract of the U.S., 1990.*

TABLE 7.4
Infant Mortality (Death by Age 2 per 1,000 Live Births)
1940–1987

Year	Infant Deaths
1940	72.9
1950	43.9
1960	44.3
1970	32.6
1975	26.2
1980	21.4
1985	18.2
1987	17.9

Maternal Mortality
(Deaths per 1,000 Live Births)
1960–1987

Year	Deaths
1960	103.6
1970	59.8
1975	31.3
1980	21.5
1985	20.4
1987	18.8

SOURCE: U.S. Bureau of the Census, *Statistical Abstract of the U.S., 1990.*

children. Unfortunately, however, this progressive coalition seems to have broken down.

The mortality rate for black infants seems stuck at the 1985 level, which is twice as high as for white infants, which in turn is much higher than in other Western industrial societies. Worse still, in modern societies and modern times, infant mortality is almost completely preventable.

Among the most effective preventative measures is early and regular prenatal care for expectant mothers. The nation could provide that care as it does immunizations against diseases. Instead, there is a tendency to blame mothers for not getting the care they need. True, many need education and nurturing themselves. But the major cause of infant mortality lies elsewhere. It resides in the structure of health care systems in the nation and in most communities.

A set of negative conditions prevail. For low-income African-American families, accessible, affordable quality prenatal care is scarce. They are over-represented among the 31 million Americans with no health insurance.[1] They also face a relative paucity of African-American health care professionals. After reaching an all-time high of 7.5 percent of all admissions to medical schools in the nation in 1974, black admissions declined to 5.9 percent in 1984.[2]

When all these conditions are positively in place, black expectant mothers get the prenatal care they deserve. In a study we conducted at San Francisco General Hospital with Dr. Jeanne Giovannoni in 1969, we found that when societal supports were in place together with an aggressive and culturally sensitive outreach program on the part of the visiting nurses association, young black expectant mothers got better prenatal care than low-income whites. What made the difference? Young black expectant mothers were part of extended families. Their mothers and grandmothers made sure that they took advantage of these resources.

Another element in the black struggle for life is reflected in the estimated life expectancies of males and females as compiled by U.S. government agencies (Table 7.5). Here again phenomenal progress has been made. A hundred years ago black males could expect to live on the average to age 32.5, black women a bit longer, to 35. The situation has improved steadily and dramatically over the years. By 1990, black males could anticipate a life expectancy of almost 68 years, more than twice the average of a hundred

TABLE 7.5
Life Expectancy
1890–2010

| | LIFE EXPECTANCY IN YEARS | |
	Male	Female
Years		
1890	32.5	35.0
1920	45.5	45.2
1930	47.3	49.2
1940	51.5	54.9
1950	59.1	62.9
1960	61.1	66.3
1970	60.0	68.3
1975	62.4	71.3
1980	63.8	72.5
1985	65.3	73.7
1988	65.1	73.8
1990	67.7	75.0
1995	68.8	76.0
2000	69.9	77.1
2005	71.0	78.1
2010	71.4	78.5

SOURCE: U.S. Bureau of the Census, *Statistical Abstract of the U.S., 1990*; also: *The Black Population, 1790–1978*.

years earlier. Black women have improved their life span even more, rising from the 35 years in 1890 to an impressive 75 years by 1990, having surpassed the longevity of white men in the middle 1970s. White women are the longest survivors, with a life expectancy in 1990 of 79.6 years as compared with 75 years for black women, 72.7 years for white men, and 67.7 years for black men.[3] However, after 1990 the racial gap would again widen.

A concomitant to the expanding life span for black males and females are declining death rates for both sexes (Table 7.6). For males the death rate declined from 11.8 per 1,000 population in 1960 to 9.9 by 1988. For females the decline was from 9.1 to 7.3 over the same period.

Both the life expectancy and death rates support the general finding that black women live longer than black men. Reasons for the shorter life span for black men include the heavier stress placed by society on them, the greater susceptibility to physical illness, and a set of unhealthy eating, drinking, exercise, and behavior patterns which will be discussed below. Still, looking over the past hundred years, African-American families have made progress with the help of their relatives, their community, and their society in protecting and sustaining the lives of their members.

Struggle Against Debilitating Diseases

But as the struggle for life continues, progress is threatened by a weakening of social and personal resolve.

Among the leading causes of death among black men and women are the eight diseases shown in Table 7.7. In some of these

TABLE 7.6
Death Rates (per 1,000)
1960–1988

	DEATH RATE	
Year	Male	Female
1960	11.8	9.1
1970	11.9	8.3
1975	10.6	7.3
1980	10.3	7.3
1985	9.8	7.3
1988	9.9	7.3

SOURCE: U.S. Bureau of the Census, *Statistical Abstract of the U.S., 1990.*

TABLE 7.7
Death Rates by Selected Causes
(per 100,000)
1970–1987

Total	Male	Female
1970	1,318.6	814.4
1980	1,112.6	631.1
1985	1,024.0	589.1
1987	1,023.2	586.2
Heart Disease		
1970	375.9	251.7
1980	327.3	201.1
1985	301.0	186.8
1987	287.1	180.8
Malignant Neoplasms		
(Cancer)		
1970	198.0	123.5
1980	229.9	129.7
1985	231.6	130.4
1987	227.9	132.0
Cerebrovascular Disease		
(Stroke)		
1970	122.5	107.9
1980	77.5	61.7
1985	60.8	50.3
1987	57.1	46.7
Chronic Obstructive		
Pulmonary Disease		
1970	N/A	N/A
1980	20.9	6.3
1985	23.9	8.7
1987	24.0	9.5
Pneumonia		
1970	53.8	29.2
1980	28.0	12.7
1985	26.8	12.4
1987	26.4	12.2
Diabetes		
1970	21.2	30.9
1980	17.7	22.1
1985	17.7	21.1
1987	18.3	21.3
Chronic Liver Disease		
1970	33.1	17.8
1980	30.6	14.4
1985	23.4	10.1
1987	22.0	9.1

TABLE 7.7 (*continued*)
Death Rates by Selected Causes
(per 100,000)
1970–1987

Acquired Immunodeficiency Syndrome (AIDS)
1981–1989

	Number of Cases (Male and Female)
Total	27,627
1981–82	249
1983	567
1984	1,116
1985	2,087
1986	3,390
1987	5,386
1988	9,115
1989 (to July 30)	5,717

SOURCE: U.S. Bureau of the Census, *Statistical Abstract of the U.S., 1990.*

the death toll has been increasing while in others it is declining. Overall, the death rate per 100,000 population declined for black men from a high of 1,319 in 1970 to 1,023 by 1987. For females the decline was from 814 to 586. For all these diseases, however, the death rates among blacks are inordinately higher than the national average. Moreover, death rates among black men are inordinately higher than black women.

Heart disease, cancer, and stroke are the big three killers. A federal government study found that between 1979 and 1981 these diseases accounted for 44 percent of the excess black deaths over whites. It is some slight comfort to note that the rates of both heart disease and stroke have been declining in recent years for both men and women. What is most striking is that for all these diseases black men die at considerably higher rates than women, with the exception of diabetes, where black women substantially exceed black men. Still, the death rates from diabetes have been declining for both sexes between 1970 and 1987.

Dr. LaSalle D. Leffal, Jr., of Howard University has concluded that the primary factors accounting for excess black deaths from cancer include "cigarettes, tobacco combined with alcohol use, occupational hazards, poor nutrition, limited access to medical care, and less knowledge and greater vulnerability to aggressive tumors, including uterus and bladder tumors."[4]

Not only is cigarette smoking a major cause of cancer, it is also implicated in heart disease, pulmonary disease, and stroke, all of which are high among blacks, who smoke much more than other groups. It is for this reason that Secretary of Health and Human Services Dr. Louis Sullivan received such plaudits from both the black community and the health care community in January 1990 when he personally confronted the tobacco industry. President Bush's only black cabinet officer, the former medical school dean was personally affronted by the tactics of the R.J. Reynolds tobacco company, which developed, packaged, and proposed to market a special brand of cigarettes primarily for blacks, under the upbeat and jazzy brand name, "Uptown." The company was all set for a test run in Philadelphia's black community. After being appealed to by black leaders and health officials, Dr. Sullivan concluded that with the already high number of cigarette-related fatalities, the last thing the black community needed was a cigarette all its own. He publicly blasted the program and the company. "This brand is cynically and deliberately targeted toward black Americans," he proclaimed all over national television and radio, as well as in the print media for several weeks. Finally, the company withdrew its special marketing program. It has been pointed out, however, that large numbers of other tobacco companies target blacks, women, and young people with the sometime willing cooperation of newspapers and magazines and other organizations that serve the black community. Indeed, one of the ironic features of life in America is the manner in which a wide range of black organizations headed by highly educated and socially conscious reformers allow themselves to be used by tobacco and alcohol companies in order to meet the expenses of their annual meetings. Their programs enable them to help improve the conditions of black Americans while their marketing of tobacco and alcohol helps to kill thousands each year.

The struggle for life in the African-American community is closely linked to the AIDS epidemic. Table 7.7 shows the heavy toll AIDS is taking. Between 1981 and 1989 some 27,627 blacks died of AIDS. This constitutes nearly 30 percent of all AIDS deaths during that period while blacks constituted roughly 12 percent of the population. Moreover, the death toll from AIDS has been expanding enormously year by year. In 1981–82 a total of 249 blacks died of AIDS. A year later this had more than doubled to 567. Over the next year the number almost doubled to 1,116 deaths. It doubled again to 2,087 in 1985. The rate of increase has slowed somewhat since then but the numbers continue to climb. By 1988, a total of 9,115 black deaths from AIDS were recorded. Moreover, during the first half of 1989 another 5,717 deaths occurred. A report by the U.S. Centers for Disease Control revealed that half of all AIDS cases among blacks result from high rates of intravenous drug use. Other contributing factors are lower education levels, reduced access to medical care, and poverty.[5] And with no vaccine or cure in sight, education and improved health care offer the best means of curbing this epidemic. Individuals, organizations, health and family specialists both within the African-American community and throughout society have important roles to play.

Other major killers of black males include pulmonary disease, pneumonia, and chronic liver disease.

In an analysis of data collected by the National Survey of Black Americans, we found a similar profile of debilitating health problems among African-Americans. We found a dozen or so health problems that regularly inflict large numbers of African-American families. These include hypertension, arthritis, nervous conditions, kidney problems, hardening of the arteries, ulcers, diabetes, stroke, cancer, liver problems, and sickle cell anemia. Two-thirds of black adults in the nation in 1980 had been diagnosed as having at least one of these conditions.[6]

Thirty-two percent of the black adults indicated that they suffered hypertension and 20 percent indicated it was so severe as to be a barrier to their working. Arthritis and rheumatism were reported by nearly one-quarter of these black adults, and nearly one-third said that this was so severe as to constitute an obstacle to their working. The third most common health complaint was nervous conditions, reported by 22 percent, and of these 28 percent indicated that these were sufficiently severe to make it difficult for them to work. Kidney problems were in fourth place, reported by 10 percent of the respondents, with 16 percent indicating it was a barrier to their working.

Women have significantly more health problems than men. Seventy percent of women as compared with 58 percent of men had one or more of the above health problems during the previous month. Despite this, women outlive men substantially. As might be anticipated there was a strong social-class distinction. Persons in low-income families with low levels of education and occupational status had more health problems than those of the middle and upper classes. Among those with family incomes under

$6,000 in 1980 dollars, a significant 76 percent had one or more health problems. Among the middle-income families, this proportion with one or more health problems fell to a slight minority of 48 percent.

The age factor was pronounced. Among persons under twenty-five years of age the proportion with one or more health problems was 40 percent. Among those of middle age this rose to 75 percent; for those 65 and over, 88 percent had one or more health problems.

Finally, family structure is relevant. Reflecting no doubt their youthfulness, never-married adults had fewer health problems. But among the married and the formerly married the difference was striking. While 64 percent of married couples had one or more health problems, this rose to 75 percent for those separated and to 88 percent for the widowed, again most likely reflecting their age. In all groups an overwhelming majority of adults over twenty-five had one or more health problems, and the percentage increased as age increased.

Diabetes is closely related to the problem of obesity, from which black women suffer in significant numbers (Table 7.8). At all ages, obesity is nearly twice as high among black females as among black males.[7] In addition to having physical causes, obesity is another symptom of societal and interpersonal stress. While both black males and females are subjected to inordinate stress, it may well be that women internalize more. This enables many to absorb the blows of life directed at them and at their loved ones. It is the internalization of worries, aggression, mistreatment, discrimination, overwork, and neglect which takes such a toll. Men, on the other hand, when faced with societal and interpersonal stress, may tend to pass it off, blame someone else, fight back, strike out at the innocent, drive too fast, or drink too much. They pay their

TABLE 7.8
Percentage in Most Obese Group
1976

Age	Males	Females
20–44	14.6	23.7
45–54	27.4	41.6
55–64	23.7	50.0
65 and over	18.6	38.5

SOURCE: U.S. Department of Health, Education and Welfare: Report of the Secretary's Task Force on Black and Minority Health 1985.

price for this behavior too. But for women obesity may be a price for the manner in which they respond consciously and unconsciously to all the stresses in their life.

THE STRUGGLE AGAINST VIOLENCE

Yet another cluster of killers involve accidents and violence. Fortunately, the overall trend in highly traumatic deaths has been downward for both males and females (Table 7.9). Still, the incidence is more than twice as high among black males. In general, the combined death rate for accidents and violence, which was 183 per 100,000 black men in 1970, had declined substantially to 130 per 100,000 by 1987. Among black females the rates declined from 52 to 38 over this period.

TABLE 7.9
Death Rates from Accidents and Violence
(per 100,000)
1970–1987

	Male	Female
TOTAL		
1970	183.2	51.7
1980	154.0	42.6
1987	129.6	37.9
MOTOR VEHICLE ACCIDENTS		
1970	44.3	13.4
1980	31.1	8.3
1987	27.7	8.6
ALL OTHER ACCIDENTS		
1970	63.3	22.5
1980	46.0	18.6
1987	37.2	14.4
SUICIDE		
1970	8.0	2.6
1980	10.3	2.2
1987	11.6	2.1
HOMICIDE		
1970	67.6	13.3
1980	66.6	13.5
1987	53.3	12.6

SOURCE: U.S. Bureau of the Census, *Statistical Abstract of the U.S., 1990.*

When specific types of accidents are considered, automobile accidents are the leading killers. Even there, the death rate has been declining, falling from 44 per hundred thousand black men in 1970 to 28 in 1987, while deaths from other accidents are also in a downward trend for both sexes.

Domestic violence seems to have had a major resurgence in recent years and is taking an extreme toll on African-American families. Child abuse by parents and caretakers came into national prominence in the 1980s. While blacks generally have lower incidence of child abuse than comparable white families, the problem is still acute.[8] A study by the U.S. Department of Health and Human Services, which examined this problem in 1979–80, found that incidents of child abuse among black families was some 15 percent of all reported incidents.[9] Studies have found that the strong kinship networks so prominent among black families serve as somewhat of a check on the apparently rising incidence of child abuse.[10]

The problem of domestic violence became so prominent that the U.S. Attorney General appointed a national task force to study it. A 1984 report concluded that it was a widespread problem in every race and social class.[11]

In his book on violence in the black family, Robert L. Hampton has affirmed that it is a major problem: "Sexual abuse, physical child abuse, family violence, and homicides are arguably among the most serious social problems in the black community."[12]

Not only child abuse, but sibling abuse, spouse abuse, and elder abuse seem to be on the rise. Women seem to be the more frequent victims of domestic abuse, leading to the establishment of shelters for battered women. Increasingly, death results from physical abuse.

Homicide, which is nearly five times as common among black men as black women, has declined significantly during recent years from a high of 68 per 100,000 in 1970 to 53 by 1987 for men. Over the same period, the rate remained at about 13 among black women. At the same time, the suicide rates climbed for males while declining for black females.

For both black men and women the highest homicide rates occur in the adult years from twenty-five through forty-four (Table 7.10). Rates are lower for both younger and older persons, up to age eighty-five when homicide rates rise sharply. Many of the victims and perpetrators are friends or relatives and often family members.

TABLE 7.10
Homicide Rates
(per 100,000)
1970–1987

	Male	Female
HOMICIDE - ALL AGES		
1970	67.6	13.3
1980	66.6	13.5
1987	53.3	12.6
15–24		
1970	234.3	45.5
1980	162.0	35.0
1987	147.6	31.8
25–34		
1970	384.4	76.0
1980	256.9	49.4
1987	207.6	44.8
35–44		
1970	345.2	77.2
1980	218.1	43.2
1987	179.9	35.7
45–64		
1970	242.4	56.0
1980	188.5	47.3
1987	133.8	41.4
65 AND OVER		
1970	220.0	107.9
1980	215.8	102.9
1987	187.1	81.2
85 AND OVER		
1970	271.8	214.3
1980	329.2	235.7
1987	364.2	193.8

SOURCE: U.S. Bureau of the Census, *Statistical Abstract of the U.S., 1990.*

With suicides, the highest suicide rates are in the adult years between age twenty and thirty-four, and for the eighty-five and over group (Table 7.11).

By the end of the 1980s homicide had become the leading cause of death among young black men and women between the ages of fifteen and thirty-four. A federal government study in 1985 found

TABLE 7.11
Suicide Rates
(per 100,000)
1970–1986

	Male	*Female*
ALL AGES		
1970	8.0	2.6
1980	10.3	2.2
1986	11.1	2.3
15–19		
1970	4.7	2.9
1980	5.6	1.6
1986	7.1	2.1
20–24		
1970	18.7	4.9
1980	20.0	3.1
1986	16.0	2.4
25–34		
1970	19.2	5.7
1980	21.8	4.1
1986	21.3	3.8
35–44		
1970	12.6	3.7
1980	15.6	4.6
1986	17.5	2.8
45–54		
1970	13.8	3.7
1980	12.0	2.8
1986	12.6	3.2
55–64		
1970	10.6	2.6
1980	11.7	1.4
1986	9.9	2.4
65 AND OVER		
1970	8.7	2.6
1980	11.4	1.4
1986	16.2	2.4
85 AND OVER		
1970	8.7	2.8
1980	18.9	N/A
1986	17.9	N/A

NA = Data not available.

SOURCE: U.S. Bureau of the Census, *Statistical Abstract of the U.S., 1990*.

that after heart disease, "homicide accounts for more excess mortality among black Americans than any other cause of death."[13] What this also tells us is that by 1986, while blacks constituted 12 percent of the national population, they accounted for a phenomenal 44 percent of all murder victims in the nation. Black men were more than six times as likely as white men to be victims of homicide, and black women were four times as likely as white women to be such victims.

Homicides represent only the tip of the iceberg of violence. It has been estimated that for every homicide there are approximately one hundred other serious assaults or attempted homicides.[14] Moreover, the conflict between black men and women had become so fierce and convoluted that despite the rampage of black men assaulting their wives there are actually more black men killed by their wives than there are wives killed by husbands. The reason for this, however, is that many of these wives are fighting in self-defense.[15]

Among the saddest features of this domestic violence is that the homicide was generally not the first act of conflict to be brought to the attention of relatives and the authorities. One study in Kansas City in 1977 found that in 85 percent of domestic homicides, the police had been called to the home at least once; and in half of the cases the police had been called to settle domestic quarrels at least five times before the fatality occurred.[16]

There are a number of features of this violence that are ominous for the historic sense of community among the African-American people. There is nothing in the values or heritage of the African-American people that produces this breach of life and dignity. The following must therefore cause considerable concern within the black community and cry out for special understanding and amelioration.

- Most cases of homicide occur inside the black community where both victim and perpetrator are black. This is true of 95 percent of black homicides. A generation ago blacks who were murdered were more likely to be murdered by the white authorities or vigilantes. It is a major matter on the agenda of the black community.
- Most of the murders occur to young blacks between fifteen and twenty, and particularly young black males. This means a great deal of agony for their parents, relatives, and friends. It means the loss of the economic potential and contribution of

these young men. It also means an exaggeration of the shortage of black males to form partnership with black females and
parenthood for black children.

· Most of the incidents are not related to robbery attempts,
theft, or other criminal behavior, but arise out of civil disputes, many of which had been ongoing for some time. Often
they are quarrels over petty items of property, actual or assumed slights, or male-female jealousy and passion. In short,
these violent deaths grow out of what would appear to be the
most ordinary aspects of life.

· Most homicides are committed not by strangers, or enemies,
but by relatives and friends. Among men, more than 60 percent are committed by persons known to the victim. Among
women an even higher percentage are known. And among
both sexes nearly 40 percent of the assailants are relatives of
the victim.

· Most of the homicides are committed with illegal but easily
available handguns.

· Increasingly, drugs and alcohol are found to be among the
factors precipitating this violence.

· The perpetrators, though still alive, generally are required to
serve long terms in prison, where they are not only removed
from the family, the community, and the economy, but where
they learn even more hardened attitudes toward violence.

What this all means is that this pattern of intracommunity violence is sapping the very heart of the black community and its
future viability. It exacerbates the decline in married-couple families. And since much of this violence occurs in the home, children
are frequently exposed to unusual emotional trauma, which can
affect them a lifetime if untreated.

Family Trauma

The impact of drugs and homicide on families is vividly illustrated
by two Washington, D.C., mothers whose sons were murdered.

Cynthia Harris was an achieving single mother of an achieving
sixteen-year-old son, Lionel Harris III, who at age seventeen was
shot and killed on the street.[17] An honor student at the city's
Coolidge High School, he was shot in a parking lot in the Georgetown section of the city. Just a year before, his mother, a D.C.
native, had decided to move back to the city from Detroit, to be

near her own parents, and to prepare her son for college. A reporter and public relations executive of her own firm, she had high aspirations and firm plans for her son and her family.

How did her son lose his life which seemed filled with so much promise? The drug culture caught up with him. A month before young Lionel Harris was murdered he had what his mother thought was his first experience in doing drugs. She noted that he left home unannounced at about 11 P.M. one night and returned about a half hour later. "I could look at him," she said, "and tell something was wrong with him. He was really high. He didn't even know where the floor was."

When the boy admitted to his mother that he had smoked PCP, she called his father, who came over to the house to be with his son. Not knowing what to do and reluctant to call in the authorities, the father just drove the boy around town for several hours hoping he would come down from his high. When they returned home at about 3:30 A.M., the boy told both his parents that he was sorry and that he loved them. They thought he had learned his lesson.

To show his concern for the problem, young Lionel, who aspired to be a journalist, began researching and writing an article for his school paper, decrying drugs and violence in the streets of the city. Ironically, his article was published the week after his own death from drugs and street violence.

One night after he finished his article, Lionel left home to go shopping for clothes in Georgetown. He had a new job and wanted to look nice. Later that night he called to tell his mother he was on his way home. Two hours later she received another phone call, this time from a friend who had accompanied Lionel to Georgetown hospital where he had died after being shot. The young man convicted of murdering young Harris, Lewis Lyons, was twenty-two years old, and he was sentenced to twenty-seven years to life in prison. At the trial, testimony disclosed that both Lionel Harris and his assailant had PCP in their systems.

Cynthia Harris wept over and mourned the loss of her son. "We were so close," she said. "Losing him was like losing an arm or a leg."

Then she went into action. She gave up her business and formed the Stop the Madness Foundation. Her activism combined with her managerial, journalistic, and public relations skills have already begun to pay dividends. The foundation has attracted strong support in the community. It has initiated peer counseling programs for teenagers, lobbied for mandatory pre-trial detention for murder cases, developed an antiviolence public service announcement for television and newspapers, and has launched plans to establish four youth houses in different sections of the city where a dozen youth will be provided treatment. It shows what highly motivated, highly able, highly dedicated leadership can do to help the community focus on this problem.

Another mother who suffered the loss of her son also launched a social-action effort, almost inadvertently.[18] Patricia Godley was part of the audience when CBS commentator Ted Koppel was conducting one of his open speakout programs about drugs. She was displeased at the drift of the program and rose to express her anger. "My son (passed two weeks ago) when he got killed," she said, "but that's not even the issue, that he's dead. I got a fourteen-year-old baby that I want to see live. I swear to God I do." Then she continued for what seemed a very long six minutes on prime-time television. "I heard the man say . . . that parents need to get more involved. What can you do to help me be something I've never been—a parent? I'm trying to assist my child. Can you do that?" Godley had her first contact with the authorities when she was thirteen. After spending three years in juvenile correction facilities she emerged at age sixteen as a drug addict. She could lie and steal with the best of them.

Her older son, Warren Jackson, was born when she was on methadone trying to cure her heroin addiction. It is almost as though he did not have a chance in life. He grew up in a drug environment. "He saw me at my worst," Godley said. By the time he was fifteen he was arrested for possession of cocaine. At sixteen he was sent to a detention center for violating his probation on the drug charge. Before his seventeenth birthday he was dead. "I tried to talk to him," Godley said. "He would not listen to me."

In what has become among the most agonizing characteristics of these drug-related homicides, the perpetrator was someone known to Godley and her son. He was Godley's previous boyfriend. When John Lee, aged forty-six, was sentenced, his attorney argued for leniency on the grounds of his history of drug abuse and incarceration. "If that's an excuse," Godley fumed, "then I can go out and kill somebody."

Godley's three children were being raised by her own mother. She had a very low opinion of herself. "I never thought I would amount to anything," she has said. Now she is an activist. Her recent road to recovery began in jail. She enrolled in a drug treatment program in 1984 and again in 1985, but was put out both times for infractions. In 1986, she was arrested on possession charge and sentenced to a year in the city jail. There she entered another drug treatment program. This time she was inspired by the progress of other inmates. "They were clean and they looked good. I got tired . . . I just got tired." When she came out this time she was in recovery and has maintained it. She got married in 1988 and brought her three children home to live with her. In November 1988, she got a job as a secretary in a nonprofit organization. "My job has been one of the best things to happen to me," she said. "They are willing to assist me with the things I don't understand. My boss accepted me, knowing everything I had done because I told him in the interview. Now I can be a secretary in anybody's office in this town." She has a new calling and a new crusade.

She speaks to audiences of drug users, telling them that she used drugs because she had a low opinion of herself. "Nobody ever told me that I could be something," she says. Now that she is receiving the help she has long sought, she can help others. "With hope and faith and the right lead, you can do anything. But you have to be willing to be led."

Still, her youngest boy, who is fourteen, does not listen to her. Since his older brother was murdered, the younger boy has been arrested for a minor drug charge. She fears he will end up like his brother. "I'm no psychologist," she said, "but from what I see, all of his behavior says pain. They were very close. He still sometimes cries about missing his brother. All I can do is hold him and tell him it's all right."

Her young son recently left home to live with his grandmother. He said that she was too strict in setting rules. "He still calls me and tells me he loves me," she said. "He'll be back. If he lives, he'll be back."

By 1990, most black leaders and health authorities were convinced that the drug epidemic was destroying the African-American community. Dr. LaSalle D. Leffall has observed that "It is not an exaggeration to say that the growing threat of chemical dependency, particularly the use of illegal drugs such as crack, marijuana, and PCP, is tearing at the very fabric of the African-American community."[19]

As early as 1987 the drug specialist Dr. Benny Primm found that the drug epidemic's dramatic impact is evidenced by increased crime, wanton violence, mental disorders, family disruptions, and social problems in school and on the job, and concluded that the drug epidemic is "the most serious and perplexing problem facing black America."[20]

It is becoming clear that innocent black children suffer the most from drug abuse. Infant mortality, sudden infant death syndrome, child abuse and neglect, and the increase in abandoned babies left in hospital wards by their mothers are all aggravated by drug abuse, especially crack cocaine. New York Police Commissioner Dr. Lee Brown, among others, has pointed to the economic benefits derived by so many from drug trafficking which makes it difficult to abolish. While the black community has an active role to play, this problem also has its major focus in the wider society.

Primary Prevention

The need is clear for more primary prevention efforts within the African-American community, and within the larger society, as well as in the voluntary sector, the private enterprise sector, and the government sector.

As Dr. Carl C. Bell explained, "Primary prevention refers to those actions that stop a problem from occurring and can be contrasted with secondary and tertiary prevention, which are remediations that occur in the early and late stages of the illness respectively."[21] Dr. Bell has urged a community-level education and awareness campaign to "increase the black community's awareness of the problem and increase black ownership of it." There are, of course, numerous and increasing efforts around the nation to this effect. He has outlined such a program involving:

- Teaching conflict-resolution skills to young people to help them develop alternatives, so that they do not turn so automatically to violence to settle disputes.
- Expanding community-based programs to encourage values, a sense of direction, and high self-esteem among black youths.
- Providing professional help for black families under stress, including parenting classes, respite care, family counseling, and family therapy.
- Establishing more alcohol and drug treatment centers in every community so that all persons who need treatment can get it.

• Expanding community programs designed to enhance racial identity and solidarity.

In all these efforts, an important role is to be played by more privileged blacks helping those in greater danger. Among the many examples of such programs, one started in Chicago by the owner of a cosmetics company has been noteworthy in its success. In its Black-on-Black-Love Campaign, the company adopted a public-housing project, providing a library with black materials, a computer lab, a ceramics shop, and outdoor murals exhibiting black pride. The results have been a decrease in gang violence, fewer fights, and less graffiti on the walls. Other examples may be cited that are equally promising. Many black churches and other black fraternal organizations and other associations have established such programs. May their numbers increase. But drugs will prevail until the federal government makes drug interdiction, alternative crops, and drug prevention and treatment national priorities. The urgent need is for what psychologist Kenneth Clark might call "a relevant war on drugs."

Increasingly, leadership elements of the African-American community are rising to confront the struggle for life, energized in part by an increased awareness of alcohol, of other drug use, and of the specter of AIDS. In 1987, a conference sponsored by the Howard University school of Human Ecology and organized by Professor Ura Jean Oyemade brought together a wide range of specialists to focus on the health problems in the District of Columbia and other urban areas.[22] Funded by the U.S. Office of Substance Abuse Prevention and addressed by Elaine M. Johnson, director of that office, the conference sought to focus on both the scientific nature of these conditions and practical approaches to their prevention. When his turn came to speak, the scholarly, articulate, and caring commissioner of health for the District of Columbia, Dr. Reed Tuckson, spoke for numerous specialists when he said:

I am pessimistic about the future. I will say that I do not see anything good on the horizon for the next couple of years. I see it being very difficult. I think that the AIDS epidemic, which is ultimately going to destroy the lives of many of our young people because of their sexual and drug-taking behavior, is going to reap incredible consequences on our community. But I also think that the AIDS epidemic will give us the opportunity for a fundamental restructuring of the urban experience in this city and around the country.

I think that the threat that AIDS represents is so severe, so serious, that it will force us to change how we behave as a civilized, or, in this case, an uncivilized society. . . . We will be forced to make changes in our sense of who we are. So in that, I will say that I am energized. I am still ready for the fight.

It was Dr. Tuckson's focus on "changing our sense of who we are" that struck such a responsive chord. He expressed not only pessimism, but realism and even optimism all in the same passage. In the appendix to the proceedings for the conference, Dr. Oyemade captured the series of hard questions and frank answers that emerged from the gathering.

Is alcohol a factor in criminal activity among African-American youth? Yes. Do African-American youths encounter barriers to effective treatment of alcohol and other drug use problems? Yes. And the final question produced what might be considered a surprising answer. Can we prevent alcohol and other drug use among African-American youth? Yes. Here the conferees pointed to long-term education and prevention programs, which when reinforced by messages in the mass media have proven to be effective in reducing the incidence of some types of drug abuse. They concluded with this upbeat message: "More progress can be made when communities and families provide full support to local prevention efforts targeted at minority youth."

Chapter 8

The Belief in Education

When Sarah Coleman of Philadelphia first met Larry Montgomery of Virginia at Morgan State College in 1953, it was far from love at first sight. She was a big-city girl from a successful family up North; he was a country boy. In time, however, they would become fast friends and love would blossom.

Nearly forty years later, Sarah and Larry could sit in their spacious, comfortable living room in Northeast Washington and speak with satisfaction of their lives together. Married in 1958, they had a great deal to be proud of. They spoke of Larry's career. Having participated in college ROTC he entered the army as a second lieutenant in 1957. By the time he retired some twenty years later he had risen through a series of tough assignments to the rank of major. He returned to his alma mater to become Director of Alumni Affairs in 1977. He said at the time that he did so in order to give something back to the institution which had given him so much. They also spoke of Sarah's role as wife, mother, citizen, community activist, and alumni booster. After earning a graduate degree she decided to devote herself part-time as a teacher in order to give full time to her family-management responsibilities.

They spoke of their upbringing and the paths that brought them together. Lawrence Montgomery, the first of two children, was born to Newburn Montgomery and Villie Belle White in the midst of the Depression. At the age of three, when his father deserted the family, he moved with his mother into the home of his grandparents in Union County, North Carolina. Soon thereafter, his grandfather Jack White went blind. Larry would grow up in the company of his grandfather as his helper. In addition, however, beginning at about age ten he took jobs in local stores as delivery boy and stock helper. In school he was a good student, an excellent swimmer, and an outstanding trumpet player. These talents would get him into and through college. He was the first of his family to get a college education.

Sarah Coleman had a more auspicious beginning in life than her husband. Born into a middle-class, Northern, urban family of professionals, she knew at a very young age that she would go to college. The question became, where? A relative had gone to Morgan and recommended it highly.

She was born into a family of Philadelphia preachers, teachers, nurses, physicians, college professors, beauticians, funeral directors, and other professionals. It was a close-knit, supportive family. It was also a family with a long line of Sarahs for whom she was named.

They spoke to us about the children. Each of them has already demonstrated the value of a strong, disciplined, and supportive family and a strong supportive college. All were graduates of Morgan State University. All had been excellent students pursuing challenging majors. Lisa, their first-born, arrived in 1958. A biology major at Morgan, she enrolled in ROTC, entered the army, and rose to the rank of captain in short order. She married John A. Jackson, an ex-military man, and they have one infant daughter.

Larry, their second, graduated with a degree in chemistry. He would serve with distinction as captain of the 21st Chemical Company, including duty in the Persian Gulf crisis in 1991. Married to Sandra Dallard, they are parents of twins, Lawrence III, and Daganita.

Their last born, Lynette, graduated with a degree in physics. Rather than enter the service, however, she became a professional cartographer with the Defense Mapping Agency. Not yet married by 1991 she was still considered the "baby" of the family.

Sarah and Larry could look back on difficult assignments, unfriendly places, and a touch of racism here and there. Overall, however, they felt that if they could live life all over again they would do it much the same way. And they gave Morgan State a great deal of credit for their achievements.

Their stories have been duplicated thousands of times. Education is the traditional opportunity through which black families find their places in life. And having found it, they replicate their experience again and again through their children.

For more than a hundred years, each generation of blacks has been more educated than the one before. This has been reflected in every area of education, including basic literacy, school attendance, highest grade level achieved, and percentage going on to and graduating college and beyond. By 1890, a short generation after slavery, and without any widespread commitment to universal schooling for black youths, an impressive one-third of the nearly 3 million black children under twenty-one years of age were attending schools (Table 8.1).[1] A major effort by black and white churches and by foundations and other voluntary agencies established schools for black children to supplement what the families did on their own and what they were able to get some reluctant public authorities to do. Only the state of South Carolina, controlled by black legislators after the Civil War, prescribed universal public education at the elementary grades.

The gains in school attendance since that time have been impressive. By 1910 about 45 percent of black children were enrolled in school. This expanded to a majority of 65 percent by 1940 at the onset of World War II. After the war there was an explosion of school attendance when the educational system generally began to match the educational aspirations of black parents. Most of the states required school attendance of all children and many jurisdictions provided assistance to the parents and schools in getting children to school. However, it was an era of blatant racism, exclusion, and inferior facilities. Education for blacks represented the most conspicuous backwater of American life until the civil rights era began in earnest after World War II. At this time, law professors at the Howard University Law School initiated their assault on the segregated school system, at first by demanding equality of resources for the black schools, and eventually by a massive attack on segregation itself. After the U.S. Supreme Court decision of 1954 outlawing school segregation, African-American families accepted hardship and danger in order to insure that the nation would remain faithful to the noble commitment of this decision. Black children marched steadily to schools across the nation; some to legally segregated schools all over the South; others to de facto segregated schools over most of

TABLE 8.1
Enrolled in School, Aged 5–20, by Region
1890–1975
(in Thousands)

Area and Year	Total	ENROLLED	
		N	(%)
UNITED STATES			
1890	2,998	987	33
1910	3,678	1,645	45
1940	4,389	2,837	65
1960	6,624	5,225	79
1970	8,405	6,886	82
1975	8,670	7,507	87
SOUTH			
1890	2,772	873	31
1910	3,403	1,489	44
1940	3,453	2,149	62
1960	4,000	3,074	77
1970	4,601	3,706	81
NORTH AND WEST			
1890	252	121	48
1910	274	156	57
1940	937	688	73
1960	2,624	2,150	82
1970	3,803	3,180	84

Regional data for 1890 and all data for 1940 and 1960 include persons of "other" races.

SOURCE: U.S. Bureau of the Census, *Current Population Reports, The Black Population in the U.S., 1790–1978,* 1980.

the North; and still others to the smattering of schools which were forced to admit them along with white children. As a consequence, by 1975 87 percent of the 7.5 million black children were in schools in all parts of the nation. This expansion of black enrollment in schools also brought about an expansion in black teachers and school officials. It was a natural relationship until after the 1960s when white-controlled school systems nationwide gave preferential treatment to white teachers and officials whatever the racial composition of the school district. Still, by 1975, after a century of freedom, the 87 percent of black children enrolled in school was the same as the white enrollment (86 percent) for the first time in history. This was surely a remarkable expression of the deep-seated commitment to learning on the part of African-American families. It was a tribute to much else as well. But none of the other assistance would have been provided had not black parents and community leaders taken the initiative, made the sacrifices, and demanded that the society respond to the educational needs of their children. Dr. Josie Johnson of the University of Minnesota has chronicled how black parents and community leaders gave inordinate impetus to the education of their own children during the generations leading up to 1954.[2]

Among all the sources of survival, achievement, and viability of African-American families, education has played a preeminent role. The thirst for learning, like the thirst for family life, crossed the Atlantic with the African captives. Their inquiring, creative, and inventive mind-set was so well developed in the era of the African Renaissance which spread to the West African Coast, that even slavery could not quench it. As a 1989 panel of black scholars led by Sarah Lawrence Lightfoot and John Hope Franklin noted: "The desire to learn to read and to write was keen in the black communities of antebellum America. . . . Even in the dilapidated log cabins of the slave quarters the desire for education was nurtured and strengthened as an integral part of the socialization patterns and kinship networks of black men and women held in bondage."[3]

Despite all the oppression of slavery, a small and valiant group consisting of some 5 percent of the 400,000 newly freed African-Americans could read and write. They formed a vanguard for what would become after the Civil War a phenomenal surge toward education on the part of the African-American people for a full century of progress. Frederick Douglass was an outstanding example of the biblical urging that "knowledge will set you free." So too was Jesse Chisholm Duke, who used the literacy he received in slavery to build a strong, achieving family and other institutions down through the generations. Dr. Josie Johnson has shown how during the years leading up to the 1954 Supreme Court desegregation decree African-American parents were in the forefront of providing education for their children. The historic commitment to education continues into the present. This is why the Lightfoot Panel in 1989 declared: "We hold this truth to be self evident: all black children are capable of learning and achieving." The panel then set forth a point of view and a strategy on behalf of the entire black community:

What we must demand is this: that the schools shift their focus from the supposed deficiencies of the black child—from the alleged inadequacies of black family life—to the barriers that stand in the way of academic success.

Dr. Lightfoot was an excellent choice to lead this panel on education. In her own pioneering work, this Harvard University Professor of Education has shown that black families have a passionate commitment to education and will cooperate with the schools to insure their success if given the proper leadership, support, and guidance.[4] Much of her work and this panel's 1989 report were influenced by the late Ronald Edmonds, a leader in black education in the 1970s. Responding to the allegations of his time that black families were responsible for school failure, he wrote:

> How many effective schools would you have to see to be persuaded of the educability of poor children? If your answer is more than one, then I suspect that you have reasons of your own for preferring to believe that basic pupil performance derives from family background instead of the school's response to family background.[5]

Although there are significant regional variations in African-American school attendance, a central finding is that despite the more adverse political and economic conditions in the South, black families there, where a majority lived (and still live), were able to close the gap between the attendance of their children and those of other regions (Table 8.1). In 1890, for example, 31 percent of black children in the South were enrolled in school, as compared with 48 percent in the North and West. By 1970, however, this differential had been progressively closed so that 81 percent in the South and 84 percent in the North and West were enrolled in school. The gender factor showed itself early. Throughout this period, a majority of black children enrolled in school at all ages has been male. This is no doubt a reflection of the fact that more black male children are born than female. But since the infant mortality rate has always been higher among male than female babies, the continuation of this preferential pattern merits attention. Black parents have long seen the necessity to prepare their young males for the world of work and to prepare their females for the dual role of domestic partner and working partner. This ambivalence in the latter role no doubt accounts for the manner in which black females lagged behind black males in educational participation and attainment in the early years. In 1950, for example, at the close of the World War II era, and on the eve of the high-tech era, 56 percent of all black males aged five to twenty-nine were enrolled in a school as compared with 47 percent of all black females (Table 8.2).

As late as 1975 black males still outnumbered black females in school. Among males aged five to twenty-nine school enrollment had increased to 69 percent while it had increased to 63 percent for females. Still, at 98 percent of all children ages five to thirteen, the elementary school grades were equally attended by males and females.

Expected Grade Level

While school attendance is high, students were not always able to keep up to their expected grade level of performance (Table 8.3). In 1950, for example, 52 percent of black students in high school, aged fourteen to seventeen, were two or more years below their expected grade level. By 1970, however, this had declined dramatically to 21 percent.

TABLE 8.2
Percentage Enrolled in School, Aged 5–29
1950–1975

Age and Sex	1950	1960	1970	1975
MALE				
Total, 5–29 Years	56	66	69	69
5–13	87	92	96	98
14–17	79	88	92	93
18 and 19	20	37	41	50
20–24	11	9	17	21
25–29	6	4	6	12
FEMALE				
Total, 5–29 Years	47	62	64	63
5–13	87	93	96	98
14–17	72	85	92	91
18 and 19	26	32	39	45
20–24	3	6	12	19
25–29	1	2	4	8

Data for 1950 and 1960 include persons of "other" races.

SOURCE: U.S. Bureau of the Census, *Current Population Reports, The Black Population in the U.S. 1790–1978, 1980.*

Literacy

Another matter which has concerned African-American families historically has been the level of literacy in the adult population.

Here again, the record of improvement has been impressive. In the U.S. as a whole a stunning 61 percent of black adults, aged fourteen and over, were illiterate in 1890 (Table 8.4). By 1969 this had been reduced drastically to only 4 percent. In the South literacy lagged somewhat behind the rest of the nation. Still, in the South illiteracy declined from 65 percent to 22 percent between 1890 and 1930, while declining from 33 percent to 5 percent in the rest of the nation.

Again, there was some considerable diversity in this attainment marked by both gender and age. Illiteracy was highest among black women in 1890 at 65 percent versus 57 percent for black men. By 1910, however, the difference had been erased. A third of both sexes were illiterate. By 1947, just after the end of World War II, black women had surpassed black men, with women's illiteracy down to 8 percent as compared with 14 percent for men. By 1969 illiteracy had been virtually eliminated, with just 4 percent of black men and 3 percent of black women still not able to read or write.

TABLE 8.3

Percentage of Enrolled Two or More Years Below Expected Grade
Aged 14–17
1950–1970

Expected Grade Status and Age	1950*	1960*	1970
Two or More Years Below Expected Grade			
Total, 14–17	52.3	31.8	21.1
14	51.6	29.1	19.0
15	53.1	31.5	20.5
16	52.8	32.6	22.0
17	51.7	35.1	24.0

* Data include persons of "other" races.

NOTE: Modal grades are: 14 years old, high school 1; 15 years old, high school 2; 16 years old, high school 3; 17 years old, high school 4. Data in this table are for the population as of spring of school year.

SOURCE: U.S. Bureau of the Census, *Current Population Reports, The Black Population in the U.S. 1790–1978, 1980.*

TABLE 8.4
Illiteracy by Region, Aged 14 and Over
1890–1969
(in Thousands)

		ILLITERATE	
Area and Year	Total	Number	(%)
UNITED STATES			
1890	4,259	2,607	61
1910	6,132	1,997	33
1930	8,027	1,445	18
1947[1]	10,471	1,152	11
1959	12,210	910	7
1969	14,280	509	4
SOUTH			
1890	3,769	2,462	65
1910	5,308	1,906	36
1930	6,116	1,351	22
NORTH AND WEST			
1890	631	208	33
1910	823	91	11
1930	1,911	94	5

Regional data for 1890 and all data for 1947 and 1959 include persons of "other" races.

[1] Data have been adjusted.

SOURCE: U.S. Bureau of the Census, *Current Population Reports, The Black Population in the U.S. 1790–1978, 1980.*

Level of School Completed

Black parents have wanted their children to go as far as they could in school, at least through high school. Improvement has been substantial if not always steady. In the nation as a whole only 7 percent of black adults aged twenty-five and over were high school graduates in 1940, on the eve of World War II. By 1975 this had increased to 43 percent. Over the same period, the median number of years of school completed had risen from 5.7 years in 1940 to 10.9 years in 1975 in the nation as a whole. In the South the increase was from 5 to 9.5 years. In the North and West median years of school completed rose from 7.6 years to 12.1 years and was virtually equal to school achievement of white adults in that region.

If we consider only adults in the restricted young adult age range of twenty-five to thirty-four, the progress that has been made in education can be even more clearly seen. In 1940, 11 percent of blacks in this age range in the nation as a whole had completed high school. By 1975 this had increased to 69 percent. At the same time, the median years of school completed for this age rose from 6.9 percent in 1940, where it trailed white attainment by 3.5 years. By 1975 this had increased to 12.4 years and had virtually closed the gap with white young adults, who had 12.8 years of schooling. Again, the South lagged somewhat behind. Median years of school rose from 6.2 years in 1940 to 12.3 in 1975, almost equalling the 12.7 years for whites. In the North and West the improvement was more substantial, rising from 8.7 years in 1940 to 12.5 in 1975 as compared with 12.8 for whites.

College Education

A final area to be considered in this historical overview is college attendance. The proportion of black adults aged twenty-five to thirty-four who had completed four or more years of college rose from a mere 2 percent in 1940 to 11 percent by 1975. In the South this rose from 1 percent in 1940 to 12 percent in 1975, slightly surpassing the North and West, where it rose from 2 percent to 10 percent. This is in large measure a reflection of the existence of the historically black colleges, most of which are located in the South. These institutions were established between 1830 and 1900 for the express purpose of educating black Americans, one hundred of them located in the South and seven in the North and West.

The overall enrollment trend for black college students is upward (Table 8.5). The total number of blacks in college expanded from 141,000 in 1960, more than tripling in that decade to 437,000 by 1970. During the 1970s, the numbers grew more slowly, but to a still impressive 718,000 by 1980. They have grown even more slowly, to 855,000 in 1987, before sliding back to 785,000 in 1988. Since 1960 black women have outnumbered black men in colleges. In 1960 there were 5,000 more black women in college than black men. By 1980 there were 134,000 more women. In 1988, the enrollment of black men declined while it increased for women. This resulted in 179,000 more black women in college than black men. For black educated women it means that their prospects of marrying an equally well-educated black man are further diminished.

Among high school graduates the proportion of men and

TABLE 8.5
College Enrollment
1960–1988

	Total	Male	Female
COLLEGE ENROLLMENT			
1960	141,000	68,000	73,000
1970	437,000	202,000	236,000
1980	718,000	292,000	426,000
1985	755,000	355,000	400,000
1987	855,000	390,000	464,000
1988	785,000	303,000	482,000
PERCENTAGE OF HIGH SCHOOL GRADUATES ENROLLED IN COLLEGE			
1960	18.7	21.1	16.9
1970	26.7	29.5	24.7
1980	46.2	44.4	47.5
1985	43.8	43.5	43.9
1987	48.7	48.3	48.9
1988	46.6	42.8	49.6

SOURCE: U.S. Bureau of the Census, *Statistical Abstract of the U.S., 1990.*

women who go on to college has diverged sharply in recent years. The percentage of black male high school graduates going on to college exceeded that of women in 1960 and 1970. By 1980, however, women had overtaken men and they have never lost the lead.

Overall, however, there have been impressive increases in the number of blacks attending college. They continued to spread out across a wide range of disciplines. Departing from their traditional and almost exclusive concentration in education and the social sciences, beginning in the 1970s blacks increased their share of degree holders in eleven of the twenty-four established disciplines. This increase occurred in fields such as public affairs and services, psychology, communications, interdisciplinary studies, health professions, biological sciences, fine and applied arts, physical sciences, engineering, architecture and environmental design, agriculture and natural resources. And by 1981 business and management was the most popular discipline of all black bachelor's degree recipients, replacing education and the social sciences. This means that in that year alone some 13,325 blacks earned

TABLE 8.6
Enrollment in Historically Black Colleges
and Universities by Race/Ethnicity
Fall 1976–Fall 1987

Race/ Ethnicity	1976	1980	1982	1984	1986	1987	Percentage Increase 1976–1987
Number of HBCUs	105	102	100	104	100		
Total	212,120	222,220	216,570	216,050	213,093	217,367	2.5
Black, non-Hispanic	185,820	185,780	177,000	175,110	176,596	182,019	−2.0
White, non-Hispanic	18,390	21,480	23,040	23,450	22,651	23,255	26.3
Asian	610	1,340	1,050	1,350	1,237	1,187	94.6
Hispanic	460	1,030	1,070	1,560	1,485	1,588	245.2
American Indian	180	400	570	240	552	519	187.2
Nonresident alien	6,660	12,200	13,840	14,340	10,572	8,829	32.6

NOTE: Details may not add to total because of rounding.

SOURCE: Susan T. Hill, *The Traditionally Black Institutions of Higher Education, 1860 to 1982.* (Washington, D.C.: Government Printing Office, 1984.) National Association for Equal Opportunity Research Institute, staff analysis of the U.S. Department of Education, Office of Civil Rights unpublished data, Fall 1984, 1986, and 1987.

bachelor's degrees in business and management; nearly 40 percent of which were earned in historically black colleges.[6]

The vitality of the historically black colleges is such that they continue to produce a disproportionate share of black college graduates for the nation's economy. Accounting for less than 5 percent of the more than 3,000 American institutions of higher education, black colleges continued to produce some 37 percent of all bachelor's degrees and 30 percent of all master's degrees awarded during the decade of the 1980s.[7] (Table 8.6)

New Ideas

The value African-Americans place on education has always been extraordinarily high. There is a deep historical and cultural belief in the efficacy of education. Blacks have sought education in every conceivable manner and at every level. Two overreaching strategies have been operative and both have been successful. They have built their own institutions in part because they were shut out of the mainstream institutions and in part because they value the ownership, control, and protection of their cultural heritage which these institutions provide. That they have been overwhelmingly successful speaks eloquently of faith, commitment, hard work, and endurance. But even while pursuing their own institutions, African-Americans have seen the necessity, the justice, and the possibilities of confronting the white institutions at every level demanding acceptance.

The evidence of blacks' successfully confronting the educational system and excelling emerges in almost every chapter of this book. When the opportunities in the educational system were opened up briefly during the 1960s and early 1970s blacks again demonstrated their capacity to take advantage of them, which is why blacks nearly closed the gap with their more privileged white high school graduates during that period. And more specifically, it is why the proportion of black high school graduates going on to college rose dramatically from around 19 percent in 1960 to nearly 50 percent by 1987 before declining slightly afterward. What this means in sheer numbers is that the enrollment of blacks in all types of colleges increased more than five-fold from 141,000 in 1960 to 785,000 in 1987.

Because of this record of achievement, there should be no mystery about how to enhance the level of black education and the contributions an educated citizenry can make to society. Opportunity structures already available include affirmative action programs to insure equal treatment, and financial aid packages as generous as the GI Bill of Rights and the Great Society could provide. The will, the talent, and the inclination are all still intact. What is needed is true educational reform. The civil rights movement pointed the way.

The lesson of the successful civil rights movement is that it could not have been conceived, designed, or led by persons outside the African-American experience; it had to be done from the inside. It is equally clear, however, that once it was initiated, and the lines of development were set forth in black communities all over the nation, it could not have been successfully executed without the massive support of persons, institutions, policies, and resources far beyond the immediate reach of the African-American people. The same is true with respect to the continuing struggle for educational equality. And if education is the sine qua non for black achievement, an educated black citizenry is equally indispensable to an orderly, equitable, and achieving America.

In many of the urban school systems, large numbers of the students are black. So too are an appreciable number of teachers, principals, superintendents, and school board members. It would be a tragedy for this collective black educational community to sit back and wait for someone in Washington, or in the larger society generally, to devise solutions for the education of urban school children—including book publishers and scholars. It is not likely to happen or to be relevant or effective.

One of the remarkable features of the spate of educational reform reports issued in the 1980s is that almost none of them came out of the African-American community or experience. As Jonathan Kozol pointed out in his book *Savage Inequalities*[8] almost none of them came to grips with the explosive issues of racism and economic deprivation in urban America. The need for black initiatives is paramount.

New ideas such as teaching African-American history and culture to all students, or teaching black boys in a specialized setting, or putting the greatest talents and resources into the schools where the need is greatest, or bringing parents into true partnership with the school-based professionals, which James Comer has found so successful in New Haven and elsewhere, will almost always face the kind of massive societal resistance that befell the community schools movement in the 1960s.[9] Not all the opposition to these initiatives will come from outside the African-American community. Nor is uniformity required. What is required is action based on sound principles of learning and teaching which have grown out of the African-American experience.

Quite apart from issues of social justice, educated people live healthier lives, they earn more, stay married longer, pay more taxes, and give more leadership to their communities than uneducated ones. Separate from the issue of social justice, education is not only the lifeblood of the African-American achievement but is equally valuable to others and is perhaps indispensable to an orderly, equitable, and achieving American society.

Chapter 9

The Influence of the Military

When Army General Colin Powell became Chairman of the Joint Chiefs of Staff of all the U.S. Armed Forces in 1989, he reached a level of responsibility no black man had ever achieved before. His appointment by the President and confirmation by the Senate marked a triumph for General Powell, his wife and family, and both their parents.

Beyond this personal victory, however, was an institutional triumph. The military system, opened to Colin Powell when few others were, paved his way to the top echelons of national and international power. His accomplishment illustrates dramatically the impact of the military on African-American families. Indeed, of all the twelve major systems of the larger society we identified in Chapter 2 which affect African-American families, it would be difficult to find one with more impact than the military, an impact which is both positive and negative with consequences that are both obvious and more subtle.

At the outset, it may be said that the military provides enormous benefits to large numbers of African-American families. One scholar has found that "Blacks occupy more management positions in the military than they do in business, education, journalism, government, or any other significant sector of American society."[1] How did this come about? It was among the unintended consequences of World War II and changes in the political system driven, in part, by the civil rights movement. After the end of the war, a number of policy initiatives by the federal government intensified the impact of the military on African-American families. First was the abolition of segregation in the armed forces. President Harry S. Truman issued an executive order abolishing segregation in the armed forces in the midst of the 1948 presidential campaign when he was locked in a close and, most observers agreed, losing race for President against Republican Governor Thomas E. Dewey of New York, Progressive Party candidate and former Vice President Henry A. Wallace of Iowa, and States Rights candidate Senator Strom Thurmond of South Carolina. Despite the liberal record of Thomas Dewey and the lingering allegiance to the Republican party among African-Americans at that time and despite the progressive agenda of Henry Wallace and the strong support he received from Paul Robeson, a cultural hero, black voters followed their leadership and were strongly supportive of Truman. He showed his appreciation by appointing the first United States Commission on Civil Rights and by accepting its strong recommendation for the abolition of segregation in the armed forces. He signed Executive Order 9981 on July 26, 1948, four months before the election. Truman won the election narrowly with strong support from the black community. The civil rights forces were in this instance able to have their demands met by a sitting President *before* the election rather than by waiting until after the election. Truman made a number of black appointments, but among his strongest contributions to black advancement was the fact that he enforced the executive order conscientiously, and so within six years segregation had virtually been eliminated in the armed forces, thus removing a long-standing grievance on the part of black leaders, organizations, and service personnel.[2] That is the single most important reason that blacks today have a broader range of acceptance, appreciation, opportunity, and utilization in the armed forces than in any civilian sector of American society.

A second policy initiative which affected African-American families was legislation in 1972, signed by President Nixon, abolishing the military draft and creating an all-volunteer armed services. This had the unanticipated effect of increasing the enlistment of black youths, a trend which has accelerated sharply since that time. There are two broad reasons black youths have been highly attracted to the military. First, they have perceived a measure of opportunity and a sense of being wanted and appreciated in a high-status system of society in which they can achieve success. Second, however, they have experienced increasingly since the 1960s severely restricted job opportunities in all the civilian sectors of society, due in large part to the dislocations caused by technological change.

A third public policy, initiated in the 1970s, was the decision to encourage the enlistment of women in the armed services in numbers and branches much broader than before. This also increased the enlistment of black youth. While it is generally known that black men are overrepresented in the armed services, it is not as well known that black women are overrepresented to an even greater extent. The same dynamics which pull black men into the military also work for black women.

Additionally, the increased and rapid utilization of new technologies in both procedures and equipment in the military has had the effect of increasing the educational level of enlistees and has helped to shape the character of the black personnel in the military. Black enlistees are more likely to be high school graduates than whites.

All of these postwar conditions have had the combined effect of increasing both the numbers and the upward mobility of African-Americans in the military. This, in turn, has had a disruptive effect on African-American families by separating large numbers of the most able youth from their families. At the same time it has helped to provide a strengthening feature to these families by creating meaningful, high-status employment with educational and career inducements, which have enabled these military personnel to do well both in the service and in civilian life afterward and thus provide for stability and upward mobility beneficial to African-American family life.

Personal Experience

The experience of my own family illustrates in parallel and divergent ways the impact of the military on African-American families. Toward the end of World War II, when my brother was nineteen and a half and I was eighteen, we were drafted within a few months of each other after completing the tenth grade in high school. We were behind a grade in school not because we were not bright and eager to learn but because of an early childhood in a rural community not supported by an elementary school for blacks. Our being drafted was a personal and family tragedy. After getting off to a slow start, we were both on our way to becoming the first members of our family to graduate from high school. The military seemed to snuff out that dream. The draft also took us away from our families for the first time, away from each other, and away from church, school, and friends. But nothing could compare with the agony of my mother at the prospect of losing both her sons at the same time to the military and the unknown.

Beyond the effect on the family there was a community impact as well. While dozens of young men had gone off to war from our neighborhood, the end of the war now seemed near and everybody felt that the military did not need two more young men. Some people were kind enough to say that our going left a particular void in the neighborhood. We had been good students in school, active participants in the St. James Baptist Church, the Boy Scouts, the Civilian Defense Corps, and a myriad of other uplifting activities, while holding down part-time jobs as dish washers in a local Birmingham department store restaurant. Still our numbers were up. Our time had come. To tell the truth I was eager to go. My brother having preceded me by a few months left a void in my life. And quite apart from my sense of patriotic duty, I did not like the idea of being left behind by my brother. And paradoxically, even as there was grieving all around, there was also a certain pride in our going off to serve our country.

In addition to these dislocations there were tangible benefits that the military system brought to our family. Because of the buildup in the war industries in the industrial city of Birmingham, my father was able to get a good job. This job enabled him to support his family, his church, his lodge, pay his union dues, buy newspapers, magazines, a radio, and other accoutrements of a better life.

In addition, by going off to war, my brother and I brought honor to the family and the community, even as we expanded our own self-concepts and sense of contribution to the world. When we came home on furlough, which we once did at the same time, we were the pride of the neighborhood. Our parents paraded us around in our freshly starched uniforms to relatives, friends, and organizations. We served as guest teachers in the Sunday School, sang in the choir, gave lectures on international affairs, and generally enjoyed our celebrity status. We were often told that we were a credit to our race and to our country—never mind that both of us were assigned to menial service units in a segregated army consisting of black troops and white officers. We were doing our bit in the nation's struggle against tyranny abroad, and both President Roosevelt and Joe Louis had assured us that we were going to win because we were on God's side. And everyone knew that our service would make things better for our people after the war.

An even more tangible reward of our military service was that my brother and I were able to send home a regular allotment from our steady if low pay which provided our mother the only savings she would ever know. In addition, our war savings bond and life insurance provided our first investments in the larger society.

Perhaps more important than all the rest, our military service took us around the world. Before the war, we had never gone more than a hundred miles beyond our birthplace in Marion, Alabama. During military service, we both served in France, Germany, the Philippines, and Korea. We were both on the same troop ship steaming toward Japan when the atomic bombs were dropped first on Hiroshima and then Nagasaki, effectively ending the war and sparing our lives while destroying millions of other innocent people. We learned something of the languages and cultures of a dozen different nations in Europe and the Pacific. We fraternized with males and females, friends and enemies, and generally expanded our own intellectual horizons. As a consequence our personal and social aspirations soared.

In addition to all this the military provided for my brother a meaningful career unmatched by what he could have achieved at that time in civilian life. Always bright, assertive, inquiring, disciplined, and highly motivated to achieve, he converted his tenth-grade education into a high school equivalency in the service, reenlisted as a career soldier, and then moved steadily up through the ranks to become the highest-ranking noncommissioned officer. As first sergeant he led large companies of men; and after 1948 these were interracial companies. After twenty years, he was able to retire at the youthful age of forty-nine with a modest pension to supplement his job as a middle-level manager in the wholesale food industry. He could, with a Veterans Administration loan, provide a home for his family and for a time medical care as well. All of which enabled him to support his large family of wife and seven children and to help support his twelve grandchildren as well. Little wonder that three of his children would be drawn to the military service while two others would be attracted to opportunities offered by higher education.

Finally, in a radically different way, the military would also make my own career possible. Unlike my brother, I could hardly wait to get out of the army after my two-year hitch and the war were both over. But during these two years my aspirations had soared. At the urging of the one man in my outfit who had ever attended college, I decided that was for me. It seemed a good way to avoid physical labor, to advance in the world and to serve others. So I returned to Birmingham, completed eleventh grade, and passed the high school equivalency exam. Then, with the GI Bill, I entered Hampton University in Virginia and later Grinnell College in Iowa becoming the first college graduate in my family. Later still I would become a social worker, a sociologist, a university professor, author, university president, and university department chair. Thus thanks to the head start I received in the military, I was able to support my small nuclear family of wife and two daughters as well as to send both girls to college.

THE MILITARY EXPERIENCE FOR AFRICAN-AMERICANS

But quite apart from its impact on this particular family the military experience brought positive contributions to black families generally. World War II was in many ways a turning point in race relations and in black progress. Because of the war and the technological revolution it hastened, there were major shifts in the occupational structure of the African-American community. According to the U.S. Census, in 1940, 70 percent of black workers were in farming or employed as domestic and unskilled labor. By 1954, this had declined to 50 percent with a concomitant expansion in the skilled and semiskilled blue-collar occupations. Meanwhile, during the war years, more than 300,000 blacks had migrated from the South to the North and West where opportunities were greater in almost every field of endeavor. Still, black leaders in the South were alert to the potential of progress in that region after the war. Meeting in October 1944, a black leadership conference in Durham, North Carolina, tried to anticipate this transition. They declared in part:

We have the courage and faith to believe that it is possible to evolve
in the South a way of life, consistent with the principles for which
we as a nation are fighting throughout the world, that will free us
all, white and Negro alike, from want, and from throttling fears.[3]

The aftermath of World War II was certainly more favorable
for black people than the previous wars. Indeed by 1948, unemployment in the black community was at a low of 5.2 percent—
only moderately higher than the white unemployment rate of 3.8
percent. After a decade of prosperity, however, the situation
would change sharply. After 1955, the unemployment rate among
blacks would soar to over twice the unemployment rate for whites,
and not fall below that ratio even to the present time. And it is this
high unemployment that has had such a deleterious effect on
black men and on the stability of black families.

Positive Functions of the Military

It can be plainly seen from the above that the military has had a
positive effect on African-American families. Daniel Moynihan
was among the first sociologists to recognize the positive functions
the military system held out for these families. One of the many
controversial features of his controversial study *The Negro Family:
The Case for National Action* was his section on military service.

Indeed, one of the very few recommendations Moynihan made
for improving the lot of the African-American family was to encourage more black men to join the armed services.[4] He cited
three major reasons for such a recommendation. First was upward mobility. He quoted the 1963 Civil Rights Commission report which observed that "Negro enlisted men enjoy relatively
better opportunities in the Armed Forces than in the civilian economy in every clerical, technical, and skilled field for which the
data permit comparison."

Second, Moynihan cited the egalitarian aspect. "There is, however," he concluded, "an even more important issue involved in
military service for Negroes. Service in the United States Armed
Forces is the *only* experience open to the Negro American in
which he is truly treated as an equal. . . . In food, dress, housing,
pay, work—the Negro in the Armed Forces *is* equal and is treated
that way."

Finally, Moynihan pointed to the masculinity feature of the
armed services. "There is another special quality about the mili-

tary service for Negro men: it is an utterly masculine world. Given the strains of the disorganized and matrifocal family life in which so many Negro youth come of age, the Armed Forces are a dramatic and desperately needed change: a world away from women, a world run by strong men of unquestioned authority, where discipline, if harsh, is nonetheless orderly and predictable, and where rewards, if limited, are granted on the basis of performance." He concluded this point with a favorable quote from the army recruitment brochure. "In the U.S. Army you get to know what it means to feel like a man." A hundred years earlier Du Bois had observed a similar parallel between military service and black manhood.

My first reaction on reading those passages in 1965 was to observe that Moynihan had not been in the same army in which I had served. His exuberance and eloquence seemed to go far beyond the merits of the case. Neither the upward mobility nor the egalitarianism were as unfettered as he purported. Still, it must be observed that if one can weave one's way through the saber rattling, chauvinism, paternalism, sexism, nationalism, and all the rest in Moynihan's treatise, there is a kernel or two of truth in his assessment of the positive functions of the armed services for low-income African-American families. It has been true for a long time that the military system provides upward mobility for large numbers of black men and now increasingly black women as well. Moreover, it provides opportunities for racial integration, for world travel, and opportunity to participate in a highly valued aspect of American life. Thus black parents are able to point with pride and promise to careers in the military as they socialize their children. At the time Moynihan wrote in 1965, however, blacks were grossly underrepresented in the military, supposedly because they could not pass the entrance tests. Now that blacks are overrepresented in the military, another sociologist has provided a contemporary assessment of the positive functions of the military for African-American families.

Charles C. Moskos, a military sociologist, has characterized the role of blacks in the military as a modern success story not generally appreciated by other sociologists, black leadership, or the public at large.[5] Moskos observed that the roughly 400,000 blacks who served in the military in 1985 constituted nearly 30 percent of the 2.1 million person armed services. A fairly high proportion of these are noncommissioned officers, though relatively few are commissioned officers. Moreover, they are fairly widely dispersed throughout almost all aspects of military life. "Blacks occupy more management positions in the military than they do in business, education, journalism, government, or any other significant sector of American society. The armed forces still have racial problems," he observed, "but these are minimal compared with the problems that exist in other institutions, public and private."[6] Specifically, Moskos pointed out that by 1985 blacks constituted 30 percent of the enlisted ranks of the army, 20 percent of those in the marines, 17 percent of the air force, and 13 percent of the navy. In the army, the largest branch of the service, blacks have the greatest opportunity for upward mobility. Ten percent of commissioned officers and one-third of noncommissioned officers were black in 1985.

Reasons for Success

There are several factors which account for the success of blacks in the military. We have already referred above to the major federal policies, initiated by President Harry Truman in 1948, abolishing segregation in the armed services plus the abolition of the draft in 1972 and reliance on an all-volunteer armed service. Still another reason for success, given the public policy resolve, is that unlike the public schools, universities, and much of civilian life where desegregation has been so slow and halting, the military is a closed system. It is also the essence of hierarchical authority. Thus when the President as Commander in Chief issues an order, it will be obeyed. Authorities all along the chain of command are sworn to obey such commands. By contrast, blacks lost ground in upward mobility in the public schools after the Supreme Court decision outlawing segregation in 1954 (this is among the grossest examples of unintended consequences of reform legislation).

More important still, the armed forces have become attractive job and career options for hundreds of thousands of young African-American high school graduates because of the dismal employment prospects for them since the early 1970s. Were it not for the military, many of these young men would be unemployed. Large numbers would hang out on street corners, get into trouble, and end up in that other major system which houses so many young black men, the criminal justice system. Even now, for those who are not able to finish high school or complete a high school equivalency program, the military is not an option and the streets are the major alternative. Unemployment among black youths in many cities approaches 50 percent. Many young men who turned eighteen in mid-1975 and left school have never been employed. Under present conditions, amid the transition from an industrial to an information society, their chances of employment are dismal indeed. All of which supports the need for an alternative, civilian, moral equivalent to the military for hundreds of thousands of black youths who now do not have a viable option.

Moreover, the military has become an attractive career in its own right. When a young black high school graduate can enter the army with an annual salary of $7,668 plus room, board, medical care, pension, and other benefits which may include a reenlistment bonus as high as $8,000, it becomes an attractive alternative to unemployment in civilian life. A study by the Brookings Institution published in 1982 indicated that 42 percent of eligible black youths enter the military as compared with 14 percent of white eligibles.[7] Blacks are also more likely to reenlist than whites, less likely to be discharged prematurely for "undisciplined behavior, lack of aptitude, psychological problems, or the like" than white soldiers.

What is not generally appreciated is that when blacks do return from the military, they do so at relatively young ages, in relatively favorable economic circumstances, with well-developed skills, and thus add to the black community a stable, self-sufficient element in the growing black middle class. Some 5,000 such men and women are expected to retire from the military each year for the next decade.

As will be discussed below, African-Americans are substantially underrepresented in the officer ranks and in the military hierarchy. Even here, however, there is important symbolic black representation and role models. Congressman Ron Dellums, who serves as chairman of the powerful Subcommittee on Military Installations of the House Armed Services Committee, has indicated that the support, cooperation, and deference he receives both from his colleagues on the committee and from members of the military establishment is surprising and gratifying. An ex-marine who rose to power by his participation in the peace movement, as chair of that important subcommittee he is in a position not only to serve as an important role model for young blacks in and out of the military but to produce substantial policy and material benefits for them as well. Not incidentally, the city of Oakland has benefited enormously from military installations, contracts, and other economic developments, because of his influence as their representative.

Two blacks have served in recent years in Cabinet level military affairs positions. Under President Carter, Clifford Alexander, a Washington attorney, served as Secretary of the Army. He has spoken of the important contribution he was able to make to race relations and black pride, quite apart from doing his job well.

Even in the Reagan administration, which did not have a good record of black appointments, two blacks served as Assistant Secretaries of the Army, out of five. These are Delbert R. Spurlock, Assistant Secretary for Manpower, and John L. Shannon, Assistant Secretary for Installations and Logistics. Then in the final year of the Reagan administration, after the Iran-contra scandal drove two other chairmen of the National Security Council from office, a black officer, Lt. General Colin Powell, was elevated to Chairman of the National Security Council. Later Powell would be promoted to four-star general and be named Chairman of the Joint Chiefs of Staff by President Bush.

The strongest black military leadership, however, is represented in the uniformed services. As of 1985, there were thirty-one black army generals on active duty, about 7 percent of the total number. Another six black generals were in the Army Reserves or the National Guard. Altogether some one hundred have received flag rank in the United States military, all but four of whom were still alive in 1988. Two of these have been four-star generals. One is legendary Air Force General "Chappie" James, for whom a School of Aerospace Sciences has been named at Tuskegee University, where he trained as a pilot in World War II. The other is Army General Roscoe Robinson, Jr. Altogether eight including two women have attained the three-star rank.

In addition to all the above factors, however, there is still another which helps to account for the success of African-Americans in the military. Again, unlike universities and other civilian institutions, the armed services have taken seriously the need to prepare their staffs for racial integration. Basic instruction in race relations and black history have become required for all military personnel. The regular efficiency reports, a type of performance evaluation of all military personnel, includes race relations skills. This mandatory requirement is rigidly enforced. Black senior officer Brigadier General Charles Hines, who holds a doctorate in sociology, has reported that these efficiency evaluations are done systematically and fairly across racial lines.[8]

A final observation on the plus side, as reported by a team of sociologists headed by Professor John Sibley Butler at the University of Texas, is that black retirees from the military earn significantly more than black individuals who have not entered the military. They found that contrary to the pattern where white veterans earn less than white nonveterans, the earnings level for both blacks and Hispanic veterans are higher than for minority nonveterans.[9] They conclude that the military offers minorities from disadvantaged backgrounds a "bridging environment" which helps prepare them for later civilian careers. Professor John Butler has estimated that at least 25 percent of all black middle-class families owe their status directly or indirectly to the military.[10]

Disadvantages of the Military

All the above advantages of the military for African-American family development are real. Yet it would be a mistake to overlook the equally serious downside to the military system. As we have argued throughout this book all complex social systems are likely to have both positive and negative potentials. Social scientists refer to this duality as "functional and dysfunctional" consequences. Some aspects of the system help to enhance the development of the people it touches while other aspects of the system hurt that development. So it is with the military.

In order to avoid the danger of portraying the military in rosy and romantic terms as Moynihan did in 1965, it is important to note the disadvantages of military service. The training of young men and women to take innocent lives and the potential for losing their own lives stand at the head of a long line of evils. An overarching problem with the military system is that it takes scarce economic and technical resources and resourcefulness out of the civilian sector of society and expends them on forces of destruction. These two aspects of the military—that it is immoral and wasteful of human development—and that the death rates were discriminatory against blacks and poor youth, were the bases of Dr. Martin Luther King, Jr.'s attack on the Vietnam War, an attack which infuriated President Lyndon Johnson. Studies have shown that Dr. King was substantially on target. At the time he made his famous anti–Vietnam War speech in Riverside Church in New York in 1967, one year before his assassination, some 13 percent of all battle deaths in Vietnam were black youth. During the two previous years the totals were even higher, amounting to over 16 percent. After 1968, however, both the numbers and percentage of black deaths in Vietnam would decline dramatically to 10.8 percent and in succeeding years progressively to 7 percent by 1972 and less than 1 percent in 1973, the final year of the war.[11]

The major reason for the excess black casualties is that blacks were assigned disproportionately to the two types of units most likely to suffer casualties, namely infantry and artillery.

In addition, the constraints and irritants of military life are legend. Harley Browning has correctly pointed out that despite all the apparent benefits to minorities, "Most veterans, whatever their ethnic status, do not have fond memories of their service experience. They are prone to recall the various constraints and irritants of military life, and even though they may have been provided with skills for surviving in bureaucratic environments, they are scarcely made happier with bureaucracies thereby, whether military or civilian."[12]

Perhaps the most pervasive dysfunctional aspect of the military for African-Americans is racial discrimination, more perhaps of the institutional variety than the personal. But as we know from the experience of servicemen in Vietnam, personal racial animosities do not vanish overnight when men and women put on uniforms. In his book *Bloods,* a study of black Vietnam veterans, Wallace Terry has drawn a graphic picture of racism in uniform.[13] Moreover, John Butler has pointed out that a time lag exists in promotions for blacks as compared with whites.[14]

A number of studies have shown that blacks in the military are not equally distributed across the enlisted ranks. There has been a tendency, however, to explain this obvious inequality on the basis of attributes such as performance on standardized tests and level of education and experience. Butler found, however, that when blacks and whites have the same test scores and level of education and experience, it takes blacks longer to move through the ranks than whites. He concludes, "One is then unavoidably led by the data in this paper to conclude that the black enlisted man in the U.S. Army is subject to inequality which is not the result of failure to meet universalistic criteria (i.e., indirect impersonal institutions), but rather a result of the direct racist actions of real-life people."[15] In support of Butler's findings, data from the Census Bureau show that blacks who enlisted in the army in recent years have higher educational levels than whites. Indeed in 1975, when it was still possible to enlist in the army without a high school diploma, while 35 percent of white enlistees had less than a high school education this was true of only 26 percent of blacks. And while only 5 percent of white enlistees had college education, 9 percent of black enlistees were college-trained.

There is also still some racial imbalance in occupational assignments. Data compiled by the military show that black enlisted men are substantially overrepresented in the relatively low-level occupational categories such as infantry, gun crews, and seamanship specialties, as well as in support service and supply units. They are substantially underrepresented in such important specialties as electrical and mechanical equipment repairmen and other technical specialties. All these areas have much more civilian transferability after service than the areas where blacks are overrepresented.[16]

Shortage of Black Officers

Still another problem with the military is the relative shortage of African-American officers. The black enlisted ranks have expanded enormously since Daniel P. Moynihan made his recommendation to that effect in 1965. It has not, however, been accompanied by an equal expansion in the black officer corps. The upward-mobility pattern diverges somewhat for black men and black women and varies substantially among the different branches of the uniformed services.

It is perhaps worth noting that in 1965 when Moynihan recommended increased induction of black men into the armed services, the number of blacks stood at about 200,000. He specifically advocated increasing that by another hundred thousand in order to reduce black unemployment and move unemployed blacks off the streets.[17] By 1967, there were 303,000 blacks in the armed services. Those who suggest that Moynihan's 1965 recommendations were ignored might reflect on this, the only specific recommendation he made, which seems, indeed, to have been followed. These numbers fell to 279,000 in 1970 during the Vietnam War and rose again in 1975 to 302,000.[18]

Black Women in the Armed Services

Black women in the armed services are even more overrepre-sented than black men (Table 9.1). Black enlisted women in-creased from 16.9 percent of all female enlistees in 1974 to nearly 30 percent in 1984.

As with men, the greatest growth and representation has been in the army. Black women constituted 20.7 percent of women in the army in 1974 and had reached 42 percent by 1984. Over the same period black women in the air force increased from 16.6 percent of all women in that service to 21.3 percent; while in the navy they rose from 9.6 percent to 18.9 percent.[19]

Between 1971 and 1981 black women officers increased from 3.3 percent of all women officers in the military to 10.7 percent (Table 9.2). Over the same decade black male officers went from 2.9 percent of all male officers to only 4.9 percent. Both genders were underrepresented. In 1981, for example, black males con-stituted 21.6 percent of all enlisted men but only 4.9 percent of all male officers. Black women accounted for 27.7 percent of enlisted women but only 10.7 percent of female officers. These data pro-vide further evidence of the "glass ceiling" in the military which, while more permeable than those in civilian institutions, is never-theless a fact of life for African-American service personnel.

Blacks fare substantially better in the army and substantially

TABLE 9.1
African-American Women in the Military as Percentage of All Enlisted Women
1974–1984

		1974		1979		1984	
		N	(%)	N	(%)	N	(%)
Army	All women	26,320		54,815		66,664	
	Black women	5,455	20.7	18,916	34.5	28,019	42.0
Navy	All women	13,143		24,751		41,579	
	Black women	1,261	9.6	3,190	12.9	7,862	18.9
Marines	All women	2,402		5,501		8,577	
	Black women	411	17.1	1,171	21.3	2,108	24.6
Air	All women	19,463		45,954		55,339	
Force	Black women	3,236	16.6	7,990	17.4	11,775	21.3
Total	**All women**	**61,328**		**131,021**		**172,159**	
	Black women	**10,363**	**16.9**	**31,266**	**23.9**	**49,764**	**28.9**

SOURCE: James R. Daugherty, "Black Women in the Military," *Focus* 13 (July 1985), Wash-ington, D.C.: Joint Center for Political and Economic Studies.

TABLE 9.2
African-Americans as a Percentage of All Enlisted Personnel and
Officers in the Military
1971–1981

	1971		1981	
Status and Gender	*N*	*(%)*	*N*	*(%)*
ENLISTED PERSONNEL				
Males	262,295	11.4	352,348	21.6
Females	4,236	14.4	45,056	27.7
OFFICERS				
Males	7,103	2.9	12,017	4.9
Females	423	3.3	2,552	10.7

SOURCE: D.R. Butler, "Equal Opportunity Policy and Practice," *Focus*, 10 (8) (August 1988), (Washington, D.C.: Joint Center for Political and Economic Studies).

worse in the navy, with those in the air force and the marines occupying a type of middle ground (Table 9.3). For example, in the army where the greatest representation of blacks occurs, they constituted 7.8 percent of the officer corps as compared with only 2.7 percent in the navy in 1981.

What further sets the military apart from many civilian institutions is that the military seems to be aware of its limitations on equality of opportunity, willing to face them honestly, and is genuinely committed to further improvements. James Blackwell has noted that in the leadership structure of all the military services, there has been distinctive improvement in recent years. Moreover, he believes that the military has the potential of having a positive impact on civilian society by showing that further improvements can be made in the realm of equal opportunity.[20] In

TABLE 9.3
Distribution of African-Americans in the Military
1981

	Enlisted Personnel *(%)*	*Officers* *(%)*
Army	33.2	7.8
Navy	12.0	2.7
Marines	22.0	4.0
Air Force	16.5	4.8

SOURCE: Alvin Schneider, "Blacks in the Armed Services," *Focus* 10 (8) (August 1982) (Washington, D.C.: Joint Center for Political and Economic Studies).

the same vein Colonel D. R. Butler, speaking at a forum on blacks in the military sponsored by the Joint Center for Political and Economic Studies in 1982, pointed to the important role black colleges have played in providing military officers. A member of the Department of Defense Equal Opportunity office staff, Colonel Butler expressed for the department the view that the military was truly open and welcoming to black personnel in all branches and at all ranks and was committed to the necessary policies and practices to assure further equality. Moreover, the department is committed, he observed, to increasing the number of black officers, retaining black officers, and creating more equitable distribution of blacks among the various military specialties.

What is also clear is that the African-American community, its leadership, its families, and individuals have a strong receptivity to the armed forces. They are extraordinarily responsive to the national needs as reflected by the call to military service. They are also responsive to the opportunities opened to them in military service, particularly since the desegregation of the armed services. Moreover, the history of blacks in the military suggests that it is indeed responsive to civilian pressure and even civilian policy recommendations. This was reflected in the desegregation of the armed services and in the increase in black enlisted personnel. All of this gives to the African-American community and leadership substantial potential for influencing the direction of the military. It would be unrealistic to expect the military to move much further toward reform on its own.

What Needs to Be Done

A number of concerns emerge from this analysis. One is that the impending demobilization and downsizing of the military services, budget, and installations in the aftermath of the cold war and the Gulf War be accomplished without an unfair share of the burden being placed on African-Americans. Another is that the obstacles to racial equality that still remain in all aspects of the military be vigorously attacked. Still another is the savings from the downsizing of the military—the so called peace dividend—be invested in the civilian economy to enhance the economic vitality of the cities.

The military experience suggests that there are ways and means of developing a comparable civilian service system—just as attractive and glamorous, just as filled with danger, discipline, status, and value as the military system—so that young adults have an alternative to enlisting in the military. The Job Corps, a partnership between government and industry, has already demonstrated the potential for preparing low-income young men and women for jobs, educational advancement, and life skills. It is one of many programs of the 1960s cut back in the 1980s that nevertheless produced positive results. Think of Head Start, Medicare, Pell Grants for Education, and the several women's, infants', and children's programs.

Planning for transition should not be left to the military alone, as now seems to be the case. There is a role for every sector concerned about black families. As Ronald Walters of Howard University has written, presidents and Congresses are reluctant to lead true reform efforts on their own initiative without sustained, well-organized public demand.

PART IV

Family Structure Is Adaptive

Chapter 10

The Functions of Marriage in African-American Families

What is the status, the dynamics, and the future of marriage in the African-American community?

A comprehensive review of research on African-American families during the 1980s shows that relatively little attention has been paid to marriage or married-couple families in this population. Much more focus has been on single-parent families. At the same time even when studies do include reference to married-couple families such studies are not well publicized and are consequently overlooked by scholars and the general public as well. This is due in part to the fact that a resilient and adaptive approach to assessing African-American families has not yet overtaken the pathological approach, which focuses heavily and often invidiously on single-parent families and teen pregnancies. Overlooked are the positive functions served by marriage. Overlooked also are patterns of diversity within and among these families.

What comes through strikingly in a careful review of this decade of studies is that among African-American families a higher level of egalitarian relations exists than among families in the nation as a whole. For men, women, and children in these families, tasks and roles are interchangeable in ways that often vary from the traditional. They do each other's work, often cooperating in patterns of collaboration not generally appreciated outside the black community. Another characteristic of black married-couple families is the prominence of women in the provider role. They make a much greater contribution to the economic viability of the family than do women in the nation as a whole. Their role is highly accepted and supported by black men. Moreover, among working couples black men provide much greater help to their wives with housework and child care than white husbands do. Even so the women bear the lion's share of housework and are more likely than men to feel overworked by these tasks.[1]

A detailed study covering this period by Robert Hill and his associates found that married-couple families are still a strong feature of African-American family life, that above the poverty level they constitute a majority of family structures, and that they are much better able to resist the negative pressures of society and take advantage of its opportunities than other types of family structure.[2]

Five generalizations will help to put the black married-couple family in perspective.

First, the African-American community is characterized by a large, growing, and diverse population. According to the U.S. Census, the black population, growing faster than the larger national population, increased from 27.2 million in 1983 to 30.3 million by 1988 and 30.4 million in 1990.[3] Moreover, this population is now represented in all the regions of the nation. A majority still live in the South despite the massive migration out of that region since the Civil War; a majority which has been on the rise since the net reverse migration back to the South since the middle 1970s. This expanding black population also now occupies all the social-class strata in society.

Second, the vast majority of these over 30 million persons live in organized households or living quarters where they cooperate in the sharing of resources and the use of common facilities. The number of black households is also expanding, rising from 8.9 million households in 1983 to 10.2 million in 1988 and to 10.5 million in 1990.

Third, while some of these households are occupied by single persons or unrelated groups, the vast majority are occupied by families, which the U.S. Census defines as persons living in the same residence who are related to each other by marriage, blood, or adoption. The number of black families rose from 6.5 million in 1983 to 7.2 million in 1988 and held steady at 7.2 million in 1990. By 1990 70 percent of all black households were family households, meaning that the vast majority of African-Americans lived in families. This is the same proportion as white households that are family households. And while this is a smaller percentage than in previous years, this 70 percent of black family households can hardly be used to sustain the "vanishing black family" thesis.

Fourth, the majority of these family households are married-couple families. The total number of black married couples has continued to increase over recent years, even as other types of family structures have increased even faster. In 1983 there was a total of 3.5 million black married-couple families in the nation. By 1988 this had risen to 3.7 million and to 3.8 million by 1990.

Finally, married couples come in two types: those with children (simple nuclear families) and those without children (incipient nuclear families). U.S. Census data show that of the 3.8 million black married-couple families in 1990 a total of 2.0 million had children of their own under eighteen while 1.8 million did not. Thus a slight majority, or 52 percent, of all married-couple families had young children of their own. These data support the following scenario. A majority of African-Americans live in households; a majority of these are family households; a majority of family households are married-couple households; and a majority of married couples have young children of their own. This in turn supports the proposition that marriage and family life are still important characteristics of the African-American community. They help to challenge the prevailing view of the vanishing black family. They suggest that the institution of marriage, and the married-couple family, while under severe attack in recent years still have some vitality, some attraction, and some important functions in the African-American community.

CHARACTERISTICS OF BLACK MARRIED-COUPLE FAMILIES

The salient characteristics of black married-couple families will suggest something of their diversity and will serve as introduction to a detailed discussion of family functions.

Geographic Location

Black married-couple families are overwhelmingly and increasingly urban dwellers. Moreover, within these urban areas, contrary to popular conception, most married-couple families live in central cities with only a minority living in suburbs. And while the suburban population is expanding, it is doing so at the expense of the rural and small-town population and not at the expense of the central cities. These central-city dwellers expanded from 49.7 percent of all black married couples in 1983 to 53.4 percent in 1988 and declined slightly to 51 percent by 1990. At the same time those who live in suburbs were expanding from 25.9 percent of the total in 1983 to 29.3 percent in 1988 and to 31 percent by 1990. Meanwhile black married couples in small towns and rural areas continued to decline, from 25.4 percent of the total in 1983 to 17.3 percent in 1988 and 18 percent in 1900. This diverse residential pattern calls into question the observation frequently made in the 1980s to the effect that black married-couple families have abandoned the central cities to single persons and single-parent families for the suburban lifestyle.

Family Size

A second characteristic of these families is that they are somewhat smaller than they were in years past, and this trend is continuing. Black married-couple families have declined from an average of 3.8 members per family in 1983 to 3.6 in 1988 and 1990.

The shrinking size of married-couple families is related to a decrease in the number of their own children. The census reports that the average number of children under eighteen in married-couple families declined from 1.97 in 1983 to 1.86 in 1988 and remained relatively steady at 1.89 in 1990. Families in the urban areas continued to have fewer children than those in small towns and rural areas.

One of the most fascinating aspects of married-couple families is the persistence of what we have termed incipient nuclear families, composed of married couples without any children of their own. These have continued to increase over the years. In 1983 some 45.5 percent of all married-couple families had no children of their own. We shall see below that this is a very highly regarded type of family structure.

Even so, a majority of black married-couple families continue to have children. In 1983 some 54.5 percent had young children of their own. This proportion remained steady in 1988, then declined slightly to 52.6 percent of all married-couple families in 1990. This more traditional type of family structure, called the simple nuclear family, continues to be a very important and highly desirable structure in the African-American community despite its relative decline in relation to other family structures. With an average of less than two children per family among these married-couple families with children, and with nearly half of married-couple families having no children, this highlights the sense in which a large share of childrearing in the African-American community has shifted to unwed parents.

Mobility

In general, black married-couple families exhibit a great deal of stability in their residential patterns. The census considers movers as those families who have moved their residence within the past five years. An impressive 86.4 percent of these families were non-movers in 1983 while only 13.6 percent had moved within the past five years. By 1988 these percentages had changed only slightly in favor of movers. Moreover, among the movers, most moved within the same county (data not available for 1990). Such residential stability enhances the ability of these families to meet their responsibilities to their family members. It also provides the basis for integration into their community institutions as well as strong basis for leadership and service to others.

Home Ownership

In the African-American community as elsewhere in society, home ownership is a major goal of almost all families. Moreover, home ownership is the principal means by which African-American families accumulate wealth or net worth. Married-couple families do much better than other types in accumulating this economic and social asset. The vast majority of black married-couple families are homeowners rather than renters, though the rate of home ownership has declined somewhat in recent years. In 1983 some 66.7 percent of all black married-couple families owned their own homes. By 1988 this proportion declined. Home-owners tend to be older than renters. In 1990, the median age of homeowners was 48.3 as compared with 34.3 for renters. What this suggests is that not only does it help to have two partners, probably with both working, but even then it takes a while to accumulate the necessary down payment and savings habits to purchase a home. Married couples fare better on all these matters than people with other types of family structure or living arrangements.

Education

Contemporary black married couples exhibit relatively high levels of formal education. In a majority of such families both partners are high school graduates. Moreover, this majority expanded from 54.9 percent of all such families in 1983 to an impressive 63.5 percent by 1988 (data not available for 1990).

Both the floor on educational attainment and the ceiling have been rising. In 1983, for example, 27.4 percent of families included both husbands and wives who had less than twelve years of education. Five years later this had declined to less than 20 percent with such low levels of education. At the same time the percent at the top of education attainment, where at least one of the partners was a college graduate, rose from 16.7 percent in 1983 to 19.2 percent in 1988. Meanwhile in the vast middle range, where at least one of the spouses had at least some college education, the proportion expanded from 34.9 percent in 1983 to 40.6 percent by 1988.

In short, there seemed to be a high level of rational appreciation for the importance of education among black married couples. High school graduation, which is the gateway to the middle class, seems to be taken as a given by nearly two thirds of them, while the proportion of college graduates increased steadily in recent years. In this manner black married couples are modeling the value of education. There is, of course, a gender difference in educational attainment, in that somewhat more wives have higher education than their husbands. For example, in 1983 some 12 percent of female high school graduates were married to husbands who had less education, as compared with 5.8 percent of male high school graduates whose wives had less education. The situation had not changed in 1988. The situation was similar, though less dramatic, at higher levels of education as well.

Labor Force Participation

In general, black married couples are active and steady participants in the labor force, often with both partners working. The long-term trend in this direction has continued in recent years. In 1983, for example, some 53.1 percent of all black married couples had both partners in the labor force. By 1988 this had expanded to 58.3 percent and remained steady at 57 percent in 1990. There are situations where the wife only is active in the labor force either because of retirement, educational pursuits, or military service on the part of the husband. These numbers are relatively small and remained steady at 7.6 percent of all these families over this period. Situations where neither partner was in the labor force, primarily because of retirement, also remained fairly steady at about 16 percent over this period.

Being in the labor force means being available to work. It does not necessarily mean employment. Even so, unemployment is relatively low among these families, falling from 9.1 percent of husbands in 1983 to 4.9 percent in 1988. Over the same period unemployment for wives declined from 6.7 percent to 5.2 percent.

In sum, black married partners, because of their numbers, their education, values, and responsibilities, continue to provide a stable work force and economic resource for the benefit of their families, their communities, and their society.

Occupations

Black married couples are generally underrepresented in the higher-level occupations and overrepresented in the lower levels. There are, however, some gender distinctions and some changes over recent years that are noteworthy (Table 10.1).

At the highest-level occupations of executive and managerial positions, black men generally outstrip their wives but not by a great deal. At the very highest level in the executive and management positions 5.3 percent of male workers could be found in 1983 as compared with 2.7 percent of working wives. Five years later, in 1988, both genders had improved their situation, with wives showing greater improvement. In that year some 5.7 percent of married men and 5.3 percent of married women held positions in this executive/managerial category.

In the second highest occupational level, professional positions, married women outstrip their husbands. In 1983 3.9 percent of men and 6.9 percent of women occupied professional positions, which generally require a college education or above. Again five years later both had improved somewhat, with 5.5 percent of men and 8.4 percent of women occupying these positions. While women outstrip men in this category, they generally occupy the middle-level professional positions, which include nurses, elementary school teachers, social workers, health workers, and counselors, while men are more highly represented in the higher-level

TABLE 10.1
Occupational Status of Husbands and Wives
1983–1988

Occupational	1983		1988	
	N	(%)	N	(%)
Total	3,564,000	100	3,752,000	100
Executive/managerial				
husbands	188,000	5.3	213,000	5.7
wives	95,000	2.7	198,000	5.3
Professional				
husbands	140,000	3.9	206,000	5.5
wives	245,000	6.9	316,000	8.4
Technical				
husbands	49,000	1.4	42,000	1.1
wives	71,000	1.9	94,000	2.5
Sales				
husbands	89,000	2.5	136,000	3.6
wives	123,000	3.5	148,000	4.0
Clerical				
husbands	196,000	5.5	208,000	5.5
wives	470,000	13.2	629,000	16.8
Service				
husbands	347,000	9.7	432,000	11.5
wives	541,000	15.2	527,000	14.0
Farming				
husbands	112,000	3.1	52,000	1.4
wives	12,000	0.3	4,000	0
Production/crafts				
husbands	376,000	10.5	466,000	12.4
wives	56,000	1.6	41,000	1.1
Machine operators				
husbands	289,000	8.1	283,000	7.5
wives	263,000	7.4	263,000	7.0
Transportation				
husbands	319,000	8.9	322,000	8.6
wives	22,000	0.6	15,000	0.4
Laborers				
husbands	232,000	6.5	247,000	6.6
wives	25,000	0.7	33,000	0.9
Unemployed				
husbands	325,000	9.1	182,000	4.9
wives	239,000	6.7	195,000	5.2
Armed services				
husbands	67,000	1.9	145,000	3.9
wives	NA	NA	NA	NA
Not in labor force				
husbands	833,000	23.4	817,000	21.8
wives	1,402,000	39.3	1,289,000	34.4

SOURCE: U.S. Bureau of the Census, *Current Population Reports, Household and Family Characteristics: 1983 and 1988.*

professions such as attorneys, accountants, physicians, dentists, and ministers.

Among technical workers black wives slightly outstrip black husbands at both time periods. Indeed the men declined slightly over this period from 1.4 percent to 1.1 percent while women were improving slightly from 1.9 percent to 2.5 percent. This represented an increase from 71,000 married black women technical workers in 1983 to 94,000 in 1988 while black husbands declined from 49,000 to 42,000 over the same period.

In the white-collar occupations of sales and clerical workers, black working wives continued to outstrip working husbands. After service jobs, by 1988 clerical jobs became the most numerous held by black working wives. They increased from 13.2 percent of all black working wives in 1983 to 16.8 percent in 1988. This meant that some 629,000 black working wives occupied clerical positions in 1988, up from 470,000 five years earlier. Meanwhile, black husbands in clerical positions remained steady at 5.5 percent of all black working husbands at both time periods.

Among black married men those in production and craft occupations rose slightly over this period from 10.5 percent to 12.4 percent. At the same time, however, those in machine operations declined slightly from 8.1 percent to 7.5 percent. Among transportation workers there was a slight decline from 8.9 percent to 8.6 percent. The falloff in these steady, well-paying, unskilled blue-collar jobs was severest among unmarried men or among men who were married and became divorced after losing their jobs. The strong association between holding good blue-collar jobs and marriage is, therefore, supported by these findings: Married black men have more success at holding these jobs. Those holding these jobs have more success at getting and staying married.

Finally, at the bottom of the occupational ladder among service workers and laborers black men and women exhibit a tradeoff. Women outstrip men in the service occupations at 15.2 percent to 9.7 percent in 1983, and 14 percent to 11.5 percent in 1988. On the other hand, black married men continued to cluster in the laborer positions of the economy. They remained steady at about 6.5 percent of the total at both time periods while black working wives comprised less than one percent of laborers at both time periods.

Although black married couples participate at every level of the occupational strata, in general men outstrip women in the higher-level and higher-paying professional and technical categories,

with the exception of middle-level professional and clerical workers. In those vanguards of the American middle class, black
women continue to outpace their husbands.

Family Income

A number of studies have pointed out that married-couple families have, in general, higher income than other types of families,
in large part because of dual earners.

Where both husband and wife were in the labor force their
median incomes rose from $26,686 in 1983 to $35,092 in 1988
and to $39,601 in 1990. By comparison, in those families where
the husband only was in the labor force, incomes were substantially lower, rising from $16,384 to $21,810 and to $25,037 over
this period. And for families where the wife only was in the work
force, incomes varied from $17,933 to $21,787, and then to
$21,400. Where neither partner was in the labor force, living
generally on retirement benefits, incomes were lowest. They
ranged from $8,794 in 1983 to $11,795 in 1988 and to $13,789 in
1990.

This family income profile shows the economic benefit of marriage, where both partners have relatively high levels of education, occupational status, and both work. For these reasons among
others married-couple families have the edge over other types of
relationships in earning income and accumulating wealth.

Contemporary black married couples constitute a substantial
element in African-American family and community life, while
continuing to decline in relative proportion to other family structures and living arrangements.

We turn now to a consideration of the internal dynamics of
African-American married-couple families.

FUNCTIONS OF MARRIAGE

The functions of the family have changed markedly over the
years even as the structure of marriage and family life have
changed. Many people have written that the traditional family has
lost its function. The sociologist Amatai Etzioni is among these.[4]
Etzioni holds that there are now only two basic functions of married couple families in contemporary times. These are childrearing and intimate companionship. Furthermore, he holds that
these two functions can be met quite well by a marriage which lasts

only till the children have reached maturity. This marriage may then be dissolved followed by a divorce without any damage in the essential functions of the family. Such a divorce after the children reach their late teens makes it possible for a second marriage during which a second set of children may be reared. After these children reach their middle or late teens, a third marriage, without children, can also be satisfactorily enjoyed by the individuals and tolerated by society.

There are at least two problems with this scenario. First it has some sexist overtones. It may be one thing for a man to have three marriages where two sets of children are raised and then have a third marriage free of children. It is quite another for a woman. A second problem is that it borders on trivializing the marital state and underestimates the emotional function it serves.

Indeed it may well be that even contemporary marriages meet more than just two basic functions. Moreover women and children may not be as interchangeable as suggested. Our secondary analysis of data in the national survey of black Americans revealed that there are six major functions for which marriage is considered very important even in contemporary African-American society.[5] These are raising children, companionship, having a sustained love life (sex), safety (for women), help with housework, and financial security. The black adults in this important national study part company with Etzioni and others who take a more restrictive view of the functions of marriage and family life in contemporary society.

A National Survey of Black Americans

The National Survey of Black Americans at the University of Michigan in 1979–80 was the first nationally representative sample of black adults in the nation. Altogether 2,107 respondents were interviewed in their homes (Table 10.2).

The respondents were predominantly female, accounting for some 62 percent of the sample. They ranged in age from eighteen to over seventy-five with the median falling between thirty-five and forty-four. By family income, education, and occupation they represented a broad cross section of socioeconomic status. For example, approximately a third were in the lowest income category, a majority were in the broad middle income range, and nearly a quarter were in the highest income levels. They lived in all the regions of the nation, with a slight majority still staying in

TABLE 10.2
Description of the Sample:
National Survey of Black Americans
1979–1980

Selected Characteristics	N	(%)
Total	2,107	100
Gender		
Male	797	38
Female	1,310	62
Family Income		
Under $6,000	586	32
$6,000–$11,999	456	25
$12,000–$19,999	380	20
$20,000–$29,999	272	15
$30,000 and over	141	8
NA	(272)	
Education		
Less than high school	919	44
High school graduate	650	31
Some college	334	16
College graduate	184	9
NA	(20)	
Occupation		
Laborers/farmers	81	7
Service	326	26
Operatives	240	19
Sales/clerical	239	19
Crafts	120	10
Professional/manager	232	19
Unemployed/NA	(869)	
Region		
Northeast	391	19
North Central	467	22
South	1,125	53
West	124	6
Urbanicity		
Large urban	1,005	48
Small urban	660	31
Rural	442	21
Age		
Under 25	320	15
25–34	539	27
35–44	342	16
45–54	317	15

TABLE 10.2 (*continued*)

Selected Characteristics	N	(%)
Age		
55–64	239	11
65–74	230	11
75 and over	112	5
NA	(8)	
Marital Status		
Never married	467	22
Married	877	42
Separated	207	10
Divorced	245	12
Widowed	305	14
NA	(6)	
Family Structure		
Single Person	451	22
Incipient nuclear (couple/no children)	252	12
Simple nuclear (couple/children)	521	25
Attenuated nuclear (single parent)	483	24
Extended families (other relatives)	354	17
Married by Gender		
Unmarried male	372	18
Unmarried female	852	40
Married male	422	20
Married female	455	22
NA	(6)	
Religiosity		
Very religious	713	34
Fairly religious	1,036	50
Not too/not at all	342	16
NA	(16)	

NA = Not Available.
SOURCE: *National Survey of Black Americans, 1979–80.*

the South and only about 6 percent in the West. They were over-whelmingly urban dwellers with nearly half living in large cities.

The family status characteristics of the sample encompassed a great measure of the diversity which has come to characterize African-Americans. This is reflected in part in their marital status. While roughly a fifth had never been married, the overwhelming majority of better than three quarters had been, although some-what fewer than half were still married at the time of the survey. There was also great diversity in family structure. Five specific structural living arrangements were identified. Roughly a fifth of all respondents lived alone in single-person households. Better than a third lived in married-couple families. About an eighth were incipient nuclear families, that is married couples living to-gether in their own household without any young children of their own. At the same time the other married couples constitut-ing a quarter of the sample were simple nuclear families who had small children living with them. Roughly a quarter of the sample consisted of segmented nuclear families consisting of one parent and children. In 1979–80 black married-couple families outnum-bered single-parent families by 37 percent to 24 percent.

Finally, the black adults in the sample were characteristically religious, with more than 80 percent indicating that they consider themselves religious and a third, very religious.

Our secondary analysis of this sample follows below. While the data was originally collected in 1979–1980, it is still current and relevant because of the pioneering nature of the study design. As

FIGURE 10.1
Functions of Marriage Considered Very
Important by Men and Women
1979–1980

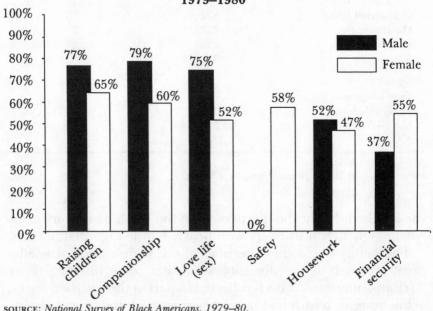

SOURCE: *National Survey of Black Americans, 1979–80.*

one of the early participants in this study has observed, "This is the first attempt to report on the feelings, attitudes, and behaviors of a national sample of the black adult population, a sample drawn to reflect the distribution of Americans of African descent across the full breadth of the United States. It was a prodigious effort involving technical innovations in sampling, questionnaire construction, and interviewing. But perhaps most importantly, it marks the first time a large-scale social science survey assessed the depths of African Americans' reflections on their lives from a black perspective."[6]

Even so, however, we recognize that some of the specific findings from this study might have changed since 1980. Still they provide insight into the complexity of African-American family life not otherwise available.

Gender Variation

While all these six activities may be considered very important functions of marriage by men and women, there are some gender differences in relative emphasis. Men seem to give greater weight to the functions of child rearing, companionship, and love life, while women give greater emphasis than men to safety and financial security, in that order. Moreover, married men outstrip married and unmarried persons of both genders in their support of the three functions men consider most important (Figure 10.2).

In this national study strong support for these six functions of marriage was expressed by a wide cross section of respondents, including never married, married, as well as separated and divorced persons; among men and women; and among those of different income levels (Table 10.3).

Variation of Family Types

As might be anticipated, married persons of both gender gave significantly higher valuation to each of these six functions of marriage than persons not married. For example, on childrearing as a function of marriage, 85 percent of married persons indicated that this was very important, while 59 percent of never married persons considered this very important. On companionship, 83 percent of married persons and 55 percent of never married persons considered this very important. On love life, 76 percent of married persons and 51 percent of never married

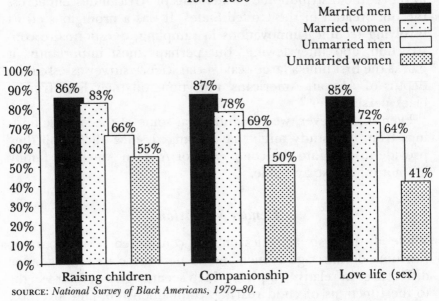

FIGURE 10.2
**Functions of Marriage Considered Very
Important by Married and Unmarried Persons
1979–1980**

Married men ■■■
Married women ⋯⋯
Unmarried men ☐
Unmarried women ▩▩▩

SOURCE: *National Survey of Black Americans, 1979–80.*

persons considered this a very important function of marriage. A similar pattern exists with respect to each of the other three functions as well. Married persons gave consistently higher valuation to all of them than did nonmarried persons.

It is important to recognize that this question did not tap the *behavior* of these respondents. Their answers, thus, do not indicate what they do or would like to do but rather what they consider important. The question, thus, taps their *standards* for their behavior, or their values. While all of the respondents gave generally high valuation to all of these six major functions of contemporary marriage, the married persons seemed more aware of the importance of marriage for each of these functions. There is no doubt, therefore, that their status and experience did indeed influence their views and their responses. But what this also tells us is that the value of marriage for meeting certain basic traditional functions is not confined to married persons alone. Even those not married or previously married attest to the value of the marital relationship in meeting these basic functions better than other types of relationships.

Moreover, while a majority of respondents tend to attach high

TABLE 10.3
Importance of Specified Functions of Marriage
1979–1980

Selected Characteristics	For Raising Children Very (%)	For Financial Security Very (%)	For Housework Very (%)	For Love Life Very (%)	For Companionship Very (%)	For Woman's Safety Very (%)
Total	69	48	49	61	67	68
Marital Status						
Never married	59	38	36	51	55	53
Married	85	58	60	76	83	75
Separated	65	41	44	48	55	47
Divorced	57	44	39	51	60	44
Widowed	53	47	49	41	52	49
Family Structure						
Incipient nuclear	76	59	62	77	86	82
Simple nuclear	88	55	56	78	80	71
Attenuated nuclear	59	43	40	46	54	48
Extended families	69	55	52	62	69	63
Married by Gender						
Married men	86	44	59	85	87	—
Married women	83	70	60	72	78	76
Unmarried men	66	30	44	64	69	—
Unmarried women	55	47	40	41	50	49
Family Income						
Under $6,000	61	50	47	51	58	56
$6,000–11,999	70	50	50	59	67	59
$12,000–19,999	70	45	47	66	72	58
$20,000–29,999	79	47	51	73	77	57
$30,000 and over	80	44	43	69	70	59

SOURCE: *National Survey of Black Americans, 1979–80.*

value to each of these functions, it is noteworthy that persons in incipient nuclear families, consisting of husbands and wives but no children, tend to give higher value to four of these six functions than those in any other type of family structure. This is true with respect to companionship, financial security, help with housework, and women's safety.

Black married men seem to cling harder to these basic traditional functions of marriage than other gender-status groups. On three of these activities, raising children, love life, and companionship, black married men rank them higher as functions of marriage than married women and higher than single persons of either gender.

What this means is that black men who have experienced marriage have stronger attachment to it than other people do. Moreover, they have greater appreciation for marriage as meeting some basic and traditional emotional and intellectual needs. This finding will come as a surprise to those readers who have formed their view of black men's attitude toward marriage based on studies of family structure which focus primarily on whether men are in or out of the home.

In terms of social class, when asked to select the *most* important functions all income groups consider the same three functions to be most important, namely raising children, companionship, and financial security. These are the big three functions among all groups of this study. At the same time, however, those from middle- and upper-income families tend to give higher value to having a marital partner for love life (sex) and companionship than those in low-income families.

What then can be said about Etzioni's proposition that the married-couple family in contemporary society has only two major functions, childrearing and companionship? Insofar as this national sample of black adults is concerned, Etzioni may be a bit premature. Among African-American adults, there are still six very important functions of marriage. Within this general finding, however, there is considerable diversity among persons of different gender, marital status, and some difference by income level and age. In keeping, however, with the gist of Etzioni's thinking, these respondents do give the highest valuation to the two functions he holds as essential, raising children and companionship.

Marriage continues as a very important type of relationship in the African-American community. It is, however, undergoing major changes in recent years. It may well be that as other living arrangements compete with marriage, the marital state will shrink in importance along the lines suggested by Etzioni. Still, for the present, we must note that in the experience of the African-American people, marriage, despite the many strains on it, is far from losing its prominent place. More than any other form of family arrangement, married-couple families continue to meet some basic functions for member as well as for the community and society at large.

Racial Socialization

If child-rearing is considered one of the most important functions of contemporary African-American marriage and family life, what are some of the most profound considerations parents give to the task? A ten-year review of black family research published in 1990 reveals that racial socialization is an important aspect of child-rearing. That is, parents must help their children accept, understand, and cope with their status as blacks in a white-dominated society.[7]

Our analysis of the survey of black Americans found strong support for this child-rearing function. Respondents were able to indicate some of the pertinent ideas and attitudes they bring to the racial socialization of their children.

Contemporary African-American parents find that they still must teach their children how to manage in a world and community where racial prejudice and discrimination are likely to be aimed against them. It is a harsh reality which the overwhelming majority of African-American parents recognize and for which they seek overtly to prepare their children. Social scientists refer to this practice as "racial socialization." What this means is that black parents recognize the double burden of preparing their children like all other parents to function successfully in society, and in addition, preparing them to function in a society that may often be arrayed against them. They cannot simply be brought up as American children. They must be brought up as American and as black in white America. This dual responsibility was recognized by Du Bois:

> It is a peculiar sensation, this double-consciousness, this sense of always looking at one's self through the eyes of others, of measuring one's soul by the tape of a world that looks on in amused contempt and pity. One ever feels his twoness—an American, a Negro; two

souls, two thoughts, two unreconciled strivings; two warring ideals in one dark body, whose dogged strength alone keeps it from being torn asunder.[8]

This makes it exceedingly difficult for parents to provide their children with positive self- and group identity. The fact that a majority of parents succeed in doing so is surely among the most remarkable strengths of black families. In carrying out this responsibility successfully, parents are called on to function as a buffer between their children and the wider society which is often hostile to them.

One of the issues in the black community is that some parents do not see the necessity of such dual education or socialization of their children. Some studies show that up to a third of black parents do not prepare their children for this duality.

There is some indication that black parents prepare their boys differently than they prepare their girls to deal with this dual experience. Some studies found that parents were more likely to caution their sons about racial barriers, and to focus more on issues of racial pride in bringing up their girls. This may be a necessary defense strategy in helping young black boys cope with greater hostilities in the wider society than black girls.

It is possible to identify nine clusters of beliefs that large numbers of black adults bring to the task of socializing their children. (Table 10.4)

Double Consciousness
Most parents feel they must teach a sense of basic identity. They have to teach their children that they are not just black, and certainly not just American, but both simultaneously. Nearly 70 percent of black adults think of themselves this way and believe that they should pass this view of themselves on to their children. In the course of fortifying their children with this double identity, 63.6 percent believe that they must teach their children what it is like to be black in white America. A slight majority indicate that their parents before them taught them specifically about being black, rather than just letting them face it and cope with it without full awareness.

TABLE 10.4
Racial Socialization
1979–1980

Beliefs About Race Relations	Percentage Who Agree
1. Double Consciousness	
Identity: black and American	69.8
Should tell children what it's like to be black	63.6
Parents told them what it's like to be black	51.5
Parents taught them how to get along with whites	38.5
Should teach children to get along with whites	48.9
2. Skin Color Not the Issue	
Skin color makes a difference in	
how blacks or whites treat you	20.0
3. African Heritage	
Feel close to people in Africa	57.2
Children should study an African language	61.7
Should give children African names	22.7
4. Racial Solidarity	
Civil rights movement helped cause	86.8
5. No Color-Blind Society	
Don't have same opportunities as whites	63.6
Most whites want to see blacks get better break	22.6
Less discrimination than 10 years ago	64.7
Less discrimination 10 years from now	57.7
6. Two Paths to Progress	
Should shop black-owned stores	65.2
Should vote black candidates	40.2
Black-elected officials help cause	71.8
Should work together as a group	89.8
Should work through present system, political	
participation	86.8
7. No Personal Bigotry	
Feel close to whites in America	23.7
Have personal friend who is white	57.7
Blacks should not date whites	35.6
8. People of Color	
Feel close to West Indians	44.4
Feel close to Native Americans	41.8
Feel close to Hispanics	34.6
Feel close to Asian-Americans	41.8
9. Feminine Issues	
Sex discrimination a real problem	47.9
Black women should fight for both blacks and	
women	74.4
Black women should work together	88.6

SOURCE: *National Survey of Black Americans, 1979–80.*

Skin Color Not the Issue

Parents teach their children by their own behavior and attitudes that being black is not a matter of color or skin tone. Fully 80 percent believe that the skin color does not make a difference in how one is perceived or treated either by whites or by other blacks.

This finding supports the view that for most blacks it is the racial identity rather than the actual skin color which binds them to their heritage and which distinguishes them from other groups both for good and for ill. The late executive director of the NAACP, Walter White, the late Congressman Adam Clayton Powell, and the actress Lena Horne are examples of blacks who though light enough to pass for white chose to identify with their African-American heritage. In general it is not believed that whites discriminate against blacks because of the actual color of their skin but because of their racial identity either self-subscribed or imposed by society. At the same time the question of skin color does arise within the African-American community in patterns of preference for mate selection and other informal behavior. Spike Lee has dramatized this issue in one of his movies, *School Daze,* where college students separated themselves into social organizations on the basis of skin color. It is not an uncommon occurrence. But for the vast majority of African-American adults, some 80 percent in our study, skin color is neither an important barrier nor an important resource in the struggle for self-development and achievement as an African-American. And this is what they seek to teach their children by precept and example. That they do not always succeed is just one more example of the limits of childhood when confronted with more powerful influences from a more powerful society.

African Heritage

Increasing is the realization that being black is a matter of heritage. Better than 60 percent believe their children should study an African language. A majority of black adults feel close to the people of Africa. Only a fifth, however, would go so far as to give their African-American children African names.

The strong identity with Africa and the interest in the study of African languages are both examples of the growing awareness of and interest in the African backgrounds of the African-American people. Despite half a century of organized efforts to celebrate African-American history, and despite the long scholarly interest in Africa among a handful of black scholars, it is only in recent times that movement toward "Afrocentric" education has come to wide-scale public attention. Indeed it was out of this increased awareness that a national movement has been mounted, not yet completely successful, to encourage blacks to identify themselves as African-Americans in preference to blacks, or Negroes, or colored people. Such a designation it is felt gives recognition to the duality of "double consciousness." Parents will need a great deal of help from professionals, organizations, scholars, and institutions in order to translate their aspirations in this regard to effective socialization of their children. The findings cited above indicate that a majority of black adults are amenable to some further exploration of the African heritage, both for themselves and for their children.

Racial Solidarity
Black adults bring to the socialization of their children a sense of racial pride, solidarity, and support of black initiatives. They still give strong support to the civil rights movement. It is an era of accomplishments against the odds that they wish their children to know, understand, and be proud of. Nearly 90 percent of adults believe that the civil rights movement has contributed to black progress.

While it became fashionable during the 1980s for a handful of black and white intellectuals to question the efficacy of the civil rights movement, this and other findings suggest that the vast majority of black adults identify quite strongly with this movement as a major source of black progress. The idea that major structural changes should be brought about, and affirmative policies should be put or kept in place in order to address systematic racial injustice, takes nothing away from the insistence of parents that their children learn, work hard, and strive to maximize their talents as individuals. And while some successful blacks may give the impression that they got where they are on their individual merits and on the good will of the wider society, a majority of blacks would still find an important place for organized racial solidarity as an aid in this upward mobility and the struggle for social justice. It is through beliefs such as this that parents are able to expose their children to their own activities in racial uplift movements, cultural activities, and various forms of self-help.

No Color-Blind Society

These parents also teach their children directly and indirectly that the struggle for equality has not yet been won, and that they do not live in a color-blind society. There are exceptions to this as with most matters. And since the end of the civil rights era there have been strong black voices urging other blacks and whites alike to operate as though a color-blind society has emerged. Prominent among these have been such economic conservatives as Harvard University's Glen Loury, George Mason University's Walter E. Williams, and Stanford University's Thomas Sowell. They were joined in the 1990s by a cadre of literary figures such as California State University professor of literature Shelby Steele and Washington State University novelist Charles Johnson. Often eloquent and sometimes carefully reasoned, these "black conservatives" receive a wide audience and strike a responsive chord in an American society which seems to have tired of the struggle for equality. Most black people, however, believe that they must teach their children another truth. Nearly two-thirds do not believe that blacks have the same opportunity as whites. An even larger number believe that most whites do not wish to see blacks get a better break. Although most believe that there is substantially less racial discrimination than ten years ago and that there will be less ten years hence, they also believe that they must teach their children that such progress is neither automatic nor easy.

Two Paths to Progress

Blacks teach their children that they must enter the mainstream of society and shoulder their rightful responsibilities to the nation. At the same time, they teach their children to support black institutions and black leaders and strive for economic, political, and social empowerment. The two approaches are not seen as mutually exclusive, but complementary. Thus almost two-thirds of black adults believe that blacks should shop at black-owned stores and other business enterprises, while an even stronger majority believe that blacks should work through the existing political and economic system by participating actively in them. And more strongly than all the rest, nearly 90 percent believe that blacks should work together as a group.

The fact that only 40 percent believe that blacks should automatically vote for black elected officials shows a level of sophistication and selectivity. Even so, however, since the power of this tendency is frequently demonstrated in contemporary elections, it calls attention to the enormous potential of the other attitudes expressed above about otherwise strong leadership.

No Personal Bigotry
Most black adults believe and seek to teach their children by precept and example that their quest for selfhood, cultural integrity, and upward mobility has no place for personal bigotry. There is no room for hatred of white persons. While a majority in our study do not claim to feel close to whites in general, a majority do claim to have a white person as a personal friend. Moreover, as shown by this fact and elsewhere in this book, a majority of black adult men and women believe that racial difference should not be a barrier to friendship, to dating, and to marriage, and needless to say to living and working together in the same place.

People of Color
There is also among black adults a certain level of personal commitment to a view which would embrace equally "all people of color." Perhaps this aspect of racial socialization will increase interaction with other minorities. Nearly four of out of ten black adults express a feeling of closeness to West Indians, as well as to Native Americans, Asian-Americans, and Hispanics.

Women's Issues
There is among African-American adults a strong awareness of and commitment to resolving women's issues. Nearly half believe that sex discrimination is a real problem in America. Overwhelmingly they believe that black women should fight equally for both blacks and women. Moreover, they believe overwhelmingly that black women should work together for community improvement.

These are the attitudes and beliefs about black-white relations in America that adults bring to the socialization of their children, and which they advocate more generally. This profile reveals a high level of self-awareness, race pride, pride in their African heritage, and a strong determination to face the future with optimism to fight institutional racism without abandoning their humanistic acceptance of people across racial lines.

This aspect of African-American culture is worth underscoring. Greater emphasis on honoring one's heritage without disparaging others, of moving ahead with optimism despite obstacles, of acceptance of others despite apparent differences, of inclusiveness of the human race rather than exclusiveness, and of sharing the resources of the community would provide a major improvement in the national climate and in the socialization of all children.

Family Structure and Personal Fulfillment

The importance of companionship in marriage was further elaborated when respondents in this national study were asked the extent of their satisfaction with various aspects of their lives (Table 10.5). Specifically they were asked to indicate the extent of their personal happiness at the present time, satisfaction with their life in general and with their families, and their feeling of self-worth. Considering the problems experienced by this cross section of Americans it was impressive to find, as a number of studies have found, relatively high levels of satisfaction among black Americans.[9] For example, this study found that 78 percent indicated that they were satisfied with their lives in general while 31 percent said they were very satisfied. In a similar manner, 80 percent indicated satisfaction with their family life, while a majority of 53 percent indicated that they were very satisfied with their family life. Similar findings were noted with respect to personal happiness and self-esteem. Because these levels were so high it was necessary to examine only those who expressed satisfaction at the highest levels in order to see how family structure might affect level of happiness.

Both men and women express higher levels of satisfaction with their family life than with life in general. While a third indicated that they were very satisfied with their life in general over half indicated the same for their family life. On the measure of self-worth, however, a somewhat higher percentage of men expressed high self-worth than did women, 41 percent to 36 percent.

Married people generally rank higher on all these measures of self-fulfillment than never married, separated, or divorced persons. Widowed persons expressed the highest levels of satisfaction. Again satisfaction with family life is higher than with life in general. Among married persons, for example, 34 percent indicated that they were very satisfied with life in general while 55 percent expressed the view that they were very satisfied with their family life. For never-married persons these percentages were 25 percent and 45 percent. The same is true with self-worth.

A third set of findings shows levels of satisfaction among the

TABLE 10.5
Satisfaction with Life and Family and Self-Worth
1979–1980

Selected Characteristics	LIFE IN GENERAL Very Satisfied (%)	FAMILY LIFE Very Satisfied (%)	SELF-WORTH High (%)
Total	31	53	35
Sex			
Male	33	54	41
Female	30	52	36
Marital Status			
Never married	25	45	36
Married	34	55	40
Separated	26	50	33
Divorced	24	45	36
Widowed	39	66	40
Family Structure			
Simple nuclear	27	49	39
Attenuated nuclear	23	48	34
Incipient nuclear	45	64	44
Extended families	32	54	36
Married by Gender			
Unmarried men	30	48	38
Unmarried women	28	53	36
Married men	35	59	44
Married women	32	50	36

SOURCE: *National Survey of Black Americans, 1979–80.*

four types of family structure. This provides us with one of the two most striking findings on this matter. We note that not only do married persons exhibit higher levels of satisfaction than never-married persons, but that married persons without children exhibit even higher levels of satisfaction in both these areas than those with children. Specifically, persons in incipient-nuclear families (married couples, no children) have higher levels of satisfaction in each of the three areas of personal fulfillment than their counterparts in simple nuclear families. Indeed, these married couples without children soar above all the other types of family structure in their levels of satisfaction. Forty-five percent of them as opposed to 27 percent of those in simple nuclear families indicate the highest level of satisfaction with life in general. An even larger 64 percent as compared with 49 percent of those in simple nuclear families indicate that they are very satisfied with their family life. Married couples without children also have higher levels of self-worth than those in other types of family structure.

A fourth set of findings reveals levels of satisfaction for married and unmarried persons by gender. Married men exhibit higher levels of satisfaction on all three of the measures of personal fulfillment than either married women, or unmarried persons of either gender.

Fifty-nine percent of married men indicated that they were very satisfied with their family life, while only 48 percent of unmarried men did so. Married men also score higher than married women in this regard by 59 percent to 50 percent. In a similar manner, married men express higher levels of self-worth than either of the other groups.

What of the high levels of personal satisfaction among black married men? African-American people make a distinction between how they are viewed in the wider society and how they view themselves. It requires a delicate balancing act, one where married people do much better than unmarried people and where married men get a greater lift than all others. Black married men know and appreciate the value of marriage which provides for them a major source of acceptance, honor, and support found nowhere else since they left their mother's house. That more married than unmarried black men find satisfaction with themselves as individuals of worth is another attraction of family life among the African-American people.

FEELING GOOD OR BAD ABOUT SELF

When the sample was asked how often they feel good about themselves a majority of 57 percent said often. Only 6 percent said hardly ever or never.

There are certain down periods in everyone's life. It may be surprising, however, to find the low frequency with which

African-American adults in this study say they feel bad about themselves (Tables 10.6 and 10.7). When asked how often they feel bad about themselves, 17 percent said often, another 38 percent said not too often, and 45 percent said hardly ever or never.

Black men have more positive feelings about themselves than black women. Specifically, 26 percent of men and 17 percent of women indicate they never feel bad about themselves. Moreover, on the positive side, 63 percent of men as compared with 54 percent of women indicate that they feel good about themselves very often. It is not clear just why this is so. It may be that black men are not as helpful in helping women overcome stresses of life as women are for them.

Widowed persons show the most positive feelings about themselves. They are less likely to fall victim to depression and more likely to feel good about themselves than all others. Again the reason is not clear. This may be in part because they tend to be older and have resolved a great deal of life's tension. They also tend to draw heavily on supportive networks of kin, friends, and church.[10]

Among the other statuses, however, the married persons show more positive feelings about themselves than unmarried persons. They are least likely to feel bad about themselves and most likely to feel good about themselves.

Beyond marriage itself, different types of family structures influence feelings about self. Once again it is the incipient nuclear family which stands out. While 25 percent of persons in these families never feel bad about themselves, this falls to 18 percent for those in simple nuclear families. Attenuated nuclear family members are most likely to feel dissatisfied. On the up side of life an impressive 66 percent of incipient nuclear family members, compared with 53 percent of those in simple nuclear families, feel good about themselves very often.

Finally, married men have more positive feelings about themselves than married women. Indeed, 26 percent of married men as opposed to 16 percent of married women never feel bad about themselves, while 62 percent of the husbands versus 54 percent of the wives feel good about themselves very often.

When respondents were asked why they feel the way they do a wide variety of reasons were advanced. They have been organized as follows:

TABLE 10.6
Attitudes About Self
1979–1980

	Feel Bad About Self (%)	Feel Good About Self (%)
Frequency (%)		
Often	17	57
Not too often	38	37
Hardly ever	40	5
Never	5	1

SOURCE: *National Survey of Black Americans, 1979–80.*

TABLE 10.7
Percentage Who Feel Good or Bad About Themselves
1979–1980

Selected Characteristics	FEEL BAD ABOUT SELF Never (%)	FEEL GOOD ABOUT SELF Very Often (%)
Total	20	57
Sex		
Male	26	63
Female	17	54
Marital Status		
Never married	17	54
Married	21	58
Separated	19	53
Divorced	14	52
Widowed	32	67
Family Structure		
Simple nuclear	18	53
Attenuated nuclear	15	52
Incipient nuclear	25	66
Extended families	22	61
Married by Gender		
Unmarried men	26	63
Unmarried women	18	54
Married men	26	62
Married women	16	54

SOURCE: *National Survey of Black Americans, 1979–80.*

TABLE 10.8
Reasons for Feeling Bad
1979–1980

	(%)
Not being effective	25.3
Lack of specific accomplishment	22.7
Poor relations with family or friends	17.1
Health and endurance problems	16.8
Personal characteristics, physical or psychological	8.9
Moral laxity	5.4

SOURCE: *National Survey of Black Americans, 1979–80.*

Feeling Bad

While our respondents do not feel bad about themselves often, when they do, they are likely to be affected by a cluster of factors (Table 10.8). They feel bad about themselves most often when they are not moving resolutely to accomplish their goals or meet their responsibilities. Other factors which bring them down are poor relationships with their family members or friends, and when they are not in good health and physical condition. Finally, when their own personal characteristics or moral laxity get in the way of their ideals and goals they feel bad about themselves.

Feeling Good

Then there is the up side of life where most black people dwell most of the time. The fact that an impressive 94 percent feel good about themselves a good portion of the time is a truly amazing level of emotional health.

African-Americans feel good about themselves when they have good relations with family and friends (Table 10.9). They feel good about themselves when they are in good health and physical condition. They feel good when they are moving effectively toward their personal goals. And, finally, they feel good when they hold to their own moral standards.

A striking feature of this study is that what most makes African-American men and women feel good about themselves is having good relations with their family members and friends. This pattern of expressive relations helps to cushion the inequities of life inflicted on them by the wider society.

The findings of this study show considerable diversity among African-American families as they experience the personal sense

TABLE 10.9
Reasons for Feeling Good
1979–1980

	(%)
Good relations with family and friends	36.5
Good health and endurance	18.4
Being effective	16.1
Specific accomplishments	10.9
Physical and personality characteristics	8.0
Moral excellence	8.0

SOURCE: *National Survey of Black Americans, 1979–80.*

of well-being of their members. What is clear, however, is that without regard to social class or geographic region, adults in these African-American families exhibit a relatively high level of satisfaction with life, happiness at the present time, satisfaction with their family life, an unexpected high degree of self-worth, and a strong tendency to feel good about themselves most of the time. Although widowed persons consistently exhibit the highest levels of satisfaction, married couples exhibit higher levels of satisfaction on all these measures than never married, separated, or divorced persons. Married couples without children exhibit even higher levels; and married men the highest levels of all.

Little wonder, then, that marriage is so popular. It is always held out as the most desirable state for African-American adults of all social classes and in all regions of the country. The strong value attached to marriage and the strong personal benefits derived from it are not strong enough forces, however, to prevent the relative decline in traditional family patterns. The reason is that there are forces in the larger society arrayed against the family traditions of the African-American people which are stronger than the values which make the people try to hold on to these traditions.

ROLE RELATIONS IN AFRICAN-AMERICAN FAMILIES

African-American families owe their existence, persistence, and resilience, in part, to the manner in which family heads execute certain role relationships. We examined three dimensions of these relationships, their personal assessment of how well they perform certain key roles, who performs the housework, and who gets more out of the relationship.

Family Roles

When a national sample of black adults was asked how well they consider they have performed certain specific family roles, an overwhelming majority gave themselves high marks in all three areas of family life (Table 10.10). They scored their greatest success in executing the parental role, where 79 percent indicated that they perform this role very well. Next came their role as spouse, where 74 percent indicated that they execute this role very well, and then came providing for the family, where a smaller but still healthy majority of 60 percent rate themselves as doing very well.

These family members see themselves as performing their essential family responsibilities at much higher levels than they are generally given credit for by outside observers.

TABLE 10.10
Percentage Who Consider That They Perform Family Roles Very Well
1979–1980

Selected Characteristics	Family Provider (%)	Good Spouse (%)	Good Parent (%)
Total	60	74	79
Sex			
Male	54	72	74
Female	63	75	82
Marital Status			
Never married	46	—	71
Married	63	74	81
Separated	60	—	78
Divorced	59	—	77
Widowed	71	—	85
Family Structure			
Simple nuclear	59	69	79
Attenuated nuclear	53	—	78
Incipient nuclear	69	82	85
Extended families	59	77	79
Married by Gender			
Unmarried men	48	—	68
Unmarried women	61	—	81
Married men	59	72	77
Married women	66	75	84

SOURCE: *National Survey of Black Americans, 1979–80.*

While both men and women rated themselves highest as parents, next as spouses, and third as family providers, there were nevertheless some distinctions. Women rated themselves higher than did men on all three of these family roles. While 82 percent of women considered that they performed the parenting role very well, this was true of 74 percent of men. The two groups rated themselves fairly evenly as spouses at 75 percent for women and 72 percent for men. In caring for their families, however, women distinctly outshone the men. In their own estimation, 63 percent of the women, as compared with 54 percent of the men, considered that they provided for their families very well.

With respect to marital status, widowed persons feel they outperform the others. Married persons do better than never-married ones, with incipient nuclear families standing out. Finally, when gender and marital status are combined, married women feel that they outstrip married men in performance of these family roles.

Help Around the House

As noted, one of the functions of marriage rated highly by both men and women was having someone to share household duties. Strong support was reflected in this study for the view that a great deal of sharing and role flexibility and reciprocity exists among African-American families. But while the degree of sharing between black husbands and wives may be greater than the national average, it is still the case that the wife and mother, even though she also works in the labor force, must do the lion's share of the housework. When asked who does the housework (cooking, cleaning, and laundry), a national sample of black adults responded as indicated in Table 10.11.

Both husbands and wives in our study indicated that women do most of the cooking, cleaning, and laundry. Black husbands share this responsibility with their wives to a certain extent; how much they share, however, depends on who is answering the question, resulting in some striking differences in perception between husbands and wives as to who does what and how much around the house. While 70 percent of the housewives indicated that they generally do the housework alone, only one-half of the husbands agree with this assessment. And while nearly one-half of the husbands felt that they help their wives with housework, only 16 percent of the wives support this assessment.

TABLE 10.11
Views of Who Performs Housework
1979–1980

	Husband's View (%)	Wife's View (%)
Wife alone	49	70
Wife and husband	47	16
Wife and other female	0	12
Husband only	4	0
Others	0	2

SOURCE: *National Survey of Black Americans, 1979–80.*

It may well be that these men do, indeed, help around the house with tasks such as taking out the garbage, repairing the dishwasher when it breaks down, and occasionally doing the dishes. The amount of their work may be so small, however, as to pale in significance in the views of their wives, who by all accounts continue to do most of the housework whatever their employment status or that of their husbands, or the ages of the children. Still, it is not necessarily the case that these men were deliberately lying. It seems more likely that men are accustomed to doing so little or nothing around the house that when they do anything at all they unconsciously exaggerate the frequency of it. It is also the case that black husbands help their wives significantly more than white husbands do. Research has shown that while white husbands of working wives devote about five hours per week to housework, black men devote seven hours. In both cases, working wives continue to do between thirty and forty hours on such household tasks. However, older children in African-American families are often relied upon as much or more than husbands to help with housework.

Givers, Takers, and Sharers

One of the more intriguing aspects of male-female relationships within marriage is the question of who gets more out of the relationship emotionally (Table 10.12). It is another way of looking inside the marriage relation to assess the expressive functions, or the socioemotional glue that makes the relationship rewarding. It is sometimes suggested that in general black men are like leeches, taking more than they give in their relationships with women. Our findings call this view into question.

TABLE 10.12
Views of Who Gets More Out of the Relationship
1979–1980

Selected Characteristics	Sharers (%)	Givers (%)	Takers (%)
Total	62	27	12
Sex			
Husbands	62	26	12
Wives	61	28	11
Family Structure			
Simple nuclear	58	30	12
Attenuated nuclear	—	—	—
Incipient nuclear	71	21	8
Extended families	60	24	16

SOURCE: *National Survey of Black Americans, 1979–80.*

When this national sample of black adults were asked "Who gets more from this relationship, you or your partner?" a very important set of findings was discovered. The most striking is that the overwhelming majority of our respondents consider themselves to be sharers. That is, they give about as much as they get from the relationship. Sixty-two percent of African-American adults indicate that both partners benefit about equally from their relationships. Another consists of one partner getting more out of the relationship than the other. We found a relatively large group of givers. A somewhat smaller group consisted of takers. Twenty-seven percent indicated that their partners get more out of the relationship than they do. The smallest group consisted of takers. A small cadre of 12 percent indicated that they get more out of the relationship than their mates. While it might be anticipated from the literature and public discourse that there are substantial gender differences in this matter, we found none. Contrary to the popular view, black men were just as likely to be seen by both themselves and their mates as sharers, givers, and takers, in that order, as were the women.

When patterns of give and take among partners in different types of family structure are examined, the incipient nuclear families stand out again. These married couples without children in the home are more likely to describe themselves as sharers than those in other types of family structure and less likely to describe themselves as givers or takers. Thus 71 percent of incipient nuclear family members described themselves as sharers, while this was true of 60 percent of those in extended families and 58 percent of those in simple nuclear families.

While it might be expected that middle- and upper-income partners would exhibit higher proportions of sharers, we found no such differences. Social class was not a significant factor.

When asked why they felt the way they did, no particular response was predominant. Givers, however, tended to indicate that they give more emotionally to their partners who need or demand more from them. To a lesser extent they also give more services and financial support than their partners. Some describe their partners as having fewer responsibilities or greater personal freedom and are thus less dependable.

Takers indicated that they get more out of the relationship also because their partners are emotionally more giving and that they seem to need or take more than their partners. A few also pointed to services and financial support received from their partners. The most prominent conclusion that emerges from this set of findings is the strong egalitarian relationship among black married couples.

MARRIAGE FOR BETTER AND FOR WORSE

Despite the substantial advantages associated with marriage and the strong desire to enter and reenter into it, the divorce rate, though tapering off somewhat in recent years, remains extraordinarily high. Moreover, not all formerly married persons would prefer their current divorced or separated status (Table 10.13).

When a national sample of African-American adults who were divorced and separated were asked whether they thought their current status was better or worse than being married, the results were exceedingly mixed, providing three categories of responses. The largest group composed of nearly one-half said their present status was better than marriage. Another group composed of 24 percent said their present status was worse than being married. Still another group, composed of 29 percent of the total, had mixed feelings on the matter, indicating that in some respects their current status was better and in other respects marriage was

TABLE 10.13
Views of Whether It's Better to Be Separated or Divorced
Than Married
1979–1980

Selected Characteristics	Better (%)	Worse (%)	Mixed (%)
Total	47	24	29
Sex			
Male	37	37	26
Female	51	19	30
Marital Status			
Never married	—	—	—
Married	—	—	—
Separated	52	24	25
Divorced	42	24	32
Widowed	—	—	—
Family Structure			
Simple nuclear	—	—	—
Attenuated nuclear	49	22	29
Incipient nuclear	—	—	—
Extended families	44	28	28

SOURCE: *National Survey of Black Americans, 1979–80.*

better. Overall, while about one-half of the formerly married people found their new status to be better than marriage, only one-quarter found it to be worse.

There is, however, a pronounced difference between men and women on this matter. Women, by a significant margin, believe that their current separated or divorced status is preferable to marriage. Some 51 percent of women as compared with a minority of 37 percent of men hold this view. By contrast, men are nearly twice as likely as women to judge their current separated or divorced status as worse than marriage. Some 37 percent of men as contrasted with 19 percent of women gave this response. Men and women of mixed feelings on the matter divided almost evenly.

What is the meaning of these findings? They may help us to appreciate why black men seem to cleave to the marriage relation more than black women. They are more often married, less often divorced, and more quickly remarried after divorce than black women. To be sure, it is partly due to the excess of women over men in the population. Just as assuredly, however, this trend toward marriage among black men supports the view that they may be more dependent and less able to cope alone than women. They need more help. If mothers, aunts, and sisters are not around to shelter and succor them after divorce, they are more likely to rush rapidly into another relationship, often leading to an early remarriage, earlier divorce, and an even shorter third marriage. Still, they opt for the marital bond over and over again.

What this also suggests is that black men are caught up in a social system which beams exceedingly contradictory signals to them. On the one hand, because they are males in a male-oriented society, they are expected to be dominant, powerful, and strong providers. They are consequently given higher status and considerably more privileges than black women. On the other hand, because they are black in a white-dominated society, they are often perceived as subservient and relatively powerless in comparison to white men, who are their role models. Consequently, they are more dependent on their women. They know and experience this contradiction keenly. They feel the unfairness of it all.

The resultant frustration regarding status and dominance is often taken out on their families. In their unconscious search for importance black men sometimes go to great lengths to put down black women in a vain effort to build themselves up. They often mistreat women even when they do not really intend to. Then, when they are deserted, they feel alone, weak, and helpless.

While these men individually are certainly responsible for their own behavior, their collective predicament and search for solutions are socially driven. What this suggests is that black families at the bottom of the socioeconomic structure have great difficulty meeting the physical needs of their members and thus in holding on to their own self-esteem. As a consequence, the emotional needs of the family are likely to be neglected as well. They will probably experience greater tension, domestic violence, and abandonment than privileged families. And, after divorce, the women are particularly more likely to view their freedom from dysfunctional marriages with higher valuation than their middle- and upper-class peers. It is this predicament of marriage as they have known it that a majority of low-income, divorced, and separated women consider worse than being separated or divorced.

The Importance of Marriage

Taken as a whole, the findings reported in this chapter support the view that the married-couple family is not dead or vanishing. Though it has lost its preeminence, it is still a widespread and attractive arrangement. In addition to performing certain basic functions, the married-couple African-American family unit is a very important context for the generation and sustaining of a sense of personal well-being. Specifically, these families have been found to be more conducive to feelings of personal happiness, satisfaction with life, and self-esteem than various rapidly expanding alternative living arrangements.

Chapter 11

Black and White Together: Trends in Interracial Marriage

The relative decline in the proportion of black married-couple families has been accompanied by a substantial increase in the incidence of interracial families involving black and nonblack marriage partners. This raises a number of questions about the place of interracial marriage in the future of African-American families.

In the nation as a whole the numbers are still small but expanding. Over the years the proportion of African-Americans married to partners across racial lines has increased from a low of 1 percent of all married couples in 1940 to over 6 percent in 1990. Interracial unions still involve greater numbers of black males than black females. By 1990, black men outnumbered black women two and a half to one in interracial unions. While the nationwide figures are fairly low, in some cities with large middle-class populations, this practice has reached alarming proportions. In the West, for example, in recent years one of every six marriage-bound black men married a nonblack woman. This is a pattern which has continued over the past few generations. Indeed, it is the relative preponderance of black men and white women in interracial unions that has given rise to the most persistent theories seeking to explain interracial marriage.[1]

TABLE 11.1
Interracial Married-Couple Families
1984–1990

	1984		1986		1988		1990	
	N	(%)	N	(%)	N	(%)	N	(%)
Total Married Couples with Black Spouse	3,604,000	100	3,812,000	100	3,844,000	100	3,931,000	100
Black husband/ black wife	3,406,000	94.5	3,598,000	94.4	3,591,000	93.4	3,687,000	93.8
Black husband/ white wife	111,000	3.1	136,000	3.6	149,000	3.7	150,000	3.8
Black wife/ white husband	64,000	1.8	45,000	1.2	69,000	1.8	61,000	1.6
Black husband/ other race wife	17,000	.6	28,000	.6	26,000	.7	24,000	.6
Black wife/ other race husband	6,000	0.0	5,000	0.0	9,000	.2	9,000	.2
Total black/ non-black couples	198,000	5.5	214,000	5.6	253,000	6.6	244,000	6.2

SOURCE: U.S. Bureau of the Census, *Current Population Reports, Population Characteristics, Household and Family Characteristics, March 1984, 1986, 1988, and 1990.*

An Expanding Phenomenon

The number of marriages involving black and white partners increased substantially after 1970. According to reports by the U.S. Census, the total number of black-white married couples increased from 65,000 in 1970 to 167,000 by 1980, representing roughly a 125 percent increase over that decade.[2] After 1980, however, a break in this trend occurred. The number of such marriages rose slightly to 175,000 in 1984 (Table 11.1). The numbers climbed again to 181,000 black-white marriages in 1986 and to 218,000 by 1988, before declining slightly to 211,000 by 1990, representing 5.4 percent of all married couples involving black partners in the nation as a whole. In some large Northern and Western cities with a substantial black middle class, the percentages were higher.

The number of black husbands and white wives increased from 41,000 in 1970 to 111,000 in 1984. Later there was an upturn to 136,000 in 1986 and to 149,000 in 1988, and to 150,000 in 1990 representing 3.8 percent of all black marriages.

Among black wives with white husbands, the numbers are distinctly smaller, and the growth pattern is less consistent. The numbers of these marriages increased from 24,000 in 1970 to 45,000 in 1980, and then to 64,000 in 1984 before declining to 45,000 in 1986. The trend rose again to an all-time high of 69,000 by 1988 before declining to 61,000 in 1990. This pattern of decline is a reflection of an extraordinary divorce rate which will be discussed below.

It is apparent that the overwhelming majority of blacks who get married marry other blacks. The proportion is somewhat less than 95 percent, however, and has been declining slightly in recent years as the proportion of interracial marriages increases. There has been a steady decline from 94.5 percent in 1984 to 93.8 in 1990.

Blacks and Other Cultures

While interracial marriages occur most frequently between blacks and whites, another pattern involves blacks and Asians.* After the deployment of black men in the armed forces in Japan, Korea, the Philippines, Vietnam, and other Asian countries, an appreciable

---

* The census lists "other race" spouses, who are mostly Asians.

number of black men married Asian women. The number of such marriages increased from 8,000 in 1970 to 20,000 in 1980. By 1984 the number had climbed to 23,000 and to a high of 35,000 in 1988 before declining to 33,000 in 1990. This increase of over 300 percent over the twenty-year period indicates that these liaisons may be the fastest-growing type of interracial marriages involving black partners. Black men outnumber black women by nearly three to one in these types of marriages.

Another variation of interracial marriages involves black and Hispanic partners.* These are not shown in the table. Many are included in the black-white figures. The number of these marriages is smaller than the number of black-white marriages but larger than the number of black-Asian marriages. In 1984, for example, there were a total of 79,000 black-Hispanic married couples. By 1986 they had increased to 101,000. They increased further to 130,000 in 1988 and to 135,000 in 1990. The Hispanic partners were largely Mexican-Americans living in the Southwest (California, Arizona, New Mexico, and Texas); and Puerto Ricans living in the Northeast, particularly New York and New Jersey. Despite the historic, political, and cultural affinity between African-Americans and Cubans, there has been very little intermarriage between the large African-American and Cuban populations of Florida, largely because the Cuban population, which migrated from Cuba after the aborted invasion at the Bay of Pigs, consisted primarily of middle- and upper-class white Cubans.

Again, black males are more likely to be involved in such crossover liaisons than black women. In 1984, of the 79,000 black-Hispanic married couples, 48,000 involved black males and Hispanic women, while 31,000 involved black women and Hispanic men. By 1986 there were 66,000 black men and 45,000 black women married to Hispanic partners. By 1990 these numbers had increased to 69,000 and 66,000 respectively.

Regional Variations

The practice of interracial marriage varies substantially from one region to another. David Heer has found that between 1960 and 1970 there was considerable regional variation in black-white marriages.[3] The numbers were highest in the West and lowest in the South. This was true of both males and females. For example, in

* Hispanics may be of any race.

1970 in the Western region, some 4.5 percent of all married black males had white wives as compared with less than 1 percent in the South.

When Thomas P. Monahan examined birth records in the United States in 1970 he found substantial regional variation among interracial parentage (Table 11.2).[4]

Hawaii and Alaska led all the other regions with 16.2 percent of children born to black-white unions. This was followed by the mountain states with 12.7 percent, and New England with 11.1 percent. The Pacific Coast states were in fourth place with 8.7 percent. No other regions came close.

An ever stronger indication of regional diversity in interracial marriage has been provided by M. Belinda Tucker and Claudia Mitchell-Kernan.[5] On the basis of their analysis of U.S. Census data for 1985, they found striking differences in this practice in the various regions and concluded that the national figures obscure much of the regional nature and impact of this practice (Table 11.3). In 1985 while in the nation as a whole 3.6 percent of black husbands and 1.2 percent of black wives had nonblack spouses, these figures rose to 12.3 percent and 3.1 percent in the West, while declining to 1.6 percent and less than 1 percent in the South. And among those married once between 1970 and 1980

TABLE 11.2
Births with Only One African-American Parent
1970

	PERCENTAGE MIXED		
Region	Total	White Parent	Other Race Parent
Total*	3.35	2.96	.39
New England	12.08	11.12	.96
Middle Atlantic	3.08	3.52	.28
East North Central	3.02	2.82	.19
West North Central	5.25	4.83	.69
South Atlantic	1.35	1.11	.24
East South Central	1.70	1.45	.25
West South Central	.92	.61	.31
Mountain	14.73	12.72	2.01
Pacific	10.05	8.73	1.32
Hawaii, Alaska**	24.68	16.17	8.51

* Parentage of both sexes known.

** States shown separately, not included in Pacific region.

SOURCE: Thomas P. Monahan, "An Overview of Statistics on Interracial Marriage in the U.S.," *Journal of Marriage and the Family* 38 (1976): 223–31.

TABLE 11.3
Black Marriages by Race of Spouse and Region of United States, for All Married Couples and Recent First Marriages (percentages)
1985

	RACE OF SPOUSE	
Category	Black	Nonblack
Total U.S. marriages		
All married couples		
Husbands	96.4	3.6
Wives	98.8	1.2
Both husband and wife married once, 1970–March 1980		
Husbands	94.7	5.3
Wives	98.3	1.7
Western region marriages		
All married couples		
Husbands	87.7	12.3
Wives	96.9	3.1
Both husband and wife married once, 1970–March 1980		
Husbands	83.5	16.5
Wives	95.4	4.6
Southern region marriages		
All married couples		
Husbands	98.4	1.6
Wives	99.4	0.6
Both husband and wife married once, 1970–March 1980		
Husbands	97.5	2.5
Wives	99.2	0.8

SOURCE: U.S. Census, 1985. Adapted from M. Belinda Tucker and Claudia Mitchell-Kernan, "New Trends in Black American Interracial Marriage," *Journal of Marriage and the Family* 52 (February 1990), 211.

the proportion of black men in the West with nonblack wives rose to an impressive 16.5 percent. This means that one of every six African-American men in the West who got married during that time married a non-African-American wife.

SOCIAL SIGNIFICANCE OF INTERRACIAL MARRIAGE

The social significance of interracial marriage, however, reaches far beyond its numbers for a variety of reasons. Rigid racial segregation in the past helps to account for the relatively low incidence of interracial marriages.[6] And increasing contact between the races at high school, college, the workplace, and other social situations helps to account for its recent increase.[7] All of which suggests a further increase in the years ahead.

Interracial Marriage Law and Society

Whatever the desires and characteristics of individuals involved, interracial marriage is preeminently an expression of the prevailing norms of the larger society. Historically, trends in interracial marriages may be viewed as a reflection of the changing societal commitment to fundamental human rights in America as expressed in public policy. Though it has existed in some form since the beginning of the nation, prior to 1940 the incidence of interracial marriage was negligible. This was due, in part, to the fact that most of the states had laws making such marriages illegal.

As many as forty of the fifty states had laws banning interracial marriage at one time. As late as 1930, thirty-one states still did so.[8] Despite these laws, there has always been a small number of such marriages even before the Civil War. There was an apparent rise in the number of such marriages after the war, most involving white husbands and black wives. Still, by 1940 less than 1 percent of blacks married across racial lines.

As recently as 1958 a judge found Richard Loving, a white man, and Mildred Jeter, a black woman, guilty of breaking the Virginia miscegenation law by getting married. When the judge sentenced them to be banished from Virginia for twenty-five years, he was being more lenient than the law allowed, which provided for banishment in perpetuity. He also inadvertently signaled that the law would not stand forever.[9]

When the Supreme Court, after several years of avoiding the issue, finally outlawed bans on interracial marriage on June 12, 1967, it affected directly seventeen states which still had such laws. As with so many reform decisions of that period, Chief Justice Earl Warren spoke for a unanimous court in declaring such statutes in violation of the due process clause of the Fourteenth Amendment.[10]

This 1967 Supreme Court decision represented a milestone not only in conjugal relations and race relations but in human freedom generally. As with other social reforms of that period, this decision upheld fundamental human and constitutional rights even in the face of public opinion to the contrary. As late as 1965, for example, two-thirds of all white Americans disapproved of interracial marriage and nearly one-half thought it should be a criminal offense. Moreover, only a slight majority of blacks (58 percent) approved of interracial marriage. During the decade after the Supreme Court decision, American attitudes would change substantially.[11]

The American attitudes have changed even more dramatically in the years since 1972, such that a majority of both white and black Americans now approve of interracial marriage. In part, these trends show a change and improvement in racial attitudes which will accordingly produce further increase in interracial marriages.

In a study of students at two college campuses,[12] Ardyth and John Stimson found that one of every three white girls and one of every three black girls were willing to date members of another race. They found men even more willing but there was significant racial difference. Sixty-seven percent of black males and forty-three percent of white males were willing to date members of another race. Black women stood out in this study in two respects. When faced with opposition from their parents to their dating whites, they were less willing to date secretly than black men or whites of either sex. Second, black females were more optimistic than the other groups that society in general was becoming more accepting of interracial marriage. The researchers concluded that a relaxation of the norms militating against interracial marriage would lead to increases in these unions and to greater interaction between the races generally.

Subsequent to the United States Supreme Court decision and the changes in public attitude an appreciable increase in interracial marriages was noted. Nationwide the number of black-white marriages increased from 51,409 in 1960 to 64,789 in 1970, representing a 26 percent increase (Table 11.4).

The increase was especially pronounced among black men with white wives. These numbers rose from 25,496 in 1960 to 41,223 in 1970, representing an increase of nearly 62 percent. Meanwhile the number of black wives with white husbands had declined slightly over the decade from 25,913 in 1960 to 23,566 in 1970 for a decline of nearly 10 percent. There was a sharp increase in the North and West and a decline in the number of interracial marriages in the South.

The preponderance of African-American men and white women in interracial marriages produced a theoretical explana-

TABLE 11.4
Number of Black-White Marriages by Type and Region
1960 and 1970

	1960	1970	Percentage Change Since 1960
United States: total	51,409	64,789	+ 26.0
Husband black, wife white	25,496	41,223	+ 61.7
Husband white, wife black	25,913	23,566	− 9.1
North and west: total	30,977	51,420	+ 66.0
Husband black, wife white	16,872	34,937	+107.1
Husband white, wife black	14,105	16,483	+ 16.9
South: total	20,432	13,369	− 34.6
Husband black, wife white	8,624	6,286	− 27.1
Husband white, wife black	11,808	7,083	− 40.0

SOURCE: U.S. Bureau of the Census, 1960 and 1970.

tion of interracial marriages. Developed in 1941 by both Robert Merton and by Kingsley Davis, and supported by Robert Staples, this theory holds that African-American men are attracted to white women because their white caste status elevates the black partner's sense of importance.[13] The same theory holds that white women are attracted to high-status black men because their high socioeconomic status elevates the white women's sense of importance.

A major challenge to this theory comes from Belinda Tucker and Claudia Mitchell-Kernan.[14] They did not find significant status differences between blacks and their spouses. They did not find significant differences in the social profiles of black men and black women who married across racial lines.

They noted that intermarriage seems most likely to occur among middle-class partners entering their second marriage who live away from home; and, among blacks, for more men than women, and more in the West and North than the South; with greater age differences between partners. These scholars concluded that something more profound than personal proclivities toward status enhancement seems to be at work. A certain lessening of social control over their behavior has taken place. The "systems of social control" against racial outmarriage or in favor of racial inmarriage in the families, hometowns, and local institutions in which these persons received their early childhood socialization are weakened as they move out from their origins in both physical and social space. Old social networks exert relatively less influence on persons moving substantially up the social-class ladder and getting married for the second time.

This social control thesis seems especially applicable to geographic mobility. In their study in Los Angeles, Tucker and Mitchell-Kernan found that there was higher incidence of intermarriage in the West, where the social climate, recent demographic settlement, and demographic diversity generated an environment more accepting of differences and more supportive of social interaction across categories. College, the entertainment industry, athletics, and the integrated workplace provide a similar social atmosphere, and indeed prove hospitable to interracial marriage. These two scholars—a sociologist and an anthropologist—made an even more profound observation, however, which brought considerable strength to their social control thesis. They noted that most of the persons consummating interracial marriages in Los Angeles were not born and reared in Los Angeles. They came from someplace else, generally far away. They came especially from the northeastern United States and from outside the continental United States, such as the Caribbean.

Tucker and Mitchell-Kernan explain: "Systems of social control that discourage racial intermarriage, in particular, may exert greater influence on mate selection for first marriages than for subsequent marriages. . . ." Moreover, "The role of geographic mobility in this scheme is a function of one's social network. Moving usually means leaving behind relatives and friends, and establishing new relationships."

Why, then, do more black men cross this racial line than black women? These scholars suggest that black girls may be socialized by their mothers differently than black boys. They may be instilled with a stronger respect for the ways of life of their parents and less likely to renounce them. This lends some support to the adage that black women love their sons and raise their daughters. Moreover, these scholars point to the differential bases on which men and women select their mates. Women give greater weight to such factors as earning capacity and ambition. Men, on the other hand, are more likely to choose their mates on the basis of physical attraction. This suggests that in contemporary American society, white women are more likely to find black men who meet their potential earning criteria than white men are to find black women who meet their European conception of physical attractiveness. Conversely, black men, many of whom have internalized the same European conceptions of physical attractiveness, are more likely to find white women who meet their criteria. It is difficult to avoid the suggestions that white men are the major obstacles to intermarriage. Their attitudes are changing, however, though they have changed more slowly than those of white women. It is this change of attitude on the part of white men that is pushing the rate of white male to black female marriages upward. As further attitude changes are noted in the society in general, and among white men in particular, the incidence of interracial marriage seems likely to spiral upward. Finally, the relative shortage of white men (though not as severe as the shortage of black men) may have the effect of making black men more attractive to white women than otherwise might be the case, particularly as black men improve their socioeconomic status, or earning capacity, and as the level of racial integration in general continues to rise.

Understanding of this phenomenon requires knowing its context. The strength of social control over behavior varies from place to place and from time to time, and may vary from gender to gender. Community sanctions against intermarriage may be stronger for black women than black men. This is consistent with the finding reported above that black college women were less likely to date white men if disapproved by their parents.

We believe that interracial marriage can best be understood as a complex social arrangement growing not only out of the complex motivations of individual actors, but growing especially out of societal values, structures, and opportunities—all of which are changing rapidly, which accounts for the relatively rapid increase in the numbers of interracial marriages. Moreover, the forces of race and race relations, as well as factors within the African-American subsociety, play important roles in the formation of interracial families. Interracial marriages are most likely to occur where white and black persons have sustained patterns of personal interactions; when the white partner takes the initiative; among middle- and upper-class individuals; in urban rather than rural communities; and in the North and West rather than the South—among persons in an age range from young to middle age and, more frequently, involving black males. In short, interracial marriage is just one more adaptation to the pushes and pulls of a changing society.

This view is particularly influenced and informed by the contributions of E. Franklin Frazier, who saw interracial marriage as a function of the structure of society and the changing state of race relations.[15] He saw interracial marriage as a function of the "two social worlds" of the black and white community. In his presidential address at the American Sociological Society in 1948 he observed:

> Intermarriage is a sociological problem which has been more or less tabooed, or when it has been subjected to study, the so-called sociological analysis has been little more than a rationalization of current prejudices.
> [Studies] have been related only inferentially to the social and economic structure of the white community and they have almost completely ignored the social reality of the Negro community and its institutions. Not only have both whites and Negroes been treated as atomized individuals without family relations and social status, but such sociologically relevant factors as the effects of urbanization and mobility upon the character of racial contacts and social status have been left out of the account. If studies of intermarriage are to have sociological significance, they must analyze intermarriage within the frame of reference of two social worlds or the social organization of the white and Negro communities.[16]

Not until the work of Tucker and Mitchell-Kernan, in 1990, have these insights been taken seriously by students of this phenomenon.

THE QUESTION OF THE STABILITY OF INTERRACIAL MARRIAGES

A major constraint facing interracial marriages is the belief that such unions will be less stable than others. Do these marriages experience greater instability, that is to say greater separation, divorce, and widowhood than marriages of two African-American persons? The prevailing view in the social science literature is that these marriages are less stable than marriages of two black partners. Albert I. Gordon, for example, has found that "Marriage out of one's faith is, according to the evidence I have examined, almost three times less likely to succeed than ordinary marriages. . . . The chances for success of an interracial marriage are, according to my research, even less than that of an interfaith marriage."[17] Sophia F. McDowell has concluded that interracial couples "necessarily bring to their relationship the burdens of history and institutions, which have become part of their personalities and attitudes. . . . The participating spouses continue to bear the psychological burdens of a culture which has defined race and sex in pathological terms."[18] Robert O. Blood holds that "the great American prejudice against blacks impacts negatively on the stability of interracial marriage."[19]

Not all students of interracial marriage, however, are as persuaded that these marriages are less stable than those of two African-American spouses. Thomas Monahan, for example, concluded on the basis of a study he did in Hawaii that the stability of interracial marriages stood in between those of all-black and all-white marriages.[20] That is, they were less stable than marriages of two white partners, but more stable than those of two black partners. In another study he conducted in 1971, he found that "contrary to popular and sociological belief in the past, for which there was no objective and quantitative proof, Negro-white marriages in Kansas [as in Iowa], have not evidenced any special proclivity to divorce, but rather probably somewhat more stability than obtains for homogamously married Negroes."[21] A number of other students of the question share Monahan's view that interracial marriages are not necessarily or generally less stable than marriages of two African-American partners. Most authorities agree that African-American marriages are less stable than white marriages. Interracial marriages are considered by these authorities to fall somewhere in between these two other patterns.

In an effort to draw a definitive answer to this question, Surinder K. Mehta did an analysis of stability of black-white versus racially homogamous marriages in the United States for the decades 1960 and 1970 based on U.S. Census data. Mehta points out at the outset of his study that "It should be noted that with few exceptions most studies concerning the stability of interracial versus homogamous marriages are based on small unrepresentative samples."[22] And while complimenting Monahan for his competent studies on this subject utilizing marriage and divorce registration data from selected states, Mehta further observed that "As Monahan is aware, however, the study of the relative instability of cross-race marriages requires 'comprehensive national figures' rather than data limited only to specific states." Mehta's reasoning was that no control is possible in the data of particular states over the "in- and out-migration differentials of marriages and divorces by race of spouses for the state." In other words, residents of Iowa may go for marriage or divorce in other states, and residents in other states may go for marriage or divorce in Iowa. National data sets are, therefore, the only control of those interstate migration potentials. All of this is to suggest that despite the competent research and findings of Monahan and the others on the subject of the stability of interracial marriages, all of which was based on data of a particular state, such findings cannot be definitive.

In order to avoid these pitfalls, Mehta utilized a national data set drawn from the 1960 and 1970 U.S. Census. His study was of interracial couples married for the first time between 1950 and 1960 and still married at the time both the 1960 and the 1970 census were taken. This included interracial couples who have been married to their one and only spouse for a substantial period of time—anywhere from ten to twenty years (Table 11.5). This is a much more substantial measure of marital stability than has been generally utilized in marital stability studies, which often use a five-year period of marriage as a measure of stability. He found strong support for the view that interracial marriages are less stable.

The attrition rate for interracial couples was higher than that for same-race couples. Thus, among the 780,239 black husbands with black wives who were married between 1950 and 1960 and still married in 1960, there were 607,089 still together in 1970. This is an attrition rate of 22 percent or a stability rate of 78 percent.

For black men married to white women, among the 7,534 couples that were married in 1960, only 4,780 were still married in 1970. This resulted in an attrition rate of 37 percent or a stability rate of 63 percent. For black women with white husbands, of the 6,082 married in 1960, only 2,842 were still listed as married in the 1970 census. This extremely high attrition rate of 53 percent is considerably greater than that for all other combinations.

TABLE 11.5
Stability of Married Couples with at Least One
African-American Spouse
1970

Racial Pair	Married* 1960 N	Still Married 1970 N	Stability Rate (%)	Attrition Rate (%)
Black husband, black wife	780,239	607,089	78	22
Black husband, white wife	7,534	4,780	63	37
Black wife, white husband	6,082	2,842	47	53

* Married between 1950 and 1960 and still married in 1970.
SOURCE: Surinder K. Mehta, 1978, p. 137

The Relevance of Education

It is widely known that higher levels of education are associated with higher levels of marital stability. This is one reason parents urge their children to finish high school at least before marriage. An important finding is that education increases the longevity of interracial marriages as well. The higher the educational level the higher the probability the marriage will last a long time.

Still, at each educational level the black husband–black wife combination was the most enduring. Among husbands with less than high school education, the black-on-black couples had the highest proportion surviving through 1960 and 1970, namely 66 percent as compared with 37 percent for black husbands with white wives and 41 percent for black wives with white husbands. At the level of high school education, again the black-black couples were the strongest survivors with a survival rate of 83 percent, as compared with 76 percent for black husbands with white wives and a low of 41 percent for black wives with white husbands. Still, at the highest education level, where husbands went beyond high school, the survival rate is so high among black husband-wife couples as to be virtually equal to the survival of white husband-wife marriages at this education level. Black married couples with husbands' education at college and beyond had the highest survival rate followed by that for black husbands with white wives, while black wives with white husbands had the lowest survival rate at this education level. Education is therefore a key factor in the longevity of interracial marriages.

THE SIGNIFICANCE OF INTERRACIAL MARRIAGES

The relevance of the two different communities that Frazier spoke of is apparent to sensitive persons involved in interracial unions. A group of interracial families have formed an organization and meet regularly at a large black church in Washington to provide mutual support. Edwin Darden, a freelance writer who is leader of an areawide organization, the Interracial Family Circle of Washington, Maryland, and Virginia, has articulated some of the concerns of interracial families in a commentary during African-American History Month in 1991:[23]

> My family consists of a black male, a white female and two biracial children. My family is as much a black family as any other one—it

just also happens to be a white family too. My children are not 50 percent of my wife and myself, but 100 percent of both.

Acutely aware of the tension between the two communities, he continues:

What I am working for—both as an individual and as president of the Interracial Family Circle of Washington—is a time when my family can attend Black History Month events free of outside judgments and without feeling out of place and undesired. There was a time when interracial couples—while shunned in white society—could find a welcome reception in a predominantly black neighborhood. Now the couple is likely to take an equal chance in either camp.

It seems likely that for some time to come the black community will continue to be more accepting of interracial couples than the white community. A firmer unambiguous identification of inter-racial families with the black community while not without some friction is the most beneficial alliance for both. For the interracial families such an alliance would provide a firm identity, an accept-ing social environment and a cause, namely racism in all its forms to struggle against with a large number of other black families. This may require what Carter G. Woodson called "taking out citizenship papers" in the black community. It would provide a place to use their talents and other resources to the maximum, while learning how to operate in two different worlds. For the black community generally and its many institutions would bring a few more dedicated hands, hearts, and minds.

Numerous black-white couples have indeed established an open and active identification with the black community. Others exer-cise their human and constitutional rights to reject all racial iden-tification, while still others most deliberately identify with the white community.

In any event, the future of interracial marriage seems likely to be guided by the fundamental rights of free association reaffirmed so eloquently by Chief Justice Earl Warren for a unanimous Supreme Court which struck down all state laws forbidding it in 1967. "Mar-riage," he wrote, "is one of the 'basic civil rights of man,' funda-mental to our very existence and survival.... To deny this fundamental freedom on so unsupportable basis as the racial clas-sifications embodied in these statutes, classifications so directly sub-versive of the principle of equality at the heart of the Fourteenth Amendment, requires that the freedom of choice to marry not be restricted by invidious racial discriminations. Under our constitution, the freedom to marry or not marry a person of another race resides with the individual and cannot be infringed by the State."[24]

With respect to the place and future of interracial families in the African-American community, perhaps W.E.B. Du Bois has already spoken the last word:

> We have not asked for amalgamation; we have resisted it. It has been forced on us by brute strength, ignorance, poverty, degradation and fraud. It is the white race, roaming the world, that has left its trail of bastards and outraged women and then raised holy hands to heaven and deplored "race mixture." No, we are not demanding and do not want amalgamation, but the reasons are ours and not yours. It is not because we are unworthy of intermarriage—whether physically or mentally or morally. It is not because the mingling of races has not and will not bring mighty offspring in its Dumas and Pushkin and Coleridge-Taylor and Booker Washington. It is because no real men accept any alliance except on terms of absolute equal regard and because we are abundantly satisfied with our own race and blood. And at the same time we say and as free men must say that whenever two human beings of any nation or race desire each other in marriage, the denial of their legal right to marry is not simply wrong—it is lewd."[25]

Chapter 12

The Caribbean Connection

In many large communities in the northern United States the black community is composed of families and individuals with three distinct geographic and social origins. Some were born in the South and migrated to the North. Others were born in the North and remained there. Still others were born outside the country, most notably in the Caribbean Island nations.

Often these diverse African descendants live together in the same neighborhoods and participate in the same institutions, including lodges, political clubs, churches, and schools. Often, too, they intermarry, suggesting a blending of subcultures. Not infrequently a certain tension develops between and among them because of their different social origins. Because of their color, all these groups face a certain amount of racial prejudice and discrimination. Their response and adaptation both to the pressures exerted by the larger society and to the opportunities it affords them may vary substantially because of socialization patterns associated with their different social origins.

Cultural diversity among people of African descent is a largely unexplored topic for social scientists, and is generally ignored by the public. But a few scholars have found it illuminating to compare native-born African-Americans to those of Caribbean descent.

There is a widespread view among them that Caribbean people do better in American society than native blacks and that the reason for this is that they have a strong and more stable family structure. Several scholars report finding superior socioeconomic attainment among West Indians relative to native blacks. Thomas Sowell, for example, is explicit about the ideological significance of focusing on West Indian successes: "The West Indian success pattern likewise undermines the explanatory power of current white discrimination as a cause of current black poverty."[1]

Do Caribbeans have a more stable family structure than native-born African-Americans? And do Caribbeans achieve greater levels of socioeconomic success because of this more stable family structure? We have found that the answer to both questions is not as simple as some have asserted. In approaching these questions we have drawn heavily on the works of Charles Green and Basil Wilson, who have done original studies among both these subgroups in New York City,[2] and the work of Robert B. Hill, who has done the only national survey of family and social characteristics that include both native African-Americans and persons of Caribbean descent.[3] First, some background information is in order to answer an overarching question: are these really two separate communities, or one?

Green and Wilson have noted a certain "interracial dialectic that exists between the African-American community and the Caribbean community."[4]

The arrival of West Indians in the early 1900s "coincided with the mass migration of southern blacks to northern cities, which was a consequence of the mechanization of agriculture and the shortage of labor that existed in the industrialized northern states during World War I."[5] West Indians began settling in Harlem along with blacks from the South to swell the small black population that already existed. These three sources of geographic origin—Southern United States, Northern United States, and Caribbean—represented three distinct subcultures. They nevertheless developed into a strong black presence in the city which became the center of black progress in the nation as represented most conspicuously by the Harlem Renaissance of the 1930s, in which members of all three groups joined together and had an enormous impact on the nation. Always, however, the absolute numbers of Caribbean people were small due to the restrictions on immigration to the U.S. from this hemisphere in favor of European populations. After 1965, however, this changed.

Passage in 1965 of the Immigration and Naturalization Act represented a significant shift in U.S. immigration policy, opening up admission to the U.S. from the Caribbean as well as Latin America, Asia, and Africa. Green and Wilson have found that "Between 1966 and 1979, European immigration was held to 22.9 percent while Caribbean people and Latin Americans changed from 15 percent to 46.6 percent."[6]

As a consequence of these changes English-speaking immigrant populations from the West Indies (including the Dutch West Indies, the American Virgin Islands, Guyana, Haiti, and Panama) have swelled to an estimated 1.7 million, constituting a significant segment of New York City's black population. According to Green and Wilson, certain sections of Brooklyn (specifically East Flatbush and Crown Heights) are now 90 percent West Indian. According to political scientist Archie Singham, those Caribbean people who came to the U.S. after 1965 came from a different Caribbean society than those who came in the period of the early 1900s through 1950.[7]

Despite cultural differences native-born blacks and Caribbean blacks have pursued courses of action mutually beneficial to each. Indeed, every major black cultural, educational, and political struggle has had the joint participation of both groups. This is particularly true of the civil rights movement and the historically black colleges.

Still, a certain degree of tension between the two groups, which can be characterized as muted in the early decades of the twentieth century, seemingly has increased as the Caribbean community has expanded in the 1980s.

Some of this tension is due to cultural differences. Some is due to the nature of racism in American society. The Caribbean people come from a region where blacks constitute a majority. They are accustomed to seeing blacks in positions of power. Consequently they are often intolerant of American racism. They sometimes seem to resent it more. Yet they do not always identify with the African-American struggle. Some have sought to avoid stigmatization from the dominant white society by distancing themselves from African-Americans. Like all such efforts, however, there can only be limited and isolated success. The Caribbean community cannot be insulated from institutionalized racism.

James Blackwell has noted that as the Caribbean population expanded, there has been a proliferation of parallel structures in the Caribbean community. Separate institutions such as schools, commercial businesses, financial institutions, and cultural associations have evolved which cater to the group's specific needs. This is seen in the numerous small businesses, which include record shops, bakeries, food stores, restaurants, shipping and export firms, and entertainment establishments.[8]

This development has led some scholars to misinterpret the relationship between African-Americans and Caribbeans. For example, Thomas Sowell has lauded the West Indians' commitment to a work ethic and a willingness to sacrifice. He holds that despite being black they have managed to acquire real estate and attain higher educational achievement, higher median incomes, and a higher rate of advancement into the professions than native-born blacks.[9] Ira Reid advanced a similar thesis. He estimated that a third of black professionals in New York City in 1939 were from the Caribbean.[10] Sowell argues further that the poor economic performance of African-Americans cannot be attributed to racism but to cultural deficiencies in black society.[11]

Nathan Glazer and Daniel Moynihan also support the thesis that African-Americans were less successful than foreign blacks. They attribute this to a lack of frugality and ambition growing out of the slave experience.[12] West Indians, on the other hand, were socialized in islands where blacks were an integral part of the professional stratum. This inhibited the rise of feelings of inadequacy and passivity which they found to be characteristic of native-born blacks. People from the Caribbean, they found, exhibited more self-confidence and a willingness to be aggressive.[13]

Other scholars have challenged this thesis of West Indian exceptionalism. For example, Harold Cruse makes the observation that the professionals and small businesses had a clientele and a ready-made market waiting to be tapped. They prospered not despite the native black community, but because of it.[14]

Green and Wilson also conclude that "These studies appear to corroborate the opinion expressed by a number of persons that African-Americans and Caribbean people are firm allies in a struggle that would seek to improve their mutual depressed social, economic, and political situation in the city."[15]

A NATIONAL PERSPECTIVE: THE BLACK PULSE SURVEY

In 1980, the National Urban League under the leadership of Robert Hill undertook a national survey of black America. This study included for the first time a national sample of Caribbean people, self-identified by descent.[16]

The study examined the extent to which the social and economic attainment of Caribbean blacks in the U.S. is significantly higher than that of native blacks. More specifically, it compared Caribbean and native blacks on such issues as population size, educational level, occupation, labor force status, earnings, household income, whether recipients of public benefits for the poor, and the kinds of discrimination experienced. The highlights from this study are discussed here.

Population Size

Most commentators usually estimate that Caribbean blacks comprise only 1 percent of the black population in the U.S. But the data from the Black Pulse Survey reveal that the actual size is about ten times as large, if all those of Caribbean descent are included. In fact, 9.6 percent of all black respondents indicated that they were of Caribbean descent. In absolute numbers, this means that about 2.5 million of the 26 million blacks in the U.S. at that time were of Caribbean origin (Table 12.1).

These are the persons who indicated that they were "of Caribbean descent" so that they include several generations. Still, nearly one-fourth of them were actually born in the Caribbean, constituting some 71 percent of all foreign-born blacks in the nation.

Table 12.1
**Characteristics of Persons of Caribbean Descent and
African-Americans
1980**

	Caribbean	African-American
Total population	2,492,000	23,413,000
Sample size	279	2,633
Percentage distribution	9.6%	90.4%
Age		
Under 30	28.0%	21.0%
30–39	23.0%	20.0%
40–59	27.0%	35.0%
60 and over	22.0%	24.0%
Median Age	39.6%	45.1%
Gender		
Male	31%	27%
Female	69%	73%

SOURCE: Robert B. Hill, Black Pulse Survey, National Urban League, 1980.

Age of Respondent

The age structure of the two populations is somewhat different. Overall, the Caribbean blacks are much younger, with a median age of 39.6 years as compared with 45.1 for African-Americans.

Socioeconomic Status

There is some support for the widely held view that Caribbean blacks in the United States have higher levels of socioeconomic achievements than African-Americans (Table 12.2). First, the former are more highly educated. At the upper levels, 28 percent of Caribbean household heads are college-educated, compared to 21 percent of African-Americans. At the opposite pole, 41 percent of Caribbean blacks did not complete high school, compared to 50 percent of African-Americans. Overall, the median years of schooling for Caribbean household heads is 12.3, compared to 11 for African-Americans.

A second dimension of socioeconomic status is occupational achievement. In keeping with their higher levels of education, Caribbean blacks also have attained higher occupational status; they are more likely to hold professional and managerial positions. One-fourth (24 percent) of all Caribbean household heads are in professional or managerial occupations, compared to 16 percent of African-Americans. Broken down according to gender, 19 percent of Caribbean men hold such jobs, compared to only 14 percent of African-American men. And 25 percent of Caribbean women are in professional or managerial positions, compared to 18 percent of African-American women.

The occupational area where Caribbean blacks particularly outstrip African-Americans is in the middle-range clerical and sales occupations. Overall, 30 percent of Caribbean blacks but only 18 percent of African-Americans occupy these middle-class positions.

The level of independent self-employment, however, is relatively low among both groups. Overall some 3 percent of Caribbean blacks and 5 percent of African-Americans work for themselves. Again, there is a small gender difference. Among men, 10 percent of Caribbean blacks are self-employed as compared with 7 percent of African-Americans. There is very little self-employment among women.

TABLE 12.2
Socioeconomic Status of Persons of Caribbean Descent and African-Americans
1980

	Caribbean (%)	African-American (%)
EDUCATION		
Less than high school	41	50
Completed high school	33	29
Some college (1–3 years)	16	14
College graduate	12	7
Median number of years completed	12.3 years	11 years
OCCUPATIONS		
Professional/managerial	24	16
Male	19	14
Female	25	18
Craft Workers	9	15
Male	12	21
Female	7	12
Clerical/sales	30	18
Male	16	9
Female	39	20
Other blue collar	38	52
Male	50	56
Female	30	50
TYPE OF WORKPLACE		
Private industry	70	67
Male	61	70
Female	73	66
Government	27	28
Male	28	24
Female	26	30
Self-employed	3	5
Male	10	7
Female	0	4
LABOR FORCE STATUS		
In labor force	63	62
Male	70	71
Female	61	58
Not in labor force	37	38
Male	30	29
Female	39	42

TABLE 12.2 (*continued*)
Socioeconomic Status of Persons of Caribbean Descent and
African-Americans
1980

	Caribbean (%)	African-American (%)
EMPLOYMENT STATUS		
Employed	76	83
Male	73	88
Female	77	80
Unemployment	24	17
Male	27	12
Female	23	20
HOUSEHOLD INCOME		
Under $6,000	36	37
$6,000–11,999	25	25
$12,000–19,999	21	18
$20,000 and over	18	20
MEDIAN EARNINGS	$217	$204
Male	250	264
Female	206	175

SOURCE: Robert B. Hill, Black Pulse Survey, National Urban League, 1980.

Earnings

The more advanced socioeconomic status of the Caribbean blacks in the United States was also reflected in their higher earnings profile. In 1980, the median weekly earnings of currently employed Caribbean household heads was $217 compared to $204 among African-American workers. However, contrary to what might be expected when the sexes are observed separately, African-American men had higher earnings ($264) than Caribbean men ($250). Findings show that the low wages of African-American women lowered the African-American earnings profile. African-American women had median weekly earnings of $175 as compared with $206 for Caribbean women.

Labor Force Participation

Despite their differing levels of formal education, Caribbean and African-American household heads have similar labor force participation rates (Table 12.2). The groups had 63 percent and 62 percent respectively of all household heads actively participating in the labor force. And these labor force participation rates were similar among both groups regardless of gender. On the other hand, contrary to conventional wisdom, Caribbean blacks had significantly higher unemployment rates than African-Americans. Overall in 1980, 24 percent of Caribbeans and 17 percent of African-American household heads were jobless. There was a striking gender difference. For example, while 12 percent of African-American men were unemployed, more than twice as many (27 percent) Caribbean men were jobless. Among women in both groups, however, the unemployment rates were similar to each other, respectively 23 percent and 20 percent.

What these findings on socioeconomic achievement suggest is that the situation is more complex and mixed than simple. In some respects, such as education and occupational status, those from the Caribbean seem distinctly ahead. In other respects, including the critical economic dimensions of life such as mean earnings, labor force participation, and unemployment, the Caribbean blacks seem to fall behind their native African-American counterparts. Gender plays a big role. African-American men lead all others in average earnings, labor force participation, and employment, while African-American women rank at the bottom. The overall picture, then, is that the two cultural groups may have much more in common with respect to socioeconomic achievement than either group has with American whites.

It is important to be reminded that the color line, which still largely distinguishes the haves and the have nots, is not confined to African-Americans versus all others. Marta Tienda's studies show that poverty follows very closely the color line.[17] Between 1960 and 1980 in husband-wife families where both members were employed, which is the most favorable situation for all families, dark-skinned minority families suffered more poverty and improved less than non-Hispanic whites (Table 12.3). For example, by 1980 the unemployment rates were 6.5 percent for non-Hispanic whites, and 16.1 percent for Hispanics. Among the various Hispanic groups, however, poverty followed the color line. The poverty rates rose to 21.7 percent for Mexican Americans and to a significant 34.9 percent for Puerto Ricans.

TABLE 12.3
All Families in Absolute Poverty by Race
1980

Race of Family	Percentage
Non-Hispanic Whites	6.5
Other Hispanics	16.1
Mexican-Americans	21.7
Native Americans	20.5
African-Americans	26.3
Puerto Ricans	34.9

SOURCE: Marta Tienda, "Poverty and Minorities," 1986.

Family Structure

How, then, does the economic status of two dark-skinned minorities, the Caribbean blacks and the African-Americans, impact on their family structure?

First, contrary to conventional wisdom, Caribbean blacks have a higher proportion of one-parent families than African-Americans (Table 12.4). Nearly half (46 percent) of all African-American families with children under fourteen are headed by one parent, and about three-fifths (58 percent) of all Caribbean families with children have one parent. This suggests that the relatively higher educational and occupational status among the Caribbean blacks

TABLE 12.4
Family Structures of Persons of Caribbean Descent and
African-Americans
1980

	Caribbean (%)	African-American (%)
Family structure: families with children		
Two parents	42	54
Single parents	58	46
Marital status		
Never married	23	15
Married	39	45
Separated	16	12
Divorced	10	10
Widowed	12	18
Families with children		
Under age 14	52	46

SOURCE: Robert B. Hill, Black Pulse Survey, National Urban League, 1980.

may not have as powerful an impact in their family structure as their relatively lower employment and earnings profile.

Another element of family structure is marital status itself. Here again, contrary to conventional wisdom we find that African-Americans have a higher preponderance of married-couple families than Caribbean blacks. While 45 percent of African-American household heads were married-couple families, this was true of only 39 percent of Caribbean blacks. Moreover, Caribbean blacks were more likely to be separated (16 percent versus 12 percent); more likely to be never-married adults (23 percent versus 15 percent); and equally likely to be divorced (10 percent) as their African-American counterparts.

Yet a third dimension of family structure is the number of children. Here again the findings are at variance with conventional wisdom. Caribbean families in the United States have slightly larger numbers of children than African-American families. Despite the fact that Caribbean adults are younger than African-Americans, they are more likely to have children. Altogether 52 percent of Caribbean families have children under fourteen years as compared with 46 percent of African-American families.

Racial Discrimination

Finally, the study disputes the often repeated allegation that Caribbean blacks experience less racial discrimination than African-Americans. In some areas—employment, housing, and transportation—the Caribbean blacks experience greater levels of racial discrimination (Table 12.5).

It may well be that Caribbean blacks are more sensitive to and indignant about racial discrimination because they have not come to know, expect, or accept it as much as African-Americans.

What do these findings tell us about the central questions raised at the outset of this chapter? Clearly, no one or two studies in this area can be definitive. Both the local community studies by Charles Green and Basil Wilson and the national survey by Robert B. Hill are pioneering efforts. It must also be noted that these studies were done more than a decade ago, and relationships between the two groups might well have changed. Still, these studies bring systematic data to bear to buttress and sometimes refute opinions based on less systematic analysis.

Do the Caribbean blacks and African-Americans who live in the

TABLE 12.5
Racial Discrimination Experienced by Black Households by Nativity
1980

Types of Bias	Caribbean (%)	African-American (%)
Total Sample	276	2,601
Percent	100%	100%
EMPLOYMENT		
Getting a job	37	27
Getting a promotion	33	23
Losing a job	27	16
HOUSING		
Renting an apartment	27	15
Buying a home	16	9
Vandalizing a home	22	3
TRANSPORTATION		
Getting a cab	19	12
Using public transportation	16	7

SOURCE: Robert B. Hill, Black Pulse Survey, National Urban League, 1980.

large cities constitute one community or two? In our view, they constitute one community in some respects. They are commonly victimized by racial prejudice and discrimination because of their color. They rise up in a fairly uniform manner to express their opposition to blatant racist activities, such as when black youths are subjected to white or police violence. They often exercise concerted political action in support of candidates and issues that touch their lives. They work together in leadership of national black organizations, black colleges, fraternities and sororities, lodges and churches. In other matters the diversity is stronger than the unity of these two cultural groups. Preferences in food, recreation, and residential living arrangements are often pronounced. However, a sense of shared destiny, and joint action on a wide range of political, economic, educational, and social matters, will benefit both groups and move them closer toward one community.

With respect to socioeconomic status and mobility strivings, the picture is somewhat mixed. Clearly, people of Caribbean descent move ahead much further than native African-Americans in a number of areas, including education and professional development. It is not at all clear, however, that accumulation of wealth, independent ownership, or self-employment is as strong as is often reported.

As for the impact of these similarities and differences on family structure, the picture is again mixed. It is not the case, as is widely assumed, that Caribbean blacks have stronger, more stable, more viable forms of family life than native African-Americans. Indeed, in the Black Pulse Survey in 1980, Caribbean descendants were somewhat less likely to constitute two-parent families than their native African-American counterparts. Here again we see that in the interaction between families and the larger society, society has the upper hand. Subcultural differences, as important as they are, are no match for the forces of powerful social systems. Family structure among Caribbean blacks and native African-Americans alike is an adaptation to the pressures and opportunities emanating from the society which controls them. But the strengths which come from a common heritage and past success in overcoming obstacles, combined with common and joint action to confront the systems of the larger society, should enable both groups to wrest for themselves their fair share of society's resources.

PART V

The African-American Community Is Generative

Chapter 13

From Working Class to Middle Class

My father and mother spent their entire lives within a one-hundred-mile radius of the sleepy little country town of Marion, Alabama, where they were born. Married to each other at age nineteen, they would remain so for thirty-seven years until the death of my father from a coronary at age fifty-six. During their marriage they would raise three children to adulthood while caring for numerous extended relatives and other people's children. But while they never traveled outside the State of Alabama, they nevertheless made the enormous transition from the agricultural era to the industrial era. Moving from the farming community of Marion, in Perry County, to the coal, iron and steel center of Birmingham, they were able to lift their own family status from the sharecropper class to the blue-collar working class. In the process they laid a foundation for the movement of their children from the working to middle class.

How were they able to accomplish these feats? First by a re-markable commitment to the value of knowledge and learning and education. They had little formal schooling themselves. My mother went through to the third grade at a country school and was never taught to read and write. She wanted the best for her children, however, and she knew that literacy was imperative. My father went through sixth grade at the private Lincoln Normal School established by the ex-slaves in Marion just after the Civil War. It was an outstanding school. There my father learned to read and write, figure and think, and speak, along with the best in the community.

My parents had a reverence for learning second only to their reverence for the spiritual. And they passed this along to their children. They were not isolated. In Birmingham there were still inordinate hardships. But there were also the multitude of wonders that is a city: indoor plumbing, electricity, telephone, radio, newspaper, and above all school and church; there was even a colored branch of the Birmingham Public Library. All were buttressed by other adults in the neighborhood who could read and write. In the next block to the right were two undertakers and a minister, all three literate. And around the corner lived a school teacher. Up the street in the other direction lived the neighborhood physician. And every day there marched proudly through the neighborhood a postman, a black postman. He could not only read *and* write, which he demonstrated often, but he also regaled the children in the neighborhood with tales of the far away places he had seen letters from, sometimes even in foreign languages.

There were other values too by which my parents lived that helped to prepare their children for upward mobility. Indeed, for my father, his family, his church, his work, and his Masonic lodge were his life. And for the first time in his life, living in the shadow of the biggest employer in Birmingham, the steel mills, he could get a good union job that paid him almost enough to support his family unaided. As for my mother, long before we would discover the ancient African moral code embodied in the seven cardinal principles of virtue, and long before Spike Lee would encapsulate these principles in the title of his movie, my mother was the living embodiment of the moral code, "Do the Right Thing."

Birmingham after World War II, the civil rights revolution, and the technological revolution would continue to present enormous opportunities. Yet progress is seldom simple. For in the midst of such expanding opportunity lurked a hidden consequence. In the wake of the post war, postindustrial era, the steel mills were closed. The new downtown high-tech medical center and the expanding financial and communications institutions which replaced the steel mills as the city's major employer, while not restricted by race, had no place for the men who lost their jobs in the steel mills.

PATHWAYS TO UPWARD MOBILITY

My family story is not an isolated case. It also illustrates what happens when the supportive forces in the larger society undergo major shifts.

The vitality of the black working class as a seedbed for upward mobility has been strongly documented. Harriette McAdoo's study of black urban and suburban families with children provides important recent evidence.[1] Each family she interviewed had income distinctly above the median for the area in which they lived and had at least one parent who attended college. In short, they were middle class in education, income, and occupation. Some 80 percent were married-couple families and 20 percent single-parent families. McAdoo interviewed these parents about their children, themselves, their own parents, and their grandparents.

She found that the largest group among them was made up of those whose parents and grandparents had been working class. These were the celebrated new black middle class.

A second group of middle-class parents had shown steady mobility over three generations. Their grandparents were lower class, their parents were working class; and they in turn, standing on the shoulders of their parents, had moved into the middle class, generally by being the first generation in their family to receive a college education and by obtaining professional occupations. This second group constituted 23 percent of the sample.

A third group of middle-class parents were following in the footsteps of the advances their parents had made. They had grandparents who were working class and parents who were middle class. This group was 6 percent of the total.

Finally, a fourth group of middle-class parents had always known middle-class status. Their grandparents and parents were middle class. These group members were following a consistent pattern of higher than average levels of education, occupation, and income in their family backgrounds. They comprised 9 percent of the total. The fourth group was the only one which did not have working-class origins.

Gary Franks

Congressman Gary Franks' family also illustrates this transition. In the 1990 congressional elections, Franks came to national attention because he was elected to Congress from the fifth district of Connecticut. His prominence was twofold. He was the first African-American to be elected to the U.S. Congress from Connecticut, and the first to be elected from New England since Edward Brooks was elected to the U.S. Senate from Massachusetts in 1960 for the first of three terms. He was also given national attention because he won on the Republican rather than the Democratic ticket. Much less attention was given to Franks's most important achievement. He, his brothers, and sisters, products of the black working class, had risen to upper-middle-class status on the strength of that working-class background.

The thirty-seven-year-old Franks grew up in a black working-class nuclear family in Waterbury, Connecticut, in the years after World War II, when industrial society was at its peak.[2] His father, although he had only a sixth-grade education, was able to get a good job as a mill worker. He sent young Gary to the Catholic high school, in part because private and parochial schools were the norm. He excelled in athletics because he had the talent. He was a good student because his family instilled in him high aspirations. He became president of his senior class because he was bright and aggressive and personable, and because the culture of the school was open to him. With all this push, support, and preparation, Franks was able to rise substantially above his social origins. He graduated from Yale University with a bachelor's degree and became a successful owner of his own small real estate firm. It is an African-American success story of the first order. He was not alone in making it up from his working class origins. All of the Franks children were able to graduate from college and five earned graduate and professional degrees. Gary Franks has said of his own status, "I'm the only one with just one degree."

Reggie Walton

Another similar story has been told by Judge Reggie Walton, of Washington, D.C., who served for a time as U.S. deputy drug czar, was born some forty years ago, and grew up in a small steel town near Pittsburgh, Pennsylvania.[3] His family was a stable, nuclear, working-class family. His father worked the night shift as a janitor at Gimbel's. Reggie lived with his father, mother, and two siblings.

This family background, however, was not enough to save him from the destructive forces of the community and the society. He fell in with the "wrong crowd." He became a delinquent, and was arrested more than once. Fortunately for him, the police turned him over to his parents. His parents made him promise to do better, but all to no avail.

Because his father worked at night, his mother had most of the responsibility for caring for him and the other children, and she had reached her wit's end. One day, she told her husband that he had to do something about their son. His father, described as a big, strong, strapping man, precipitated a crisis that was the turning point in Judge Walton's life.

One Saturday morning, young Walton was in the kitchen making breakfast for himself, having missed eating with the family. He had slept late into the day because he had been out late the night before. He heard some heavy footsteps behind him and sensed danger. His father came up to him and stared him straight in the face. He tried to move away, but his father advanced toward him. He realized that he could not escape.

Walton tells it this way. "He grabbed me by the collar, and told me that he was sick and tired of my coming home late, being disrespectful to my mother, and getting into trouble. He said that I had just one more time to do that, and it was going to be him and me. I knew then that I couldn't win. He put the fear of God in me, and I straightened up."

So Walton stopped getting into trouble, and stayed in high school long enough to graduate. Though he had poor grades he was able to get admitted to one of the historically black colleges, West Virginia State College. There he joined the Alpha Phi Alpha fraternity. These men exuded pride in themselves, their group, their heritage, their race, and their country.

One of their members came to campus one day to give a speech. He was Supreme Court Justice Thurgood Marshall and, as was his habit, he visited with some of the fraternity brothers after the program. They sat around and talked. Of this experience, Walton says, "My goodness, I discovered that I didn't have to be a high school coach. I could be anything I wanted to be. I could even be a lawyer."

By the time he graduated from college, he and nine of his classmates decided to go to law school. At the age of thirty-two he was a Superior Court judge in the District of Columbia, and by age forty he had been appointed by the President to become deputy drug czar.

Someone asked him why he was giving up his cushy, prestigious job to work on the drug problem. Walton said, "Well, I'll tell you why. Most of the friends I grew up with are either dead, in jail, alcoholics, or junkies, and I know that—with the right guidance and a different mindset—all these guys would have had the ability to do at least as much as I've done in life, if not more. And knowing that, I feel a special responsibility to reach out to try to do all I can."

It was not simply the physical confrontation with his father that made the difference in Reggie's life. It was the forceful, psychological, and social presence of his father, his community, and his college and fraternity. It was a powerful combination. Most especially it was his anchor in a working-class family that kept him from downward mobility that represented such a strong and tempting threat.

Charles Albert

Charles Albert and Cheryl Strong represent still another approach to this transition. By 1985 they were solidly middle class. Albert, a thirty-year-old attorney, was associated with a large Chicago law firm.[4] His cohabitating partner, Cheryl Strong, was employed working as a design consultant for a large department store in Chicago. After living together for three years, they became engaged and decided to get married. They were financially ready to take this step, in part because Albert had been preparing for marriage and other major events.

He was fortunate to have been born into a stable working-class family. His father, a longtime laborer in the steel industry, was working class, but his income allowed the family to live in a middle-class neighborhood and maintain a middle-class lifestyle. Because his mother was a full-time housewife, Albert and his siblings grew up in a traditional American family and neighborhood which protected them from some of the harsher elements of growing up black in America. Albert currently lives about a mile from his parents and keeps in close touch with them. He is proud of and grateful for the type of upbringing he was provided by his hardworking parents and once remarked, "Although my parents, who have been married thirty-eight years, were never rich, where I lived has never been considered a ghetto."

Albert's father had the good fortune, as many other black workers did, of getting into the relatively high-paying, unionized steel industry before the middle of the 1950s when that industry and other basic elements of the industrial era began to crumble. He was able to assist Albert financially, using in part the equity acquired from the family's modest home on the Southside of Chicago to send Albert through college and law school. Albert was the first member of his family to attend college.

Albert has followed a path since leaving law school which increasingly departs from the more traditional dependent, civil service, consumer-oriented black middle class. With a good education, strong earning potential, and positive self-image, he has moved steadily toward building the kind of independence that is characteristic of the American middle class in general. He has set his career goals high. He is determined to become a partner in his law firm, though he knows this will take hard work and will require a nonrefundable contribution to the firm of about $15,000. Even on his salary of $64,000, this will require some planning.

After determining his career goals, Albert set about liquidating his college and university debts. Even with help from his parents and his own part-time job, he could not make it through school without government loans since his family's economic status made him ineligible for low-income government grants. Consequently, he took out $6,000 in loans while at Princeton and another $15,000 while at Harvard Law School. Unlike many other professionals, however, he began an intensive repayment program as soon as he started working. Within five years of leaving law school, he had paid $11,000 of his $15,000 loan for law school and $4,000 of his $6,000 loan for college.

In addition to looking backward to clear up his indebtedness, Albert began simultaneously to look forward, building his own investment program to start him on the path toward financial independence.

Albert's next step is to buy a house, particularly as he anticipates moving from the temporary though stable stage of cohabitation to the more permanent state of marriage. With his customary foresight, he is looking the housing market over carefully. He says, "I have recently become engaged and we want to be certain before we move from this spacious low-rent apartment that we have a good deal." The data suggest that Charles Albert and Cheryl Strong already have in each other a good deal indeed.

ROLE OF THE EXTENDED FAMILY

There is a certain downside to having achieved middle-class status while other relatives are still in the working class, and it is a situation most black middle-class families face. The average income of factory workers has continued a twenty-year decline from 1970. Workers who had an average of $187 per week in 1970 had fallen to $172 in 1980 and $167 in 1989 when inflation was taken into account.[5] In this climate it was not unusual for working-class families with earnings as high as $35,000 to drop to less than $6,000 in a few short years. African-American families without relatives to turn to for help became prime candidates for the poverty of the working poor or the nonworking poor. They also became prime candidates to experience depression and to engage in acts of domestic violence and abandonment.

A perceptive article by reporter Isabel Wilkerson of *The New York Times* in November 1990 provided a revealing insight into some of these pressures.[6] She found, with a clarity that sometimes escapes social scientists, that "Two main things tend to distinguish black middle-class people from middle-class whites. One is the likelihood that many more of their relatives will come to them for help. The other is that they tend to lack the resources of people who started life in the middle class."

The following family profiles illustrate this situation.

Joyce Ford

Joyce Ford, the daughter of laborers, grew up in a public housing project. Now she has a good government job and the amenities of her status. But she still has the bone-deep worries of the poor.

Sitting at her desk one day, she received a call. "Your brother's sick," the caller said. "He needs to see somebody."

She spent the better part of the day trying to figure out where her out-of-work brother should go for treatment, and how to pay for it.

Donald Sheppard

Donald Sheppard is an assistant professor of social work at Texas Southern University in Houston. His father was a wool presser at a Houston dry cleaners. Sheppard became the only one of eight children to get a college degree and carry a briefcase to work. A sister once told him, "You're almost like a god in our family."

He and his wife, Gin, both social workers, earned their master's degrees at the University of Chicago in the mid-1980s and raised five children at the same time. They returned to Houston to an extended family of relatives and friends who needed them. The augmented family was a reality as well. Once a childhood friend of Sheppard's who was down on his luck and recently evicted asked Sheppard if he could move his family in with him and his family. The answer was yes, and Sheppard's children slept on the floor to make room. They stayed for five weeks. "Every day, I had to buy milk and bread and cereal," Sheppard said. "I had twelve people in the house, and I was the provider."

His goal is to build up reserves so he can provide for relatives without depleting his own money. But he is a long way from that.

Marjorie Ellis

Marjorie Ellis further illustrates this complex situation.

Ellis's father was a cement finisher who died when she was in grade school; her mother was a maid. She and her sister were the first to graduate from high school and work behind a desk. Now thirty-eight, she is a drafting clerk at the Southern Bell Telephone Company. She shares her two-bedroom ranch house with her sister, her sister's children, her elderly aunt, and her mother.

They are all in transition. Her sister has a job as a civilian worker in the military and is trying to get on her feet, one of the nephews is in college, the aunt is recovering from hip surgery, and her mother is struggling on a pension. They all turned to Miss Ellis when they needed help and now share space in the house, chipping in whenever they can.

Their fortune is tied to her fortune. "If there's a middle class, I'm in the poor section," Miss Ellis said.

She doesn't have the $2,500 she needs to get the engine fixed for her 1984 Thunderbird so she must take the 5:30 bus each dark morning to get to work by 7.

"I'm behind and it's hard to catch up," said Ellis, who earns about $30,000 a year. "I pay one bill one week, the others when I can. I might be late a month. That doesn't mess your credit up too bad. Sometimes I sit and pray and cry. Then I figure it'll be all right somehow. I'm not going to let any of my relatives go wanting if I can help them."

She remembers her minister's words when she got her house: "You're coming up in the world. You're coming up slow, but you're coming up in the world."

Under the strain, Ellis has developed a bleeding ulcer, diabetes, and chronic depression for which she takes regular medication. She often has nightmares about becoming homeless.

Jared Samples

Finally, Jared Samples shows the mixed blessings of upward mobility. Jared Samples presumably went from working poor to middle class overnight when he won a seat on the Atlanta City Council last year. One of the first things he did when he got his first paycheck was to move out of the Perry Homes housing project where he grew up. The next thing he wants to do is get his mother out.

He is saving for the house he wants to buy for her, but he is finding that the $25,000 he makes as a full-time public servant doesn't go very far, especially when he still tries to give money to his nephew in college or a sister to pay her car insurance when he can. "We're four generations out of slavery and one generation out of the projects," he said. "My life is pretty much set. I can work every day but I can't get but so far."

It is clear that each of these families has risen to the middle class on the strength of their working-class parents, and often with the assistance of other relatives as well, most of whom are still working class with an insufficient amount of resources in order to manage. The question for scholars and policymakers alike is: what is the bearing of the extended family on the upward mobility of African-American families? Some hold that extended families facilitate upward mobility of their members, while others maintain that they are a liability. In reality, as has been demonstrated above, both tendencies exist.

Taking an approach consistent with the wholistic perspective now emerging, Harriette McAdoo has suggested the following:

> A third theoretical view may be that instead of viewing the two theoretical approaches as competing, it may be possible that they are both operative, but at different periods within the life of an upwardly mobile black adult. The extended family may be a source of strength when the person is poor, but is seen as being less essential when the higher status is achieved. This may account for some of the alienation and antagonism that appears to exist between working and middle-class blacks. This social class division *appears* to be stronger among blacks than apparently is the case within white families.[7]

The Achievement and Challenge of the Black Middle Class

There are certain distinct pathways to upward mobility among African-American families. The black middle class may be characterized by its origin in the black working class, generally in the previous generation. Most middle-class blacks are still first-generation middle class. In the foreseeable future they may continue to be characterized by their precariousness, as more dependent than independent, more employees of others than owners and managers, and with relatively little accumulated wealth. Moderate and even high salaries and income will not automatically translate into wealth, which refers to the net value of assets over liabilities. Still, the black middle class is a major achievement sustained by education, two earners, extended families, religion, and service to others.

Chapter 14

Room at the Top:
The Rising Black Business Class

For American families, the route to the top of the socioeconomic structure requires ownership of property, other financial assets, and ownership of business and professional practices. Business ownership exists at every social-class level, not just the upper class. Yet public discussions of the black community and especially of black families generally ignore altogether the place of business ownership. When it is discussed, the emphasis is on the relative absence of a strong black business class in comparison with the white community.

In the 1989 issue of the National Urban League's *State of Black America,* the economist David Swinton confirmed this assessment: "As we have pointed out in previous editions of *The State of Black America,* blacks own a very small share of American businesses." He continued: "Overall, the black-owned business sector only originated about 13.8 billion dollars in receipts in 1982 in an 8.4 trillion dollar economy."[1] Moreover in his 1990 survey, describing the 1980s as a "decade of limited progress," Swinton reported that the relatively low level of black ownership of wealth and business enterprises constitutes the major cause of the huge disparities between black and white economic well-being. This ownership factor ranks far ahead of the problems of black employment and earnings.[2]

In our view, however, it is difficult to make the case that $13.8 billion is an insignificant figure. The same is true of the roughly

$300 billion aggregate annual income that flows into the African-American community. The question is, how are these funds utilized and invested? To what extent do they turn over in the African-American community before going out again? Indeed, it is in the utilization of such capital accumulation to build strong independent black institutions and simultaneously to build strong independent reciprocal connections with the larger society that such income generation holds promise.

Often such analyses as those cited above are followed with the assertion that African-Americans just do not have the entrepreneurial spirit, or talent, or interest that other people have. They'd rather try to get ahead by working for others and let others take the risks of ownership. We take a somewhat different view. A broad view of the African-American experience will show that there is indeed a strong entrepreneurial spirit. Historically, business ownership has played a major role in the stabilization and achievement of African-American family and community life.

Two recent studies lend considerable support to this view. John Sibley Butler, professor of sociology and business at the University of Texas, Austin, finds strong entrepreneurial development in certain areas of the nation, which he calls "enclaves." In Durham, North Carolina; Tulsa, Oklahoma; and Philadelphia, black business enterprises blossomed during the period when the constraints against them emanating from the larger society were less stringent than today.[3]

Shelly Green of the Institute for the Study of Economic Culture at Boston University and Paul Pryde of Washington, D.C., have together produced a comprehensive overview of this topic. They argue that there is strong history and strong potential in black entrepreneurial development and they urge blacks to galvanize the entrepreneurial potential in their own families and communities.[4]

This view is advocated also by Mayor Sharon Pratt Kelly of Washington. In a commencement address at Howard University in 1991 and elsewhere she has extolled the virtue of black entrepreneurial enterprise. The civil rights revolution, she holds, opened up enormous opportunities for blacks in a wide range of political, social, and educational areas, and helped to expand the black, white-collar middle class. The next logical base of that revolution, she believes, must be primarily economic and must focus on the expansion of the ownership of the economic life of the community. She has urged blacks to look beyond the secure base of work for the federal government, which has served the community well in the past, to a new era of ownership. "It can not be," she said in a television appearance on Martin Luther King's birthday in 1992, "that business ownership is good for Eastern Europe and the former Soviet Union, and not good for black America." She believes that the entrepreneurial talent is present in the African-American community and that the task of leadership is to create the opportunity structures, support systems, and incentives necessary for expansion. She has committed her administration to give leadership in this direction because she sees the value of such ownership to the stability of family and community life.

There are strong indications that entrepreneurial spirit, talent, and interest are not dormant in the African-American community but instead constitute vital aspects of its culture and promise much for its future development.

In a society dominated by the entrepreneurial spirit—where private business ownership is at the center of the national ethic and where private business provides most of the jobs, most of the wealth, and most of the political influence—it has been argued that the absence of a strong entrepreneurial class among African-Americans has been a crippling condition.[5] Some families have been able to penetrate this barrier. To understand the full range of African-American family life, they must be taken into account.

Surveys of minority-owned business enterprises by the United States Bureau of the Census showed substantial growth in this sector between 1977 and 1987. The total number of black-owned firms increased from 231,203 in 1977, with total sales of $8.6 million, to a total of 424,165 firms in 1987, with total sales of $19.8 billion. This represented a 90 percent increase in the number of firms and an even more substantial increase in sales over that ten-year period. Much of this growth was due to the impetus given to minority business ownership by Congress and the Nixon administration, a policy which was continued under Carter and Ford. And while these and other affirmative action policies would come under sharp attack after 1980, the black entrepreneurial sector would continue to expand at least through 1987. The specific comparisons between 1982 and 1987 as compiled by the U.S. Census are shown in Table 14.1.

This table shows that the total number of black-owned firms had increased from 308,260 in 1982 to 424,165 by 1987, showing a 37 percent increase over that most recent five-year period. And while this is a smaller increase than the previous five-year period, it is still substantial. Most of these firms are sole partnerships with

TABLE 14.1
African-American-Owned Firms
1982–1987

Type	1982 N	1987 N	Change (%)
All Firms	308,260	424,165	+ 37
Firms with paid employees	37,841	70,815	+ 89
Number of employees	121,373	220,467	+ 81
Annual payroll	$ 948,108,000	$ 2,761,105,000	+191
Sales and receipts	$5,704,545,000	$19,762,876,000	+280

SOURCE: U.S. Bureau of the Census, *Survey of Minority-Owned Business Enterprises, Black, 1982 and 1987.*

nobody employed outside the family. Even so, however, the number of firms with paid employees doubled over this period, increasing from 37,841 in 1982 to 70,815 by 1987. A critical element in the significance of these firms is their capacity to hire other employees. The total number of paid employees in all black firms rose from 121,373 in 1982 to 220,467 in 1987, reflecting an 81 percent increase. Still another measure of their impact is the size of their payroll to these employees. This too expanded, from $948 million in 1982 to $2.8 billion in 1987, showing a 280 percent increase over the five-year period.

A final overall measure of the economic contribution of black-owned firms is their total sales and receipts. This aggregate expression of black economic power more than tripled, rising from $5.7 billion in 1982 to $19.8 billion in 1987.

Black-owned firms are scattered widely throughout the nation (Table 14.2). All states except Wyoming had a net increase in such firms. The largest number of firms in 1987 were in California, New York, and Texas. These were followed by Florida, Maryland, and Georgia. Among these six states the greatest percentage increases were in Florida, Maryland, and Georgia followed by New York, Texas, and California in that order.

This increase in black company ownership was accompanied by an opening up of career opportunities in privately owned mainstream companies. Combined with the entrepreneurial opportunity structures, this caused a shift in education as well. When I became president of predominantly black Morgan State University in 1975, the largest professional school was education, training elementary and secondary teachers, the bastion of the historic black middle class. By the time I left (ten years later) the largest school was the business school, training professionals and entrepreneurs

TABLE 14.2
African-American-Owned Firms by State
1982–1987

State	1982 N	1987 N	Change (%)
United States	308,260	424,165	+37
Alabama	6,806	10,085	+48
Alaska	433	507	+17
Arizona	1,274	1,811	+42
Arkansas	3,323	4,392	+32
California	38,876	47,728	+23
Colorado	2,163	2,871	+33
Connecticut	2,455	4,061	+65
Delaware	982	1,399	+42
District of Columbia	8,179	8,275	+1
Florida	15,596	25,527	+64
Georgia	13,490	21,283	+58
Hawaii	271	399	+47
Idaho	84	94	+12
Illinois	14,785	19,011	+29
Indiana	5,011	5,867	+17
Iowa	603	703	+17
Kansas	1,903	2,323	+22
Kentucky	2,814	3,738	+33
Louisiana	12,359	15,331	+24
Maine	109	131	+20
Maryland	13,776	21,678	+57
Massachusetts	2,782	4,761	+71
Michigan	10,947	13,708	+25
Minnesota	1,042	1,448	+39
Mississippi	6,464	9,667	+50
Missouri	5,782	7,832	+35
Montana	55	77	+40
Nebraska	682	863	+27
Nevada	636	1,002	+58
New Hampshire	123	229	+86
New Jersey	9,121	14,556	+60
New Mexico	466	587	+26
New York	24,044	36,289	+51
North Carolina	13,333	19,487	+46
North Dakota	54	57	+5
Ohio	12,390	15,983	+29
Oklahoma	2,837	3,461	+22
Oregon	644	848	+32

TABLE 14.2 (continued)
African-American-Owned Firms by State
1982–1987

State	1982 N	1987 N	Change (%)
Pennsylvania	9,501	11,728	+23
Rhode Island	283	489	+73
South Carolina	9,129	12,815	+40
South Dakota	51	63	+24
Tennessee	7,200	10,423	+45
Texas	27,361	35,725	+31
Utah	164	202	+23
Vermont	63	98	+56
Virginia	13,192	18,781	+42
Washington	2,046	2,583	+26
West Virginia	622	727	+17
Wisconsin	1,844	2,381	+29
Wyoming	90	81	−9

SOURCE: U.S. Bureau of the Census, Survey of Minority-Owned Business Enterprises, Black, 1982 and 1987.

for the private sector. New schools of architecture, transportation, and engineering were likewise oriented to the private entrepreneurial sector. Thus black parents had more options in preparing their children for life, options which historically had been absent.

It is important, therefore, for students of black families to understand something of the black entrepreneurial tradition. An appreciation of the one helps in understanding the other. The entrepreneurial talent may therefore be considered one of the strengths of black families. Indeed John Sibley Butler has done studies which suggest that black children brought up in entrepreneurial families do as well in certain areas of upward mobility as children brought up in Japanese, Jewish, or other ethnic families with a stronger reputation for upward mobility.[6]

The growth of the black entrepreneurial class has been chronicled by Black Enterprise magazine, which since 1973 has profiled the top one hundred black firms, both in terms of annual gross sales and in number of employees (Table 14.3).[7]

By highlighting these hundred firms, we leave out many significant economic enterprises. Blacks have made a major incursion into four areas not included in the table but regularly chronicled by Black Enterprise magazine. These are insurance, banking and thrift, and automobile retail.

TABLE 14.3
The Top 100 African-American Industrial/Service Companies 1990

Rank	COMPANY	LOCATION	CHIEF EXECUTIVE	YEAR STARTED	STAFF	TYPE OF BUSINESS	1990 SALES*
1	TLC Beatrice International	New York	Reginald F. Lewis	1987	5,000	Food products	1,496.000
2	Johnson Publishing Co.	Chicago	John H. Johnson	1942	2,382	Publishing; broadcasting	252.187
3	Philadelphia Coca-Cola Bottling	Philadelphia	J. Bruce Llewellyn	1985	1,000	Soft-drink bottling	251.300
4	H.J. Russell & Co.	Atlanta	Herman J. Russell	1958	668	Construction and development	143.295
5	Soft Sheen Products	Chicago	Edward G. Gardner	1964	532	Hair-care products	92.100
6	Barden Communications	Detroit	Don H. Barden	1981	308	Communications and real estate	86.000
7	Trans Jones/Jones Transfer	Monroe, MI	Gary L. White	1986	1,189	Transportation services	75.000
8	Garden State Cable TV	New York	J. Bruce Llewellyn	1989	300	Cable TV broadcasting	74.000
9	Stop Shop and Save	Baltimore	Henry T. Baines	1978	600	Supermarkets	65.000
10	The Bing Group	Detroit	Dave Bing	1980	173	Steel processing	61.000
11	Technology Applications	Alexandria, VA	James I. Chatman	1977	800	Information systems integration	59.739
12	Advanced Consumer Marketing	Burlingame, CA	Harry W. Brooks, Jr.	1985	250	Information systems	51.250
13	Community Foods	Baltimore	Oscar A. Smith, Jr.	1970	430	Supermarkets	47.500
14	The Maxima Corp.	Rockville, MD	Joshua I. Smith	1978	785	Systems engineering	45.804
15	The Thacker Organization	Decatur, GA	Floyd G. Thacker	1970	115	Construction and management	45.600

* In millions of dollars to nearest thousand. As of December 31, 1990. Prepared by BE Research. Reviewed by Mitchell/Titus & Co.

TABLE 14.3 (continued)
The Top 100 African-American Industrial/Service Companies 1990

Rank	COMPANY	LOCATION	CHIEF EXECUTIVE	YEAR STARTED	STAFF	TYPE OF BUSINESS	1990 SALES*
16	Crescent Distributing Co.	Harahan, LA	Stanley S. Scott	1988	170	Beverage distributor	45.250
17	Network Solutions	Herndon, VA	Emmit J. McHenry	1979	450	Systems integration	43.000
18	Granite Broadcasting Corp.	New York	W. Don Cornwell	1988	356	TV broadcasting	42.614
19	Essence Communications	New York	Edward Lewis	1969	80	Magazine publishing; TV production	42.392
20	Integrated Systems Analysts	Arlington, VA	C. Michael Gooden	1980	600	Engineering; electronic	42.000
21	Systems Management American	Norfolk, VA	Herman E. Valentine	1970	273	Computer systems integration	40.260
22	Surface Protection Industries	Los Angeles	Robert C. Davidson, Jr.	1978	175	Paint and specialty coatings	40.000
23	Wesley Industries	Flint, MI	Delbert W. Mullens	1983	340	Industrial coatings	36.400
24	Pro-Line Corp.	Dallas	Isabel P. Cottrell	1970	290	Hair-care products	35.416
25	Westside Distributors	South Gate, CA	Edison R. Lara, Sr.	1974	115	Beverage & foods distributor	35.400
26	Johnson Products Co.	Chicago	Eric G. Johnson	1954	232	Hair and personal care	34.000
27	Beauchamp Distributing	Compton, CA	Patrick L. Beauchamp	1971	110	Beverage distributor	31.600
28	Brooks Sausage Co.	Chicago	Frank B. Brooks	1985	145	Sausage manufacturer	31.100
29	The Gourmet Companies	Atlanta	Nathaniel R. Goldston III	1975	1,395	Food service management	30.210
30	Calhoun Enterprises	Montgomery, AL	Greg Calhoun	1984	520	Supermarkets	30.000

TABLE 14.3 (*continued*)

The Top 100 African-American Industrial/Service Companies 1990

Rank	COMPANY	LOCATION	CHIEF EXECUTIVE	YEAR STARTED	STAFF	TYPE OF BUSINESS	1990 SALES*
31	Superb Manufacturing	Detroit	Dave Bing	1985	130	Automotive parts supplier	28.400
32	Orchem	Cincinnati	Oscar Robertson	1981	55	Specialty chemicals	27.000
33	Commonwealth Holding Co.	New York	James H. Dowdy	1967	286	Real estate and manufacturing	26.900
34	Trumark	Lansing, MI	Carlton L. Guthrie	1985	205	Metal stampings and products	26.400
35	Parks Sausage Co.	Baltimore	Raymond V. Haysbert, Sr.	1951	245	Sausage manufacturer	26.037
36	Queen City Broadcasting	New York	J. Bruce Llewellyn	1985	160	TV broadcasting	26.000
37	Yancy Minerals	Woodbridge, CT	Earl J. Yancy	1977	8	Industrial metals; minerals	25.840
38	Crest Computer Supply	Skokie, IL	Gale Sayers	1984	45	Computer hardware	25.000
38	Inner City Broadcasting Corp.	New York	Pierre Sutton	1972	200	Radio, TV, and cable TV	25.000
38	Summa-Harrison Metal	Royal Oak, MI	Charlie J. Harrison, Jr.	1978	170	Engineering and metal stampings	25.000
41	H. F. Henderson Industries	West Caldwell, NJ	Henry F. Henderson, Jr.	1954	181	Industrial process controls	24.100
42	Restoration Supermarket Corp.	Brooklyn	Roderick B. Mitchell	1977	116	Supermarkets and drugstores	24.000
43	Regal Plastics Co.	Roseville, MI	William F. Pickard	1985	250	Custom plastic ejection molding	22.369
44	National Capital Systems	Falls Church, VA	Sy O. Smith	1976	260	ADP professional services	22.000

TABLE 14.3 (*continued*)

The Top 100 African-American Industrial/Service Companies 1990

Rank	COMPANY	LOCATION	CHIEF EXECUTIVE	YEAR STARTED	STAFF	TYPE OF BUSINESS	1990 SALES*
45	Input Output Computer	Waltham, MA	Thomas A. Farrington	1969	200	Computer software and systems	21.000
46	African Development Corp.	Hollywood, CA	Dick Griffey	1985	8	African commodities	20.550
47	Dick Griffey Productions	Hollywood, CA	Dick Griffey	1975	74	Entertainment	20.000
47	Viking Enterprises Corp.	Chicago	Fletcher E. Allen	1990	170	Commercial printing	20.000
49	Delta Enterprises	Greenville, MS	Harold L. Hall	1969	300	Electronics; railroad parts	19.500
50	Dual & Associates	Arlington, VA	J. Fred Dual, Jr.	1983	210	Engineering services	19.339
51	Simmons Enterprises	Cincinnati	Carvel E. Simmons	1970	80	Aerospace engineering	19.250
52	Accurate Information Systems	So. Plainfield, NJ	Stephen Yelity	1983	110	Software development	18.300
53	Bronner Brothers	Atlanta	Nathaniel Bronner, Sr.	1947	250	Hair-care products	18.200
54	V-Tech	Pomona, CA	James E. Parker	1982	248	Biomedical test products	18.000
55	Metters Industries	McLean, VA	Samuel Metters	1981	303	Systems engineering; computers	16.960
56	Telephone Advertising Corp	Atlanta	Herbert H. Hamlett, Sr.	1988	16	Advertising kiosks	16.832
57	Keys Group Co.	Detroit	Brady Keys, Jr.	1967	1,400	Fast food	16.100
58	Earl G. Graves Ltd.	New York	Earl G. Graves	1970	62	Magazine publishing	16.000
59	Williams-Russell—Johnson	Atlanta	Pelham C. Williams	1976	210	Construction and engineering	15.300
60	C.H. James & Co.	Charleston, W VA	Charles H. James III	1883	25	Wholesale food distribution	15.056

TABLE 14.3 (continued)
The Top 100 African-American Industrial/Service Companies 1990

Rank	COMPANY	LOCATION	CHIEF EXECUTIVE	YEAR STARTED	STAFF	TYPE OF BUSINESS	1990 SALES*
61	Terry Manufacturing Co.	Roanoke, AL	Roy D. Terry	1963	280	Apparel manufacturing	15.000
62	Mandex	Springfield, VA	Carl A. Brown	1974	270	Telecommunications; computer services	14.961
63	American Development Corp.	N. Charleston, SC	W. Melvin Brown, Jr.	1972	187	Manufacturing and sheet metal	14.819
64	Burns Enterprises	Louisville	Tommie Burns, Jr.	1969	450	Janitorial services; supermarkets	14.800
65	Consolidated Beverage Corp.	New York	Albert N. Thompson	1978	20	Wholesaler; Caribbean exporter	14.500
66	Powers & Sons Construction	Gary, IN	Mamon Powers, Sr.	1967	60	Construction	14.464
67	Ozanne Construction Co.	Cleveland	Leroy Ozanne	1956	40	General construction	14.000
68	James T. Heard Management	Cerritos, LA	Lonear Heard	1971	490	Fast food	13.965
69	Am-Tech Export Trading Co.	Detroit	Robert E. Ellis, Sr.	1984	14	High-technology products	13.600
70	TEM Associates	Emeryville, CA	Berah D. McSwain	1981	150	Computer support services	13.400
71	Systems Engineering	Falls Church, VA	James C. Smith	1985	194	ADP technical support services	13.250
72	A Minority Entity	Norco, LA	Burnell K. Molerie	1978	1,000	Janitorial and food services	12.939
73	Carter Industrial Services	Anderson, IN	Will J. Carter	1976	241	Shipping containers; trucking	12.586

Table 14.3 (*continued*)
The Top 100 African-American Industrial/Service Companies 1990

Rank	COMPANY	LOCATION	CHIEF EXECUTIVE	YEAR STARTED	STAFF	TYPE OF BUSINESS	1990 SALES*
74	NBN Broadcasting & Companies	New York	Sydney L. Small	1973	105	Radio broadcasting and telephone	12.500
74	Best Foam Fabricators	Chicago	Keith A. Hasty	1981	105	Corrugated boxes and cushioning	12.500
76	Management Assistance Corp.	El Paso	Louise E. Johnson	1979	190	High-technology services	12.000
76	Stephens Engineering Co.	Greenbelt, MD	Wallace O. Stephens	1979	120	System integration; computer	12.000
78	Eltrex Industries	Rochester, NY	Matthew Augustine	1968	155	Office products; printing	11.950
79	Williams & Richardson Co.	Detroit	Eddie C. Williams, Sr.	1978	40	General contracting	11.500
80	Black River Mfg.	Port Huron, MI	Isaac Lang, Jr.	1977	87	Auto parts supplier	11.400
80	Ellis Electronic	Detroit	Robert E. Ellis, Sr.	1984	24	Environmental engineering	11.400
82	Drew Pearson Enterprises	Addison, TX	Drew Pearson	1985	16	Sportswear manufacturer	11.257
83	Texcom	Lanham, MD	Clemon H. Wesley	1981	93	Telecommunications services	10.774
84	Burrell Communications Group	Chicago	Thomas J. Burrell	1971	120	Advertising; public relations	10.684
85	Specialized Packaging	New Haven	Carlton L. Highsmith	1983	6	Packaging design; engineering	10.680
86	Watiker & Son	Zanesville, OH	Al Watiker, Jr.	1973	130	Heavy construction and mines	10.538
87	Production Dynamics	Chicago	Charlie Banks	1985	10	Electrical, industrial supplier	10.425

TABLE 14.3 *(continued)*

The Top 100 African-American Industrial/Service Companies 1990

Rank	COMPANY	LOCATION	CHIEF EXECUTIVE	YEAR STARTED	STAFF	TYPE OF BUSINESS	1990 SALES*
88	Highbeam Business Systems	East Orange, NJ	Henry E. Davis, Jr.	1978	115	Business equipment dealership	10.100
88	Correction Connection	Philadelphia	Larry D. Depte	1987	30	Health products manufacturer	10.100
90	Jet-A-Way	Roxbury, MA	Eddie Jeter	1969	56	Rubbish removal; recycling	10.000
90	Universal Software	Southfield, MI	Shirley F. Moulton	1983	28	Computer reseller; imaging	10.000
92	Michael Alan Lewis Co.	Union, IL	Wayne Embry, Sr.	1978	86	Automotive interior trim	9.880
93	RPM Supply Co.	Philadelphia	Robert P. Mapp	1977	19	Electrical and electronic	9.820
94	William Cargile Contractor	Cincinnati	William Cargile III	1956	63	Construction; real estate	9.700
94	Apex Construction Co.	Boston	Jack E. Robinson	1983	230	General construction	9.700
96	The Mingo Group	New York	Samuel J. Chisholm	1977	45	Advertising; public relations	9.450
97	C.G. Enterprises	Southfield, MI	Phillip M. Ingram	1982	35	Computer products sales	9.448
98	Uniworld Group	New York	Byron E. Lewis	1969	80	Advertising	9.392
99	Solo Construction Corp.	N. Miami Beach	Randy Pierson	1978	37	Underground engineering	9.362
100	Compliance Corporation	Lexington Park, MD	Harold Thomas Herndon	1980	170	Computer software and hardware	9.200

Other black-owned enterprises should also be noted, particularly production companies in the communications and entertainment industries. William Cosby Productions, Oprah Winfrey's Harpo Productions, Quincy Jones Production, and Suzanne de Passe of Motown Productions are leading examples. These and others have joined the long-standing Jackson family enterprises. Already they have shown that blacks can operate as independent owners at the highest levels of the white establishment. They have long ceased to be highly paid employees working for and dependent on the whims and tastes of others.

Analysts tend to dismiss black-owned firms because they are so much smaller than many white-owned firms. However, there are numerous reasons to consider them carefully.

First, these companies demonstrate the existence of the entrepreneurial spirit among African-Americans. In this regard they show a strong leadership model for black males. Black men serve as chief executive officers in 90 percent of the top 100 firms. These firms provide various and progressive levels of economic well-being, security, and vitality for participating African-American families, and relative social and political independence.

As family-owned enterprises, many of these firms have the active participation of several family members. The Johnsons of Chicago, the Russells of Atlanta, the Graveses and Suttons of New York, the Henry F. Henderson family of New Jersey, and John Berfield and Sons of Michigan provide conspicuous examples. They challenge the prevailing idea that in contrast to the Asians, African-Americans cannot work together to build a business.

These businesses often provide quality goods and services to the black community that would not have been available otherwise. This includes the insurance companies, and banks and savings and loan associations. It also includes the newspapers, magazines, communications production companies, beauty supply products manufacturing and supply companies, and the like. Often these small firms pave the way for larger white-owned firms, which give them extraordinary competition. The case of the beauty products manufacturers is a good example. This is among the many hazards of doing business.

In 1991 the one hundred largest black-owned industrial and service companies employed some 31,351 persons, down from 33,300 in 1990 and from 37,000 in 1989.

Even with the general economic recession and the severe reces-

sion in the auto industry, the top one hundred black auto deal-
erships in the nation employed some 6,427 persons, holding
steady with 6,400 in 1990 and 6,500 in 1989.

At the same time there were thirty-five black-owned banks in
1991, down from 37 in 1990. Still, they employed some 1,624
persons in 1991, down from 1,806 in 1990 and 1,641 the previous
year. Meanwhile the hard-hit black-owned savings and loan companies were reduced to twenty in 1991 from twenty-four in 1990
and a high of thirty-three in 1989. Even so, these twenty thrifts
employed 538 persons in 1991, down from 636 in 1990 and a
high of 850 in 1989.

Finally, the black-owned insurance companies, a mainstay of
the black entrepreneurial tradition, saw their numbers decline
through mergers. The fifteen largest insurance companies employed some 3,839 workers in 1991, down substantially from the
4,700 employees in this industry in 1990 and the 5,000 in 1989.

As has been shown above, employment, especially meaningful
employment, is perhaps the single most important key to family
stability. Despite economic setbacks, by providing jobs these firms
make a contribution to black family stability. The Joint Center for
Political Studies found that "although the minority business sector
is relatively small, it is an important source of employment for
minority workers, often providing career opportunities unavail-
able elsewhere."[8]

While all their workers are not black, in business as in other
areas, African-American institutions continue to provide more
interracial employment than white institutions. Some 60 percent
of black firms report that between three-quarters and 100 percent
of their employees are black.

A word must be said about the variation in earnings and employment of black firms depending on the industry. In some industries black-owned firms outpace those of other groups. The
Joint Center for Political Studies found that African-Americans
are trailing Hispanics and Asians in most fields, but forging ahead
in others. In finance, insurance, and real estate, black entrepreneurs showed higher average sales and receipts than other
minority-owned firms.

The major firms make a sizable contribution to their local economies by their purchases of goods, services, equipment, and basic
materials as well as by their investments, deposits, and loan port-
folios. Some appreciation of this economic contribution is gained

from an overview of the total sales as well as total assets of these firms.

The top one hundred black industrial and service companies had total sales of $4.3 billion in 1990, down by four percent from $4.5 billion a year earlier. Funds come into these institutions and go right out again in the form of payroll, purchases, investments, loans, and other expenses, all of which help to enrich the local economies and contribute taxes at all levels of government. Many black leaders are grappling with methods to keep more of these funds circulating within the black community before they go out again into the larger economy. In the meantime, funds flow through, including going to the operation of local, state, and national governments through property, income, Social Security, and other taxes.

Black-owned firms also provide a measure of support to the strong humanitarian and philanthropic tradition in the African-American community. There has been a view in the wider society for some time that the African-American people were principally recipients of charity and not givers. Perhaps that myth was shattered by a pioneering study directed by Dr. Emmett D. Carson at the Joint Center for Political Economic Studies in 1987. He confirmed that charity and volunteerism have been prominent features of the African-American cultural heritage. After a two-year intensive study of the contemporary situation he was able to establish definitively that the tradition is still alive. He concluded that "contrary to widespread beliefs, blacks are as active as whites in supporting charitable organizations." Moreover, he found that "blacks and whites at all income levels are equally involved in volunteer activity."[9] Owners of black firms have been among the leading participants in both the charitable giving and in volunteer activities.

Because of all these positive features, black-owned business enterprises offer culturally tested models by which to teach children that they can be anything they want to be if they develop the proper habits, attitudes, and behaviors. No longer do parents need to overlook ownership in favor of teaching their children to work for others, for the government, in the military, or in the professions. Business ownership in a wide variety of fields is visible to them. Persons who make these businesses successful are available to them in the media, in their organizations, and in their communities—though not yet in their textbooks.

The black-owned business sector helps to connect the black community with mainstream society, and at the same time provides the larger society with vehicles through which to reinforce strong black communities and families.

BLACK ENTREPRENEURIAL FAMILIES

The following case studies illustrate the relationship between achievement of African-American families and business success. Even though they cannot be considered representative of the full range of entrepreneurial families, their stories provide insight into several success factors.

While it is true that black men often precede black women in moving into the front offices of both black and white business enterprises, they do not do so alone. Both the families into which they were born and the families which they form in later life are helpful to them. And the women in these families play significant roles.

The Johnson Family of Chicago

John H. Johnson, for example, one of the wealthiest and most powerful black businessmen in America, would not be where he is today, and would not be able to secure the future of his enterprises, without the partnership of three generations of black women—his mother, his wife, and his daughter.[10]

The economic and social impact of this company and this family are impressive. In 1991, the Johnson companies reported total gross sales of $252 million, up from $241 million the year before. Moreover, they employed 2,382 people, up from 2,370 the year before. The family has been listed by *Forbes* magazine as possessing a net worth of over $200 million, which makes them among the 400 wealthiest families in America. And while their wealth is still small by American corporate standards, it has been estimated that the Johnson empire touches the lives of at least one-half of the adult blacks in the United States. All of which helps to secure this family's place in the black upper class. Throughout its history, since its founding in 1942, this company has been a family affair.

Johnson owes his start in business to his mother. Bringing up her son as a single mother in Arkansas prior to World War II, she brought him to Chicago so he could attend high school. Johnson began the company in 1942 with a $500 loan from his mother. In order to raise the money, his mother allowed him to pawn some of her furniture. Johnson's wife, Eunice, a college graduate from a middle-class family, has been a longtime business associate and currently heads two of the companies within the Johnson enterprises. She is chief executive of the Fashion Fair Cosmetics line and of Ebony Fashion Fair. The cosmetics products were carried in more than 1,500 stores in 1986. Tragically, his son died at the age of twenty-five in 1981 of sickle-cell anemia. Johnson's daughter, Linda, worked her way up through the company. She earned a degree in journalism and worked in the business for a number of years, then enrolled in 1986 in an MBA program to learn the more technical aspects of business operation. On the day she graduated her father appointed her president and chief operating officer of all the Johnson enterprises, elevating himself to chairman.

Not only family members but other women as well have played important roles along with the men in the Johnson company. He once explained to a visitor that he had more female vice presidents than male and that he found them to be, as a group, much more able, dedicated, and loyal. Moreover, although he built his own commercial enterprise "without a dime of government money," he is a strong advocate of affirmative action programs for minorities and women.

The Russell Family of Atlanta

Another giant of the black entrepreneurial class is the Herman J. Russell family, owners of the H.J. Russell Construction Company in Atlanta, Georgia. Three generations of the Russell family have developed along with the family business.[11]

For 1990, H.J. Russell & Company, a construction, development, and communications company in Atlanta, ranked number four on the list of top one hundred black firms, and has ranked among the top ten black businesses since the beginning of these annual surveys in 1973. As an umbrella company for some thirteen different enterprises, the H.J. Russell Company includes construction, airport concessions, beverage, real estate, communications, and property management firms.

These companies reported $143 million in gross sales in 1990 up from $132 million in 1989, and employed 668 people, the same as the year before. The Russell family net worth has been estimated in the neighborhood of $100 million.

As in the case of Johnson, Russell's family played an important role in the success of his enterprises. He has reported that his father made substantial contributions to his entry into business. Unlike Johnson, Herman J. Russell was born into a business family. His father was a skilled plasterer who owned his own business, and who brought young Russell into the business as laborer and helper at the age of ten. His father taught him to work hard, he has said, and he has been working hard ever since.

In addition to the experience and opportunity, his father also gave him a set of values. Russell looks back on his father as "a great inspiration to me. He taught me some of the basic fundamentals: to always be true to yourself, to be punctual, and the art of saving a dollar." His father also taught him to value land and property. "My father believed in land, and that rubbed off on me. He made a believer out of me when it came to real estate. It's hard for me to give up land once I get it." Thus despite an inherited speech impediment, Russell has negotiated some of the most intricate and lucrative land deals in Atlanta and throughout the Southeast to build his present enterprises.

A further gift from his father was the opportunity to pursue higher education. His father both encouraged and helped him financially to study at Tuskegee Institute in Alabama, where he learned the professional and highly technical aspects of construction and business. It took some farsightedness on the part of his father to see the value of dispensing with one of his most able and loyal workers so that he could obtain the higher education which the father himself never had.

The family Russell made has also played an important role. His wife, Otelia, has been a strong supporter and booster. His daughter, Donata Major, at twenty-eight was executive vice president of one of his companies, Concessions International. One son, H. Jerome, at twenty-four was executive vice president of another company, City Beverage Company. Another son, Michael, twenty-two in 1986, was a civil engineering major at the University of Virginia. He represents a particular occupational ladder in the Russell family. From his father, a self-taught plasterer, Herman Russell became a college-trained construction specialist; his son Michael has carried the occupational line even higher with advanced professional study of civil engineering. One son describes his father as "a very complex person" who can "communicate with lots of different people and get action from them." Another said that "He is a caring and good father, and definitely a role model for me."

Like a number of other wealthy upper-class blacks, Russell has placed the headquarters of his companies within the black community so that the economic benefits circulate within it. As an avid tennis player and strong churchman, he attends to the physical and spiritual aspects of his life as well.

It is said that Russell is a consummate family man and that the company is a family affair. He still works twelve hours a day, lives in a modest house, drives a modest car, rides coach class on airplanes, and eats lunch at inexpensive restaurants. Active politically, he has benefited from city contracts. Unlike John H. Johnson, he has not seen the necessity of avoiding involvement with government. Under three mayors of Atlanta, one white and two black, he has prospered and made enormous contributions to the life and tax rolls of the city. A strong believer and supporter of black institutions, he is a favorite of the local charities. "We will only control our destiny," he has said, "when we learn to master whatever we are doing." And, as a result of his now favorable position when doing joint ventures with largely white companies he says, "I insist not only that we pick up our equal part in the proceedings, but that we have black people in key positions where they can learn. If all we are going to get out of it is a buck and we don't develop the human resources then we are missing the boat."

The Llewellyn Family of New York

Another entrepreneurial role model for African-American families is J. Bruce Llewellyn, principal owner of three major business enterprises, the Coca-Cola Bottling Company of Philadelphia, Garden State Cable TV Company of New York, and Queen City Broadcasting of New York, ranked number three, number eight, and number thirty-six among top black enterprises in 1990.[12] They reported total gross sales in 1990 of $251 million, $74 million, and $26 million, all showing growth over the previous year. They employed a combined total of 1,460 persons. Llewellyn attributes much of his head start in life to his family. His parents, Charles and Vanessa, were both born in Jamaica. Ambitious, they came to the United States in 1921 like countless other ambitious immigrants, and like so many black immigrants, they settled in

New York's Harlem. His father got a job as a linotype operator with a prominent newspaper. His mother was a full-time home-maker and caretaker for Llewellyn and his younger sister, who is now a New York District Supreme Court judge. He says that his parents taught them a strong work ethic and instilled in them a belief that they could compete with anyone. A powerful sense of self-worth and high self-esteem was the result.

This process was helped along considerably in the Llewellyns' case when they moved from Harlem before he was two years old to a nearby suburban community. He believes that growing up in an integrated community—even though he lived in the segre-gated portion of that integrated community—exposed him to black and white children of substantial resources and abilities and taught him to compete effectively with all of them. "It's important that you have no sense of inferiority about what you're learning or about your abilities."

Llewellyn also learned from his parents the value of money and of operating a business. His father owned a restaurant, where he was allowed to work as a young boy. He was encouraged to sell magazines at a very young age, and he also sold Fuller Brush products. "My father used to tell me," he has said, "that this is a great country with great opportunity but that you're going to have to work twice as hard to get half as much."

In addition, however, to what he learned from his family, his school, and his community, he learned valuable lessons also when at the age of sixteen and not yet a high school graduate he joined the army. There he learned through hard and bitter experience the requirements of leadership. He rose quickly through the ranks to become a company commander at nineteen. He was so small, he said, that he began smoking cigars to add to his stature with the older men under his command. After five years in the service, he came out in 1948 to a time of enormous economic optimism and upward mobility for black Americans. He invested his savings in a business and simultaneously enrolled in school. Eventually earn-ing a law degree, he has moved from one level of successful and not so successful operations to the next in government and busi-ness. Along the way, his family, his community, his school, the army, the political and economic structures in combination have provided him first the head start, then the continuing support which are indispensable to the level of achievement to which so many aspire.

BLACK POLITICAL POWER AND ECONOMIC POWER

Washington, D.C., Mayor Sharon Pratt Kelly's concern to move beyond political power to substantial economic power in the next phase of black community development is not without support. In cities governed by black mayors, for example, there is a much fairer distribution of contracts to business groups. Black business owners, their employees, and their families benefit from this exercise of political power. A study by Dr. Timothy Bates found that "Black political power in City Hall creates an environment in which black businesses flourish."[13]

In general, Dr. Bates found that black businesses are more successful in cities run by black mayors. Specifically, he found that along with the increase of black mayors has been an increase in college-educated black entrepreneurs and that they have increasingly entered what are called the emerging minority industries, including wholesale, construction, finance, and business services. In black-led cities emerging black firms employed an average of 4.3 persons as compared with 2.3 in cities led by non-black mayors. Average sales were also higher. In black-led cities, average sales per firm in 1982 were $53,793 as compared with $35,953 in white-led cities. Black firms survived longer in black-led cities. The percent of firms in 1982 that were still operating in 1986 was 73 percent in black-led cities and 67 percent in white-led cities. The capitalization of black firms was higher in black-led cities. In 1982 the mean financial capital (per firm) in black-led cities was $25,432 as compared with $18,915 in other cities.

There Is a Black Upper Class

Many students of African-American families and of upward mobility have ignored the black business class and the contribution it makes to the black upper class. Some even continue to argue against the existence of a black upper class. In 1991 Professor Bart Landry, author of the *New Black Middle Class,* gave a speech in which he repeated his thoughtful if arguable belief that there is no black upper class. When this came to the attention of prominent black columnist Carl Rowan, he exploded, not because he was left out of Dr. Landry's definition of upper class but because a lot of his friends were. Landry's definition is clear. "I have maintained throughout this study that blacks lack an upper class."

And by upper class he means "owners of the means of production." He continues: "Included in this group are those families and individuals who own or have controlling shares of large corporations and banks or have amassed large fortunes through business enterprises or through inheritance."[14]

What makes this definition provocative is that it uses wealth as the sole criteria. Then Landry proceeds to set the wealth curve rather high, eliminating "simple millionaires" from the upper class. But the matter that caused the ire of Carl Rowan is that Professor Landry apparently listed names of a few whom others might consider upper class and then excluded them. All of which prompted Rowan to write:

> I've seen a lot of nonsense written in the past few weeks to "celebrate" black history month, but few things more absurd than a sociologist's assertion that "blacks don't have an upper class."
>
> The last thing we ought to be telling American youngsters, especially black ones, is that you can't be "upper class" unless you have money to burn, plus second and third homes in places like Paris and Palm Springs. Landry asserts that upper class "is about owning large corporations that keep producing more income, corporations with massive stocks."
>
> I'll wager that both John H. Johnson and Reginald Lewis would say "rubbish" to what Landry is writing and saying. I think they would say that being upper class may suggest having a comfortable amount of money, but that "class" also is about other things as well.[15]

Then Rowan listed some of his favorite candidates for the upper class: Dr. LaSalle D. Leffall, the former president of the American Cancer Society; Clifton R. Wharton, Jr., the former president of Michigan State University; James Earl Jones, the actor; Barbara Jordan, the former congresswoman; William Gray, who ranked third in the House of Representatives; L. Douglas Wilder, the governor of Virginia; and General Colin Powell.

Finally, Rowan objected to Landry's dismissing Bill Cosby from the upper class.

> Landry dismisses Bill Cosby with the assertion that "When you are talking about the upper class, you are not talking about a few million dollars. That's peanuts." Well, any guy who gives $20 million to a black college is upper class enough for me.

While the entire concept of social class is rather arbitrary, it would seem that the columnist comes closer than the sociologist in expressing the meaning of class in the African-American community generally. Income, wealth, education, occupation, all play a part. But so do social standing, contribution to community and society, and above all the esteem accorded by the community. Members of the upper class, including the leading entrepreneurial families, operate at the highest levels of recognition, impact, and respect.

It has been pointed out by a number of observers that private business ownership is less well developed in the African-American community than in the nation as a whole. Such observations often overlook or underestimate, however, the significance of black business ownership. They often conclude that there is a relative absence of the entrepreneurial spirit and talent in this community in comparison with others. The above findings, however, show the large and growing entrepreneurial sector in the African-American community. They show that there is no absence of entrepreneurial spirit and talent among the African-American people. Nor is there absence of opportunity for successful black enterprise. The presence of business enterprises in the African-American community is not minimal but substantial. What needs to be more fully appreciated is that such business enterprises are highly related to strong, achieving, and productive African-American families.

Chapter 15

Stumbling Blocks and Stepping Stones: Traditional African-American Family Values

The history of family life among the African-American people is a history of struggle. It is a struggle to keep life and limb, and body and soul together. It is filled with inordinate hardships and handicaps. This same history, however, is also a lesson in endurance. It is a history of overcoming obstacles, of turning stumbling blocks into stepping stones. And because of the high value placed on kinship and community, the struggle to maintain and enhance family and the sense of belonging and of well-being which it fosters often brings forth the best efforts and the most creative adaptions of the African-American people.

Successive generations can turn the stumbling blocks of life into the stepping stones of success. Although it can be dangerous, and sometimes seems all but impossible, somebody in the family keeps moving along. As a consequence the family moves beyond survival to higher levels of achievement.

Stepping stones exist at every level of the social structure. One family's success may flow from the extraordinary, unanticipated assistance of an especially caring, talented individual. Others may get a boost from their nuclear, extended, or augmented families. Social support may come from a friend, neighbors, and even strangers, or from community institutions such as the church, school, or various other organizations. Still others may benefit from institutions or conditions in the larger society.

Families who have achieved a measure of success may think that they succeeded all by themselves. The two families profiled in this chapter harbor no such illusions. The Curry family of Marion, Alabama, honored as family of the year in 1984 by the Hampton University Black Family Institute, points to an institution in their local community which is largely responsible for their status. The Duke family of Montgomery, Alabama, Pine Bluff, Arkansas, and Chicago, pays its respects to an ancestor who paved the way.

THE CURRY FAMILY

When Hampton University selected the Curry family as family of the year it was honoring more than a set of individuals related to each other by blood and marriage. The university was recognizing the interaction among a set of values, relationships, and institutions that are at the core of African-American culture and survival.

All the Curry siblings, Helen, Pauline, Minnie, James, Lorenzo, Tommy, and Gladys, were there. So were their spouses and children, who came from all over the country to Hampton, Virginia, to be honored by one of black America's oldest and most distinguished institutions, one which has played a crucial role in this family's evolution. The contemporary James Curry was there with Eloise, his wife of more than a quarter century, and their two grown children. As one of the more effective principals of a Washington, D.C., inner-city high school, senior deacon in one of the city's oldest and largest Baptist churches, leader in its program for neighborhood boys, leading citizen and devoted husband and father, he was an outstanding representative of this remarkable family, having grown up poor in rural Alabama after the turn of the century. He would be among the first, along with his brother Lorenzo, to acknowledge that members of this achieving family had not succeeded on their own. They would point to family members, extended relatives, nonrelatives, friends, neighbors, and especially the church, the school, and the workplace as among the major sources of their achievement. They would also point to individuals and institutions in the wider society which helped to hone their values, beliefs, and actions. A central place would be assigned to the Lincoln School, founded by blacks in the years immediately after the Civil War.

James and Sally

The recorded history of the modern Curry family dates to the slave era.[1] James Curry, the elder, the patriarch of the family, was born into slavery in Perry County, Alabama, in 1848. Sally, his only wife, was born into slavery a few years earlier in 1842. Still, she outlived her husband by a decade, dying in 1944 at the age of 102. He died in 1934 at the age of 86.

Reflecting the high level of literacy in antebellum Perry County, James had emerged from slavery with the ability to read and write. His grandchildren recall him as the resident intellectual, always collecting books, magazines, and newspapers and helping them learn to read them. He worked after slavery for a white family on Polk Street in Marion. He later purchased property from them and built a small house next door at 310 Polk, which still stands today in modernized form. The Polk Street house would be the center of life for the Curry family for more than a hundred years.

Although Sally could not read or write, she was remembered as possessing a good command of the language, with impressive speech and diction; she carried herself erect and with great personal pride. She did cooking and housework for white families in Marion after her marriage until later life, when she took a strong hand in rearing her grandchildren while their mother worked in the local laundry trade.

Of the six children born to James and Sally Curry, three lived into adulthood. Lucy, one of their daughters, would be remembered by the grandchildren as a loving family member who lived with them in the Polk Street house. She worked as a maid and cook in Marion until the late 1920s when she went off to New York to do similar work. She wrote back fascinating tales about life in the big city. She later returned to the house on Polk Street in Marion where she died in 1930.

Irving Curry and the Lincoln School Legacy

One of the three surviving children born to James and Sally Curry was Irving, the eldest son. Born in the Polk Street house in 1895, he died there at the age of seventy-eight in 1973. As a boy, he was enrolled in Lincoln Normal School.

On May 17, 1866, a small band of newly freed African-American men concerned about the education of their children conceived the founding of a school. It took shape a year later, when on July 17, 1867, nine former slaves drew up a petition to incorporate the Lincoln School of Marion, Alabama, named in honor of the recently slain President. These men did what they could. They agreed on the school. They pooled their resources and their labor, bought the land, and built the school. But they could not do the teaching. So they did the next best thing; they appealed to the American Missionary Association to send teachers from the North.

For better and for worse the school would endure for a century until it was closed permanently in 1970 by the state authorities on the pretext that it was a segregated black school, in conflict with the 1954 Supreme Court decision declaring school segregation unconstitutional.

Irving Curry had to quit Lincoln in order to care for his own elderly parents. He became a house painter and did well at this skilled trade until ill health forced him to retire. His children remember that he lived an exemplary life, and according to family members and acquaintances he exhibited the finest qualities of manhood. He was a devoted family man, generous to his fellows, full of integrity, honesty, and forthrightness.

Irving and Minnie

Irving married Minnie Webb in 1915 and moved her into his family home on Polk Street. They lived there together for fifty-eight years until his death in 1973. On the occasion of their fiftieth wedding anniversary, all their children and grandchildren came back to the Polk Street house in Marion to give them a surprise anniversary party. Minnie studied at Lincoln Normal School in the early years, and subsequently she worked at Lincoln in the school laundry to help pay the tuition for her children to attend the school. Her children remember her as an industrious mother. She often rose early in the morning to work at the laundry. Then she would stay up till late at night doing ironing from her private laundry business by the light of a kerosene lamp. Her children also remember her being kind, thoughtful, loving, and attentive. A devoted Christian, she imparted to them strong values about justice and mercy. Mama Minnie fell ill in 1975 and spent ninety-eight days in the hospital. Her friends and relatives were as attentive to her as she had been to them when she was well. She died in 1976, three years after the death of her husband.

Their firstborn son, Irving, died in childhood. All the other six of Minnie and Irving's children attended Lincoln Normal School. All graduated from the high school department. All attended and graduated from college. Most have advanced degrees. All their children who are old enough have also completed college. What helped to account for such achievement? In sum, they were surrounded by a social environment which propelled them forward.

The Role of the Teachers

While the curriculum and the instruction were uniformly excellent at Lincoln, there was a human dimension as well. James Curry has said, "Our teachers told us that we could be anything we wanted to be. And most of us wanted to be just like them, schoolteachers." The interest of the teachers in their graduates was expressed over and over again. When one of the Curry siblings graduated from Lincoln, two of her teachers, a husband and wife team, contributed $100 toward her college tuition. They requested that she not repay them, but urged her when she was able to make a similar contribution to another struggling student. In college, the student worked after school, received lots of help from her siblings, and by her second year in college was able to make a $100 contribution to another needy student. After graduation from Hampton, she continued to contribute $100 a year to some needy student throughout her professional career.

One Curry sibling reported that when he graduated from Lincoln, he could not afford to go straight to college because he had to help support the three older siblings who were already in college. So two of his teachers, another married couple, took him home with them to Muncie, Indiana, gave him free room and board for a year, and helped him find a job. Then when he entered the army during World War II, he reported that "Then I could really help my brother and sisters finish college." Later he would finish himself with the support of the GI Bill.

The Curry children's strong sense of family solidarity, industriousness, and sharing was encouraged by their parents and their teachers. The spirit of sharing with nonfamily members was also nurtured in their family, the church, and the school. It is no wonder that all the Curry siblings entered the helping professions—teaching, social work, and related fields.

The Curry family is far from an isolated example. Horace Mann Bond found that an unusually large number of highly achieving

black professionals have roots in the Lincoln School.[2] Coretta
Scott King, in an interview in 1988, spoke of Lincoln preparing
her for the rigors of Antioch College. And in her autobiography
she has written:

> The faculty at Lincoln was brave and dedicated and the school had
> a strong tradition of service to humanity which was communicated
> to its students. I feel that the chance to go to such a school made a
> real difference in my life. Looking back now, so many things that
> happened to me when I was younger seem to have been preparing
> me for my life with Martin. Going to Lincoln School was one of the
> most important of these.[3]

Another Lincoln graduate, Jeanne Childs Young, who first met
her husband, Andrew Young, the former United Nations Ambas-
sador and mayor of Atlanta, when he came for an internship as a
young minister at the Congregational Church in Marion, also
spoke about how Lincoln prepared her for a life of service.

Lincoln Support Systems

The close association of spiritual values and educational aspirations among African-American families was reflected in the important role assigned to the church and to religion in the
curriculum of the school. The local Congregational Church was
constructed in 1880 under the leadership of Thomas C. Steward,
who had come from Ohio in 1867 to serve as the principal of
Lincoln School. Over the years the close cooperation between the
church and the school helped to insure the future of each. Moreover, members of the community helped to build the buildings,
pay the teachers, and assisted the teachers in teaching their children.

Mary Elizabeth Phillips, who was named the sixth principal of
Lincoln School in 1892, was a New England educator who first
came to Alabama to teach at Talladega College, sponsored by the
American Missionary Association AMA. She presided over the
school for thirty-five years until 1927, the year she died. In 1935
Lincoln alumni established Phillips Hall as a memorial to her
work.

Among the obstacles the school constantly faced was the hostility to the school and particularly to the white teachers by local
white citizens. On at least one occasion, vigilantes organized a
posse with shotguns and planned a march on the teachers' resi-

dence late in the night to run the white teachers out of town. They were deterred by the black men of the community, who organized an armed posse and took turns standing guard over the teachers' residence at night.

The state was also hostile to Lincoln School throughout its history. The education of the ex-slaves was not a state responsibility. It was the state which, against the wishes of the African-American people, made Lincoln a segregated black school in 1953 by expelling all the white teachers; and it was the state, against the wishes of the African-American people, which closed the school in 1970 because it was a segregated black school, in violation of the 1954 Supreme Court decision.

Lincoln was not the only private school which had such positive effects in the lives of African-American families. All over the South, schools sponsored by the American Missionary Association for the newly freed former slaves helped to lift them from the depths of degradation produced by the slave system. William J. Edwards, the black founder of Snow Hill School in Alabama in 1893, has paid tribute to others who did similar work. Writing in 1918, he observed:

> [T]o me, these have been twenty-five years of self-denial, of self-sacrifice, of deprivation, even of suffering, but when I think of the results, I am still encouraged to go on; when I think of the work that Mr. McDuffie is doing at Laurinburg, N.C., Brown at Richmond, Alabama, Knight at Evergreen, Alabama, Mitchell at West Butler, Alabama, Carmichael at Perdue, Alabama, Brister at Selma, Alabama, and hundreds of others, I feel that the sacrifice has not been in vain, so I continue believing that after all the great heart of the American people is on the right side.[4]

As Henry A. Bullock has pointed out, long before public schools were developed for the ex-slaves, Northern philanthropy sought to establish public schools for the blacks all over the South.[5]

Scholars have pointed out that factors which enhance the self-esteem of individuals are paramount in their successful coping and achievement.[6] Several aspects of the Lincoln legacy reflect this. The curriculum was rigorous and soundly based on the best principles of the New England enlightenment. The instructors were competent and compassionate. They believed, or knew, that their pupils could master all branches of knowledge despite their disadvantageous circumstances. They went far out of their way to demonstrate this faith in their pupils. The school maintained discipline. Attendance was required. Tardiness was discouraged. The teachers demanded order and decorum in school and on the playground and even in the community. The teachers were in intimate contact with the parents. The importance of parents to the education process has been reemphasized by recent studies.[7]

Lincoln School stressed moral and spiritual values and concern for others. For years the Congregational Church was led by the principal or a teacher at Lincoln. Students were required to attend regular religious services. Religion was an important part of the curriculum.

The school encouraged students to learn and appreciate their own African-American history along with other cultural and artistic developments. They studied the abolition movement. My father reported that Booker T. Washington was a frequent visitor to Lincoln when he was a student there in the early 1900s.

The school was not isolated but highly interrelated with other institutions in the community. Family life, work life, and church life were all important to the school and reinforced by it. In all these ways Lincoln Normal School provided a cultural oasis which served as a community-level screen of opportunity which enabled the children and their families to cope effectively with their circumstances.

THE DUKE FAMILY

In July of 1989, a family reunion held in Chicago drew some fifty members of the Duke family. Coming together for the first time were members of three generations and four branches of this strong extended family representing four of the eight children of a remarkable man, Jesse Chisholm Duke. He was born a slave in Alabama twelve years before he was freed by the Civil War. When he died in 1916, at the age of sixty-three, his brief obituary in the *Crisis* magazine read as follows:

> A prominent citizen, J.C. Duke was born in 1853 in Alabama. He became editor of the *Montgomery Herald,* but was driven from the state because of his fearless editorial policy. Settling at Pine Bluff, Arkansas, he became editor of the *Pine Bluff Herald*. He served as a lieutenant of the Seventh United States Volunteers in the Spanish-American War, and for a number of years was Grand Chancellor of the Knights of Pythias of the State, making that Order notable among colored men. For twenty-five years, he was prominent in the civic and political life of the state. He died in Chicago last January.[8]

This obituary gave only a cursory picture of the life and contributions of this man, and told little of the institutions he touched or the family he built which have persisted to the present generation. The full story is told by historian Allen W. Jones, archivist at Auburn University in Alabama, and by Duke's oldest daughter, who at the age of eighty, in 1976 dictated her memoirs to one of Duke's great-great-grandchildren.[9]

Family Background and Marriage

Jesse Chisholm Duke was born in Dallas County, Alabama. His slave mother, Ellen, had been brought to Alabama from Maryland. His father, Abner, a slave on a neighboring plantation, had been brought to Alabama from Virginia. Jesse's mother died in 1859 and he continued to live on the same plantation until 1863, when at the age of ten he was hired as a servant to a family of French refugees who lived nearby. The eldest daughter of the family, a schoolteacher, taught young Jesse to read and write. He would use this skill to the utmost. Early literacy gave him a headstart. Two years later he was hired out as a servant to a local physician who sent him to night school for a short time. After a group of local white bigots raided and wrecked this school for black children, the physician's daughter took the responsibility of providing Jesse's education.[10]

Reflecting on what had been handed down to her through the years, Jesse Duke's oldest daughter, Esther, described his early family experience.

> My father's mother, Easter, was a mulatto. Her father was Old Marster. She married a man named Abner Duke. To that union of Abner Duke and Aunt Easter came three boys: Green, Noah, and Jesse Chisholm Duke being my father.
>
> My father's master was named Chisholm. And that's why his name was Jesse Chisholm Duke. But his mother hated white people so, because of the way they treated women. She said she did not want to be called Chisholm, because some of those young people had tried to insult her and she didn't want their name. So she asked, in some way, I don't know how they changed their names in those days, but she asked that they change their name to Duke.
>
> After a certain length of time, Aunt Easter died and my father's father married a woman named Mary Jane, and to that union there were two daughters, Charlotte and Willie.
>
> Abner Duke was a laborer; he worked in the fields. And so did his

wife. His children were not educated, that is, they did not have the push that my father had. My father was the only one of Mr. Duke's children who went on and continued his education; went to school, and studied at home.

My father left Demopolis as a young man and went to Montgomery, Alabama. He went into politics immediately and his aim was to change a lot of the conditions that he saw. He was always a very good speaker. The two families, the Dukes and the Blacks, didn't know of each other during slavery time. But my father met my mother later in Demopolis while he was running on the road.[11]

In his research on Jesse Chisholm Duke, Professor Jones corroborated much of the oral history as repeated by Duke's oldest daughter, Esther. He found that Jesse Duke's earlier political activity had earned him a job in the post office, and in 1876 he was appointed Republican county clerk of elections. His job was to register blacks to vote. The Democratic inspector of elections, however, had a different goal, namely to keep blacks from voting.

Duke on one occasion defied the Democratic inspector by opening the polls and holding the elections. In 1876 the Republican Executive Committee rewarded Duke by employing him to canvass the Fourth Congressional District for the presidential ticket and for James T. Rapier, a black Republican candidate for Congress. Both his candidates won. Blacks went to polls in overwhelming numbers, a practice that would soon be suppressed for a century.

At every turn, Duke faced threats and physical intimidation by local white Democrats. Once a crowd of white men marched into his grocery store and demanded that he close his business and leave town. According to Professor Jones, "Duke challenged the leader of the crowd with a pistol and forced the men to leave his store."[12] Throughout the county, Duke and other blacks were harassed and taunted at polling places by white Democrats. He stood his ground and usually succeeded in helping blacks to register and vote.

At the age of twenty-four, he returned to his position as mail clerk in the post office at Selma. Then in short order he joined the St. Phillip Baptist Church and married Willie Evelyn Black of Selma on January 10, 1878. They had six boys and two girls over the next seventeen years before her premature death.

The Dukes' eldest daughter remembered a family of strong values, strong convictions, and indomitable spirit. They used these gifts to build their own business enterprises. She recounted in her memoirs:

My mother's father had a trade, architect, and right today his grand-children and descendants live in Demopolis and they live on Black Street, named after him. Not a one will ever work for a white man. Every one has his own business. They are tailors. They are contractors. They are beauticians. They have dress shops where they sew and all that. One of the nephews even taught at Tuskegee University.

Now, the Blacks were aristocrats. My mother even had a cousin, a Mr. Turner who was a Congressman in Washington, from Alabama.

The Dukes were not aristocrats. Furthermore, my father had been running around, like so many fellows do, and had an illegit-imate child. This child was named J.C. Duke. But my mother and father could never name a child after my father. He didn't take care of that child, but he was the father of it. And the girl didn't want him to take care of it. I don't think she thought much about it. You know how those women were. And there was no love between them. It was an affair. The Blacks knew about this illegitimate child. When my mother and father met at a church social, or something like that, he had really grown up. He considered himself just as good as the Blacks. When he asked to marry Willie Evelyn Black, the Blacks blew their top. Oh, the idea of marrying a man with a child.

My father said once, he and my mother went for a walk. They were sitting on a log discussing their future. He was very much hurt because the Blacks didn't want him to marry my mother. So she said, "Well, let's run off and get married. I'll go with you wherever you go."

But he told her, "No, I have my pride. I will try to win their respect. And if I don't, we will never marry." So when he was running on the road, and became prominent in politics, and they saw they were really in love and wanted to marry, they consented and they had a very nice wedding in Demopolis.[13]

On the occupational front, Duke left his job with the post office in 1879 and opened a grocery store in Selma. He remained po-litically active, serving a two-year term on the Republican State Executive Committee. After 1885 when the Democrat Grover Cleveland was elected President, Duke's political career suffered a fatal blow. He abandoned active politics and turned his consider-able energies to his other pursuits.[14]

Churchman

Duke moved rapidly to the top of the ranks at the Baptist Church.

He served as a delegate to most of the Colored Baptist State Conventions in Alabama from 1881 to 1887 and was frequently appointed to committees of the Convention. He was appointed to the Board of Trustees of Selma University, a school founded and supported by the black Baptists of Alabama. In December 1886 the Colored Baptist Convention appointed Duke "State Printer and Business Manager" for the black Baptists in Alabama.

Journalist

He launched a long and eventful career as a journalist. Professor Jones writes:

> In less than thirty days after his removal from the postal service, Duke began his career in journalism. On May 8, 1886, he published the first issue of the *Montgomery Herald,* a weekly paper which pledged "Equal and Exact Justice to All Men."
>
> Jesse Duke's reputation as a journalist spread rapidly, and within a few months he had gained the respect of other black editors in the state and throughout the South.[15]

Educator

Duke teamed up with Booker T. Washington to advance the cause of black education and institution building. At first both men opposed moving a black university from Marion to Montgomery, fearing that it would be too close to Washington's Tuskegee Institute some fifty miles away and provide unwelcome and unnecessary duplication and competition. Let it stay in Marion or move to Birmingham, they argued. Professor Jones continues:

> But after the Alabama legislature passed an act in February 1887 appropriating $10,000 to build a "colored university" and $7,500 annually for its support, Duke changed his position and joined a committee of black citizens who sought to move the university to Montgomery. Duke used his Montgomery *Herald* to solicit donations from the black citizens of the city for the university. A rivalry for the university developed between Birmingham and Montgomery during the summer. When the black citizens of Montgomery offered $5,000 and three acres of land for the university, it was accepted unanimously by the Board of Trustees of the State University on July 26, 1887. The conservative Montgomery *Advertiser,* the voice of white supremacy in the state, applauded the decision of the board and predicted that "only good will come of it, good to the school and good to Montgomery."[16]

The manner in which the citizens of Montgomery followed black leaders to win out over industrial Birmingham would be instructive.

But while Duke's victory for blacks in Montgomery was both sweet and enduring, he was not to enjoy it personally for very long.

Fighter for Justice

In early August 1887 Jesse Duke witnessed a lynching. A black boy who was accused of raping a white girl was hanged by a white mob and then his body was dragged by a rope through the streets of the black section of the city. Duke responded to this event in his *Montgomery Herald* on August 13 with an editorial about lynching:

> Every day or so we read of the lynching of some negro for the outraging of some white woman. Why is it that white women attract negro men now more than in former days? There was a time when such a thing was unheard of. There is a secret to this thing, and we greatly suspect it is the growing appreciation of the white Juliet for the colored Romeo, as he becomes more intelligent and refined. If something is not done to break up these lynchings, it will be so after a while that they will lynch every colored man that looks at a white woman with a twinkle in his eye.[17]

Some whites were so incensed by Duke's audacity and implied accusations about white female honor that they called a meeting for early Monday morning to discuss the best plan to pursue. They decided to pay Duke a visit. When the committee went to the *Herald* office, Duke was gone. He had left town on Friday to attend the Eufaula District Sunday School convention.

According to Professor Jones, excitement continued to spread through the city during the night. Rumors that Duke was in Selma and would come in on the train sent a crowd to the depot to greet him. Another rumor that he was seen sitting in a restaurant on Monroe Street with fifteen other men caused a delegation to search the streets and cafés in the black section of town. The search led one angry group to Duke's home. "His wife and children hid in the cellar while the mob banged on the doors and broke out some windows."[18] Duke secretly reentered the city and then escaped, with the help of the white Democratic mayor whom Duke had befriended. Once he was safely out of the state, Duke wrote a letter to the *Montgomery Advertiser* defending himself and absolving all other blacks of having any knowledge or association with his editorial. He disclaimed any intention of reflecting "upon the moral inflexibility of the white women of Alabama, or any implication that their inclination is towards amalgamation." Duke's letter concluded: "My only ambition has been to elevate my race, which you and humane journalists profess to encourage; and when in my conception—however erroneous it may be—of the proper course to conduct a colored newspaper, such an intolerant spirit is evidenced as now prevails at Montgomery, I am astonished as I am persuaded that men have lost their reason."

Duke settled in Pine Bluff, Arkansas, bought a house and a farm, which was located about three miles from the city, and sent for his family.

In Arkansas the Duke family thrived and rose to the top of the socioeconomic structure. Jesse Duke's daughter Esther comments on this period:

> When he got to Pine Bluff, he bought a farm about 3 miles in the country from the city limits, a beautiful home on a big highway. Then he sent for my mother and the four boys. There was a colored family in Montgomery named Loveless, who helped my mother pack the things and sell what things they couldn't possibly take.
>
> He wasn't there too long before he sent for his father, Abner Duke and Mary Jane, Uncle Noah, Uncle Green and his half-sisters, Charlotte and Willie. Charlotte lived with my father and mother to help with the children because they didn't have any help at that time. But after they became established, they always had a woman come in and help with the children.[19]

Military Officer

After nine years as a prominent editor, churchman, community leader, educator, and gentleman farmer, Jesse Duke became a soldier. Always a patriot, in 1898 at the age of forty-five he joined the army to help in the Spanish-American War. Professor Jones writes:

> He enlisted as a second lieutenant in Company I of the U.S. Volunteer (Colored) Infantry Regiment at Jefferson Barracks, Missouri. He was later transferred to Camp Haskell in Macon, Georgia. He rose to the rank of first lieutenant in January 1899 and was discharged at Camp Haskell about two months later. He returned to Pine Bluff and resumed his career in journalism as editor of the *Pine Bluff Weekly Herald* from 1901 to 1908.[20]

Lodge Leader

Finally as agent, officer, and head of the Knights of Pythias lodge in Arkansas, Duke was extraordinarily successful. His daughter has recounted:

> For a long time he made his money from his newspaper. But first, before he went in the newspaper, he was a principal of the high school in Pine Bluff. And then he went into the newspaper. And then lodges were popular at that time. Pythians, Masons, and my father was the Grand Chancellor of the Knights of Pythias for the whole state of Arkansas. Now that's where he coined money, and that's when I went off to school. He'd travel from one tiny horse-and-buggy town to the other setting up lodges. It took 50 men to set up a lodge and each man had to pay $10 to join the lodge. Five dollars went to him and $5 went in the lodge treasury. And sometimes when he'd come home, he'd have so much money that he would have to have a police escort.[21]

Duke remained on his farm at Pine Bluff until a few months before his death in Chicago on January 23, 1916.

Charles Sumner Duke

Of the eight children born to Jesse Chisholm Duke and his wife, Willie Evelyn Black Duke, two died in infancy, Leslie (1877) and Rosebud (1895–96). Thomas (1887-1904) was accidently drowned at age seventeen. The other five grew to adulthood in this privileged, devout, service-oriented, and highly achieving environment. They benefited from their own head start. Four of them went on to historically black colleges. Charles Sumner (1879–1952), David (1881–1928), Esther Pauline (1889–1986), and Edward (1882–1943). Harrison Reed (1892-1923) did not go to college.

While all the surviving children of Jesse Chisholm Duke and Willie Evelyn Black Duke were influenced by their illustrious father, and all acquitted themselves well in life building solid careers and strong families, it was their oldest son, Charles Sumner Duke, who followed most closely in his father's footsteps in further distinguishing the family name. Highly gifted intellectually, he would take to education with a thirst and a passion that has become legend down through the generations. By the time he was sixteen he had not only completed high school but had graduated from a two-year junior college in Arkansas. It would be but the first of a series of four colleges and universities from which he would graduate. His older sister, Esther Pauline spoke of him fondly while dictating her memoirs at age eighty, to one of his great granddaughters:

> Charlie graduated when he was sixteen, and went to Washington.
> . . . Charlie lived with some man that my father knew. He went to Howard University. But Charles would come home in the summer and he was a page to one of the senators. Pages and things like that were politically appointed. This man in Washington had this senator make Charles a page and he worked there to help himself through school. I don't know what state he was from, but he was a Northern senator. [Charlie] was there for I don't know how many years while he was in school.[22]

Something about Charles's rectitude and reputation can be gleaned from this recollection by his adoring older sister:

> I remember when Charles—I loved my brother. I thought he was perfect. That's the truth. I didn't think he could do anything wrong.
> . . . I remember one summer when he was home we were working in the field and a blade of that corn fodder cut his hand and he said "Damn it." Why did he say that? Oh, I cried for months. The idea! I couldn't believe that my brother would say that ugly word. That hurt me so bad. Other little incidents that my sister-in-law, my brother Dave's wife, would tell me about Charles—I couldn't believe it to save my life; that is, going out with women and what not. Oh, I just couldn't believe it.

Whatever might have been his proclivities, it is clear that Charles allowed nothing and nobody to interfere with his education. He graduated from Howard University in a timely manner with a degree in engineering.

Charles Sumner Duke and Eileen Estelle Taylor were married in 1908 in Detroit, Michigan. Longtime members of the Chicago black upper-middle class, they had four children. Two, Charles Sumner, Jr., and a twin, died in infancy in 1912. His surviving son, Jesse Chisholm Duke II, would also earn a degree in engineering from Howard University, while his daughter, Inez Estelle, would graduate from the University of Chicago as did her husband, Herman Tate. Years later, when Inez would come to Washington to visit her own daughter and son-in-law and grandchildren at Howard University, she would be moved almost to tears when taken to the Engineering School to view a portrait of her own father hanging on the wall.

The bachelor's degree in engineering from Howard would be just one more stepping stone for Charles Sumner Duke. His older sister remembers the story of his education well:

> He graduated in engineering from Howard University. From there he went to Exeter and from there to Harvard. He was very, very smart in mathematics. I remember, he graduated before his class in mathematics. This was Harvard.

Indeed after spending two years at Exeter during which he distinguished himself academically, Duke was able to complete his course of study at Harvard in two years, graduating with a bachelor's degree in mathematics in 1904. Later he would earn still another degree, this time a master's degree in civil engineering at the University of Wisconsin. His thesis, *The Scientific Investigation of Deep Water Tunnels,* was highly regarded and widely published. Duke would follow his famous father's footsteps in several respects. He entered the teaching profession, serving as the principal of the first public high school for African Americans in Indianapolis, Indiana in 1907. Later in 1916 at the age of thirty-seven, he enlisted in the all-black 8th Infantry of the Illinois National Guard. On July 6, 1916 the unit was called into federal service. Duke served at Camp Wilson, Fort Sam Houston, Texas. Legend has it that Duke was part of the force that crossed into Mexico in 1916, pursuing the revolutionary Pancho Villa.

Duke's major work, however, was as an architect and engineer. He accumulated a large number of buildings and other projects to his credit. Then in 1929 he was convener of a group of black architects, engineers, and scientists who formed the National Technical Association, a professional association functioning to the present day.

TRADITIONAL AFRICAN-AMERICAN FAMILY VALUES

What do we learn from the fruitful lives of Jesse Chisholm Duke and his progeny that may speak to our time? And how are these insights related to the story of Lincoln School and the Curry family? Both cases highlight for us a number of family values, generated in Africa, which survived slavery and the exodus and which have relevance to African-American family life today. Parents, teachers, counselors, and others who aim to help children grow and help strengthen family life may benefit from insights derived from these two case studies.

First is the value of learning, knowledge, education, and skills development. From the ancient teachings at the university of Ipet Isut on the west bank of the Nile River, the love of learning has been a deeply ingrained cultural value among the African people.

The high value African-American families place on education and their strong commitment to self-help have been documented in a study by Dr. Josie Johnson of the University of Minnesota. After examining the autobiographies of fifty successful African-Americans who were born during the half century after the Civil War, Dr. Johnson concluded:

> The Reconstruction autobiographies revealed that parents, communities, and organizations initiated a variety of activities that resulted in schooling for black children. These activities ranged from mothers taking in laundry to pay tuition for the children and fathers risking their lives in order that their children might go to school, to communities meeting for the express purpose of building a school structure.[23]

In addition she writes: "They paid tuition for children to attend schools away from home, assisted in salaries of teachers when salaried teachers were available, provided land, materials, and labor in the building of schools."[24]

The African-Americans who conceived Lincoln School after the Civil War shared this love of learning. Jesse Chisholm Duke practiced it.

We also learn from these cases that a head start is critical. Early literacy is the key to success. And one of the major tragedies of our contemporary educational system is that some have forgotten that and others never knew it.

In 1990, I began a term on the national evaluation commission for the High Scope Foundation in Ipsilanti, Michigan, one of the most successful of the head start–type programs for minority children under four from disadvantaged backgrounds. Among the ingredients that make for the success of such early intervention, the most apparent is low-income black parents' commitment to their children's learning.

These two case studies also demonstrate that at the elementary and high school levels black teachers have played an important and historic role. The erosion of this source of upward mobility and achievement for black children after the 1954 era of desegregation has been among the most crippling, even if unintended, consequences of that remarkable contemporary reform.

Professor Faustine Jones-Wilson has described the basis of success of black youths at Dunbar High School in Little Rock prior to desegregation in 1954:

> To most graduates of Dunbar the whole was greater than the sum of the parts. . . . From 1930 to 1955 if one were a black youth of secondary-school age in Little Rock, Dunbar was the place to be. Students did not want to be absent, since school was "where it was happening." Dunbar was one's home away from home, where students were taught, nurtured, supported, corrected, encouraged, and punished if/when it was necessary to do so. . . .
>
> There never was a choice for the student between "learning" and "not learning." To fail to learn what was being taught in school was unacceptable to teachers, family, peers, and the community.[25]

Second, after the love of learning, the African people have traditionally held deep spiritual values. In both these family histories, this value was operative. The black church has become a vehicle for the expression of this sense of reverence and search for transcendence over life and death.

A third value highlighted in the case studies is the quest for self-governance. Politics is spread throughout these stories. It could not be otherwise in the years just after the Civil War. The governments at the local, state, and national levels were perceived as belonging to all the people. In the brief years before the end of Reconstruction African-Americans took to the ballot as they did to education and to their church. And for a time their participation paid off for them as it would later pay off for the Irish, the Italians, and the Jewish people of New York and elsewhere in the nation. Politics was a way out and up, a stepping stone to influence; it provided a sense of belonging to the whole and a feeling of pride.

A fourth African-American family value reflected in both these stories is service to others. It runs all through the lives and careers of these two distinguished families. A fifth value is cooperation with other people for economic, political, and social goals. Sixth, race pride shines like a beacon throughout the several generations.

Finally, we are reminded that there was and are no substitutes for strong black-owned private enterprises, neighborhood institutions, and political power to create the conditions for strong black families. In the private enterprise sphere one area exploited by Jesse Duke and his sons is the newspaper business. Numerous great black newspapers have historically been associated with great black families. The *Afro-American* newspaper and the Murphy family of Baltimore; the *Chicago Defender* and the Barnett family of Chicago; the *Pittsburgh Courier,* and the *Norfolk Journal and Guide* are some other outstanding examples. In modern times newspapers have given way to black-owned magazines and broadcast companies in association with achieving families. The Johnson family's *Ebony* magazine, the Graves family's *Black Enterprise,* and the Sutton family's Inner City Broadcasting Company are ranked among the top one hundred black businesses in the nation today out of some 300,000.

Another private initiative associated with strong families historically has been the Fraternal Lodge Movement. Duke was an organizer, entrepreneur, leader, and beneficiary of the Knights of Pythias. The Masonic Lodge, Odd Fellows, Elks, and several others likewise have helped to build strong families.

It can now be seen that the relative preponderance of blacks as employees and consumers in enterprises owned and controlled by others is a major source of weakness in African-American family life today. Conversely, the historic roots and the small but expanding growth of such enterprises augurs well for enhanced black family life in the years ahead.

The basic values and belief systems which have sustained African-American families over the years have been attested to by a number of scholars. Our own work in 1968 identified a set of values as among the sources of family stability and achievement. Among these high priority was given to spiritual values, educational achievement, family ties, and economic independence.[26] The most celebrated work in this area has been done by Robert Hill in his pacesetting delineation of the five strengths of black families in 1971 which included strong kinship bonds, strong work orientation, adaptability of family roles, strong achievement orientation, and strong religious orientation.[27] Hill used the same Census data that others had used to show the pathology of African-American families to show their strengths as well. Without denying the existence of problems, Hill maintained that a balanced approach would identify both problems and strengths and that any successful effort at assisting these families must be based on their strengths, not their weaknesses. Both Carol Stack and Joyce Aschenbrenner have found that low-income two-parent, and single-parent families in the inner city place strong value on relationship and kinship ties, reciprocity, fidelity to family obligations, and a strong commitment to the children.[28]

Harriette McAdoo has shown that the values of kinship and mutual assistance extend far beyond the function of helping poor people meet their basic necessities. It is a characteristic feature of relationships and middle-income families as well as both single-parent and two-parent types in both city and suburb.

Royce and Turner tested the values identified by Hill in a study conducted in Dayton, Ohio in 1980. In addition to validating the findings of Hill, they found that African-American families place strong values on teaching children to have self-respect, to be happy, on cooperation within the family, and on discipline.[29]

Christopherson conducted studies in 1973, 1977, and 1978 which highlight African-American family values in eight rural Oklahoma communities. There he found love for children, acceptance of children born out of wedlock, and strong resilience and adaptability of family coping skills.[30]

Finally, Lawrence Gary and his associates at Howard University have found that among strong achieving black families of both single-parent and two-parent structures, the values they rely on to facilitate their achievement include strong kinship bonds, strong achievement orientation, positive parent-child relations, strong religious orientation, intellectual-cultural orientation, and strong work orientation. In other words, the family, the church, the school, and the work place.[31]

Gary and his associates asked community leaders to nominate stable black families for the study and then to indicate the characteristics which made them strong (Table 15.1). Finally, the participants themselves were asked to identify common strengths in black families. They specified that in black families generally and in their own families, the most important attributes were family unity, religion, coping strategies, mutual support, and sharing responsibilities.

The researchers noted that "Female-headed families were twice as likely as were husband-wife families to be cited by informants because of their ability to deal with crises. Husband-wife families were more likely than were female-headed families to be cited because of their love, kindness, compassion, and their ability to be supportive and caring."

And in all these studies, love of children and emphasis on family cooperation are important values. Indeed, since Hill's pioneer-

TABLE 15.1
Characteristics of Strong African-American Families Cited by Community Leaders
1983

	N	(%)
Total Families Nominated	74	100
Characteristic		
Strong kinship bonds	40	54
Strong achievement orientation	34	46
Parenting skills	34	46
Strong religious-philosophical orientation	24	32
Intellectual-cultural orientation	23	31
Ability to deal with crisis	23	31
Strong work orientation	19	26
Independence	14	19
Organization	13	18
Active recreation orientation	12	16
Appreciation for each other	10	14
Adaptability of family roles	10	14
Self-expression	10	14
Love, kindness, compassion	10	14
Supportiveness, caring	9	12

SOURCE: Gary et al., *Stable Black Families,* 1983.

ing work, other scholars have begun to study strengths of families more generally as a basis for family support policies.

A group of black scholars at the Joint Center for Political and Economic Studies in Washington, D.C., has pointed to the value the community has always placed on family life, education, work, and collective action.[32] Moreover, Marian Wright Edelman has reminded her readers that African-American families have always placed high value on children and their well-being, while Moynihan has reminded us that the nation as a whole has not done so.[33]

Clearly then there is a place for teaching moral and ethical values in the family. Just as clearly other institutions in the community can help. Beyond values, however, is the need for a caring society to provide opportunity structures for all families. The family, church, school, and workplace in dynamic interaction can become an ecosystem which surrounds, protects, and enhances the emotional, intellectual, physical, social, and economic well-being of all our children.

Chapter 16

And Still We Rise: Single-Parent Families in Helping Communities

When the same factors and values which enabled traditional black families to achieve high levels of viability operate in today's single-parent families, these young people may also rise above the constraints of their status.

During the 1980s a myth developed about single parents. Black teenage, unwed mothers and their households became synonymous with the black family. And because the myth was perpetrated by television as well as scholars and political analysts, it quickly took on a life of its own.

Lost in these discussions were some simple facts. Most single parents are adults, not teenagers. Most are white, not black. We have already noted that teen parenting among white girls in America—leaving aside black girls altogether—is higher than in any of the other industrialized Western countries. Not all black teens succumb to the worst features of this predicament. Once pregnancy and childbirth occur, they need not wreak havoc.

The following stories suggest that there is potential for upward mobility even among black single-parent families. They defy the dysfunctional stereotype. They too are diverse. Each demonstrates that the obstacles commonly faced by single parents can be overcome with timely and appropriate social support.

Charlene Carroll

Charlene Carroll grew up in a female-headed family. Her mother and father separated when she was a year old.[1] When she was eleven, her mother became disabled and she was placed in a foster home. Like so many other such children, she was moved from one foster home to another until she was eighteen. At nineteen, she dropped out of high school. Like many other young women, she became an unwed teenage parent. The long arm of the extended family reached out to her and an aunt took her in, even though she herself was poor and lived in a public housing project. So far, the story seems typical of what we often read of poor high school dropouts who became pregnant before they have grown up themselves. This story, however, is different. By the time Carroll was thirty-five, she owned three beauty salons, earned more than $100,000 a year, and was a pillar of her community.

Carroll's rise from the bottom to the top of the socioeconomic structure, from the underclass to the upper class in a single generation was partly due to her own personal attributes—her intelligence, curiosity, and determination—as well as the strong work orientation received from her mother. It was partially due to the care and guidance she received in foster care, a service which is as often maligned as single-parent families. But her success also had to do with the guiding hand of her aunt, who took her in when she became pregnant. She always liked fixing hair, so with the encouragement and support of her aunt she went to cosmetology school. She was bright, learned fast, and became proficient at her trade. Pretty soon she was doing the hair for all her aunt's friends in the housing project. Later, she got a job in Olive Benson's salon in Boston. There she was encouraged to do further study in some of the leading cosmetology schools in San Francisco, London, New York, and Montreal. After six years she was ready to branch out on her own.

There is still another feature of Carroll's experience not generally included in descriptions of women who get pregnant out of wedlock. She got married and had another child. With the help of her husband and $5,000 of family savings, she applied for and received a government loan of $15,000 from the Small Business Administration in order to set up her own business. Thus in 1976, this young mother, wife, and hairdresser became an entrepreneur. During the next ten years her business grew from one place, Charlene's Hair Salon—with five employees and a gross of

$80,000 during the first year—to a flourishing business embracing three salons in Boston, Cambridge, and Brockton, Massachusetts, which by 1983 employed twenty-six people and grossed over $474,000. She took home $87,000 that year from the business and earned another $23,000 as a consultant and representative of Soft Sheen hair-care products.

Now with her firefighter husband and three children, Carroll enjoys the benefit of a strong, stable, modern family. "We try to do as many things together as possible," she has said, "because my time is limited." She continues, "I'm lucky, though, because my husband does all the cooking. I hate to cook. I clean up and organize. My husband calls me an army sergeant because I make sure that everyone has a job." As a hedge against slipping back into the poverty class, Carroll and her husband invest their profits in her business for expansion and tax advantages. In 1984, they bought a five-story apartment building in Boston's gentrified south-end neighborhood. The building is large enough to house the offices of her company and one of her salons, with other modern office and recreation facilities. To finance the purchase of this building she needed $120,000. This time she went to a commercial bank instead of the Small Business Administration. And this time she was not given the runaround. Now her economic and social achievements buttress the stability of her marriage and family life. She is clearly an outstanding example for young black girls to follow.

Phyllis Tucker Vinson

Another example of a young woman who did not let becoming pregnant out of wedlock deter her from upward mobility is Phyllis Tucker Vinson, who rose to vice president of NBC Television in charge of Saturday programming.[2] Vinson moved up from being an unwed mother on welfare to the top echelon of the communications industry. The eldest of three children, she grew up in a close-knit middle-class black family in Los Angeles. Her mother, all her aunts, and her grandmother before her were schoolteachers, the bulwark of the black middle class. She was expected to follow their example. Unfortunately, however, like increasing numbers of middle-class girls, she became pregnant in high school. She managed to graduate at nineteen before the baby was born. Still, she was in a bind. She had no husband, no job, and a baby to care for. Although her close-knit family was both supportive and helpful to her, she still needed to work. Having made no specific plans for higher education, Vinson took a job as a clerk-typist in the Los Angeles Police Department at $470 a month in order to support herself and her son.

Soon, however, her higher aspirations took hold. She quickly realized that being a clerk-typist was not a meaningful career for her. So she went to college. In order to do so, however, she went on welfare, primarily in order to get health care for her child.

As might be anticipated, her middle-class family offered to help her and did not approve of her going on welfare. "They didn't like it," she said, "but it was my mistake; and I said to them, 'Let me take care of it.' "

After receiving her B.A. in child development from California State University at Los Angeles in 1972, Vinson took another secretarial job—this time with NBC. Her plan was to work there just long enough to get credentials so that she would follow the other women of her family into the teaching profession. But her inquiring mind soon became fascinated with the world of television. She was particularly interested in children's programs, a reflection of her child-development training.

By 1985, Vinson was vice president of NBC Television, responsible for overseeing all five hours of Saturday morning children's television. Her programs have consistently won top awards. Thus by age thirty-eight, she was not only earning top ratings for the children's programs but top dollar as well, earning more than $100,000 a year.

How did she get to the top? She did it in part by perseverance in the face of handicaps; she did it also by creative application of her talents, her curiosity, and her daring. Her superior and sponsor at NBC, Steve Waterman, said, "I've never seen anyone with so much endurance . . . She even gets up now at four in the morning to read scripts!"

She has also branched out to produce family shows for prime time. Even with her success, she recognizes some racially imposed limitations. "From the outside it might look like I've moved quickly," she says, "but from the inside you see yourself moving much slower than your white male counterparts, who make these tremendous leaps." Vinson's long-range goal is to own her own production company.

Patricia Locks Schmoke

Another example of outstanding achievement against the odds is Patricia Locks Schmoke, who overcame her handicap to become a physician.[3] Those who know her know her to be as friendly, warm, and pleasant as she is bright, competent, and professional. It was not always so. Patricia might well have been a negative statistic instead. She was born in a public housing project to a mother whose husband was absent because of military duty. She was a teenage, unwed mother and welfare recipient. None of this, however, defined Patricia or her family.

She became pregnant at the age of seventeen and gave birth to a child while still in high school. Her parents were very supportive of her, and so she continued to live at home while she completed high school. Her father, having returned from the military, moved the family out of the public housing project. He then became a mortician and entered the family business, following in his father's footsteps. After high school, she took a menial job to support herself and her child but soon realized that she would not have a future as a working mother without a college education. She enrolled at Coppin State College, a small historically black college in the middle of the west side of Baltimore.

At first Patricia continued to work to support herself and her son. Soon, however, the government made a modest investment in her which has paid off handsomely. She was persuaded by her college advisor that if she went on welfare she would then be able to devote her time to her studies and caring for her child without the additional responsibility of work. She did so and with the aid of federal and state aid progressed rapidly through college. Even before she graduated she was admitted to medical school with a full scholarship at the University of Florida. So with permission she skipped her last year of college and went straight to medical school. Again, her parents were highly supportive and kept her child while she was away at school.

Her father says that "she was very inquisitive, very interested in science." When he was going to mortuary school, he often brought science books home and she took a special interest in them. Patricia, who was the oldest of four children, was an avid reader. Even in elementary school, according to her mother, she often read two to three books a week in addition to her required studies.

When she was twenty-two years old with her first year of medical school under her belt, she went home to Baltimore for vacation and added another achievement to her blossoming career. A friend arranged a blind date for her with Kurt Schmoke, a young Harvard Law School student, who was already a Rhodes Scholar, former captain of the local high school football team, and a leader in the Sunday School of one of the city's historical black churches. Patricia was later to say of Kurt, "You know, I had heard about all of his degrees and I thought for sure he would be snobbish." She found instead that, "He was one of the nicest people you'd ever want to meet."

Four months after they met, they eloped. If this all seems like a fairy tale, it is not yet over. Kurt persuaded Harvard to let him spend his third year away so he could be with Patricia. Patricia graduated medical school after transferring to the University of Maryland and Kurt graduated from Harvard Law School. They both went on to develop distinguished careers as a dual-career family with two children.

By 1987, Patricia and Kurt had been married twelve years, a long time in these days of frequent divorce. They had climbed several mountains separately and together. Together they now had two children, aged sixteen and seven, Kurt having earlier adopted her son. Those who know the family know that as is traditional with black families no distinction is made between two children based on paternity. Both Patricia and Kurt, and now the son, have spoken publicly and proudly about their family relationship. She became a distinguished physician-ophthalmologist at the Johns Hopkins University Hospital, while he joined a prestigious law firm and became a member of the White House Staff under President Jimmy Carter.

In 1984, he was elected District Attorney; and on November 11, 1987, he became the first elected black mayor of Baltimore, a city that has had a majority black population for more than a decade, and which had its first black candidate for mayor nearly twenty years ago.

Meanwhile, as Patricia received the congratulations from family and friends on becoming Baltimore's first black first lady, there was no doubt in her mind that the one volunteer activity she would not give up was her work with other black professional women who provide volunteer service at the local high school for unwed teenage mothers. She wanted to continue to encourage these young people to finish high school, go to college, and reach their personal and professional goals despite the severe disadvantage of teenage pregnancy. It would be difficult to find a better role model. "I hope," she said, "that for the young girl who had a child or some other setback, that she would see through my life that she can overcome obstacles. But at the same time, for the girl who is not pregnant, I don't want her to consider having a baby as an alternative lifestyle. It was very, very difficult." She continued: "Obviously, I'm very pleased with the way things happened to me in meeting Kurt and having a very happy family and good marriage. But had this not happened to me, I still think I would have had a good life. Finding a good man and the good life is sort of like icing on the cake. But had that not happened, I probably still would have gone to school and become a physician. And I would have raised my son the best I could. Basically," she concludes, "you don't have to look for a rescuer to be rescued."

Regina Thomas

Regina Thomas represented all the statistics so commonly associated with what some call the black underclass.[4] She was a high school dropout, an unwed mother at eighteen, and a double unwed mother by twenty. She served a stint on welfare. And by the time she was twenty-one she and her two children were living in a shelter for the homeless. But she was not without personal resources. She had her pride and self-esteem; she was industrious; and with her eleven grades of schooling she could read and write. And she also had a supportive extended family. Her mother made a home for her and her two children as long as she could. Then the mother got married. With the husband moving in there was no room for Thomas and her children. So she had to move out of her mother's house. And in the African-American family tradition her older brother took her into his home with his family. Unfortunately, however, when the landlord discovered that seven people lived in the apartment he considered only big enough for four, he demanded that somebody move out. So Thomas and her children ended up in the homeless shelter.

Thomas was fortunate that she landed in a homeless shelter in a northern Virginia community where the booming economy meant that low-wage jobs in the service sector were available. She found a full-time job as a nurse's aide in a home for the elderly, earning $13,000 a year, which placed her just above the poverty line. Now she was no longer on welfare, no longer poor, and no longer unemployed. Still, she was a "card-carrying member" of the urban black underclass. Her situation as a female head of family and her shelter residence guaranteed her that label. Moreover, Thomas had to pay an enormous portion of her salary for child care and had trouble getting to work because of a poor public transportation system. She could not afford to make payments and insurance on a car. She was not alone in her predicament. A survey by the Virginia Coalition for the Homeless found that better than 80 percent of the more than 7,000 people in homeless shelters in northern Virginia had jobs. *The Washington Post* reported that while low-income service jobs paying just above the minimum wage were plentiful in the Washington, D.C., suburban area, affordable housing was not, "forcing many working people such as Thomas to use a public shelter."

Even though Thomas became a member of this celebrated underclass she did not need the kind of lectures on values or on get-up-and-go which became so fashionable in the 1980s. Nor would welfare reform or antipoverty legislation be of help to her. What she needed was a social system that would respond to her needs as effectively as it did to the needs of those more favored, more powerful, and more privileged. Eventually, thanks to some very constructive reporting by *The Washington Post,* she got a measure of that social support.

By bringing her situation to the attention of the authorities in an unusually positive manner, the newspaper was able to stimulate people's humanitarian impulses as well as eventually elicit the help of the bureaucracy. Some offered to care for her children free until she could get on her feet. One offered to take in the whole family. One friend walked with her each day to the bus.

The local county government assigned her to a federally subsidized two-bedroom apartment for which she would pay $300 a month. This was still more than one-third of her income but a bargain nevertheless—compared to prices in the regular housing system.

The transportation system continued to fail her. But a neighbor with two cars sold her a 1982 Datsun for $500 down, plus another $500 later. The neighbor realized that one car was enough if it works and if a neighbor has a greater need.

Regina now had a job above the poverty level, a decent place to live, and a reliable means of transportation. And she had help with caring for her children.

Thomas and her two children still faced enormous problems and they continued to benefit very little from the much vaunted decade of economic recovery; but having the social system begin to work for and with her instead of against her gave her a fighting chance to further improve the viability of her family.

Posing in front of her new car with her well-dressed children, and resplendent in her plain white dress and corn-rowed hairstyle, she said: "I've always wanted to be independent, to do things myself. But it's nice to know all these people out there care."

Some raised questions about the shiny car. But it was clearly more a necessity than a luxury. *The Washington Post* reported that "Social workers point out that transportation is critical because affordable housing is often far from job centers and mass transit routes." It is a lesson which should have been learned from the inner-city uprisings of the late 1960s and the *Kerner Commission Report* which analyzed them. It is a lesson that will not be learned by policymakers until scholars and other analysts are able to help them place low-income African-American families in a much broader perspective than the conventional deficit model so prevalent at the present time.

Beatrice Clark

Beatrice Clark became pregnant when she was a senior in high school.[5] After giving birth to her son she returned to finish high school. Then she moved out of her parents' home, against the advice of her father, got a job, and entered Temple University. This was in part, however, a reflection of the strong achievement motivation she had received from both her parents. "My mother cleaned houses for a living and my father was a janitor at a local high school. We were poor, but not poor-poor. My mother always had the potential of doing so much more with her life. But she came from a poor family, too. She died when she was forty-five and never had the opportunity to do the things I've done. But she provided me with the kind of influence I'll always remember." Her mother was a strong motivating force in her early life, though the mother died when Beatrice Clark was quite young. "My mother was bright, extremely bright. She died before I had my son, but I'll always remember her telling me that she wanted me to do well."

After graduating from college, Clark worked for several large computer companies including IBM. Now both her education and her earnings placed her squarely in the lower rungs of the growing black middle class. Her motivation showed in her behavior and her attitude. "There was no luck involved," she says of her achievements. "It was very, very hard. You have to be unwilling to accept the average. You can't be afraid to make changes in your life." Moving out of her father's house was one move. Moving for job mobility was another. "Already, I've relocated more than once for a job. If you are going to go anywhere you've got to be willing to make sacrifices."

Now thirty years old, Clark has never been married and does not seem anxious about her single status. She lives alone with her son in a comfortable apartment and enjoys her friends and acquaintances. She has no plans to seek a marital partner. "It's not that I'm opposed to marriage. I just haven't found a person that could hold my interest. When I think about where I'm going to be five or ten years from now, I never see myself married or living with somebody." It is a status increasingly being chosen by large numbers of black single adults.

Patricia Cason

As discussed above, most black single mothers are not teenagers but adults. Moreover, increasing numbers of them have been married and are victimized by separation and divorce. Patricia Cason's experiences are relevant in this regard.[6] Her husband was a returning Vietnam veteran with numerous health and personal problems. She concluded that she could no longer bear the pain of their troubled relationship. "I told him I was going to leave him. He didn't believe me. He came home one day and I was completely packed, waiting for him." For her, the extended family offered the stability her marriage did not. "He was carrying a lot of pain. I just didn't know it, I was too young. I left him and stayed with my aunt . . . I had to get my act together." She had to plan for herself and her two children, aged four and eight. So she was busy "trying to figure out what am I going to do with these little babies here." With determination and the help of her family and the educational system, she did quite well indeed.

She was twenty-six when she left her husband and moved in with her aunt. After separation and later divorce, she experienced the difficulty of supporting her family with only a high school education. She knew that her job as a checkout clerk in a grocery store did not hold much of a future. "I kept asking myself, 'Is this what I have to live for for the rest of my life? Well, what the hell is the use of trying?' I don't want to live like this. . . . And this other part of me would come out and say, 'Girl, don't matter what you don't want. You chose to have children. . . . You can't give up.' " So she decided to go to college. At first she entered the local community college, then transferred to Temple University.

During her college years, she arose at 5:00 A.M. and took her younger daughter to a nearby child-care center. Then she would take her older daughter by trolley to school. Cason would board the trolley again to go to her own classes. After classes she reported to her part-time job. "It almost killed me," she said looking back over the years. "I had to do something to feel like I was worth something."

She graduated in four and a half years with a degree in criminal justice. This enabled her to begin a professional position with a salary just above the poverty line. Still she was able to save enough for a down payment on a Philadelphia row house that had been abandoned for ten years. She and her two daughters, now twelve and fifteen, set to work and transformed it into a livable home.

Now her daily life was filled with small and large challenges. She became an active volunteer serving as president of her neighborhood association. During the intervening years, she has had strong and stable support both from her own family and from her children's father, who makes regular payments and visits the children at least once a week. Still, she is called on by life to assume a major share of the responsibility herself. "What I'm proud of," she says, "is my inner strength, my ability to sit down and admit what I can do, what I can't do, and then to attack these things." It is a combination that has served her and countless other single parents well.

Vivian Wells

Professionals and other adults who work with teen parents are often impressed with several aspects of ignorance or naivete on the part of adolescents. The first is how unaware many of them seem to be about sex and the mechanics of getting pregnant. Many had no desire or intention of getting pregnant and assumed that it would not happen to them. The other is ignorance of the actual responsibilities associated with child care as a single parent. Vivian Wells, an eighteen-year-old single mother, has told of her own experience.[7] She did not plan to get pregnant. "I never really planned to have children until I was married," she said. "I was dumbfounded when it happened. I knew that birth control was out there, but I just didn't know how to get to it. All this time I'd been having intercourse and I didn't get pregnant. [She was fifteen and a half.] So, I said, 'Well, I'll just keep on doing it.' . . . And when it happened, I didn't want to get an abortion. I was totally against it. I felt like I was taking someone else's life."

Vivian Wells also illustrates the ignorance about what is involved in caring for a child alone. She was without support in part because the father of the child provided no assistance. "He never even brought her one Pamper," she said of the father. Having moved out of her mother's house she supported her child with a combination of a job and welfare benefits. "I have to struggle to pay the rent," she said. "There's a lot of things I would like to have." Yet because Vivian was determined to make it for herself and her daughter, she was wise enough to return to high school, at a special school for young mothers.

Part of the ignorance is about the habits of babies. "I can't stand crying," Wells said, "and my daughter, she really whines a lot, and I have to have a lot of patience with her. I don't have that much time to spend with her—that's the whole problem."

Now a typical day in her life goes like this: She gets up in the morning and takes her daughter to the day-care center where she pays what she considers extremely high fees to get quality care. Then she goes to work at her part-time clerical job. After a half day of work, she goes to trade school for classes, then returns to the job and works till 5:30. After work she picks up her daughter and takes her home. They spend the rest of the day in their one-room apartment. "We eat dinner," she said, "and then we go to bed." Next day the routine begins all over again.

Still another observation frequently made by professionals and others is that teen pregnancy does not just happen to wayward girls. It happens to good girls too. Vivian Wells tells of her own upbringing. "On my mother's block, people used to look at me as Miss Sweet Innocent Vivian. . . . We were all into the church thing. And then I pop up pregnant. I was a disappointment to a lot of people."

Still there is often an amazing degree of optimism and high aspiration among these young mothers. Vivian Wells says of her situation, "I'm going to raise her so that she can talk to me about anything. I always say, when she gets older, if she is ready to do her thing, just don't be ashamed to let me know. I understand she's going to have those needs and I'm going to take her to get birth control, whatever kind she wants." It is a resolution often expressed by teen parents but not as often lived up to. It is not a matter that is completely in their hands.

RISING ABOVE THE ODDS

Clearly, Charlene Carroll, Phyllis Vinson, Patricia Schmoke, Regina Thomas, and the others are not typical of black girls who get pregnant in their teens without husbands. Neither are they isolated examples of achievement on the part of single-parent females. What is also clear is that the variety and complexity of this family form also includes various levels of socioeconomic status. Some are struggling in the underclass. Others have a solid niche in the working class. Still others are middle class. And a few female-headed families rise to the upper class.

When we look carefully at this phenomenon, we observe a wide variety of pathways out of the teen-pregnancy and single-mother dilemma.

None of this is to suggest that African-American female-headed families are without problems. From these data, however, it is clear that while the welfare mothers get a great deal of attention among both social scientists and common citizens, as well as in family policy considerations, there is a substantial segment of single-parent families who operate above the poverty level, many in the economic comfort zone shared by Phyllis Tucker Vinson, Charlene Carroll, and Patricia Locks Schmoke. Moreover, the vast majority of these mothers, even the very poor ones, are self-supporting through their own labor. This is far from the stereotype of the "typical" black female family head.

And while the reasons for the achievement for these families are varied, they all include high school graduation, supportive family systems, welfare, work, and high career goals, which means that an understanding and supportive human and resource environment is necessary. This is a feat accomplished by only a minority of unmarried mothers. Even so, however, the numbers who do so are sufficiently impressive to be encouraging to other young women, their parents, schools, and policy analysts.

PART VI

———

The Future Is
Already Here

Chapter 17

The Black Church: Spiritual Values and Community Reform

The black church is at the leading edge of the African-American community's push to influence the future of its families. As we shall see, there are several reasons why the church is so important. Robert Hill has shown that religious orientation is one of the greatest historic strengths of black families. Over the centuries, the church has become the strongest institution in their community. It is prevalent, independent, and has extensive outreach.

Its relevance to the future of black families was dramatically underscored by the president of the 8.7 million member National Baptist Convention U.S.A. during its 1991 annual convention in Washington, D.C. Speaking to the 40,000 delegates representing 33,000 churches and 100,000 pastors in this, the largest black organization in the nation, the Reverend T. J. Jemison declared that the group would give highest priority to the family in the years ahead. He also announced plans for programs to support black businesses, provide jobs, and sell "everything black people use."

"We must take care of our own," he said. "We have tried other institutions and they have failed. The church must bring the black family back to where it belongs."

The Reverend Mr. Jemison is keenly aware of how difficult it will be to convert millions of members into supporters of his ideas. The massiveness of the Baptist church is a limitation. It is perhaps the most decentralized and democratic of the large, national, African-American organizations. Each local congregation is its own supreme governing body. Moreover, family-centered programs may need to share priority with paying the balance on the new $10 million headquarters the association built in Nashville in 1989.[1]

But in addition to what it does for its members, the black church as an institution has always reached out to serve important functions for the black community as a whole. It is in this respect both a preserver of the African-American heritage and an agent for reform. Indeed no successful movement for improving the conditions of life for the African-American people has been mounted without the support of the church. The second largest Baptist denomination, the National Baptist Convention of America, with some 11,000 churches and more than 2.4 million members, has also increasingly encouraged churches to develop community programs. The president of the association is minister of a church in Shreveport, Louisiana. The smallest of these Baptist denominations, the Progressive National Baptist Convention, with 775 churches and more than 1.2 million members, is even more oriented toward community outreach activities than the older associations. Having split off from the older groups during the civil rights era in order to provide more consistent support to the social justice movement led by Martin Luther King, a Baptist minister, this national association has remained in the forefront of social reform.[2]

Three of the Progressive National Baptist Convention contemporary leaders have come to our attention during the course of our study, as they have built strong community-oriented churches that have provided the basis for their national leadership. Rev. J. Alfred Smith was elected president of this association in 1987 largely on the basis of his achievements in building Allen Temple Baptist Church in Oakland, California, from a congregation of 1,000 members in 1970 to over 4,000 today largely by an extensive program of community outreach activities.[3] With his son, Rev. J. Alfred Smith, Jr., as his assistant pastor, and a large cadre of religious and lay leaders, he has led this and other churches to move considerably beyond their walls, their members, and their spiritual mission into new levels of community service. Dr. Smith, Sr., is also a founder of the Congress of National Black Churches, an umbrella organization of the major black denominations, whose major purpose is to stimulate more community reform.

The current president of the Progressive National Baptist Convention, which regularly hosts 10,000 or more attendees at its annual national conventions, is Charles Adams, minister of the Hartford Memorial Baptist Church in Detroit. His church is a leader and pioneer in community work, and Dr. Adams has become a national leader in political, economic, and educational affairs.

The final member of this progressive triumvirate to come to our attention during this study is Rev. J. Otis Moss of Cleveland. Not only is his Institutional Baptist Church a leader in building coalitions with other churches and with political, economic, educational, and social agencies, but Dr. Moss has become a national leader in these fields. Formerly an associate of Martin Luther King, he has served as president of the PUSH organization founded by Rev. Jesse Jackson, and chairman of the National Urban League convention.

In some ways and in many places the Methodist denominations have become even more active than the Baptists in community reform activities. The 6,200 churches in the African Methodist Episcopal denomination are in the forefront of this movement with more than 2.2 members. An outstanding example is the First AME Church of Los Angeles under the leadership of Rev. Cecil L. "Chip" Murray. This former U.S. Air Force pilot turned minister has led this church from a membership of some 300 when he was appointed in 1977 to over 7,500 by the end of 1991. He attributes this growth in major part to the philosophy and activity of the church in reaching "beyond the walls" of the church into a massive array of community outreach programs.[4] Rev. Murray has told Iris Schneider of the *Los Angeles Times* that "If we don't change the community, the community corrupts the individual." He continued, "The coming-to-church-for-personal-salvation days are over. Now we are looking not only for personal salvation but for social salvation."[5] During our site visits Rev. Murray amplified on this theme. The community outreach role of this church is so extensive that it was given a national award by President Bush in 1989 as one of the nation's "thousand points of light." As we shall see, this dual role of the black church has a long and honorable tradition among the roughly 2 million African Methodist Episcopal churches, whose founder Richard Allen, who established this church in 1787 in Philadelphia, has become one of the most celebrated pioneer leaders in African-American history.

In the same city, the Ward AME Church under the leadership of Rev. Frank Madison Reid III has pioneered in work with black and Hispanic youth gangs and with the drug problem long before these became of nationwide concern.[6] Finally, some black churches in the historically white United Methodist denomination have also established strong community outreach programs. In Los Angeles, the Holms United Methodist Church under the leadership of Rev. James Lawson, an early associate of Martin Luther King, is outstanding in this regard. Rev. Lawson has continued to head the Western regional operations of the Southern Christian Leadership Conference and is in the forefront of political leadership in the city.

Meanwhile up north in San Francisco, the Glide Memorial United Methodist Church, under the longtime leadership of radical activist Cecil Williams, whose title is minister of liberation, has established a national network of black churches fighting the crack cocaine epidemic.[7] This is built upon the long and successful outreach of this church into all the corners of the most devastating social problems in that city.

It is a mistake, then, to think of the black church in America as simply, or even primarily, a religious institution in the same way the white church might be conceived.

From the beginning, community service has been an element of black religious expression. Indeed, some 200 years ago when Absalom Jones, Richard Allen, and others walked out of the white Methodist church in Philadelphia what they formed right away was not a new church. Instead, they formed the Free African Society with forty-two members, which had a number of functions, including "socioeconomic cooperation in the form of savings, mutual aid, education to children and charity to indigent, widowed, and orphaned members."[8] Only three years later did Richard Allen form Mother Bethel, the first African-Methodist-Episcopal Church in America.

Every black neighborhood and many nonblack ones have black churches as a major institutional presence.

We have estimated that there are over 75,000 black churches in the nation (Table 17.1). The overwhelming majority are Protestant. The 30,000 congregations in the National Baptist Convention, U.S.A., as late as 1984 embraced 40 percent of all black local congregations. The other Baptist denominations also have large numbers of churches.

TABLE 17.1
African-American Churches
1989

Major African-American Denominations	N (in thousands)	(%)*	Source**
National Baptist Convention, U.S.A.	30,000	40.0	(1)
National Baptist Convention of America	11,398	15.0	(2)
National Primitive Baptist Convention	2,198	2.9	(1)
Progressive National Baptist Convention	775	1.0	(3)
African Methodist Episcopal	6,200	8.2	(1)
African Methodist Episcopal Zion	6,060	8.0	(1)
Christian Methodist Episcopal	2,340	3.1	(3)
Apostolics	300		
Pentecostals	550	1.6	(2)
Holiness	28		(2)
Bible Way	350		(3)
Church in God in Christ (COGIC)	9,982	13.2	(2)
Major White Denominations			
Church of God			
Anderson, Indiana	509	1.7	(2)
Cleveland, Tennessee	772		(2)
Episcopalian	358		(2)
Lutheran			
Evangelical Lutheran Churches	1		(2)
Presbyterian			
Presbyterian Church (U.S.A.)	440		(1)
United Methodist	2,455	3.2	(2)
Seventh Day Adventist	340		(2)
United Church of Christ (Congregational)	279	1.4	(1)
Christian (Disciples of Christ)	446		(2)
Total	75,781		

* May not add up to 100% due to rounding.

** (1) = Melton (1988), *Encyclopedia of American Religions*

(2) = Jacquet (1989), *Yearbook of American and Canadian Churches*

(3) = Denominational lists from black denominations

SOURCE: Andrew Billingsley, Cleopatra Howard Caldwell, Robert B. Hill, and Victor Rouse, "The Role of the Black Church in Family-Oriented Community Outreach Programs," 1991.

Prevalence of Churches

The three historically black Baptist denominations account for nearly half of all black church members (Table 17.2). The three historic black Methodist denominations are second with nearly 20 percent of the total. The rapidly growing Church of God in Christ

Table 17.2
Estimated Distribution of Church Membership
1989

Church Denomination	N (in millions)	(%)
African Methodist Episcopal	2.2	9.3
African Methodist Episcopal Zion	1.2	5.1
Christian Methodist Episcopal	0.9	3.8
Church of God in Christ	3.7	15.6
National Baptist Convention, U.S.A., Inc.	7.5	31.6
National Baptist Convention of America	2.4	10.1
Progressive National Baptist Convention	1.2	5.1
Smaller black communions	1.4	5.9
Predominantly white Protestant groups	1.2	5.1
Roman Catholic	2	8.4
Total	23.7	100.0

SOURCE: C. Eric Lincoln and Lawrence H. Mamiya, *The Black Church in the African American Experience* (Durham: Duke University Press, 1990), p. 407.

is in third place with about 16 percent. The 2 million black Catholics in 1989 accounted for some 8 percent of the 24 million black Christians.

The multiple functions of the black church were described by Benjamin Mays and Joseph Nicholson: "Despite its problems and failures, there was a certain "genius of soul" of the black church "that gives it life and vitality, that makes it stand out significantly above its buildings, creeds, rituals and doctrines; something that makes it a unique institution."[9]

At the center of this genius was complete ownership and control by the African-American people. It represented freedom, independence, and respect for its leadership, as well as the opportunity for self-esteem, self-development, leadership, and relaxation. Moreover, they found that the black church was a community center and recreational center that encouraged education, business development, and democratic fellowship beyond its members.

In more recent times C. Eric Lincoln has called attention to this multiplicity of functions:

Beyond its purely religious function, as critical as that function has been, the black church in its historical role as lyceum, conservatory, forum, social service center, political academy and financial institution, has been and is for black America the mother of our culture, the champion of our freedom, the hallmark of our civilization.[10]

Religious Expression

What do African-Americans tend to believe in and how strong are those beliefs? How do they express their religion? We look for the answers because both beliefs and behavior can be powerful inducements to well-being in families.

A study reported at the 1991 meetings of the Association of Black Sociologists showed that the strongly held belief in God, quite apart from religious participation, had a positive effect on the outcome of pregnancies among low- and moderate-income unmarried black women. Women with the strongest beliefs were more likely to have healthy babies. It is already widely known among health and family specialists that families and individuals actively involved in religious life also tend to have more positive life outcomes than those who are not actively involved.

In a secondary analysis of data from the National Survey of Black Americans we found firm support for both these dimensions of religious orientation (Tables 17.3 and 17.4).[11]

An overwhelming 84 percent consider themselves religious. A substantial majority of 76 percent indicated a belief that religion was very important in their lives when they were growing up. An equally strong majority of 77 percent indicated that they believe the church is still a very important influence in their lives. Finally, an even greater majority indicated a belief that it is very important to send children to church (80 percent). In all these beliefs, women and men evidence high levels of religiosity though women score substantially higher.

In addition to people's beliefs, behavior with respect to religious practices was analyzed (Table 17.4). While their reports of the religious practices do not indicate as strong an involvement as their beliefs do, they are still quite strong. Indeed, on three out of

TABLE 17.3
Percentage Citing Church as Very Important
1979–1980

	Total (%)	Male (%)	Female (%)
Consider self religious	84	76	86
Religion very important when young	76	75	72
Church very important now	77	72	80
Very important to send children to church	80	77	82
Member of church	68	59	73

SOURCE: *National Survey of Black Americans, 1979–80.*

TABLE 17.4
Percentage Reporting Religious Activities
1979–1980

	Total	Male	Female
Attend church (at least monthly)	71	61	76
Pray daily	78	68	84
Watch religious broadcasts (weekly)	68	63	71
Read religious books (weekly)	50	40	57

SOURCE: *National Survey of Black Americans, 1979–80.*

four measures of religious activity, the overwhelming majority of men and women participated actively.

A substantial majority of 78 percent indicate that they pray daily. Women outnumber men in this activity by 84 percent to 68 percent. Further, some seventy-one percent indicated that they attend church with some regularity or at least once a month. Women outnumber men in this activity as well by 76 percent to 61 percent. In addition, a majority of 68 percent listen to weekly religious broadcasts and 50 percent read religious books and other materials weekly. In all these activities, women also outnumber men.

The fact that black men seem to have a strong set of religious beliefs but do not convert these into practice as frequently as women do raises questions about the structure of society or the structure of the church that restrains men's religious participation. One minister in the black church study indicated that there may be something about the manner in which churches are organized.

Reverend Johnnie Ray Youngblood of the St. Paul Community Baptist Church in Brooklyn, New York, spoke to us emphatically about this matter, "I don't blame black men for staying home and watching TV on Sunday," he said. He holds that activities at most churches are not designed with the interests and talents of men in mind. He has begun a "male ministry" to correct that oversight. When asked if women resent the special attention this gives men, he responded that the opposite is true. They appreciate having their husbands, fathers, and sons actively involved.[12]

COMMUNITY SERVICE

Dean Lawrence Jones of Howard University's School of Divinity once reported that in a single recent week he attended religious gatherings where special collections were taken for Fisk University; for a family burned out of their home; for scholarship help to a needy student; for an NAACP special appeal; for the home-less; and for a food bank.

The wide array of social-service activities on the part of black churches has recently come to the attention of the concerned national public. *The New York Times* took note of these activities in a May 23, 1988, editorial. "Increasingly," said the *Times*, "the black churches have stepped in to try to repair the breaches in black family life left by social, economic and political change. Their efforts range from complex, foundation-financed child develop-ment programs to simple but sensible adopt-a-family projects."[13]

BLACK CHURCH RESPONSES TO CURRENT SOCIAL CONDITIONS

In a pilot study of seventy-one churches along the Eastern Sea-board, we found substantial variation in these community out-reach programs.[14] The following churches illustrate the range of community outreach programs. One of the churches we visited is the Third Shiloh Missionary Baptist Church in New Orleans.

One of the smallest and newest of the fifteen or so Baptist churches which surround the Desire Public Housing Project, which houses 8,000 people, Third Shiloh is only twenty years old. Composed mostly of low-income blue-collar workers and their families, the congregation has been saving money for nearly twenty years with the dream of building a new church building.

In 1988, drug traffickers became so bold that they set up two crack houses in abandoned property across the street from the church. Three times burglars broke into the church and took typewriters, air conditioners, a public-address system, and other church property. They made off with anything they could sell in order to buy drugs. Instead of moving away the church took action.

The church took the funds it had been saving for a new church building and bought these abandoned houses for $35,000. It tore them down and built ten new apartments. This action alone pro-vided work for a few of the local people in a neighborhood where the unemployment rate is above 60 percent. The project cost the church a total of $150,000, of which the federal government agreed to provide some $60,000. The church then rented these apartments for up to $400 per month, thus turning a profit, which it will use for supporting a tutoring program for youth, a schol-arship fund for students, and that long-awaited new church building. Their priorities are clear: social rehabilitation in the neighborhood, decent affordable housing for low-income families, educational support for the youth, and then a new church building.[15]

Even as a pacesetter, Third Shiloh is not alone among black churches joining the war on drugs. The late-night talk show host, Arsenio Hall, made news when in late 1991 he announced that he had purchased a crack house in Los Angeles for $165,000 and donated it to his church, the First AME, to convert to facilities for its war against drugs.[16] Rev. Murray, the minister, has told us that the church has decided to spend some $50,000 to renovate this property and turn it into a youth center, which will be named Hall House in honor of its donor. Completed and officially dedicated in July 1992, this particular project is just one of a wide attack on drugs that this church has incorporated into its extensive community outreach program. Altogether some six crack houses in the nearby area have been put out of business by the men of the church as part of their regular neighborhood patrols. Three of these facilities have been renovated and turned into housing and other constructive uses. The church has invested more than $800,000 each to acquire and repair these facilities.[17] These community patrols by groups of well-organized and disciplined men of First AME church march through four adjacent neighborhoods in groups of 50 to 200 every Friday, Saturday, and Sunday night. According to reports by the Los Angeles Police Department since these patrols began five years ago, the crime rate has dropped in all these neighborhoods by better than 60 percent.

Another church in our pilot study was the 6,000 member Shiloh Baptist Church in Washington, D.C., founded by a handful of ex-slaves in 1863. It has even more extensive community outreach programs. In order to provide a home for many of its community activities as well as church organizations, the church, under the leadership of the late Reverend Henry C. Gregory III built the Hugh Shiloh Family Life Center at a total cost of $5 million. It provides a wide range of facilities for the whole family: a full-scale restaurant, full basketball court, racquet ball courts, exercise rooms, banquet hall, meeting rooms, rooftop garden overlooking the neighborhood, all of which are open to the community.

This church sponsored a nationally recognized child-care development center that has attracted numerous visitors, including the President of the United States. It conducts a parent-child math and science learning center. It sponsors a Male Youth

Health Enhancement Program whereby the men of Shiloh have embraced about a hundred young males from the neighborhood, largely from low-income, single-parent families. This project, which has attracted foundation support, has a small staff. The men volunteers and the staff work closely with the parents, who are organized into a parents group that meets regularly. They keep in touch with the schools in order to monitor the progress of the boys. They provide an after-school program each weekday, weekly seminars on life, drugs, sex, health, African-American history; as well as a wide range of local and regional field trips to scientific, educational, and cultural facilities. These are all in addition to sponsoring a local branch of the Boys' and Girls' Clubs of America, the Boy Scouts, and the Girl Scouts.

These programs provide opportunities for volunteers not only from the church membership but nonmembers as well—particularly for students pursuing careers in education, social work, the ministry, or family sciences. It also provides a major bridge between the social classes.

Meanwhile, further north in Columbia, Maryland, another small church has tackled the AIDS epidemic. Veronica Jennings has brought to public attention the leadership of this church in organizing other black churches to expand AIDS education.[18] While blacks accounted for 12 percent of the national population, they accounted for some 27 percent of the nearly 100,000 AIDS cases reported by the U.S. Centers for Disease Control in 1988.

Armed with such data and alarmed by the fact that her own teenage daughter knew very little about AIDS, Mrs. Gwendolyn Clark took her concerns to her minister. The quick response and leadership of the minister, the Rev. Herbert H. Eaton, propelled the eighteen-year-old, 500 member largely middle class St. John Baptist Church into a leadership role in the fight against this fatal disease. "We are a black church," he said, "and a disproportionate number of AIDS patients are black and other minority people. Yet there is very little education focused on minorities." The church then launched an AIDS education program for the black community. The program consists of recruiting volunteers from the church and training them to teach AIDS education and provide counseling to affected patients. Some volunteers have already signed up. They will conduct seminars in some twenty-five black churches in the area. In addition, the church conducts regular seminars on AIDS for community leaders and professionals. Recently the church won a $60,000 grant from the state of Maryland to develop a model AIDS education program for black communities throughout the state.

The need for such education is widespread among professionals as well as lay persons. To illustrate this need, the Reverend Mr. Eaton tells about the time a local minister was called to the hospital to visit one of his members with AIDS. Instead of going to the patient's beside, the minister put on a hospital gown and rubber gloves, then stood outside the patient's door and prayed for him.

St. John's is not alone in responding to this crisis; the Congress of National Black Churches, representing 60,000 black churches in seven historically black denominations with 15 million members, has also become active in AIDS education together with other social problems. Still, St. John's is unique in taking an advanced leadership position in fighting this problem. It demonstrates again what a small black church can do under effective socially oriented leadership. Even a small church can command the respect and support of all sectors of the community.

Meanwhile further north, we visited in our pilot study one of the nation's oldest, largest, and wealthiest black Baptist churches which is making a similar response to the social needs of its community. In the Bedford-Stuyvesant section of Brooklyn, New York, the 141-year-old, 10,000-plus member Concord Baptist Church is composed of a cross-section of middle-class and working-class parishioners, a majority of whom give 10 percent of their earnings to the church. Concord has been pastored by Rev. Gardner C. Taylor for forty years. Its community outreach programs include an entire square block of institutions, including an academic school through twelfth grade, a scouting program (which proudly boasts that Ford Foundation President Franklin Thomas was once a member), nursing home, homes for the elderly, and a housing rehabilitation program. Recently, over a two-year period the church raised a million dollars from its members and established its own foundation, which uses the interest to support a wide range of political, economic, and social development activities in the community. Each year the church awards about $75,000 in grants to community agencies for such social-service projects as teen pregnancy prevention, housing, health, education, recreation, art, music, and political education.

Each of these churches represents what Bishop Roy Calvin Nichols (retired) of the United Methodist Church has characterized as "vital churches." In a national study, Bishop Nichols found that "A vital congregation is one in which the redemptive and liberating power of the Gospel is applied with ever-increasing effectiveness to the real needs of people in the context of their personal and social situation in the world."[19]

These churches also come close to the type of community service center that Dr. Kenneth B. Smith, president of the Chicago Theological Seminary, believes that black churches have the special mission to provide. A distinguished former pastor of one of Chicago's leading black churches, the Reverend Mr. Smith is also an exceptionally active leader in the community, having served as chair of the Chicago Urban League, president of the Chicago School Board, and in other community positions. In the interview with us he spoke of his deeply held conviction about the dual mission of the church as both a spiritual and a social institution. In the same vein, Dr. Vincent Harding, professor of religion at the Iliff School of Religion in Denver, observed that the genius of the black church is that it sees these two missions—the spiritual and the social—as one.

Ten Exemplary Churches

While the above churches are exceptional, they are not alone. The following profiles drawn from our pilot study show how extensively churches are involved in their nonreligious community outreach roles.

1. *Allen African Methodist Episcopal, Jamaica, Queens*
The 154-year-old, 3,000-member Allen AME Church in Queens has been under the leadership of Rev. (Congressman) Floyd Flake since 1976. Members are drawn from working-class and middle-class families. The church has thirteen assistant ministers, eight of whom are women. The extensive social-service programs, which span the entire life cycle, include the following:

1. *Senior Citizen Housing.* This complex was launched eight years ago to provide affordable housing and a healthy and safe environment for senior citizens. About 325 seniors are currently residing in this facility, which was financed through HUD funds for housing the elderly.

2. *Allen Christian School.* This school was formed six years ago to provide quality private education from prekindergarten to the eighth grade. In addition to a strong academic curriculum, the school provides spiritual and cultural enrichment as well. Foreign language, computer instruction, and African-American studies

span the entire curriculum. About one hundred paid staff operate this school, which is financed by the church and tuition fees.

3. *Allen Senior Citizens Community Center.* It provides a broad range of social and recreational activities for senior citizens and also has a food cooperative.

4. *Allen Women's Resources Center.* This center was established two years ago to provide support and services to abused low-income women of all races. In addition to emergency shelter for ninety days, the center's services include counseling, child care, and housing and job referrals. Three paid staffers operate the center, which is financed by the church and local government.

5. *Multi-Service Center of the Allen Housing Corporation.* This center was formed five years ago to promote a broad range of educational, health, employment, and recreational services to community residents of all ages and is financed by rental income and federal, state, and local government funds.

6. *Allen Homecare Agency.* This agency was established about four years ago to provide home care to the home-bound elderly. Home attendants are sent to the homes of the aged for as little as four hours or as much as twenty-four hours a day. Currently, about 282 senior citizens are clients. It has nineteen paid staff members and is funded mainly by the state and local governments.

7. *Allen Housing Corporation.* This program buys dilapidated houses, hires and trains local citizens to repair them, then arranges low-interest loans from local lenders so that low- and moderate-income families can become home owners.

8. *Allen Commercial Properties.* This is a city block of commercial properties owned by the church. The income goes to further the social service programs.

2. *Bridge Street African Methodist Episcopal, Brooklyn*

The 223-year-old, 2,000-member Bridge Street AME Church in Brooklyn has been under the leadership of the seminary trained husband-wife team of Rev. Lawrence and Rev. Barbara Lucas since 1982. Its members are both working class and middle class. The church has thirteen assistant ministers, six of whom are women. Its social-service programs include the following:

1. *Parenting Program.* The Parenting Program, founded in 1986 by Reverend Barbara Lucas, provides a broad range of support to one- and two-parent families, who are mostly poor or working class. It includes such activities as Big Brother, Big Sister, Foster Grandparents, and Family Crisis Intervention. With a paid staff

of five, the program is financed by state and local funds as well as by contributions from the church.

2. *After-School Tutorial Program.* The tutorial program, initiated in 1984, provides after-school academic assistance to underachieving black boys and girls between the ages of seven and seventeen from diverse socioeconomic backgrounds and family structures. This program, staffed by fifteen, is supported by funds from the church, foundations, and state and local government.

3. *Adult Education.* This program was established in 1986 to improve the education of adults in the community. In addition to teaching English as a second language to Haitian and Hispanic immigrants, this program helps many adults complete their high school (or GED) equivalency. It is staffed by four volunteer certified teachers and financed solely by the church.

4. *Food Distribution.* In operation since 1984, this program distributes surplus federal food to the hungry and homeless monthly. Approximately 1,500 persons receive such items as cheese, rice, and honey each month. Staffed by forty-two volunteers, this program is financed by the church and state and local government.

5. *Other Programs.* Other programs operated by the church include the Share Food Cooperative, Counseling Consortium, Senior Citizens Center, Federal Credit Union, and Social Action program (which focuses on voter registration).

3. St. Paul Community Baptist, Brooklyn

In the East New York section of Brooklyn, the relatively young sixty-one-year-old, 2,000 member St. Paul Community Baptist Church, under the leadership of Rev. Johnny Ray Youngblood since 1973, has three men who serve as assistant ministers. A woman chairs the extensive array of social-service programs, including the following:

1. *Nehemiah Housing Project.* This project, which began four years ago, is designed to provide affordable low-income housing and a decent community environment for residents in the East New York section of Brooklyn. This nationally acclaimed effort is sponsored by an interracial and interdenominational consortium of churches, which provides the major source of funding. To date, 1,000 families have been provided homes. Another 1,000 homes are in the planning stages. Funding comes from a variety of public and private sources.

2. *St. Paul Christian School.* This school was established four

years ago to provide quality private elementary school education to disadvantaged children from nursery through sixth grade. In addition to a strong academic curriculum, the school provides wholesome spiritual and cultural enrichment. The school, which has twenty-two paid staff, is financed by tuition fees and church contributions.

3. *Share.* This program, which has been in operation for six months, is designed to enhance the accessibility of nutritious food to low-income individuals and families. Major program activities include facilitating more cost-effective and nutritious food purchases, and distributing fruits and vegetables to families in need.

4. *St. Paul Corporation.* This program was established five years ago to foster the development of community-owned small businesses that enhance the quality of the neighborhood stores and rent them to neighborhood residents at no profit. The corporation, which has twenty-two paid staff, is financed mainly by the church and revenues from their business enterprises.

5. *Creative Hands.* This program was formed six years ago to increase the participation of senior citizens in wholesome social activities. Program activities include: arts and crafts, Bible study, field trips, cultural events, and educational seminars.

4. *The Bethel African Methodist Episcopal, Baltimore*
The 202-year-old, 6,000-member church was for thirteen years under the leadership of Rev. (now Bishop) John R. Bryant and his wife, Rev. Cecilia Bryant. Members are both working class and middle class. The church has seventeen assistant ministers, eleven of whom are women. It is currently pastored by Rev. Frank Madison Reid. Social-service programs include the following:

1. *Outreach Center Ministry.* The center was established to provide a broad range of services to needy individuals and families. Its components include a "Faith Store" to provide clothing for the needy, a food pantry, employment referrals, emergency shelter, Alcoholics Anonymous, and counseling services. There are eight staff members, seven of whom are volunteers. It is financed mostly by the church.

2. *Teen Parenting Enrichment Place.* This program was formed about three years ago to prevent adolescent pregnancy and to enhance the parenting skills of male and female teen parents. This multiservice support center provides assistance to the children of teen parents and to the grandparents on both sides. The

center has eleven paid staff and is financed by the church and the state government.

3. *Senior Citizens Program.* This program was formed eleven years ago to provide wholesome social, cultural, recreational, and educational activities for senior citizens. It is staffed by two volunteers and is financed completely by the church.

4. *Bethel Christian School.* This school was established five years ago to provide affordable, quality private education to children of low-income families. The school also provides spiritual and cultural enrichment. It has seventeen staff members, fourteen of whom are paid, and is financed through tuition fees and church contributions.

5. *Prison Ministry.* This program, established nine years ago, provides spiritual enrichment to prison inmates. Major program activities include Bible study, group discussions, church services, and individual counseling. It is staffed by seven volunteers and financed completely by the church.

6. *Other Programs.* Other programs include the Bethel Women's Center to provide support to abused and disadvantaged women and the Bethel Bible Institute to provide ministerial training for lay persons.

5. *Union Temple Baptist Church, Washington, D.C.*

In the Anacostia section of Washington, D.C., the Union Temple Baptist Church has extensive social-service programs. This twenty-year-old, 1,000 member church composed primarily of working-class members has been under the leadership of Rev. Willie Wilson since 1973. The church has four assistant ministers, one of whom is a woman. Prominent among its extensive array of social-service programs are the following:

1. *Harambee House.* This facility was established four years ago to provide residential care for girls who had been adjudicated as delinquent by the courts. It tries to enhance the self-esteem and positive social development of these troubled girls by providing a comprehensive array of educational, cultural, spiritual, and recreational activities. About four girls reside there at one time and remain on the average for about three or four months. This program has twenty-four staff members, half of whom are volunteers. The program is funded by the church and the D.C. Youth Services Administration.

2. *Soul Bowl.* This program was set up six years ago as a feeding program for the homeless. Between seventy and a hundred home-

less and other poor persons are fed each day. It is operated by fifteen staff members, thirteen of whom are volunteers. The program is funded mainly by the church.

3. *Agape Town Square.* This housing complex was completed two years ago to provide affordable, quality housing for low-income and working-class families. This fifty-seven-unit facility was financed by the church and through HUD's Section 8 subsidized rent program for low-income families.

4. *Orita Rites of Passage.* This program was instituted eight years ago to provide formalized educational, cultural, and spiritual instruction and ceremonies to facilitate the transition of black youth to responsible manhood and womanhood. A major component of Orita is to instill proper understanding of the importance of their African heritage. This program is administered by volunteers and is funded completely by the church.

5. *Alcohol and Drug Counseling.* This program was established twelve years ago to help alcoholics and drug abusers to overcome their addiction. Abusers receive individual and group counseling and support in weekly meetings. Adults comprise the bulk of program participants. This program has ten volunteers and is financed completely by the church.

6. *Metropolitan Baptist Church, Washington, D.C.*
In the Northwest Shaw section of Washington, D.C., the 124-year-old, 4,000 member Metropolitan Baptist Church has extensive social-service programs. Under the leadership of Rev. H. Beecher Hicks, Jr., since 1978, the church has four male assistant ministers. It has a largely middle-class membership. The community outreach programs of the church focus heavily on education. They include the following:

1. *Project Literacy U.S.* The PLUS program was instituted last year to combat the high rates of illiteracy in the black community. Each week individuals are provided basic instruction in reading, writing, and arithmetic. The program is staffed by twenty volunteers and is funded by the church and the Delta Sigma Theta Sorority, a major co-sponsor.

2. *Food and Clothing Program.* This program was set up nine years ago to provide food and clothing to the homeless and other individuals and families in need. It is staffed by thirty-five volunteers and is funded by the church.

3. *Prison Ministry.* This program was established four years ago to provide emotional and spiritual support to prison inmates. Ma-

jor program activities include counseling services, lectures, Bible study, information referral, and employment counseling. It is staffed by about twelve volunteers and is funded completely by the church.

4. *Adopt-a-School—Sharp Center.* Four years ago, the church "adopted" the Sharp Health Center, a school for handicapped children and youth. Church volunteers provide a broad array of services and support to these children. About seven volunteers staff this program, which is funded completely by the church.

5. *Adopt-a-School—Garrison Elementary.* The church "adopted" Garrison Elementary School four years ago to provide Big Brothers and Big Sisters to children with poor academic performance. The program is staffed by about seventeen volunteers and is funded completely by the church.

6. *Scouting Programs.* Over eight years ago, various scouting programs were instituted to enhance the social development of black children and youths. It currently has Boy Scout, Girl Scout, Cub Scout, and Brownie programs. About twelve volunteers staff these programs, which are financed by the church.

7. *Other Programs.* Other programs include modern ballet, GOD Brothers and Sisters, basketball teams, computer classes, martial arts, and Metro Voices.

7. *Bible Way Church, Washington, D.C.*

In northwest Washington, D.C., the sixty-year-old, 3,000 member Bible Way Church composed of working-class and middle-class members has been under the leadership of its founder Bishop Smallwood E. Williams since its inception sixty years ago. He has one male assistant minister. The church is also the mother church for some 300 other Bible Way churches throughout the world. The community outreach programs of this church include the following:

1. *Senior Citizens Program.* This program was established twenty-nine years ago to provide a broad array of services and support to the elderly. Major activities include providing hot meals every first and third Sunday and on Thanksgiving; transportation assistance; food distribution on holidays; counseling and recreation. This program is staffed by three volunteers and is financed by the church and special fund-raising events.

2. *Golden Rule Apartments.* These apartments were constructed twelve years ago to provide affordable, quality housing for low-income and working-class individuals and families. This high-rise

complex has 184 units with air conditioning, laundry facilities, day care, and recreational facilities. This program, which is staffed by volunteers, was financed through HUD's housing program for low-income families.

3. *Golden Rule Center.* This center was established eleven years ago to provide affordable housing and a wholesome living environment for low-income individuals and families. These facilities consist of twenty town houses, some with four bedrooms for large families, and were financed by the church and through HUD's low-income housing program.

4. *Golden Rule Supermarket.* Bible Way constructed a supermarket that was vitally needed in its low-income neighborhood. After operating the supermarket for the first eighteen months, the church now leases it to local businessmen.

5. *Youth Programs.* These provide wholesome educational, recreational, and spiritual activities for young people, staffed by volunteers, financed by the church.

8. *New Hope Church of God in Christ, Atlanta*

In Atlanta the forty-year-old, 350 member New Hope Church of God in Christ, composed of working-class and middle-class members, has been under the leadership of Bishop J. P. Husband for six years. Its social-service programs include the following:

1. *Day Care Center.* The Hinsely Day Care Center has been in operation since the church was founded in 1948. It provides preschool basic education to children from two to six years old. It was established to provide affordable child care for working black mothers. Mrs. Howard, the director of this center, was formerly a principal in the public school system in Atlanta. Its staff consists of eight paid instructors, who are deeply committed to the center's objectives.

2. *Prison Ministry.* This program, which started in 1973, attempts to provide social and emotional support to black women prisoners in the Fulton County Jail. Each Wednesday volunteers provide some assistance to the prisoners, their children, and other family members. This program, which is staffed by volunteers, is funded completely by New Hope. Contributions for the Prison Ministry are collected every third Sunday.

3. *Tutoring Program.* This program provides educational assistance to students having academic difficulty. It is sponsored by New Hope's Young People's Department and is targeted to black

children between the ages of seven and fourteen. Young people in the program do their homework in the study hall where they are assisted by tutors. Members of the AKA Sorority at Spelman comprise the bulk of the volunteer tutors. During its four years of operation, this program has significantly improved the grades of many students.

4. *Ministry for Economic Development.* MED is a nonprofit effort to harness the resources of black churches to enhance the economic development of the black community. It plans to spur the development of small businesses, a job bank, a food bank, and a clothing bank. This program, which started in 1982, is sponsored by the consortium of local churches in the Church of God denomination.

9. *Holy Ghost Roman Catholic Church, Rural Louisiana*

In Opolousas, Louisiana, the sixty-eight-year-old, 1,000 member Holy Ghost Roman Catholic Faith Community Church was under the leadership of Father Albert J. McKnight for six years. He had two male assistant pastors. The aggressive, extensive, and innovative outreach programs of this rural Catholic church included the following:

1. *Southern Development Foundation.* In 1972, in order to spur community and economic development among blacks in rural areas, Father McKnight helped to launch this foundation, which is headquartered in Lafayette, Louisiana. Major functions of the SDF businesses are to provide mini-grants to stimulate rural development projects, and to conduct research and test programmatic models for agricultural development.

2. *BUST.* Father McKnight also contributed to the creation of the Black Unity and Spiritual Togetherness, a nonprofit organization dedicated to stimulating business development. Community BUST corporations have evolved, along with BUST Enterprises, Inc., an investment group created to finance business development, and BUST Landlorders, Inc., whose main goal is to enhance and maintain land acquisition among rural blacks. Because of these successes, BUST chapters are forming throughout the South.

3. *Feeding Program.* This program, financed mainly by the church, provides food and hot meals to poor individuals and families in rural areas. Staffed by volunteers, 200 persons are fed daily.

4. *G.E.D. Preparation.* This program, staffed by volunteers and

financed completely by the church, was established to help school dropouts to pass their high school equivalency tests.

5. *Fitness Center.* The church has a full, Universal fitness center to enhance the physical development of children and adults in rural areas.

6. *Counseling Program.* This program was instituted to help individuals and families cope more effectively with personal problems and family crises. It is staffed by volunteers and is funded by the church.

10. *Valley Queen Baptist Church, Marks, Mississippi*

In rural Marks, Mississippi, the sixty-eight-year-old, 200-member Valley Queen Baptist Church is composed mostly of working-class members. It is under the leadership of Rev. Carl Brown. Among its extensive social-service outreach programs are the following:

1. *Quitman County Development Organization.* The Reverend Mr. Brown helped to create QCDO eleven years ago as a nonprofit organization dedicated to addressing the social, political, and economic needs of poor and black people in that rural county. QCDO's major functions include leadership training, community development, and economic development. Some of QCDO's accomplishments are establishing a Federal Credit Union; developing a laundromat, thrift store, and rental office and business space as part of the Marks Mini Mall Development Center Project; and coordinating the METS Public Transportation System.

2. *Economic Development Project.* In 1985, the Reverend Mr. Brown, with the assistance of the Ford Foundation, helped to launch QCDO's Black Church Community and Economic Development Project to facilitate their "reinvolvement" in developing the total black community. This is an ecumenical endeavor embracing a broad spectrum of denominations. QCDO provides technical assistance and/or enhances the social and economic well-being of black children, youths, adults, families, and the total community.

3. *Feeding Program.* This program was instituted to provide food to needy individuals and families. About fifty-six people are served each day. It is staffed by volunteers and funded mainly by the church.

4. *Homeless Shelter.* This program was established to provide emergency shelter to the homeless. It accommodates up to twenty homeless persons at a time. This effort was initiated by a grant from Riverside Church in New York.

5. *Nursing Home Program.* This program was set up to provide emotional and social support to senior citizens through regular visitations to nursing homes. It is staffed by volunteers and funded completely by the church.

BLACK CHURCHES IN THE NORTHEAST

On the basis of this pilot study a comprehensive and systematic nationwide study was launched in all the four regions of the nation.[20] Our findings from the Northeast region of the United States help to establish the important role of the black church as a community agent with remarkable actual and potential impact. Telephone interviews were conducted with a random sample of 315 black churches representing at least twenty denominations in fourteen specific cities of the six Northeast states of Massachusetts, Connecticut, Rhode Island, New York, New Jersey, and Pennsylvania.

There is a great range of denominations represented in the study (Figure 17.1). Baptist churches predominate in this sample as they do in the nation generally, constituting nearly 38 percent of all churches. The historically black Baptist denominations are well represented. Methodists represent the next largest group comprising some 15 percent of the churches in the study. The

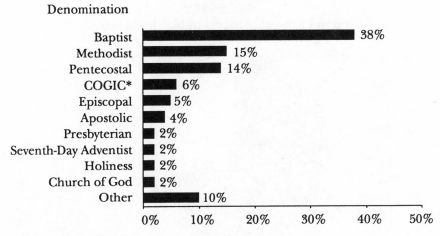

FIGURE 17.1
Faith Traditions and Denominations in Northeast Sample
1991

Denomination

* Church of God in Christ
SOURCE: Billingsley et al. "The Role of the Black Church," 1991.

historically black Methodist denominations are well represented. And these are followed by Pentacostal at 14 percent. After these come the Church of God in Christ with 6 percent, the Episcopalians with 5 percent and the Apostolics with nearly 4 percent.

Several major findings stand out in this random sample of black churches in the Northeast region conducted in 1990–91.

The churches were found to represent the economic independence referred to by Benjamin Mays and J. W. Nicholson in their 1933 study and by C. Eric Lincoln and Lawrence Mamiya in their 1990 publication.[21] Specifically we found that 69 percent of the black churches in this region owned their buildings outright, having completely paid off the mortgage (Figure 17.2). Another 23 percent were in the process of buying their buildings.

We found that black churches represent a broad spectrum of social classes (Figure 17.3). Roughly 60 percent of them were composed of a mixture of both working-class and middle-class members. Only 30 percent were primarily working class and 8 percent had mostly middle-class members.

Churches are stable fixtures that tend to stay in one neighborhood for long periods of time (Figure 17.4). Twenty-seven percent of the churches have never moved and another 27 percent have moved only once in their history.

These churches are heavily supported by female members (Figure 17.5). A majority have over 50 percent female members and nearly half are 75 percent or more female. At the same time, however, 91 percent of the senior ministers are male.

FIGURE 17.2
Church Ownership Status in Northeast Sample
1991

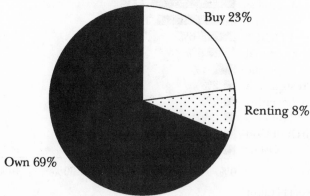

SOURCE: Billingsley et al. "The Role of the Black Church," 1991.

FIGURE 17.3

**Social Class of Church Members in Northeast Sample
1991**

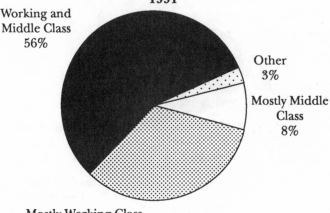

Working and
Middle Class
56%

Other
3%

Mostly Middle
Class
8%

Mostly Working Class
33%

SOURCE: Billingsley et al. "The Role of the Black Church," 1991.

FIGURE 17.4

**Church Movement Patterns in Northeast Sample
1991**

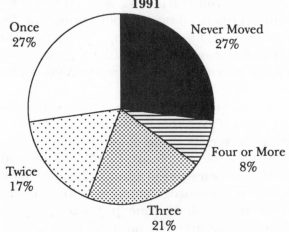

Once
27%

Never Moved
27%

Four or More
8%

Twice
17%

Three
21%

SOURCE: Billingsley et al. "The Role of the Black Church,"
1991.

Ministers had relatively high levels of education and were actively involved in community leadership activities. A majority of the ministers were college graduates; a majority had seminary or Bible college training; and more than a third had a master's or doctorate degree. Most were full-time pastors with no outside jobs.

FIGURE 17.5
Female Church Membership Northeast Sample
1991

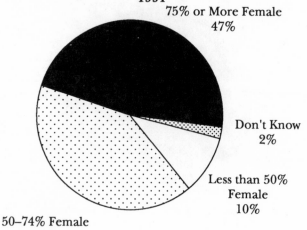

75% or More Female
47%

Don't Know
2%

Less than 50%
Female
10%

50–74% Female
41%

SOURCE: Billingsley et al. "The Role of the Black Church,"
1991.

Most churches were actively involved in providing family-oriented community outreach programs. Altogether 70 percent of these churches operated one or more programs. Only 30 percent operated none. Those operating programs represented all the major denominations included in the study. Moreover, the average number of outreach programs operating by the churches was four.

These programs span a wide range of types across the entire life cycle (Figure 17.6). Taken together some 31 percent of these programs were aimed specifically at children and youth. Another 51 percent were of the more inclusive family support and assistance type, 8 percent were directed to adult and elderly individuals. Finally, 10 percent of these programs were more general community service and community development activities.

These churches are involved not only in their own programs but in extensive collaboration with other churches and other community agencies. This collaboration with other churches is both within and across denominational lines, and there is an even more extensive collaboration with other nonreligious social agencies (Table 17.5 and Figure 17.7). Primary among these are local police (84 percent) and local schools (77 percent), followed by welfare departments (74 percent) and hospitals (70 percent).

FIGURE 17.6
Types of Outreach Programs Sponsored by Churches in Northeast Sample
1991

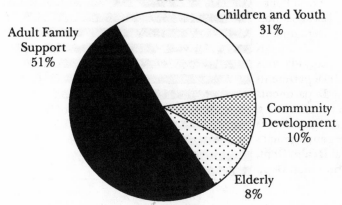

SOURCE: Billingsley et al. "The Role of the Black Church," 1991.

TABLE 17.5
Community Involvement of Churches in Northeast Sample
1991

Outreach Activities with Churches in Same Denomination	N	(%)
Yes	140	65
No	75	35
Outreach Activities with Churches in Other Denominations		
Yes	139	65
No	75	35
Cooperation with Nonreligious Social Agencies		
Yes	156	74
No	56	26

SOURCE: Billingsley et al. "The Role of the Black Church," 1991.

THE FUTURE ROLE OF THE BLACK CHURCH

Black churches in the Northeastern region serve as important social-service institutions for families and the community. Fully seven out of ten have established one or more family-oriented community outreach programs. They engage in a wide range of outreach activities, including programs for children and youth, adults and families, and the elderly, as well as broadly based community development projects. Churches of all denominations engage in these activities.

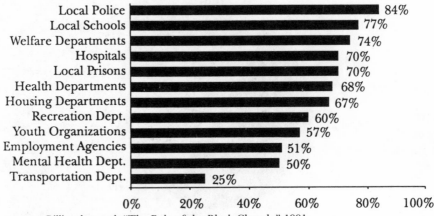

FIGURE 17.7
Church Cooperation with Social Agencies in Northeast Sample
1991

SOURCE: Billingsley et al. "The Role of the Black Church," 1991.

What is it that distinguishes churches that engage in community outreach from those that do not? Age and size seem to be principal factors associated with the development of outreach programs. The older, larger churches are more likely to sponsor outreach programs. Other prominent factors include the number of paid clergy and presence of other paid staff members, the level of education of the senior minister, and ownership of its facilities. Each of these factors reflects the relative level of resources or wealth of the church. The churches with greater resources in these areas are more likely to engage in community outreach programs.

A third set of characteristics also distinguishes these community-oriented churches. Specifically, if the senior minister or other church leader interviewed perceives the role of the church to be serving both its members and the community, the church is much more likely to engage in community outreach than if his or her perception is that the church should only serve its members. Further, if the church frequently makes available its facilities for nonreligious activities, that same church is more likely to sponsor community outreach programs. Finally, if the senior minister is himself active in community activities—such as the NAACP, local ministerial alliances, the Urban League—the church is more likely to sponsor community outreach programs.

The church has the strong potential to bring the community together—upper class, middle class, the working class, and the poor—to focus on helping poor families regain hope for their future. In its search for a focus of concern about those families, Americans would do well to remember the black church has a track record.

While there is a certain amount of skepticism in the nation about the capacity of the black churches to coalesce around priority issues, the long-term research we have reported on in this chapter has already established that some two-thirds of black churches in the study are already actively involved in family-oriented community outreach programs at the local level. Moreover, the overwhelming majority are disposed to cooperative arrangements with nonreligious community agencies as well.

This analysis provides considerable support for the proposition that the church, in cooperation with other institutions, will play a pivotal role in the future of African-American families.[22] It also confirms the insight of the Reverend Wallace Charles Smith in his book, *The Church in the Life of the Black Family*. He noted that no other institution is as completely accepting of black families in all their complexity, nor as supportive. Writing of his very practical experience as a pastor, Reverend Smith has pointed out the importance of the family-oriented community outreach mission of the contemporary black church, particularly in the urban areas of the nation. He writes:

> As a pastor . . . I have watched families struggle with an assortment of devastating problems. I have shared the pain of families in which members have been accused or convicted of theft, drug addiction, prostitution, rape, and murder. I have been involved with homeless families who have been so desperate for a place to live that squatting in abandoned houses was their only recourse. I have witnessed elderly persons lose all sense of autonomy because of homelessness, illness, and loneliness. I have heard the cries of children, parents, and the elderly as they faced conditions of hopelessness. Through it all I have witnessed a remarkable fact—for these persons the church has been the central authenticating reality in their lives. When the world has so often been willing to say only "no" to these people, the church has said "yes." For black people the church has been the one place where they have been able to experience unconditional positive regard.[23]

Then Dr. Smith, in his role as scholar, sets forth a conceptual framework by which the black church can address this family crisis. In doing so he moves beyond a focus on the problems to a broader, more wholistic perspective. Arguing for what he calls "a cooperative strategy" between church and community, he observes that "the black family and the black church have drawn on each other for support and nurture. For them to develop a cooperative strategy suitable for dealing with the enormity of the problems, several shared realities must be understood." He lists these realities as recognition that the black community is a suffering community, a community of extended families, an inclusive community, an adoptionist community, and finally, a hopeful community.[24] There is no questioning the strategic role of the black church. Its centrality is captured brilliantly by Pulitzer Prize–winning playwright August Wilson in *Fences, Joe Turner's Come and Gone, The Piano Lesson*, and his 1991 production, *Two Trains Running*. He has shown how a heritage of spirituality and religiosity can be redemptive in the resolution of complex family problems.

Both Dr. Smith, the theologian/scholar, and August Wilson, the playwright, lend meaning in their work to the multiple roles of the black church as it interacts with families. And as the majority of churches in our study seem to confirm, it is by moving out beyond its membership, by opening up its facilities to the community, and by moving out resolutely into secular community issues that the black church shows the greatest potential for helping contemporary African-American families harness their strengths and move to greater levels of viability.

Chapter 18

———

Climbing Jacob's Ladder: Self-Help Redefined

Will more people in the black community place the viability of struggling families at the top of their personal, professional, and organizational agendas? Will they accept their responsibility to interpret black families' needs and aspirations to the larger society? Will they be able to press society to play its proper role? Will they cooperate across racial, organizational, and physical boundaries? These are controversial questions, because they imply that the black community must take profound initiatives in the coming years, and inspire society to do the same.

We believe that self-help is fundamental to African-American progress in an often, though clearly not always, hostile society. Ultimately, the future of African-American families depends on how well the black community itself understands this. To a greater or lesser degree, there are promising signs that many sectors of the community already do.

INDIVIDUAL INITIATIVES

Responsible Parents

Nearly three percent of all black families are headed by single men. It is an expanding phenomenon. Larry Tolson may not be typical of them all, but he is an outstanding example of one dimension of our meaning of individual self-help.[1]

In 1991 at age twenty-seven, Tolson was already father of nine children, whom he was raising alone. It all began when he was twenty-one and decided to get married and settle down. He did and in rapid-fire order three children were born: Lawrence, now aged seven, plus twins Perry and Larry, Jr., now six. Then the mother moved out. He soon struck up a relationship with another woman who was eager to help him make a family. Together for five years, they produced six additional children, including two sets of twins: Lance and Leonard, Latise and Lakita, Lisa, and LaShawn. Then she left.

While numerous local authorities and others who do not know him frequently question whether he can possibly raise these nine children well, Tolson continues to do what seems impossible.

Who is this determined young man? He works part-time as an auto mechanic. He is a full-time student at a local technical institute. In addition, he finds time to do volunteer work for the local senior citizens group and the neighborhood council. An observer has confirmed that Tolson's children are always clean, well fed, and well dressed. Those old enough to attend school always test in the top levels of their class.

A local community leader and member of the city council, Wilhelmina J. Rolark, who helped Tolson find housing for his family has described him as "an exceptional father. He's determined to make something of himself and he is totally dedicated to his children." Tolson has described his own source of strength. "My saving grace," he told reporter Courtland Malloy, "is that I took home economics from seventh grade through high school. Even changing diapers is not so bad," he said, "when you get used to it."

Their five-bedroom public housing apartment is well kept. He has taught the children to help him with the cooking and cleaning and other chores. Tolson also gets a hand from the neighbors. His volunteer work pays off. "There are many elderly women out here, and they help me a lot," he said. "They baby-sit, braid hair, and sew. So my volunteering is one way to say thanks."

He also gets strong moral support from his mother. When asked if he feels burdened by such responsibility at such a young age, Tolson responded as though these responsibilities have saved his very life. "A lot of my friends are either in prison, strung out on drugs, or dead," he said. "And I was heading along the same path until these babies started coming. I no longer get high, unless it's on my kids. Through them, I've experienced the joy of true devotion, and now I know what love really means. I can't give that up."

Larry Tolson has learned that none of these achievements is his alone. Yet many successful African-American individuals fall victim to the urge to forget about their group identity and group responsibility and seek only to raise themselves and to vanish into the American mainstream. It reflects an American individualism which tends to ignore the common good. It leads to enhancing the well-being of the few over the welfare of the many.

Parenting Other People's Children

There are, however, strong indications that the traditional commitment of the individual to the whole of African-American family life is far from dead and may even be on the verge of a renaissance across class lines. Kent and Carmen Amos have shown that middle-class and privileged black people still can reach out and parent other people's children.[2] In 1981 Kent Amos was a thirty-seven-year-old, successful Xerox Corporation executive. His wife, Carmen Harden, was also employed. They had two children aged sixteen and twelve. Though they could afford the best private school for their son, they decided to put him in the local high school from which Amos himself had graduated nearly two decades earlier. In a short time, with the encouragement of his parents, their son began bringing his friends home from school. It was apparent to Kent and Carmen that those children needed help and they elected to give it.

Kent Amos, the successful businessman and Vietnam veteran, went into action on the local home front. He was knowledgeable and proud of his heritage. "I believe in myself," he once told an interviewer, "and my aim is to be the best black man I can be. If I do that, I will be the best man there is."

He quietly designed an after-school program for their son Wesley and his friends in their home. "You are welcome in this house," he said. "Here you will be treated like our own kids. But you'll also be held to the standards we set for them." He also told the youths, "Work hard and get an education. You can be whatever you want to be."

Soon the routine was set. After school a group of boys came to the Amos home for fellowship and parenting, as well as chores, homework, dinner, and recreation and conversation. Amos and

Carmen were surrogate parents to them all. Within six years the number of these boys had reached fifty. They were too many for Carmen to do the cooking so the boys were taught to help her and to help Amos with the shopping. In 1987 the evening study sessions outgrew the Amos home and moved to the neighborhood school, with the monitoring of the athletic director, Arthur Riddle. After nearly ten years Amos could give the following report of how two individuals can make a difference in the lives of often wayward black youth. Of the fifty members of this augmented family, eighteen had graduated from college, and another eighteen were still in college. Most of the others were employed or in school. Only a few had been lost to the streets.

Amos had a word for all his kids: "When you make it in life, it will be your role to reach out and help others." He told one reporter that he considers his major contribution to the youths to be "consistency."[3] He estimates that it costs them between $15,000 and $20,000 a year to sustain this program. But when questioned about this he puts it in perspective: He can afford it. "I'm living in a pretty nice house, I have a good life and manage my money well.... My wife and I each drive a Mercedes.... What am I giving up—stocks?"

And what about Carmen? She says that Kent has more patience with the youths and she needs more quiet time. "I'm more private than he is," she says. "Once I get everybody situated and fed, I'll take my quiet time. Kent thrives on having the kids around."

Amos believes that their example can be contagious. "These kids don't need to drown," he told a reporter. "There are enough substantial adults out there who can make a difference and who—if they would just walk into the water and lock arms—would stop these kids from being swept downstream."

Dorothy Perry of Miami, for example, has become the surrogate mother of dozens of children from first through tenth grade for an after-school program very similar to that run by Kent and Carmen Amos.[4] After her own five children grew up, she began helping children whose parents needed an extra support system. Every day after school they come to her home. She keeps in touch with their parents and their teachers.

She told reporter William Raspberry about her dream. "My dream is a big house by a lake with different sections for cooking, sewing, and other skills taught by senior citizens, so they can feel useful, too. It would be a safe haven for young and old." When he asked how about money for herself, she said, "You know, I never thought about that."

A Personal Crusade

Allen Paige, another successful black adult, was named one of the ten outstanding young men in America in 1981. He was once voted most valuable player for the National Football League. He is a nine-time All-Pro defensive tackle and member of the Football Hall of Fame. By 1990 he was Assistant Attorney General of Minnesota. He had not forgotten the black youths still caught up in the struggle for life and meaning in life. "Even when I was playing professionally," he told an interviewer, "I never viewed myself as a football player. There is far more to life than being an athlete." Moreover, he believes "that black athletes have an obligation to influence the way young minority people grow up in a positive way."[5]

Paige has launched an extensive personal crusade in the inner-city high schools of Minnesota, bringing this message to young people who need it most. After the Hall of Fame induction he gathered a few friends and together they established a foundation. The Minnesota Vikings donated the proceeds from one game to help launch it. By fall 1989, ten students from Minneapolis high schools were helped to go to college. By fall 1990, thirty-one students were beneficiaries of awards of up to $2,000.

Although Paige has a demanding job, a wife, and four children, he is still able to devote the necessary time to keep this project going. He is both realistic and visionary about this project. "We can get them focused on the idea that education is important, that it can help them achieve whatever their hopes and dreams are. Thirty kids a year doesn't sound like a lot, given the scope of the problem we have in this country, but if you get thirty kids working with thirty other kids, and repeat that again and again, the numbers just get bigger. You can change some attitudes."

Advocates and Mentors

Spencer Holland, director of the Morgan State University Center for Educating Black Males, is a man with a mission.[6] He believes that the most disadvantaged and intractable black boys can be motivated to learn and achieve if black men take a special interest in them. He did not always have so much faith in education. He confesses that when he graduated from high school, it took inordinate persuasion from his mother for him to go to college. A longtime educator, he became a celebrated dropout from the field for three years. "I couldn't stand it anymore," he told a reporter. "I finally threw it all over. I went into computers. No people, no children."

Then on the day when Dr. Martin Luther King's birthday became a national holiday, Holland decided to return to education. At fifty-one, with two advanced degrees from Columbia University, he reflected on his own personal achievements. "I knew I had gotten all my money, all my scholarships because of people like Dr. King. . . . So, I thought, 'Okay, Dr. King. I will go back. I will grit my teeth and I will go back.' "

Many of his initiatives are fraught with controversy—especially his advocacy of special inner-city schools exclusively for black boys. But one of his initiatives has caught on both in Baltimore and Washington, D.C. He designed a long-term mentoring program that brings black professionals into the schools and into the lives of youths who often have no effective role models. Project 2000 has been adopted by an organization of black men called Concerned Black Men. In Washington, D.C., they have adopted an inner-city public school class of ninety-three boys and girls and plan to work with them through the year 2000 when they will graduate from high school. Under this program African-American men are persuaded to spend one-half day, once or twice a week, helping the teachers and the pupils in classes of both boys and girls. Holland still has a special interest in the boys. "We're looking for men to help the teachers discipline and boys respond better to men."

At Stanton Elementary School in the southeast section of Washington, D.C., Yolanda Coleman is the only school counselor for 530 mostly low-income students. "This is like manna from heaven," she said. "You can see the effect the men have. The students' faces light up. And when the men leave, you hear the boys ask the same question, 'Will you be back? Will you be back?' "

Tenina Southerland, a second-grade teacher at Stanton, welcomes the mentors. "Many of these boys lack family support and aren't being taught to respect each other," she said. "Their needs are tremendous." One of the mentors at Stanton School is Ray Casey, an architect. His presence in the school has been described as follows:

"One recent afternoon, Southerland's second graders were in class matching numbers with letters to spell words such as flower, cake, and apple. Southerland patrolled the room, helped by a Howard University student volunteer. Some students were still goofing off. Then Ray Casey, the architect, arrived. The boys erupted into a chorus of cheers. They left their desks and tugged at his arms and waist to show good grades on homework or ask for help with words and number work."

During his visit to four classes, Casey, huddled with a group of third-grade boys, asked about their work, shook their hands, coached a second-grade quiz. "Soon the bell rang, and the halls filled with students bound for the doors." Teachers thanked Casey for coming. He asked how he could help during his next visit. Meantime, boys bounced off each other to tell him good-bye.

What is the central insight to be derived from these illustrations? It is that one highly able, motivated, dedicated, and persistent individual can still make a difference even in today's complex society. Whether working with their own children as Larry Tolson does, or with other people's children as Kent and Carmen Amos or Dorothy Perry or the others do, they send a message to the African-American community that is as old as Africa and as effective as their grandparents' home remedies. Kent Amos puts it this way: "These are all our children" and "Love is truly the answer." When it is realized that some 20 percent of all the nearly 10 million black households are composed of single adults living alone and that another fifth are composed of married couples with no children of their own in the home; that an expanding pool of black elderly are retiring in fairly good health; that a majority of African-Americans are no longer poor; and that more than a third of all black families are middle and upper class, the enormous potential of Kent Amos's vision is apparent.

All over the nation individuals of talent and means are reaching out to supplement the role of other people's families in meeting the taxing needs of their members. But the task is much too great for individual self-help efforts alone. There is a critical need for more organized and institutional forms of self-help. For while it is true that strong families make strong institutions, it is equally true the other way around.

INSTITUTIONAL INITIATIVES

In 1984, the nation's two oldest and largest black national organizations, the NAACP and the National Urban League, sponsored a national black family summit at Fisk University.

All the national black organizations were represented. These national leaders were told that they were called together to address this problem in its broadest possible dimensions because the black family crisis is no provincial matter. It is a national problem. They were reminded of a statement issued a few months earlier by a distinguished group of black intellectuals under the leadership of the psychologist Dr. Kenneth Clark and the historian Dr. John Hope Franklin:

> One of the legacies of racial oppression in America is that a large segment of the black population is structurally excluded from the American society. . . . [Today] at least three societies exist in America: the mainstream, the assimilated minorities, and the excluded. These societies are separate and unequal and the disparities among them threaten to destroy the national fabric.[7]

It was also pointed out to this largely middle-class assembly that the very initiatives which had elevated many of them into the black middle class were in danger.

When these leaders, professionals, activists, theologians, historians, and social-science scholars who study families returned to their organizations, almost everyone who had not done so already launched a program of education, networking, collaborating, self-help efforts, and social advocacy on behalf of black families.

To add to this national resolve on the part of the black community to understand and deal with this problem, a few months later the leading national black women's organizations called another conference to focus specifically on the problem of teenage pregnancy. Meeting at Spelman College under the leadership of Dorothy Height of the National Council of Negro Women, Marian Wright Edelman of the Children's Defense Fund, Jewell Jackson McCabe of the National Coalition of One Hundred Black Women, and Hortense Canady of Delta Sigma Theta Sorority, they fashioned a nationwide plan of action against teenage pregnancy. Each year at the annual meeting of the Children's Defense Fund, they report their progress.

There are other women and men, to be sure, all over the nation giving leadership to a variety of efforts to revitalize the African-

American family. Further initiatives are being spearheaded by Girls, Inc. (formerly Girls Clubs of America), the Links, and Jack and Jill of America, as well as other national groups. But by any reckoning there is a small group of black women mentioned above who are setting the pace, calling on both the black community and the rest of the nation to place high priority on family values, family integrity, family solidarity, family supports, and family policy. Thus, as with their lineal ancestors—Harriet Tubman and Sojourner Truth, Fannie Lou Hamer and Rosa Parks—these women and the organizations they affect are leaving their mark on the future of African-American families.

Throughout the voluntary, nonprofit sector, black women have moved into national roles in the family restoration movement. These include Evelyn Moore of the National Black Child Development Institute, Mary Futrell, former president of the National Education Association; Faye Wattleton, former president of the Planned Parenthood Federation of America; Geneva B. Johnson, president of Family Service America; and Glendora Putman, former president of the National YWCA.

A most moving example of the increasing institutional focus on African-American families is the National Council of Negro Women, which produces the annual African-American Family Reunion Celebration. It is a celebration of the remarkable mosaic that is African-American family life. It proclaims through laughter and tears, we are still here, still struggling, still determined to be free and to live in community with ourselves and with free persons everywhere.

A description of the 1988 reunion helps to explain its appeal:

> A family album of black mothers, fathers and children stretched a full four stories high, welcoming everyone to the Philadelphia Black Family Reunion Celebration.
> Dr. Betty Shabazz, widow of Malcolm X, summed up the mood as she spoke during the opening ceremony. . . . "We must celebrate our successes as a people," she told those gathered before her. "It used to be against the law for blacks to marry and have children that we could keep with us," she said. "Now that we can have families, we need to keep black families together. . . ."
> Assembled in West Philadelphia's Fairmount Park on June 18, 1988, the 11 pavilions featured exhibits and lectures on family values, education, children and young adults. Other tents had presentations on sports, beauty, work, ethics, spirituality, health, films and the African diaspora.[8]

Dorothy Height pointed out in the summer of 1991 that after four consecutive summer reunions in four of the nation's largest cities involving more than 5 million participants not a single police incident had occurred. No knifing, no shooting, no looting—and no arrests.

Business Ownership

Among the institutional initiatives in the black community perhaps none is more powerful or more underestimated by family specialists than business and economic development. Some sociologists are beginning to see the connection between a viable black-owned economic base and strong black families. John Sibley Butler, for instance, argues not only that ownership of business enterprises is good for family viability, but that the community has a long tradition of entrepreneurial initiative. He points out that in enclaves around the nation such as Tulsa, Oklahoma's "Little Africa"; Durham, North Carolina's "Negro Wall Street"; and Chicago's "Black Metropolis," thriving black business activity helped to stabilize family life during the early 1900s.[9] Along with eyewitnesses, he also points out how the larger society frustrated these self-help initiatives.

THE WIDER SOCIETY'S ROLE

During the 1980s it became fashionable among American leaders and scholars to ask whether the government should help African-American families with the many problems they faced or whether the time had come for the black community to help itself. Some commentators argued that the government had done enough and most of what it had done had not helped the situation but had made it worse and, therefore, black self-help was the only sound path to follow.

These advocates were harshly critical of civil rights leaders, organizations, and the black middle class for having given strong support over the years to civil rights legislation, affirmative action, and other government policies on behalf of the disadvantaged. It was argued that these leaders and organizations should have been supporting black self-help instead. It was argued that blacks should solve their social problems without depending on the government.[10] Those who advocated vigorous government action on behalf of blacks were placed on the defensive throughout the decade.

The argument over whether the government or the black community was responsible for correcting the problems black families face was confounded with another argument over whether racism was still a powerful force in American society, or whether there was a "declining significance of race" so profound that race and racism no longer were major obstacles to black progress.[11]

This argument throughout the decade had a rather unreal quality to it. Could these proponents be serious? In what America did they live? Where did they go to school? Where did they go to church? Where did they work?

There are several fallacies in the argument that the government has no further responsibility for bringing about racial justice. The first is the inherent assumption that government money was white money; that government action was white people's generosity; that the government belonged to white people. If this were not the case, how could a distinction be made between the government and the black community?

The problem with this reasoning is that it flies in the face of the facts. Take the question of government money. It is generally known that numerous kinds of taxes are levied against the poor. Income taxes, Social Security taxes, sales taxes, user fees, property taxes, all are collected disproportionately from the poor.

It is also generally known that blacks are disproportionately arrayed among the poor. While a majority of white American families are middle income and above and live in suburbia, a majority of black American families are low income and live in the inner cities.

Those who underestimate the contributions blacks make to the government would do well to remember that blacks not only pay a disproportionately high portion of taxes but through their spending make it possible for many merchants to realize great earnings, enabling them to pay taxes as well. Moreover, they would do well to reflect on history. The wealth generated by the Southern agricultural economy could not have been possible without the contributions of the Africans who labored without pay for over 200 years. And the industrial wealth of the North was secured when blacks joined the Civil War during its last two years assuring victory for the Union army.

An even more profound fallacy with the argument that black

people should help themselves rather than rely on the government is its either-or perspective. Either the government helps black people or black people help themselves. We have argued throughout this book that such a false dichotomous way of thinking obscures reality more than it highlights it. Surely *both* the government *and* the black community have important responsibilities, obligations, and roles to play in the eradication of racial injustice.

The argument ignores the fact that the black community both historically and at the present time is not a passive entity in the struggle for improvement but is activated by self-help. The self-help tradition of black Americans is long and deep.

Finally, the argument about blacks helping themselves is too narrowly drawn. Among those who argue for black self-help rather than government help there is a conspicuous absence of analysis of how African Americans could save, invest, and spend the more than $300 billion income earned by them each year to support and build more enterprises, institutions, and agencies which they controlled. Not even the conservative black economists set forth such analyses.

Perhaps it was in part the vigor of the argument as well as these fallacies that impelled a group of some thirty black intellectuals to issue a report titled *Black Initiative and Governmental Responsibility*.[12] Under the leadership of the historian John Hope Franklin, the psychologist Kenneth Clark, the attorney Eleanor Holmes Norton, sociologist William J. Wilson, children's advocate Marian Wright Edelman, and others called together by the Joint Center for Political Studies in Washington, a pamphlet was issued that effectively pierced the essence of this false dichotomous argument. John Hope Franklin read a portion of his cogently succinct executive summary to this document at the 1986 Congressional Black Caucus weekend:

> We believe that solutions to the problems facing black Americans require simultaneously three distinct areas of activity:
>
> • that we draw more explicitly and openly upon the extraordinarily rich and vibrant tradition of black values that continues to sustain us;
> • that we do more to mobilize and, in some instances, redirect the strong self-help tradition that is hard at work but too often hidden from public view; and,
> • that we lay out the much obscured case for government's re-

sponsibility for disadvantaged citizens in a stable democracy and indicate specific steps that government should take.[13]

Expanding on these themes, the report held:

- The black community has always been an agent for its own advancement.
- The "self help" tradition is so embedded in the black heritage as to be virtually synonymous with it.
- We must reach more broadly and more deeply to levels of participation that include the poorest blacks and that draw them closer to blacks who have been more fortunate.
- Persistent poverty has eroded but not destroyed the strong deep value framework that for so long has sustained black people.
- The black community must take the lead in defining the new and the continuing problems it faces, in communicating the urgency of these problems, and in both prescribing and initiating solutions.
- Many fruitful strategies are in place and should be expanded.
- Many of the most pressing problems of the black community are well beyond its capacity or that of any community to resolve.
- We urge a concentrated effort by government to invest first in models and then in programs and strategies for human development that will facilitate economic independence and encourage the poor to take charge of their own lives.
- The inexcusable disparities between whites and blacks . . . can be eradicated only if the government assumes its appropriate role in a democratic, humane, and stable society.[14]

The government and the black community are not separate entities. Each is an expression of the other.

Some forecasters are beginning to see indications that the larger society is preparing to come to grips with the needs of all its citizens. Marvin Cetron and Owen Davies have captured much of this mood:

> By 2000, there will be no mistaking the trend toward a more comfortable, more equal America. The richest and poorest segments of the American population will be much smaller than they are today, the middle class correspondingly larger. Poverty will not be a thing of the past; there will still be economic problems that urgently require attention. But the worst will be behind us. We will have built the kinder, gentler America that today is only a pious slogan.[15]

It is difficult to share such optimism considering the Reagan legacy. David Swinton has pointed out that African-Americans suffered disproportionately during the Reagan era.[16] All age groups and all types of family structures have fared badly in comparison to white families.

Even the Republican analyst Kevin Phillips, who showed how the rich have been getting richer, especially the super-rich, at the expense of all others and the nation as a whole during the Reagan era, professed some optimism:

> One could reasonably assume that the 1990's would be a time in which to correct the excesses of the 1980's, for the dangers posed by excessive individualism, greed and insufficient concern for America as a community went beyond the issue of fairness and, by threatening the ability of the United States to maintain its economic position in the world, created an unusual meeting ground for national self-interest and reform. As the 1980's ended, other events were also suggesting new political directions.[17]

What is needed to reverse the fortunes of African-American families is suggested by David Swinton:

> A solution to the longstanding economic difficulties of the black community will require two major changes in public policy. First, there must be a more effective national economic policy to end the erosion of the American industrial structure. The living standards of American workers must be preserved and improved. The economy must also be strong enough to provide equal and adequate opportunities to all citizens who are willing to work.
>
> Second, black Americans must insist on a major commitment from the federal government as the representative of the American people to make the effort to repair once and for all the damages of centuries of exploitation and mistreatment. The failure of past policies stems directly from their failure to go far enough in repairing the damages of the historic legacy of discrimination. The repair of these damages cannot be considered complete until the black population is able to attain the same economic results as whites.[18]

These large-scale economic policies will require the leadership of the public sector and the cooperation and support of the private sector. They cannot be the responsibility of the African-American community or any sub-society within the nation.

In all the major reforms benefiting African-Americans in the past, there had been substantial response from each of these sectors. It was true of the war on slavery, the war on Jim Crow, and the war on poverty. We have devoted several chapters to the proposition that society exerts extraordinary influences on African-American families both to their benefit and to their detriment. Substantial support must be elicited from all sectors of the larger society if African-American families are to have a viable future. Families cannot be understood or enhanced apart from the community which nurtures them, or the society which sustains them.

At the outset of this book we identified twelve key systems of the larger society: the economic system, the political system, the health system, the housing system, the educational system, the welfare system, the criminal justice system, and the military system, as well as the transportation, recreation, communications, and religious systems. Extraordinary reforms can spring from any of them if proper attention is paid.

The challenge is to make this society more responsive to, and supportive of, all its members. Without vigorous, organized, and persistent advocacy on the part of the collective African-American community, however, it is not likely that the society will abandon its hegemony over the resources and amenities largely enjoyed by the wealthiest, most powerful, and most privileged elements of the nation. Frederick Douglass said it well: "Power concedes nothing without a demand. It never has. It never will."

Notes

CHAPTER 1

1. Hylan Lewis, *Blackways of Kent* (Chapel Hill: University of North Carolina Press, 1967).

2. D. T. Gurak, et al., *The Minority Foster Child: A Comparative Study of Hispanic, Black, and White Children* (Bronx, NY: Hispanic Research Center, Fordham University, 1982).

3. Robert Hill, *Informal Adoption Among Black Families* (Washington, D.C.: National Urban League, 1977); Reynolds Farley and Walter R. Allen, *The Color Line and the Quality of Life in America* (New York: Russell Sage Foundation, 1987), p. 168; Robert Hill, memorandum to author, November 7, 1991.

4. Children's Defense Fund, *A Children's Defense Budget: An Analysis of the President's FY 1987 Budget and Children* (Washington, D.C., Children's Defense Fund, 1986).

5. Andrew Billingsley, *Black Families in White America* (Englewood Cliffs, NJ: Prentice Hall, 1968).

6. J. A. Williams and R. Stockton, "Black Family Structures and Functions: An Empirical Examination of Some Suggestions Made by Billingsley," *Journal of Marriage and the Family* 35 (February 1973): 39–49; Ludwig L. Geismar, *555 Families: A Social-Psychological Study of Young Families in Transition* (New Brunswick, NJ: Transaction Books, 1973); Carol Stack, *All Our Kin: Strategies for Survival in a Black Community* (New York: Harper and Row, 1974); Dimitri Shimkin, E. M. Shimkin, and D. A. Frate, eds, *The Extended Family in Black Societies* (The Hague: Mouton Publishers, 1978); Isabel S. Payton, "Single-Parent Households: An Alternative Approach," *Family Economics Review* (Winter 1982): 11–16; Robert K. Merton, *Social Theory and Social Structure* (Glencoe, IL: The Free Press, 1957); Robert Hill, et al., *Research on the African-American Family: A Holistic Perspective* (Boston: University of Massachusetts, 1989); Robert B. Reich, *The*

Work of Nations: Preparing Ourselves for 21st Century Capitalism (New York: Knopf, 1991).

7. William Dressler, Susan Haworth-Hoeppner, and Barbara J. Pitts, "Household Structure in a Southern Black Community," *American Anthropologist* 87 (1985): 853–62.

8. William E. Cross, "The Ecology of Human Development of Black and White Children: Implications for Predicting Racial Preference Pattern," in M. Cochran and C. Hendersen, eds., *The Ecology of Urban Family Life* (Ithaca: Cornell University, 1982).

9. U.S. Bureau of the Census, Current Population Reports, Series P–20, No. 411, *Household and Family Characteristics: March 1985 and March 1990* (Washington, D.C.: U.S. Government Printing Office, 1985 and 1990).

10. These trends are taken primarily from U.S. Census data. See especially U.S. Bureau of the Census, Current Population Reports, *Household and Family Characteristics: March 1983, 1986, 1988, and 1990.*

11. Kathryn A. London, "Cohabitation, Marriage, Marital Dissolution, and Remarriage: United States 1988," Advance Data, Vital and Health Statistics, National Center for Health Statistics, 194 (1991).

12. Daniel Patrick Moynihan, *Family and Nation* (San Diego: Harcourt Brace Jovanovich, 1986); Marian Wright Edelman, *Families in Peril: An Agenda for Social Change* (Cambridge, MA: Harvard University Press, 1987).

13. William Julius Wilson, *The Truly Disadvantaged* (Chicago: University of Chicago Press, 1989).

14. U.S. Bureau of the Census, Current Population Reports, *Household and Family Characteristics: March 1983 and 1986.*

15. U.S. Bureau of the Census, Current Population Reports, *Household Economic Status: 1984 and 1988.*

16. Carnegie Council on Adolescence, *Turning Points* (New York: Carnegie Corporation of New York, 1989).

17. W.E.B. Du Bois, "The Study of the Negro Problem," *Annals* 1 (January 1898), 1–23.

CHAPTER 2

1. Marian Wright Edelman, "Black Children in America," in Janet Dewart, ed., *The State of Black America* (New York: National Urban League, 1989), 63.

2. Children's Defense Fund, *A Vision for America's Future: An Agenda for*

the 1990s: A Children's Defense Budget (Washington, D.C.: Children's Defense Fund, 1989), xviii.

3. Jewelle Taylor Gibbs, "Health and Mental Health of Young Black Males," in Jewelle Taylor Gibbs, ed., *Young, Black, and Male in America: An Endangered Species* (Dover, MA: Auburn House, 1988), 219.

4. Haki R. Madhubuti, *The Black Male: Obsolete, Single, Dangerous? The Afrikan American Family in Transition* (Chicago: Third World Press, 1990).

5. Patricia Raybon, "A Case of 'Severe Bias,'" Letter to the Editor, *Newsweek*, 2 Oct. 1987.

6. James Blackwell, *The Black Community: Diversity and Unity* (New York: Dodd, Mead, 1985), 14.

7. John Hope Franklin and Eleanor Holmes Norton, eds., *Black Initiative and Governmental Responsibility: An Essay by the Committee on Policy for Racial Justice* (Washington, D.C.: Joint Center for Political and Economic Studies, 1989), 3–4.

8. Roger Wilkins, "Mandela: Our Cousin, a King: Black Hands Across the Ocean," *The New York Times*, 22 Feb. 1990, A–23.

9. Robert N. Bellah, et al., *Habits of the Heart: Individualism and Commitment in American Life* (New York: Harper and Row, 1985), 154.

10. Ibid.

11. Taken from secondary analysis of data from James Jackson, et al., "National Survey of Black Americans," University of Michigan, 1980.

12. Nathan Glazer, "Introduction," in E. Franklin Frazier, *The Negro Family in the United States* (Chicago: University of Chicago Press, 1966).

13. Daniel Patrick Moynihan, *The Negro Family: The Case for National Action* (Washington, D.C.: U.S. Government Printing Office, 1965), 5.

14. See especially Harriette Pipes McAdoo, "The State-of-the-Art of Black Family Research: A Review of Black Family Research" (Bethesda, MD: The Center for Minority Group Mental Health Programs of the National Institute of Mental Health, January 1981, unpublished); Reynolds Farley and Walter R. Allen, *The Color Line* (New York: Russell Sage Foundation, 1987); Robert Staples and Alfredo Mirande, "Racial and Cultural Variations Among American Families: A Review of the Literature on Minority Families," *Journal of Marriage and the Family* 42 (1980): 157–73; Robert B. Hill, et al., *Research on African-American Families: A Holistic Perspective* (Boston: William Monroe Trotter Institute, University of Massachusetts, 1989); Robert J. Taylor, et al., "Developments in Research on Black

Families: A Decade Review," *Journal of Marriage and Family* 52 (November 1990), 993–1014.

15. Aristotle, *The Politics*, rev. ed., trans. Trevor J. Saunders (New York: Penguin, 1981), 60.

CHAPTER 3

1. E. Franklin Frazier, *The Negro Family in the United States* (Chicago: University of Chicago Press, 1966).

2. Melville J. Herskovitz, *The Myth of the Negro Past* (Boston: Beacon Press, 1958).

3. Nathan Glazer and Daniel P. Moynihan, *Beyond the Melting Pot* (Cambridge: MIT Press, 1963).

4. Donald Johanson and Maitland Edey, *Lucy: The Beginnings of Humankind* (New York: Warner Books, 1981).

5. Kenneth F. Weaver, "Stones, Bones, and Early Man: The Search for Our Ancestors," *National Geographic* 168 (November 1985): 601; see also Richard Leaky and David L. Brill, "A Fossil Skeleton 1,600,000 Years Old: Homo Erectus Unearthed," *National Geographic* 168 (November 1985): 624–29.

6. John Tierney, et al., "The Search for Adam and Eve: Common Ancestor, A Woman Who Lived 200,000 Years Ago and Left Resilient Genes That Are Carried by All of Mankind," *Newsweek*, 11 Jan. 1988, 49.

7. Rebecca L. Cann, Mark Stoneking, and Allan C. Wilson, "Mitochondrial DNA and Human Evolution," *Nature* 325 (January 1987): 31–36; see also Rebecca L. Cann, "DNA and Human Origins," *Annual Reviews of Anthropology* 17 (1988): 127–43.

8. Tierney, "The Search for Adam and Eve," 49.

9. Ibid., 48.

10. Ibid., 47.

11. Quoted in John Anthony West, *Ancient Egypt: A Guide to the Sacred Places of Ancient Egypt* (London: Harrap Columbus Books, 1987), 2.

12. Ibid., 3.

13. Martin Bernal, *Black Athena: The Afroasiatic Roots of Classical Civilization*, vol. 1, *The Fabrication of Ancient Greece 1785–1985* (New Brunswick, NJ: Rutgers University Press, 1987), 8.

14. Ray Winfield Smith, "Computer Helps Scholars Re-create an Egyptian Temple," *National Geographic* 138 (November 1970): 648.

15. E. A. Wallis Budge, *The Dwellers on the Nile: The Life, History, Religion and Literature of the Ancient Egyptians* (New York: Dover, 1977).

16. Asa G. Hilliard III, Larry Williams, and Nia Damali, eds., *The Teachings of Ptah Hotep: The Oldest Book in the World* (Atlanta: Blackwood Press, 1987): 17–34.

17. Ibid.

18. Ibid.

19. John Hope Franklin, *From Slavery to Freedom* (New York: Knopf, 1956), 11.

20. Niara Sudarkasa, "Interpreting the African Heritage in Afro-American Family Organization," in Harriette P. McAdoo, ed., *Black Families* (Beverly Hills, CA: Sage Publications, 1981), 40.

21. Niara Sudarkasa, "African and Afro-American Family Structure: A Comparison," *The Black Scholar* (November/December 1980): 45.

22. Ibid.

CHAPTER 4

1. Lerone Bennett, Jr., *Before the Mayflower: A History of Black America*, rev. ed. (New York: Penguin, 1987), 240; see also John Hope Franklin and Alfred A. Moss, Jr., *From Slavery to Freedom: A History of Negro Americans*, 6th ed. (New York: Knopf, 1988).

2. Sidney Kaplan and Emma Nogrady Kaplan, *Black Presence in the Era of the American Revolution*, rev. ed. (Amherst: University of Massachusetts Press, 1988), 209–11.

3. Ibid., 217.

4. Ibid., 216.

5. E. Franklin Frazier, *The Negro Family in the United States* (1939; revised, Chicago: University of Chicago Press, 1966).

6. E. Franklin Frazier, *The Negro Family in Chicago* (Chicago: University of Chicago Press, 1932); E. Franklin Frazier, *The Free Negro Family* (Nashville: Fisk University Press, 1932); E. Franklin Frazier, "The Negro Slave Family," *Journal of Negro History* 15 (April 1930): 198–259.

7. Frazier, "The Negro Slave Family," 1.

8. Andrew Billingsley and Marilyn C. Greene, "Family Life Among the Free Black Population in the 18th Century," *Journal of Social and Behavioral Sciences* (Winter 1973–74): 172–80.

9. George Rawick, *From Sundown to Sunup: The Making of the Black Community* (Westport: Greenwood Publishing, 1970), 93.

10. Ibid. This work is an extensive collection of slave narratives compiled by Rawick. A small sample has been selected in order to highlight the extensive references to family relationships and regional

differences. We express our appreciation to Terry Stephens, Linda L. Bracken, Maryanne C. Dearborn, Susan M. Dulaney, and Alice Turner of the University of Maryland for assistance with the reading, coding, analysis, and preparation of the materials included here.

11. Franklin and Moss, *From Slavery to Freedom*, 110–12.

12. Deborah Gray White, *Ar'n't I A Woman? Female Slaves in the Plantation South* (New York: Norton, 1985). Filomina C. Steady, ed., *The Black Woman Cross-Culturally* (New York: Schenkman Publishing, 1981), 29–30.

13. White, *Ar'n't I A Woman?*, 109.

14. Ibid., 160.

15. Herbert G. Gutman, Personal communication, Morgan State University, Fall 1978.

16. Harriet Jacobs, "The Perils of a Slave Woman's Life," in Mary H. Washington, ed., *Invented Lives* (Garden City, NY: Doubleday, 1987), 16–67.

17. Eugene P. Feldman, *Black Power in Old Alabama: The Life and Stirring Times of James Rapier, Black Congressman from Alabama: 1839–1883* (Chicago: Museum of African American History, 1968).

18. Fawn M. Brodie, *Thomas Jefferson: An Intimate History* (New York: Norton, 1974).

19. Ira V. Brown, *The Negro in Pennsylvania History, Pennsylvania History Studies*, No. 11 (University Park: Pennsylvania Historical Association, 1970), 35.

20. Dorothy Sterling, *Captain of the Planter* (Garden City, NY: Doubleday, 1958); Robert Smalls log in *Boston Advertiser*, 18 June 1962.

21. Sterling, *Captain of the Planter*.

22. Franklin and Moss, *From Slavery to Freedom*.

23. Ibid., 162.

24. Ibid., 168.

25. Sarah Bradford, *Harriet Tubman: The Moses of Her People* (Secaucus, NJ: Citadel Press, 1961), vii.

CHAPTER 5

1. John Hope Franklin and Alfred A. Moss, Jr., *From Slavery to Freedom: A History of Negro Americans* (New York: Knopf, 1988), 201.

2. Ibid., 209.

3. Arnold H. Taylor, *Travail and Triumph: Black Life and Culture in the South Since the Civil War* (Westport: Greenwood Press, 1976), 5.

4. Ibid., 5.

5. Lerone Bennett, Jr., *Before the Mayflower: A History of Black America*, 5th ed. (New York: Penguin, 1987), 222.

6. Edmund L. Drago, "The Black Household in Dougherty County, Georgia, 1870–1900," *Journal of Southwest Georgia History* (Fall 1983), 47.

7. Nell Painter, *The Exodusters: Black Migration to Kansas After Reconstruction* (New York: Knopf, 1977).

8. U.S. Bureau of the Census, Current Population Reports, Series P–23, No. 80, *The Social and Economic Status of the Black Population in the U.S.: An Historical View, 1790–1978* (Washington, D.C.: U.S. Government Printing Office, 1980).

9. Edmund L. Drago, "The Black Household in Dougherty County, Georgia," 41–42.

10. Herbert G. Gutman, *The Black Family in Slavery and Freedom, 1750–1925* (New York: Vintage, 1976), 11.

11. Robert Francis Engs, *Freedom's First Generation: Black Hampton, Virginia 1861–1890* (Philadelphia: University of Pennsylvania Press, 1979), xviii-xix.

12. Ibid., xix.

13. Ibid., 201.

14. Ibid., 190.

15. Ibid., 190.

16. Ibid., 167.

17. Kenneth L. Kusmer, *A Ghetto Takes Shape: Black Cleveland, 1870–1930* (Urbana: University of Illinois Press, 1976).

18. Ibid., 190.

19. W.E.B. Du Bois, *The Philadelphia Negro: A Social Study* (1899; reprint, New York: Schocken, 1967).

20. Kusmer, *A Ghetto Takes Shape*, 174.

21. Ibid., 224.

22. Ibid.

23. Paul J. Lammermeier, "The Urban Black Family of the Nineteenth Century: A Study of Black Family Structure in the Ohio Valley 1850–1880," *Journal of Marriage and the Family* 35 (1973): 452.

24. James Weldon Johnson, "Lift Every Voice and Sing," in Langston Hughes and Arna Bontemps, eds., *The Poetry of the Negro, 1746–1949* (Garden City, NY: Doubleday, 1949), 32.

CHAPTER 6

1. Nicholas Lehman, "Origin of the Black Underclass," *Atlantic Monthly*, July 1986.

2. Alvin Toffler, *The Third Wave* (New York: William Morrow, 1980).

3. Daniel Bell, *The Coming of Post Industrial Society: A Venture in Social Forecasting* (New York: Basic Books, 1973), xiii.

4. Amitai Etzioni, *An Immodest Agenda: Rebuilding America Before the 21st Century* (New York: McGraw-Hill, 1984), 109.

5. Reynolds Farley and Walter R. Allen, *The Color Line and the Quality of Life in America* (New York: Russell Sage Foundation, 1987), 2.

6. Ibid., 3.

7. Daniel Patrick Moynihan, *Family and Nation* (New York: Harcourt Brace Jovanovich, 1986), 146.

8. Ibid., 146.

9. Ibid., 47.

10. See special issue on technology, *Home Economics Forum*, vol. 1, no. 2 (Spring 1987).

11. Tom E. Larson, "Employment and Unemployment of Young Black Males," in Jewelle Taylor Gibbs, ed., *Young, Black, and Male in America: An Endangered Species* (Dover, MA: Auburn House, 1988), 97–128.

12. Barry Bluestone, *Deindustrialization of America* (New York: Basic Books, 1982), 6–7.

13. Ibid., 54–55.

14. Ibid., 64–65.

15. Margaret Heckler, *Report of the Secretary's Task Force on Black and Minority Health, Executive Summary*, vol. 1 (Washington, D.C.: U.S. Department of Health and Human Services, 1985).

16. Margaret C. Simms, "Falling Behind Despite Employment Gains: While Blacks Gained Jobs in 1988 They Made Little Advancement Compared to White Workers," *Focus* 17 (April 1989): 5–6.

17. Ibid., 5.

18. Ibid., 5.

19. Ibid., 6.

20. Bart Landry, *The New Black Middle Class* (Berkeley: University of California Press, 1987), 74–75.

21. The Editors, "The Top 100 Black Businesses: Defining a New Generation," *Black Enterprise*, June 1988, 103–234; Bernard Anderson, "Black Enterprise Board of Economics Report," *Black Enterprise*, June 1988, 258.

22. J. D. Leckenby, "Incidental Social Learning and Viewing Race: 'All in the Family' and 'Sanford and Son,'" *Journal of Broadcasting* 20 (Fall 1976): 481–94.

23. James Comer, "The Importance of Television Images of Black Families," in Anthony W. Jackson, ed., *Black Families and the Medium of Television* (Ann Arbor: Bush Program Child Development and Sociology, University of Michigan, 1988), 19.

24. Gordon Berry, "Research Perspectives on the Portrayals of Afro-American Families on Television," in Anthony W. Jackson, ed., *Black Families and the Medium of Television* (Ann Arbor: Bush Program Child Development and Sociology, University of Michigan, 1988), 47.

25. Vincent Harding, *Hope and History: Why We Must Share the Story of the Movement* (Mary Knoll, N.Y.: Orbis Books, 1990), 160.

CHAPTER 7

1. U.S. Bureau of the Census, *Statistical Abstract of the United States: 1990*, 110th ed. (Washington, D.C.: U.S. Government Printing Office, 1990), 100.

2. James E. Blackwell, "Graduate and Professional Education for Blacks," in Charles V. Willie, Antoine Garibaldi, and Wornie L. Reed, eds., *The Education of African-Americans* (Boston: William Monroe Trotter Institute, University of Massachusetts, 1989), 104.

3. U.S. Bureau of the Census, *Statistical Abstract of the U.S.: 1990*, 72.

4. LaSalle D. Leffal, Jr., "Health Status of Black Americans," in Janet Dewart, ed., *The State of Black America 1990* (New York: National Urban League, 1990), 127.

5. Ibid., p. 136.

6. These findings are taken from a secondary analysis of data from the National Survey of Black Americans, conducted by University of Michigan Institute for Social Research, James Jackson, director. We are thankful to Dr. Jackson for providing us access to this data set and for generous assistance in its utilization. Robert Hill and Deborah Robinson assisted with the analysis.

7. Margaret Heckler, *Report of the Secretary's Task Force on Black and Minority Health* (Washington, D.C.: U.S. Department of Health and Human Services, 1985).

8. Robert B. Hill, et al., *Research on African-American Families: A Holistic Perspective* (Boston: William Monroe Trotter Institute, University of Massachusetts, 1989), 17.

9. Ibid.

10. Robert B. Hill, *Informal Adoption Among Blacks* (Washington, D.C.: National Urban League, 1977).

11. Robert L. Hampton, ed., *Violence in the Black Family: Correlates and Consequences* (Lexington: Lexington Books, 1987).

12. Ibid.

13. Secretary's Task Force on Black and Minority Health, U.S. Department of Health and Human Services, 1985.

14. Carl C. Bell with Esther J. Jenkins, "Preventing Black Homicide," in Janet Dewart, ed., *The State of Black America 1990*.

15. Ibid.

16. Ibid.

17. Donald Huff and Jenice Armstrong, "McKinley Star's Death Hurts So Bad," *The Washington Post*, 17 Jan. 1990, B–4.

18. Keith Harriston, "Channeling Grief into Activism," *The Washington Post*, 10 Feb. 1990, 1.

19. Leffal, "Health Status of Black Americans," 127.

20. Benny J. Primm, "Drug Use: Special Implications for Black America," in Janet Dewart, ed., *The State of Black America 1987* (New York: National Urban League, 1987), 145–58.

21. Bell and Jenkins, "Preventing Black Homicide," 148.

22. Ura Jean Oyemade and Delores Brandon-Monye, eds., *Ecology of Alcohol and Other Drug Use: Helping Black High-Risk Youth* (Rockville, MD: U.S. Department of Health and Human Services, 1990), 34, 210.

CHAPTER 8

1. Reginald Wilson, "The State of Black Higher Education: Crisis and Promise," in Janet Dewart, ed., *State of Black America 1989* (New York: National Urban League, 1989), 121–36.

2. Josie Johnson, "An Historical Review of the Role Black Parents and the Black Community Played in Providing Schooling for Black Children in the South, 1865–1954," Ph.D. diss., University of Massachusetts, Boston, 1986.

3. Sarah Lawrence Lightfoot, et al., *Visions of a Better Way: A Black Appraisal of Public Schooling* (Washington, D.C.: Joint Center for Political Studies, 1989), ix.

4. Sarah Lawrence Lightfoot, *Worlds Apart: Relationships Between Families and Schools* (New York: Basic Books, 1978).

5. Ronald Edmonds, "Effective Schools for the Urban Poor," *Educational Leadership* (October 1979): 23.

6. Antoine M. Garibaldi, "Blacks in College," in Charles V. Willie, et al., eds., *The Education of African Americans*, vol. 3 (Boston: William Monroe Trotter Institute, University of Massachusetts, 1990), 93.

7. Ibid.

8. Jonathan Kozol, *Savage Inequalities: Children in America's Schools* (New York: Crown Publishers, 1991).

9. James Comer and Norris M. Haynes, "Meeting the Needs of Black Children in Public Schools: A School Reform Challenge," in Willie, et al., eds., *The Education of African Americans*, III, 63.

CHAPTER 9

1. Charles C. Moskos, "Success Story: Blacks in the Army," *Atlantic Monthly*, May 1986, 64–72; see also Moskos, "Blacks in the Armed Services: Issues for Society" (Paper prepared for symposium on Blacks in the Military, Joint Center for Political Studies, June 3–5, 1982).

2. James E. Blackwell, *The Black Community: Diversity and Unity*, 2nd ed. (New York: Harper & Row, 1985); see also Edwin Dorn, ed., *Who Fights for America: Race, Sex and Class in the Armed Forces* (Washington, D.C.: Joint Center for Political Studies, 1987) and Edwin Dorn, "Truman and the Military," *Focus* 16 (May 1988): 3–4.

3. Benjamin Quarles, *The Negro in the Making of America*, rev. ed. (New York: Macmillan, 1961), 228.

4. Daniel P. Moynihan, *The Negro Family: The Case for National Action* (Washington, D.C.: U.S. Government Printing Office, 1965), 42–43.

5. Moskos, "Success Story," 64.

6. Ibid., 66.

7. Ibid., 67.

8. Ibid., 67.

9. John Sibley Butler, "Inequality in the Military: An Examination of Promotion Time for Black and White Enlisted Men," *American Sociological Review* 41 (October 1976): 807–18.

10. John Sibley Butler, Personal communication, October 1989.

11. Felix (Pete) Peterson, "Vietnam Battle Deaths: Is There a Race or Class Issue?" *Focus* 15 (July 1987): 3.

12. Harley L. Browning, et al., "Income and Veteran Status: Variations among Mexican Americans, Blacks and Anglos," *American Sociological Review* 38 (February 1973): 74–84.

13. Wallace Terry, *Bloods: An Oral History of the Vietnam War by Veterans* (New York: Random House, 1984).

14. Butler, "Inequality in the Military," 817.

15. Ibid.

16. Colonel D. R. Butler, "Equal Opportunity Policy Practice," *Focus* 10 (August 1982): 4.

17. Moynihan, *The Negro Family*, 42.

18. Edwin Dorn, *Who Fights for America*, 12.

19. Ibid., 12.

20. Blackwell, *The Black Community*, 299.

CHAPTER 10

1. Robert J. Taylor, et al., "Developments in Research on Black Families: A Decade Review," *Journal of Marriage and Family* 52 (November 1990), 993–1014. Other scholars who co-authored this study with Dr. Taylor are Linda M. Chatters, M. Belinda Tucker, and Edith Lewis.

2. Robert B. Hill, et al., *Research on African-American Families: A Holistic Perspective* (Boston: William Monroe Trotter Institute, University of Massachusetts, 1989). Other scholars who co-authored this study with Dr. Hill are Andrew Billingsley, Eleanor Ingram, Michelene R. Malson, Roger H. Rubin, Carole B. Stack, James B. Stewart, and James E. Teele.

3. U.S. Bureau of the Census, Current Population Reports: *The Black Population in the United States, March 1990 and 1989* (Washington, D.C.: U.S. Government Printing Office, 1991).

4. Amitai Etzioni, *An Immodest Agenda: Rebuilding America Before the 21st Century* (New York: McGraw-Hill, 1984).

5. The National Survey of Black Americans was conducted by Dr. James Jackson at the University of Michigan Institute for Social Research. We are indebted to Dr. Jackson for making this data available to us, and to Dr. Robert Hill and Dr. Deborah Robinson for assistance with the analysis.

6. Anderson James Franklin, Foreword to James Jackson, ed., *Life in Black America* (Newbury Park, CA: Sage Publications, 1991), vii.

7. Robert J. Taylor, et al., "Developments in Research on Black Families: A Decade Review," *Journal of Marriage and Family* 52 (November 1990), 993–1014.

8. W.E.B. Du Bois, *The Souls of Black Folk*, reprinted in *Three Negro Classics* (New York: Avon Books, 1965), 215.

9. Clifford L. Broman, "Satisfaction Among Blacks: Significance of Marriage and Parenthood," *Journal of Marriage and the Family* 50 (February 1988): 45–51; Clifford L. Broman, "Household Work

and Family Life Satisfaction of Blacks," *Journal of Marriage and the Family* 50 (1988): 743–48; Christopher G. Ellison, "Family Ties, Friendships, and Subjective Well-being Among Black Americans," *Journal of Marriage and the Family* 52 (May 1990): 298–310.

10. James Jackson, ed., *Life in Black America* (Newbury Park, CA: Sage Publications, 1991).

CHAPTER 11

1. Robert K. Merton, "Intermarriage and the Social Structure: Fact and Theory," *Psychiatry* 4 (1941): 361–74; see also Kingsly Davis, "Intermarriage in Caste Societies," *American Anthropologist* 43 (1941): 376–95; Robert Staples, "Negro-White Sex: Fact and Fiction," in Robert Staples, ed., *The Black Family: Essays and Studies* (Belmont, CA: Wadsworth Publishing, 1971), 288–91.

2. U.S. Bureau of the Census, *Statistical Abstract of the U.S. 1987*, 107th ed. (Washington, D.C.: U.S. Government Printing Office, 1987), 39; Andrew D. Wineberger, "Interracial Marriage: Its Statutory Prohibition, Genetic Import, and Incidence," *Journal of Sex Research* 2 (1966): 157–68.

3. David M. Heer, "Prevalence of Black-White Marriage in the United States," *Journal of Marriage and the Family* 36 (May 1974): 246–57.

4. Thomas P. Monahan, "An Overview of Statistics on Interracial Marriage in the U.S.," *Journal of Marriage and the Family* 38 (1976): 223–31.

5. M. Belinda Tucker and Claudia Mitchell-Kernan, "New Trends in Black American Interracial Marriage: The Social Structural Context," *Journal of Marriage and the Family* 52 (February 1990): 207–18.

6. Doris Y. Wilkinson, *Black Male/White Female* (New York: Schenkman, 1980).

7. Delores P. Aldridge, "Interracial Marriage: Empirical and Theoretical Considerations," in Delores P. Aldridge, ed., *Black Male-Female Relationships* (Dubuque: Kendall/Hunt Publishing, 1989), 125–34.

8. Ernest Porterfield, "Black-American Intermarriage in the United States," *Marriage and the Family Review* 5 (1982): 17–34.

9. Ibid.

10. David M. Heer, "Prevalence of Black-White Marriage," 249.

11. Tucker and Mitchell-Kernan, "New Trends in Black American Interracial Marriage," 215.

12. Ardyth Stimson and John Stimson, "Interracial Dating: Willingness to Violate a Changing Norm," *Journal of Social and Behavioral Sciences* 25 (Spring 1979): 36–44.

13. Merton, "Intermarriage and the Social Structure"; Davis, "Intermarriage in Caste Societies"; and Staples, "Negro-White Sex."

14. Tucker and Mitchell-Kernan, "New Trends in Black American Interracial Marriage," 214.

15. E. Franklin Frazier, "Race Contacts and the Social Structures," Presidential address read before the annual meeting of the American Sociological Society, Chicago, December 27–30, 1948, reprinted in G. Franklin Edwards, *E. Franklin Frazier on Race Relations* (Chicago: University of Chicago Press, 1968), 43–64.

16. Ibid., 49.

17. Albert I. Gordon, *Intermarriage: Interfaith, Interracial, Interethnic* (Boston: Beacon Press, 1964), 348.

18. Sophia F. McDowell, "Black-White Intermarriage in the United States," *International Journal of Sociology of the Family* 1 (1971): 57.

19. Robert O. Blood, Jr., *Love Match and Arranged Marriage: A Tokyo-Detroit Comparison* (New York: The Free Press, 1967), 303.

20. Thomas Monahan, "Intermarriage and Divorce in the State of Hawaii," *Eugenics Quarterly* 13 (March 1966): 46.

21. Thomas Monahan, "Interracial Marriage and Divorce in Kansas and the Question of Instability of Mixed Marriages," *Journal of Comparative Family Studies* (Spring 1971), 119.

22. Surinder K. Mehta, "The Stability of Black-White vs. Racially Homogamous Marriages in the United States, 1960–1970," *Journal of Social and Behavioral Science* 24 (1978): 133.

23. Edwin Darden, "My Black History Paradox," *The Washington Post*, 24 Feb. 1991, B–5.

24. Monrad G. Paulsen, et al., *Domestic Relations: Case Studies and Materials*, 2nd ed. (Mineola, NY: Foundation Press, 1974).

25. W.E.B. Du Bois, "The Marrying of Black Folk," *The Independent* 69 (13 Oct. 1910): 812–13.

CHAPTER 12

1. Thomas Sowell, *Ethnic America* (New York: Basic Books, 1981): 194.

2. Charles Green and Basil Wilson, *The Struggle for Black Empowerment in New York City* (New York: Praeger, 1989) 117.

3. Robert B. Hill, *The Black Pulse Survey* (New York: National Urban League, 1980).

4. Green and Wilson, *The Struggle for Black Empowerment in New York City* (New York: Praeger, 1989) 117.

5. Ibid.

6. Ibid.

7. Archie W. Singham, "Coalition Building: Race, Culture, Play Critical Roles," *City Sun*, 17–23 April 1985, 19.

8. James E. Blackwell, *The Black Community: Diversity and Unity* (New York: Harper and Row, 1975).

9. Thomas Sowell, *Ethnic America*.

10. Ira De Augustine Reid, *The Negro Immigrant: His Background, Characteristics and Social Adjustment, 1899–1937* (New York: Columbia University Press, 1939); see also Ron Bryce-Laporte, "New York and the New Caribbean Immigrants," *International Migration Review* 12 (1979): 212–19.

11. Sowell, *Ethnic America*.

12. Nathan Glazer and Daniel Patrick Moynihan, *Beyond the Melting Pot* (Cambridge: MIT Press, 1970).

13. Ibid.

14. Harold Cruse, *Plural but Equal: A Critical Study of Blacks and Plural Society* (New York: William Morrow, 1987).

15. Green and Wilson, *The Struggle for Black Empowerment*, 132.

16. Hill, *The Black Pulse Survey*.

17. Marta Tienda and Lief Jensen, "Poverty and Minorities: A Quarter Century Profile of Color and Socioeconomic Disadvantage" (Paper delivered at the conference on "Poverty and Social Policy: The Minority Experience," Arlie, Virginia, November 5–7 1986).

CHAPTER 13

1. Harriette McAdoo, "The Impact of Extended Family Structure on Upward Mobility of Blacks," *Journal of African-American Issues*, vol. 3, no. 4 (1975): 295.

2. Nick Ravo, "New Star for G.O.P. Is Conservative and Black," *The New York Times*, 25 Nov. 1990, 1.

3. "Desperate to Save a Generation: D.C. Judge Picked for U.S. Drug Post Gives Stiff Terms and Talks," *The Washington Post*, 6 May 1989, B–1.

4. Lloyd Gite, "Living Hell," *Black Enterprise* (May 1986): 44–50.

5. William E. Schmidt, "Hard Work Can't Stop Hard Times," *The New York Times*, 25 Nov. 1990, 1.

6. Isabel Wilkerson, "Middle Class Blacks Try to Grip a Ladder While Lending a Hand," *The New York Times*, 25 Nov. 1990, 1.

7. Harriette McAdoo, "Transgenerational Patterns of Upward Mobility in African-American Families, in Harriette McAdoo, *Black Fam-*

ilies, 2nd ed. (Beverly Hills, CA: Sage Publications, 1986), 148–67.

CHAPTER 14

1. David Swinton, "The Economic Status of Black Americans," in Janet Dewart, ed., *The State of Black America 1989* (New York: National Urban League, 1989), 26–27.

2. David Swinton, "The Economic Status of Black Americans during the 1980s: A Decade of Limited Progress," in Janet Dewart, ed., *The State of Black America 1990* (New York: National Urban League, 1990), 40.

3. John Sibley Butler, *Entrepreneurship and Self-Help Among Black Americans: A Reconsideration of Race and Economics* (New York: State University of New York Press, 1991), 6.

4. Shelly Green and Paul Pryde, *Black Entrepreneurship in America* (New Brunswick, NJ: Transaction Publishers, 1989).

5. Thomas Sowell, *Ethnic America* (New York: Basic Books, 1981).

6. Butler, *Entrepreneurship and Self-Help*.

7. *Black Enterprise*, "19th Annual Report on Black Business, June 1991," 89–124.

8. Timothy Bates, "Black Political Empowerment and Economic Advancement," *Focus* 17 (May 1989): 5–6.

9. Emmett D. Carson, "Survey Dispels Myth That Blacks Receive but Do Not Give to Charity," *Focus* 15 (March 1987), 5.

10. Derek T. Dingle, "Doing Business John Johnson's Way," *Black Enterprise*, June 1987, 151–64; see also John H. Johnson with Lerone Bennett, Jr., *Succeeding Against the Odds* (New York: Warner Books, 1989).

11. Nathan McCall, "How Herman Russell Built His Business . . . Brick by Brick," *Black Enterprise*, June 1987, 176–84.

12. Ken Smikle, "Bruce: The Boss," *Black Enterprise*, September 1986, 36–42.

13. Bates, "Black Political Power and Economic Advancement."

14. Bart Landry, *The New Black Middle Class* (Berkeley: University of California Press, 1988), 228.

15. Carl T. Rowan, "Blacks and Class," *The Washington Post*, 1 March 1991, A–15.

CHAPTER 15

1. Most of the material for this family history was provided by Lorenzo Curry, the third son of James and Sally Curry, during interviews at

his home in Marion, Alabama, while he served as host to an institute on Lincoln School and to the author during the fall of 1988. He also shared certain family records. Additional information about this family has been provided by James Curry, the second son, mostly informally over the period 1985–90 as we worked together on various projects at Shiloh Baptist Church in Washington, D.C. We express to them our appreciation.

2. Horace Mann Bond, *Black American Scholars: A Study of Their Beginnings* (Detroit: Balcamp Publishing, 1972).

3. Coretta Scott King, *My Life with Martin Luther King, Jr.* (New York: Holt, Rinehart and Winston, 1969), 36.

4. William J. Edwards, *Twenty-five Years in the Black Belt* (1918; reprint, Westport: Negro University Press, 1970), 20.

5. Henry A. Bullock, *A History of Negro Education in the South: From 1619 to the Present* (Cambridge: Harvard University Press, 1967).

6. George V. Coelho, et al., eds, *Coping and Adaptation* (New York: Basic Books, 1974).

7. Josie R. Johnson, "An Historical Review of the Role Black Parents and the Black Community Played in Providing Schooling for Black Children in the South, 1865–1954" (Ph.D. diss., University of Massachusetts, Amherst, 1986) 46; Sarah Lawrence Lightfoot, *Worlds Apart: Relationships Between Families and Schools* (New York: Basic Books, 1978); Reginald Clark, *Family Life and School Achievement: Why Poor Black Children Succeed or Fail* (Chicago: University of Chicago Press, 1983); James Comer: *School Power: Implications of an Intervention Project* (New York: The Free Press, 1980).

8. *Crisis*, vol. 11, April 1916 (New York: National Association for the Advancement of Colored People), 290.

9. Allen W. Jones, "The Black Press in the 'New South': Jesse C. Duke's Struggle for Justice and Equality," *Journal of Negro History* 64 (Summer 1979): 215–28; Esther Pauline Duke Hamilton, "Memoirs and Reflections" (as dictated to Amy Tate Billingsley, Spring 1968).

10. Hamilton, "Memoirs and Reflections," 1.

11. Ibid., 2.

12. Jones, "The Black Press in the 'New South,' " 217.

13. Hamilton, "Memoirs and Reflections," 7.

14. Jones, "The Black Press in the 'New South,' " 217.

15. Ibid., 218.

16. Ibid., 220.

17. Jesse C. Duke, editorial, *Montgomery Herald*, 13 August 1887.

18. Jones, "The Black Press in the 'New South,' " 222.

19. Hamilton, "Memoirs and Reflections," 13.

20. Jones, "The Black Press in the 'New South,'" 225.

21. Hamilton, "Memoirs and Reflections," 35.

22. Ibid., 38.

23. Johnson, "An Historical Review of the Role Black Parents," 65.

24. Ibid.

25. Faustine Childress Jones, *A Traditional Model of Educational Excellence: Dunbar High School of Little Rock, Arkansas* (Washington, D.C.: Howard University Press, 1981), 2.

26. Billingsley, *Black Families in White America*.

27. Robert B. Hill, *The Strengths of Black Families* (New York: Emerson Hall, 1971).

28. Carol B. Stack, *All Our Kin: Strategies for Survival in a Black Community* (New York: Harper & Row, 1974); Joyce Aschenbrenner, "Extended Families Among Black Americans," *Journal of Comparative Family Studies* 4 (1973): 257–68.

29. D. Royce and G. Turner, "Strengths of Black Families: A Black Community Perspective," *Social Work* 25 (1980): 407–9.

30. V. Christopherson, "Implications for Strengthening Family Life: Rural Black Families," in N. Stinnett, et al., eds., *Building Family Strengths: Blueprints for Action* (Lincoln, Neb.: Lincoln University Press, 1979).

31. Lawrence E. Gary, et al., *Stable Black Families: Final Report* (Washington, D.C.: Institute for Urban Affairs and Research, 1983).

32. John Hope Franklin and Eleanor Holmes Norton, eds., *Black Initiative and Governmental Responsibility: An Essay by the Committee on Policy for Racial Justice* (Washington, D.C.: Joint Center for Political and Economic Studies, 1987).

33. Marian Wright Edelman, *Families in Peril: An Agenda for Social Change* (Cambridge, MA: Harvard University Press, 1987); Daniel Patrick Moynihan, *Family and Nation* (New York: Harcourt Brace Jovanovich, 1986).

CHAPTER 16

1. Herschel Johnson, "We're in the Money," *Black Enterprise*, August 1984, 40–46.

2. Jube Shriver, "Child's Play," *Black Enterprise*, August 1986, 30–34.

3. Jean Thompson, "Patricia Schmoke, Laughing in the Whirlwind," *Baltimore Morning Sun*, 27 Nov. 1987, B1–B3.

4. Mary Jordan, "A Steady Job but No Home," *The Washington Post*, 29 Aug. 1988, D–1, D–5.

5. Fawn Vzaro and Terry E. Johnson, "Three Single Mothers Tell Their Stories," *Philadelphia Inquirer*, 10 June 1984, 16.

6. Ibid.

7. Ibid.

CHAPTER 17

1. David Briggs, "Baptists Exhorted to Pay for Dream," *The Washington Post*, 8 Sept. 1991, D–9.

2. G. Willis Bennett, *Effective Urban Ministry: Based on a Case Study of Allen Temple Baptist Church* (Nashville: Broadman Press, 1983).

3. J. Alfred Smith, Sr., and J. Alfred Smith, Jr., *Annual Report, 1987* (Oakland, CA: Allen Temple Baptist Church, 1987).

4. Cecil L. Murray, *Annual Report and Forecast, 1992* (Los Angeles: First AME Church, 1992).

5. Iris Schneider, "Refuge and Strength: Black Church Life in Southern California," *Los Angeles Times*, 9 Feb. 1992, E–1.

6. Frank Madison Reid III, *1985–86 Annual Report* (Los Angeles: Ward AME Church, 1987).

7. Cecil Williams, *Facts on Crack* (San Francisco: Glide Memorial Church, 1987).

8. Ida R. Mukenge, *The Black Church in Urban America: A Case Study in Political Economy* (Lanham, MD: University Press of America, 1983).

9. Benjamin Mays and Joseph Nicholson, *The Negro's Church* (New York: Arno Press and *The New York Times*, 1969), 278.

10. C. Eric Lincoln, "The Black Church and Black Self-Determination" (Paper read before the Association of Black Foundation Executives, 15 April 1986, Kansas City, Missouri).

11. Andrew Billingsley, Robert Hill, and Deborah Robinson, "Secondary Analysis of Data from the University of Michigan, Institute for Social Research National Survey of Black Americans," unpublished working paper, 1989.

12. Rev. Johnny Ray Youngblood, Senior Minister, St. Paul Community Baptist Church, Brooklyn, NY, personal interview, Fall 1988.

13. *The New York Times*, editorial, "Black Churches, Endangered Children," 23 May 1988.

14. This pilot study was funded by the Ford Foundation. We are grateful to the foundation and particularly to Lynn Walker for faith in this project and for generous support. We also especially thank Rob-

ert Hill, Robert Beasley, Terry Stephens, Victor Rouse, Jualynne Dodson, Ida R. Mukenge, Elaine Cannon, and Dianne Walls-Tabon for research support.

15. Frances Frank Marcus, "New Orleans Journal: Project on Piety Street Reclaims Crack House," *The New York Times*, 12 May 1989, 8.

16. Daniel Cerone, "The Arsenio Way," *Los Angeles Times*, 5 Jan. 1992, 4; see also Aldore Collier, "Arsenio Hall Dispels Nasty Rumors and Talks about His 'Crack' Cocaine House," *Jet*, 27 Jan. 1992, 58.

17. Murray, *Annual Report and Forecast, 1992*.

18. Veronica Jennings, "Black Churches Allying Against AIDS," *The Washington Post*, 3 July 1989, B–51.

19. Roy C. Nichols, "Components of a Vital Congregation," in *Report of the Consultation on Vital Congregations* (The Council of Bishops, United Methodist Church, 15 Nov. 1987), 109.

20. This ongoing nationwide study of a representative sample of black churches and their family-oriented community outreach programs is supported by the Ford Foundation, the Lilly Endowment, and the University of Maryland, College Park. A national research advisory committee of social scientists and religious leaders is headed by Dr. Lawrence Jones, former dean of the Howard University School of Divinity. The author is principal investigator of the study and Dr. Cleopatra Howard Caldwell is study director. We are indebted to Dr. Robert Hill, Dr. Victor Rouse, Terry Stephens, Valery Drake, Angela Dungee Greene, Andrea Anderson, Kelly Nippes, and Dianne Walls-Tabon for service on the senior research staff.

21. Mays and Nicholson, *The Negro's Church*; and C. Eric Lincoln and Lawrence Mamiya, *The Black Church in the African-American Experience* (Durham, Duke University Press, 1990).

22. Andrew Billingsley and Cleopatra Howard Caldwell, "The Church, the Family and the School in the African-American Community," *Journal of Negro Education* 60 (1991): 427–40.

23. Wallace Charles Smith, *The Church in the Life of the Black Family* (Valley Forge, PA: Judson Press, 1985), 14.

24. Ibid., 25–28.

Chapter 18

1. Courtland Malloy, "Single Father and His Nine Children Have a House Full of Love," *The Washington Post*, 27 Jan. 1991, B–3.

2. Peter Michelmore, "The Kids of Kent Amos," *Reader's Digest*, September 1990.

3. Kathleen McCormick, "By Any Means Necessary," *City Paper*, College Park, Maryland, 21 Dec. 1990, 17–23.

4. William Raspberry, "Miz Dot's Beautiful Expression," *The Washington Post*, 29 Sept. 1991, A–23.

5. Michael Ryan, "He Gives Kids a Chance to Win," *Parade*, September 9, 1990.

6. Holly Selby, "Unorthodox Educator," *Baltimore Sun*, 2 Dec. 1990, 1–6, G–8.

7. Kenneth Clark and John Hope Franklin, *A Policy Framework for Racial Justice* (Washington, D.C.: Joint Center for Political Studies, 1983), p. 5.

8. Charyn D. Sutton, "Black Family Reunion Celebration in Philadelphia," *Sisters*, National Council of Negro Women, Fall 1988, 13.

9. John Sibley Butler and Kenneth L. Wilson, *Entrepreneurial Enclaves in the African-American Experience* (Washington, D.C.: National Center for Neighborhood Enterprise, Neighborhood Policy Institute, 1988).

10. See especially Charles Murray, *Losing Ground: American Social Policy 1950–1980* (New York: Basic Books, 1986).

11. William J. Wilson, *The Declining Significance of Race* (Chicago: University of Chicago Press, 1978).

12. John Hope Franklin and Eleanor Holmes Norton, *Black Initiative and Governmental Responsibility: A Policy Framework for Racial Justice* (Washington, D.C.: Joint Center for Political Studies, 1987).

13. Ibid., ix.

14. Ibid., 4–15.

15. Marvin Cetron and Owen Davis, *American Renaissance: Our Life at the Turn of the 21st Century* (New York: St. Martin's, 1989).

16. David Swinton, "Economic Status of Blacks in 1986," in Janet Dewart, ed., *The State of Black America* (New York: National Urban League, 1987), 49–74.

17. Kevin Phillips, *The Politics of Rich and Poor* (New York: Random House, 1990), 220–21.

18. Swinton, "Economic Status of Blacks in 1986."

Selected Bibliography

BOOKS

Battle, Stanley F., ed. 1987. *The Black Adolescent Parent*. New York: Haworth Press.

Billingsley, Andrew. 1968. *Black Families in White America*. Englewood Cliffs, NJ: Prentice Hall.

Blackwell, James. 1985. *The Black Community: Diversity and Unity*. New York: Dodd, Mead.

Cherlin, Andrew J. 1981. *Marriage, Divorce, Remarriage*. Cambridge: Harvard University Press.

Comer, James P. 1988. *Maggie's American Dream: The Life and Times of a Black Family*. New York: New American Library.

Coner-Edwards, Alice, and Jeanne Spurlock, eds. 1988. *Black Families in Crisis: The Middle Class*. New York: Brunner/Mazel.

Diop, Cheikh Anta. 1978. *The Cultural Unity of Black Africa: The Domains of Patriarchy and of Matriarchy in Classical Antiquity*. Chicago: Third World Press.

Du Bois, W.E.B. 1967. *The Philadelphia Negro: A Social Study*. New York: Schocken.

———. 1969. *Souls of Black Folk*. New York: Penguin.

Edelman, Marian Wright. 1987. *Families in Peril: An Agenda for Social Change*. Cambridge: Harvard University Press.

Engram, Eleanor. 1982. *Science, Myth, Reality: The Black Family in One-Half Century of Research*. Westport, CT: Greenwood Press.

Etzioni, Amitai. *An Immodest Agenda: Rebuilding America Before the 21st Century*. New York: McGraw-Hill.

Farley, Reynolds, and Walter Allen. 1987. *The Color Line and the Quality of Life in America*. New York: Russell Sage Foundation.

Felder, Henry E. 1984. *The Changing Patterns of Black Family Income, 1960–1982*. Washington, D.C.: Joint Center for Political Studies, 1984.

Franklin, John Hope, and Eleanor Holmes Norton. 1987. *Black Initiative and Governmental Responsibility: A Policy Framework for Racial Justice.* Washington, D.C.: Joint Center for Political Studies.

Frazier, E. Franklin. 1932. *The Negro Family in Chicago.* Chicago: University of Chicago Press.

———. 1966. *The Negro Family in the United States.* Chicago: University of Chicago Press.

Gibson, William. 1980. *Family Life and Morality: Studies in Black and White.* Washington, D.C.: University Press of America.

Giddings, Paula. 1984. *When and Where I Enter: The Impact of Black Women on Race and Sex in America.* New York: Bantam.

Green, Charles, and Basil Wilson. 1989. *The Struggle for Black Empowerment in New York City: Beyond the Politics of Pigmentation.* New York: Praeger.

Gutman, Herbert G. 1976. *The Black Family in Slavery and Freedom, 1750–1925.* New York: Vintage.

Hampton, Robert L., ed. 1987. *Violence in the Black Family: Correlates and Consequences.* Lexington, MA: Lexington Books.

Harding, Vincent. 1990. *Hope and History: Why We Must Share the Story of the Movement.* Mary Knoll: Orbis Books.

Hare, Nathan. 1984. *The Endangered Black Family: Coping With the Unisexualization and Coming Extinction of the Black Race.* San Francisco: Black Think Tank.

Hendricks, Leo E. 1981. *An Analysis of Two Select Populations of Black Unmarried Adolescent Fathers: Final Report.* Washington, D.C.: Mental Health Research and Development Center.

Hill, Robert Bernard. 1977. *Informal Adoption Among Black Families.* Washington, D.C.: National Urban League, Research Department.

Hill, Robert, et al. 1989. *Research on the African-American Family: A Holistic Perspective.* Boston: University of Massachusetts Press.

Jewell, K. Sue. 1988. *Survival of the Black Family: The Institutional Impact of American Social Policy.* New York: Praeger.

Jones, Jacqueline. 1985. *Labor of Love, Labor of Sorrow: Black Women, Work, and the Family From Slavery to the Present.* New York: Basic Books.

Kerner, Otto. 1968. *Report of the National Advisory Commission on Civil Disorders.* Washington, D.C.: U.S. Government Printing Office.

Landry, Bart. 1988. *The New Black Middle Class.* Berkeley: University of California Press.

Lewis, Hylan. 1967. *Blackways of Kent.* Chapel Hill: University of North Carolina Press.

Lewis, Jerry M., and John G. Looney. 1983. *The Long Struggle: Well-*

Functioning Working-Class Black Families. New York: Brunner/Mazel.

Lightfoot, Sarah Lawrence. 1978. *Worlds Apart: Relationships Between Families and Schools*. New York: Basic Books.

Madhubuti, Haki R. 1990. *The Black Male: Obsolete, Single, Dangerous? The Afrikan American Family in Transition*. Chicago: Third World Press.

Martin, Joanne Mitchell, and Elmer P. Martin. *The Helping Tradition in the Black Family and Community*. Silver Springs, MD: National Association of Social Workers.

McAdoo, Harriette Pipes, ed. 1988. *Black Families*. 2nd ed. Newbury Park, CA: Sage Publications.

McGhee, James D. 1982. *A Dream Denied: The Black Family in the Eighties*. Washington, D.C.: National Urban League.

Moynihan, Daniel Patrick. 1986. *Family and Nation*. San Diego: Harcourt Brace Jovanovich.

———. 1965. *The Negro Family: The Case for National Action*. Washington, D.C.: U.S. Government Printing Office.

Rawick, George. 1970. *From Sundown to Sunup: The Making of the Black Community*. Westport: Greenwood Publishing.

Redford, Dorothy, and Michael D'Orso. 1988. *Somerset Homecoming: Recovering a Lost Heritage*. New York: Doubleday.

Roberts, James Deotis. 1980. *Roots of a Black Future: Family and Church*. Philadelphia: Westminster Press.

Stack, Carol. 1974. *All Our Kin: Strategies for Survival in a Black Community*. New York: Harper and Row.

Staples, Robert. 1986. *The Black Family: Essays and Studies*. Belmont, CA: Wadsworth Publishing Company.

Tatum, Beverly Daniel. 1987. *Assimilation Blues: Black Families in a White Community*. New York: Greenwood Press.

Washington, Joseph R. 1988. *Black-Race Family Binds and the White-Ethnic Kinship Ties: Reflections on Religion, Race, and Ethnicity in the Reagan Era*. Tampa: Department of Religious Studies, University of South Florida.

White, Deborah Gray. 1985. *Ar'n't I A Woman? Female Slaves in the Plantation South*. New York: Norton.

Williams, Richard. 1986. *They Stole It, but You Must Return It*. Rochester, NY: HEMA Publishers.

Willie, Charles Vert. 1981. *A New Look at Black Families*. 2nd ed. Bayside, NY: General Hall.

Wilson, William J. 1978. *The Declining Significance of Race*. Chicago: University of Chicago Press.

———. 1987. *The Truly Disadvantaged*. Chicago: University of Chicago Press.

Zollar, Ann Creighton. *A Member of the Family: Strategies for Black Family Continuity*. Chicago: Nelson-Hall.

JOURNAL ARTICLES

Allen, Walter R. February 1987. "The Search for Applicable Theories of Black Family Life." *Journal of Marriage and the Family* 40.

Anderson, Elijah. January 1989. "Sex Codes and Family Life Among Poor Inner-City Youths." *Annals of the American Academy of Political and Social Science* 501: 59–78.

Anderson, Kristine L., and Walter R. Allen. Summer 1984. "Correlates of Extended Household Structure." *Phylon* 45(2): 144–57.

Aoyagi, Kiyotaka. Autumn 1988. "The Realm of Personal Attachment in Kinship Behavior of Black Families in the U.S.A." *International Journal of Sociology of the Family* 18(2): 215–31.

Baptiste, David A. 1986. "The Image of the Black Family Portrayed by Television: A Critical Comment." *Marriage and Family Review* 10(1): 41–63.

Barnett, Bernice M. June 1985. "Self Perception of the Husband/Father in the Intact Lower Class Black Family." *Phylon* 46(2): 136–47.

Barnett, Bernice M., Ira E. Robinson, and Wilfred C. Bailey. 1984. "The Status of Husband/Father as Perceived by the Wife/Mother in the Intact Lower-Class Urban Black Family." *Sociological Spectrum* 4(4): 421–41.

Beckett, Joyce O., and Soraya M. Coley. 1987. "Ecological Intervention With the Elderly: A Case Example." *Journal of Gerontological Social Work* 11(1-2): 137–57.

Bray, Thomas, J. Winter 1988. "Reading America and the Riot Act: The Kerner Report and Its Culture of Violence." *Policy Review* 43: 32–36.

Bryant, Z. Lois, Marilyn Coleman, and Lawrence H. Ganing. Fall 1988. "Race and Family Structure Stereotyping: Perceptions of Black and White Nuclear Families and Step Families." *Journal of Black Psychology* 15(1): 1–16.

Bullard, Robert D. March 1984. "The Black Family: Housing Alternatives in the 80's." *Journal of Black Studies* 14(3): 341–51.

Burton, Linda M. Fall 1987. "Young Grandmothers: Are They Ready?" *Social Science* 72(2-4): 191–94.

Carlson, Shirley. Autumn 1988. "Family and Household in a Black Community in Southern Illinois." *International Journal of Sociology of the Family* 18(2): 203–13.

Collins, Patricia H. Fall 1986. "The Afro-American Work/Family Nexus: An Exploratory Analysis." *Western Journal of Black Studies* 10(3): 148–58.

———. July 1986. "Getting Off to a Good Start: The First Class in Black Family Studies." *Teaching Sociology* 14(3): 193–95.

Cox, Arthur J. June 1983. "Black Appalachian Families." *Journal of Sociology and Social Welfare* 10(2): 312–25.

Darity William, A., Jr., and Samuel L. Meyers, Jr. Fall 1981. "The Class Character of the Black Middle Class: Polarization Between the Black Managerial Elite and the Black Underclass." *Black Law Journal* 7: 21–31.

———. Summer-Fall 1984. "Public Policy and the Condition of Black Family Life." *Review of Black Political Economy* 13(1-2): 165–87.

———. November 1984. "Does Welfare Dependency Cause Female Headship? The Case of the Black Family." *Journal of Marriage and the Family* 46(4): 765–79.

———. Summer-Fall 1987. "Public Policy Trends and the Fate of the Black Family." *Humboldt Journal of Social Relations* 14(1-2): 134–64.

Downs, Susan Whitelaw. 1986. "Black Foster Parents and Agencies: Results of an Eight State Survey." *Children and Youth Services Review* 8(3): 201–18.

Dressler, William W. March 1985. "Extended Family Relationships, Social Support, and Mental Health in a Southern Black Community." *Journal of Health and Social Behavior* 26(1): 39–48.

Dressler, William, Susan Haworth Hoeppner, and Barbara J. Pitts. December 1985. "Household Structure in a Southern Black Community." *American Anthropologist* 87(4): 853–62.

Edwards, Cecile H. Spring 1982. "Low-Income Black Families: Strategies for Survival in the 1980's." *Journal of Negro Education* 51:85–89.

Edwards, Ozzie L. Spring 1982. "Family Formation Among Black Youth." *Journal of Negro Education* 51: 111–22.

Farley, Reynolds, et al. December 1978. " 'Chocolate City, Vanilla Suburbs': Will the Trend Toward Racially Separate Communities Continue?" *Social Science Research* 7(4): 319–44.

Fine, Mark, Andrew I. Schwebel, and Linda James-Myers. Spring 1987. "Family Stability in Black Families: Values Underlying Three Different Perspectives." *Journal of Comparative Family Studies* 18(1):1–23.

Foster, Herbert J. December 1983. "African Patterns in the Afro-American Family." *Journal of Black Studies* 14(2): 201–32.

Fratoe, Frank A. Spring 1988. "Social Capital of Black Business Owners." *Review of Black Political Economy* 16(4): 33–50.

Gaston, John C. June 1986. "The Destruction of the Young Black Male: The Impact of Popular Culture and Organized Sports." *Journal of Black Studies* 16(4): 369–84.

Gill, Robert Lewis. July-October 1982. "The Effects of the Burger Court Decisions Upon the Lives of Black Families." *Negro Educational Review* 32: 230–51.

Gimenez, Martha E. November 1987. "Black Family: Vanishing or Unattainable?" *Humanity and Society* 11(4): 420–39.

Hampton, Robert L. Spring 1979. "Husband's Characteristics and Marital Disruption in Black Families." *Sociological Quarterly* 20(2): 255–66.

Jewell, K. Sue. Winter 1984. "Use of Social Welfare Programs and the Disintegration of the Black Nuclear Family." *Western Journal of Black Studies* 8(4): 192–98.

Krech, Shepard, III. Winter 1982. "Black Family Organization in the 19th Century: An Ethnological Perspective." *Journal of Interdisciplinary History* 12(3): 429–52.

Lammermeier, Paul J. 1973. "The Urban Black Family of the Nineteenth Century: A Study of Black Family Structure in the Ohio Valley 1850–1880." *Journal of Marriage and the Family* 35.

Lantz, Herman R. March 1980. "Family and Kin as Revealed in the Narratives of Ex-Slaves." *Social Science Quarterly* 60(4): 667–75.

McAdoo, Harriette P. 1975. "The Impact of Extended Family Structure on Upward Mobility of Blacks." *Journal of African-American Issues* 3(4).

———. Fall-Winter 1985. "Strategies Used by Black Single Mothers Against Stress." *Review of Black Political Economy* 14(2-3): 153–66.

Peterson, Gary W., M.E. Stivers, and D.F. Peters. July 1986. "Family Versus Nonfamily Significant Others for the Career Decisions of Low Income Youth." *Family Relations* 35(3): 417–24.

Redd, Lawrence N. September 1988. "Telecommunication, Economics, and Black Families in America." *Journal of Black Studies* 19(1): 111–23.

Robinson, Jeanne B. July 1989. "Clinical Treatment of Black Families: Issues and Strategies." *Social Work* 34(4): 323–29.

Rutledge, Essie Manuel. December 1988. "African-American Socialization Experiences by Family Structure." *Journal of Black Studies* 19(2): 204–15.

St. Pierre, Maurice. Spring-Summer 1982. "Black Female Single Parent Family Life: A Preliminary Sociological Perspective." *The Black Sociologist* 9: 28–47.

Sampson, Robert J. September 1987. "Urban Black Violence: The Effect of Male Joblessness and Family Disruption." *American Journal of Sociology* 93(2): 348–82.

Shireman, Joan F., and Penny R. Johnson. May-June 1986. "A Longitudinal Study of Black Adoptions: Single Parent, Transracial, and Traditional." *Social Work* 31(3): 172–76.

Simms, Margaret C. Fall-Winter 1985. "Black Women Who Head Families: An Economic Struggle." *Review of Black Political Economy* 14(2-3): 141–51.

"Slipping Through the Cracks: The Status of Black Women—Single-Parent Families." Fall-Winter 1985. *Review of Black Political Economy* 14(2-3): 139–40.

Smith, Eleanor J., and P.M. Smith, Jr. September 1986. "The Black Female Single Parent Family Condition." *Journal of Black Studies* 17(1): 125–34.

Spitze, Glenna. November 1984. "Black Family Migration and Wives' Employment." *Journal of Marriage and the Family* 46(4): 781–90.

Staples, Robert. November 1985. "Changes in Black Family Structure: The Conflict Between Family Ideology and Structural Conditions." *Journal of Marriage and the Family* 47(4): 1005–13.

———. March 1987. "Social Structure and Black Family Life: An Analysis of Current Trends." *Journal of Black Studies* 17(3): 267–86.

———. Spring 1988. "Reflections on the Black Family Future: The Implications for Public Policy." *Western Journal of Black Studies* 12(1): 19–27.

Taylor, Robert J., et al. November 1990. "Development in Research on Black Families: A Decade Review." *Journal of Marriage and the Family* 52.

———. February 1986. "Receipt of Support From Family Among Black Americans: Demographic and Familial Differences." *Journal of Marriage and the Family* 48(1): 67–77.

Tolnay, Stewart E. September 1984. "Black Family Formation and Tenancy in the Farm South, 1900." *American Journal of Sociology* 90(2): 305–25.

Wharton, Clifton R. Spring 1986. "The Future of the Black Community: Human Capital, Family Aspirations, and Individual Motivation." *Review of Black Political Economy* 14(4): 9–16.

White, Barnetta McGhee. Spring 1988. "The Paper Trail: A Historical Exploration of the Black Family." *Western Journal of Black Studies* 12(1): 1–8.

Wilkinson, Doris Y. Fall-Winter 1984. "Afro-American Women and Their Families." *Marriage and Family Review* 7(3-4): 125–42.

Williams, J.A., and R. Stockton. February 1973. "Black Family Structures and Functions: An Empirical Examination of Some Suggestions Made by Billingsley." *Journal of Marriage and the Family* 35.

Wilson, Karen R., and Walter R. Allen. Winter 1987. "Explaining the Educational Attainment of Young Black Adults: Critical Familial and Extrafamilial Influences." *Journal of Negro Education* 56(1): 64–76.

Wolf, Ann Marie. January 1983. "A Personal View of Black Inner-City Foster Families." *American Journal of Orthopsychiatry* 53(1): 144–51.

Young, Philip K.Y., and Ann H.L. Sontz. Spring 1988. "Is Hard Work the Key to Success? A Socioeconomic Analysis of Immigrant Enterprise." *Review of Black Political Economy* 16(4): 11–31.

Ziter, Mary Lou Politi. March-April 1987. "Culturally Sensitive Treatment of Black Alcoholic Families." *Social Work* 32(2): 130–35.

Zollar, Ann Creighton. Fall 1982. "Variations Interdependencies Between and Among Members of Lower Class Urban Black Extended Families." *The Western Journal of Black Studies* 6: 131–37.

———. November 1986. "Ideological Perspectives on Black Families Related Typologies." *Free Inquiry in Creative Sociology* 14(2): 169–72.

Zollar, Ann Creighton, and Julie Honnold. Spring 1988. "Socioeconomic Characteristics and Kin Interaction in Black Middletown." *Western Journal of Black Studies* 12(1): 9–18.

Popular Articles

Blount, Carolyn S. March 1986. "Characteristics of the Black Family." *About Time* 14(3): 4.

———. September 1988. "Stephen G. Vassiannie, Sr.: Family Business With a Quality Reputation." *About Time.* 16(9): 22–25.

Bray, Rosemary L. August 1982. "Two Career Families: The Struggle for Success." *Black Enterprise* 13: 39–44.

Brewer, Rose M. Winter 1987. "Black Women in Poverty: Some Comments on Female-Headed Families." *Signs* 13(2): 331–39.

Brown-Collins, Alice R. Spring 1981. "Contributions of Cross-Cultural Research to Family Studies: The Inadequacy of the Nuclear Family." *Umoja* 5: 34–44.

Davis, Angela, and Fania Davis. September-October 1986. "The Black Family and the Crisis of Capitalism." *Black Scholar* 17(5): 33–40.

Dingle, Derek T. June 1984. "Diversification: Meeting Today's Challenges." *Black Enterprise,* 14: 170–74.

Dupree, Adolph. September 1983. "Through a Magnifying Glass: An Examination of Family Relations. *About Time.* 11: 14–20.

Graves, Earl G. April 1984. "Our Families and Business." *Black Enterprise* 14: 11.

———. December 1988. "Challenges for the Black Family." *Black Enterprise* 19(5): 9.

Hooks, Benjamin L., and John E. Jacob. February 1984. "Black Family Summit Conference to Convene May 3–5, 1984, at Fisk University, Nashville, Tennessee: Joint Statement of Purpose." 91:2–15.

Johnson, Herschel. April 1985. "The Carmichaels: A Corporate Family." *Ebony* 40(6): 147.

Karenga, Maulana. September-October 1986. "Social Ethics and the Black Family: An Alternative Analysis." *Black Scholar* 17(5): 41–54.

Knight, Elizabeth. November 1984. "The Black Family: A 'Wholistic' Approach Work for Urban League." *About Time* 12(11): 14–17.

Kunjufu, Jawanza. January-February 1987. "The Strengths of the Black Family or the Vanishing Family: CRISIS in Black America—You Decide." *Black Collegian* 17(3): 122–24.

Ladner, Joyce A. September-October 1986. "Black Women Face the 21st Century: Major Issues and Problems." *Black Scholar* 17(5): 12–19.

———. Summer-Winter 1987. "Black Teen Pregnancy: A Challenge for Educators." *Urban League Review* 11(1-2): 236–44.

Lehman, Nicholas. July 1986. "Origin of the Black Underclass." *Atlantic Monthly*.

Malveaux, Julianne. May-June 1988. "Race, Class, and Black Poverty." *Black Scholar* 19(3): 18–21.

McGhee, James D. Winter 1982. "A Dream Denied: The Black Family in the Eighties." *The Urban League Review* 7: 25–37.

Monagan, Alfrieta Parks. Winter 1985. "Rethinking 'Matrifocality.' " *Phylon* 46(4): 353–62.

Nelson-Ricks, Jill. May 1984. "The Black Family in Crisis: Mothers Struggling Alone." *Essence* 15(1): 85.

Platt, Tony. 1987. "E. Franklin Frazier and Daniel Patrick Moynihan: Setting the Record Straight." *Contemporary-Crises* 11(3): 265–77.

Pressley, Patsy V. March 1987. "Families That Work." *Essence* 17(11): 75–127.

Riley, Norman. November 1988. "Single Motherhood." 18–22.

Smith, Earl. Fall-Summer 1987. "The Black Family: Daniel Patrick Moynihan and the Tangle of Pathology Revisited." *Humboldt Journal of Social Relations* 14(1-2): 281–305.

Staples, Robert. September-October 1986. "The Political Economy of Black Family Life." *Black Scholar* 17(5): 2–11.

Stevenson, Rosemary M. September-October 1986. "The Black Family: A Bibliography of Recent Works." *Black Scholar* 17(5): 55–57.

Still, Lawrence A. September 1984. "The Quanders: America's Oldest Black Family." *Ebony* 39(11): 130.

Tramel, Essie Seck. Summer 1986. "The Impact of Unemployment on the Social Well-Being of the Black Family." *Urban League Review* 10(1): 87–97.

Tucker, Sheilah L. April 1988. "Pro-Line Corporation." *Crisis:* 48.

Washington, Robert O. Summer-Winter 1988. "Strategy of Responsible Militancy: A Template for Today's African-American Youth." *Urban League Review* 12(1-2): 39–53.

DISSERTATIONS AND PAPERS

Dunlap, Eloise Emma. May 1989. "Male/Female Relations and the Black Family." *Dissertation Abstracts International, A: The Humanities and Social Sciences,* 49(11): 3517-A. Available from UMI, Ann Arbor, MI, Order No. DA8902079.

Floyd, James Earl. August 1988. "Black Family in Transition: A Multigenerational Study of Crisis Resolution." *Dissertation Abstracts International, A: The Humanities and Social Sciences, 1988,* 49(2): 350-A. Available from UMI, Ann Arbor, MI. Order No. DA8807521.

Hunter, Andrea Gail. June 1988. "Making a Way: Economic Strategies of Southern Urban Afro-American Families, 1900–1936." *Dissertation Abstracts International, A: The Humanities and Social Sciences, 48,* 12(1): 3206-A. Available from UMI, Ann Arbor, MI. Order No. DA8804598.

Madison, Patricia Lee. 1987. "Effects of Unemployment on the Black Married Males' Self-Esteem and Family Relations." *Dissertation Abstracts International, A: The Humanities and Social Sciences,* 48(6): 1548-A. Available from UMI, Ann Arbor, MI. Order No. DA8719308.

Tienda, Marta, and Lief Jensen. November 1986. "Poverty and Minority: A Quarter Century Profile of Color and Socioeconomic Disadvantage." (Paper delivered at the conference on Poverty and Social Policy: The Minority Experience).

Acknowledgments

The book was begun in 1973 while I was professor of sociology and social work and vice president for academic affairs at Howard University in Washington, D.C. The university, my graduate students, and Marilyn C. Greene, my research assistant for several years, were especially helpful for the two years of research in the National Archives, as was Robert Johnson of the National Archives staff.

During my nine years as professor of sociology and president of Morgan State University in Baltimore, Maryland, the project was largely placed in abeyance, except for helpful service in record keeping by Linda McClure and support from Brenda Ferguson and Fred Douglass. In 1983 with an assist from Robert B. Hill the book was placed back on my agenda. Since 1984, it has been a major undertaking and some would say preoccupation. I am grateful to the Morgan State University Board of Regents for a one-year sabbatical, which enabled me to work on it full-time. Thereafter, a visiting professorship at the University of California, Berkeley, with special assistance from Troy Duster, Director of the Center for the Study of Social Change; Harry Specht, Dean of the School of Social Welfare; and Reginald Jones, Chair of the Department of Afro-American Studies, provided the opportunity and support for scholarly reflection. Later, a stint as visiting scholar on the James R. Dumpson Chair in Family and Child

Welfare at Fordham University with enormous assistance from former Dean Dumpson, Dean Mary Ann Quaranta, and Assistant Dean Patricia Morrisey enabled me to try out several ideas and acquire valuable insights.

Since 1985 as professor of sociology and Afro-American Studies and as professor and chair of the Department of Family and Community Development at the University of Maryland, College Park, I have been provided with a reasonable teaching load and enormous technical, professional, and financial assistance toward the completion of this work. I am especially indebted to Terry Stephens, who has served as my faculty research assistant and has been a strong support system for most of that time.

Then, when after nearly five years of intensive work I still needed another period of support to complete some special analyses, three angels at the Ford Foundation, Shelby Miller, Lynn Walker, and Robert Curvin, came to my rescue. A timely grant enabled me to engage Dr. Robert B. Hill and Dr. Deborah Robinson to do special analyses of a data set from the University of Michigan National Survey of Black Americans that Dr. James Jackson graciously made available to us. Meanwhile, Dr. Roger Rubin generously served as acting chair of the department in my absence, while Professors Sally Koblinsky, Leigh Leslie, and Flora Millstein offered their classes as guinea pigs for earlier drafts of this book.

For a monumental job of typing the manuscript, Terry Stephens has been ably assisted by Diane Walls-Tabron and Florence Curley, while Michelle Moore tried valiantly to keep track of me and my varied responsibilities.

To my students at the University of Maryland and several audiences around the nation who have given valuable feedback to the prepublication drafts that I have inflicted on them, I am deeply grateful.

My family, Amy, Angela, and Bonita, have been encouraging, patient, supportive, and sustaining beyond measure. Amy, Angela, Harriette McAdoo, Jeanne Giovannoni, Robert B. Hill, Leanor Boulin-Johnson, and Terry Stephens read the entire manuscript and gave me valuable advice on improving it. For more than thirty years Amy Tate Billingsley has been the "wind beneath my wings." This book is no exception.

In the publishing world two remarkable women early saw the merit of this book and stuck with it to the end. They are my agent, Marie Dutton Brown, and Carole Hall, then executive editor.

Carole demonstrated that an editor truly committed to a project works as hard and effectively as the author in bringing it to fruition. A fateful lunch meeting with Marie, Carole, and Terry Stevens in spring of 1988 provided a major stepping stone for the realization of this project. Fred Chase did a yeoman's job of copy editing it. And in the final stages of *Climbing Jacob's Ladder* Sheila Curry and Diane Aronson at Simon & Schuster teamed up to put the book over the finish line.

To these and all others who contributed so much to me and this work, I say thank you. Despite all their assistance and advice, however, it no doubt suffers a number of shortcomings for which I alone am responsible.

Finally, I wish to acknowledge those scholars who have chronicled the changing dynamics of African-American family life. Preeminent among them are Marie Peters, Harriette McAdoo, Robert B. Hill, Joyce Ladner, Niara Sudarkasa, Robert Hampton, John Scanzoni, Joyce Aschenbrenner, Carol Stack, Debra White, Bob Staples, Walter Allen, and Margaret Spencer. They have made seminal contributions to our knowledge of African-American family life. Their prodigious scholarship and personal insights have served as important guideposts for my own research and reflection.

In the process of writing this book a number of more limited by-products have been published by the author. These include "Single Parent Families" (with Jeanne Giovannoni), *Encyclopedia of Social Work*, 1976; "The Other Side of Slavery" (with Marilyn G. Greene) in Robert L. Clark, *Afro-American History: Sources for Research*, Howard University Press, 1981; "Building Strong Faculties in Historically Black Colleges and Universities," *Journal of Negro Education*, 1983; "The Conception of the Black Family in the Fiction of Waters E. Turpin" in Burney Hollis, *Sword Upon This Hill*, Morgan State University Press, 1984; "Families: Contemporary Patterns," *Encyclopedia of Social Work*, 1987; "Black Families in a Changing Society," *The State of Black America*, National Urban League; "Black Families and the Elderly" in Wilbur Watson, *Health Care and the Elderly*, Atlanta University Press, 1987; "The Impact of Technology on Afro-American Families," *Journal of Family Relations*, October 1988; "Understanding African American Family Diversity," *State of Black America 1990*, National Urban League; "The Church, the Family and the School in the African American Community," *Journal of Negro Education*, Summer 1991; "The Black Church as a Family Support System" (with Cleopatra

Howard Caldwell), *National Journal of Sociology*, forthcoming; "The Black Family and the Black Church," *Journal of the Association of Christian Education*, forthcoming; "The Sociology of Knowledge of William J. Wilson: Placing the Truly Disadvantaged in its Socio-Historical Context," *Journal of Sociology and Social Welfare*, December 1989.

Data from this manuscript have also been used in a number of endowed lectureships, including "Social Change and Urban Black Families," the 1985 James R. Dumpson Lecture, Fordham University; "African-American Families and Children at Risk," the 1989 Gisela Konopka Lecture, University of Minnesota; "African-American Families in a Changing Society," the 1989 Marie A. Peters Memorial Lecture, National Council on Family Relations; "African-American Families," the 1990 Werner and Bernice Boem Distinguished Lecture, Rutgers University; "The Family and the Church in the African-American Experience," the 1992 Distinguished Hamilton Visiting Lecture, Emory University.

Index

(*continued from Copyright page*)

C. Eric Lincoln and Lawrence Mamiya. *The Black Church in the African American Experience*. Copyright 1990, Duke University Press, Durham, North Carolina. Reprinted with permission.

C. Eric Lincoln, "The Black Church and Black Self-Determination" Paper read before the Association of Black Foundation Executives. April 15, 1986, Kansas City, Missouri.

Crisis. Vol. 11, April 1916 (New York: National Association for the Advancement of Colored People), 290.

David S. Broder. "Desperate to Save a Generation: D.C. Judge Picked for U.S. Drug Post Gives Stiff Terms and Talks." *The Washington Post*. May 6, 1989. B–1.

Faustine Childress Jones. *A Traditional Model of Educational Excellence: Dunbar High School of Little Rock, Arkansas*. (Washington, D.C.: Howard University Press: and the Institute for the Study of Educational Policy, 1981) 2.

Fawn Vraro and Terry E. Johnson. "Three Single Mothers Tell Their Stories." *The Philadelphia Inquirer*. June 10, 1984. 16.

Fawn Vraro, et. al. "Homes Without Fathers." *The Philadelphia Inquirer*. June 10, 1984. 1–A.

Harriette P. McAdoo. "The Impact of Extended Family Structure on Upward Mobility of Blacks." *Journal of African-American Issues*, vol. 3, no. 4 (1975): 295–6.

Herschel Johnson. "We're In the Money." *Black Enterprise*. 40–46. Copyright: August 1984, The Earl G. Graves Publishing Co., Inc., 130 Fifth Avenue, New York, New York 10011. All rights reserved.

"Top 100 Black Owned Industrial/Service Companies" (chart). © 1992, The Earl G. Graves Publishing Co, Inc. 130 Fifth Avenue, New York, New York 10011. All rights reserved.

Asa G. Hilliard III. "The Ages of Black African Rule in KMT (Egypt)," (chart) 1983.

Holly Selby. "Unorthodox Educator." *The Baltimore Sun*. December 2, 1990. 1–6, 8–G.

Yearbook of American and Canadian Churches, Jacquet. (1989). (Data from this was used in Table 17.1.).

James Jackson provided secondary analyses of data for the National Survey of Black Americans by which Table 17.3 and figures 10.1 through 10.13 were constructed by Deborah Robinson and Bob Hill.

James Weldon Johnson. "Lift Every Voice and Sing." Langston Hughes and Arna Bontemps eds. *The Poetry of the Negro 1746–1949* (New York: Doubleday and Company) 32.

Jean Thompson. "Patricia Schmoke, Laughing in the Whirlwind." *The Baltimore Morning Sun*. Nov. 27, 1987. B1–3.

Mary Jordon. "A Steady Job But No Home." *The Washington Post*. August 29, 1988. D1, D5. © 1988, *The Washington Post*. Reprinted with permission.

Michael Ryan. "He Gives Kids a Chance to Win." *Parade*, September 9, 1990. Reprinted with permission from *Parade*.

Peter Michelmore. "The Kids of Kent Amos." *Reader's Digest*, September 1990. The Reader's Digest Association, New York. Reprinted with Permission.

Robert Francis Engs. *Freedom's First Generation: Black Hampton, Virginia 1861–1890*. (Philadelphia: University of Pennsylvania Press, 1979): xviii–xix.

Surinder K. Mehta. "The Stability of Black-White vs. Racially Homogamous Marriages in the United States, 1960–1970." *Journal of Social and Behavioral Science*. 24 (1978): 137.

Jube Shriver. 'Child's Play." *Black Enterprise*. 30–34. Copyright: August 1986, The Earl G. Graves Publishing Co., Inc., 130 Fifth Avenue, New York, New York 10011. All rights reserved.

Veronica Jennings. "Black Churches Allying Against AIDS." *The Washington Post*. July 3, 1989. B–51. © 1989, *The Washington Post*. Reprinted with permission.

W.E.B. Du Bois. "The Marrying of Black Folk." *The Independent.* 69 (October 13, 1910): 812–3.

William Raspberry. "Miz Dot's Beautiful Expression." *The Washington Post.* September 29, 1990. A–23. Reprinted with permission.

Coretta Scott King, *My Life with Martin Luther King, Jr.* (New York: Holt, Rinehart and Winston, 1969) 36.

Isabel Wilkerson, "Middle-Class Blacks Try to Grip a Ladder While Lending a Hand." *The New York Times,* November 25, 1990, 1.

M. Belinda Tucker and Claudia Mitchell-Kernan. "New Trends in Black American Interracial Marriage: The Social Structure Context." *Journal of Marriage and the Family.* 52:1 (February 1990): 211.

Paul J. Lammermeier. "The Urban Black Family of the Nineteenth Century: A Study of Black Family Structure in the Ohio Valley, 1850–1880." *Journal of Marriage and the Family.* 35 (1973): 452.

Thomas P. Monahan. "Percentage of Births with a Negro Parent which were of Mixed Race, United States, 1970" (table). "An Overview of Statistics on Interracial Marriage in the United States." *Journal of Marriage and the Family.* 38 (1976): 223.